THE PUERTO RICANS

THE
PUERTO
RICANS
A DOCUMENTARY HISTORY

EDITED BY
Kal Wagenheim
AND
Olga Jiménez de Wagenheim

 Markus Wiener Publishers
Princeton

Third Printing 1996

For information write to:
  Markus Wiener Publishers
  114 Jefferson Road
  Princeton, New Jersey 08540

Library of Congress Cataloging-in-Publication Data

The Puerto Ricans: a documentary history/edited by Kal Wagenheim
  and Olga Jiménez de Wagenheim.—Updated 1994 ed.
    Includes bibliographical references and index.
    ISBN 1-55876-077-6
    1. Puerto Rico—History.   2. Puerto Ricans—United States—History.
  I. Wagenheim, Kal II. Wagenheim, Olga Jiménez de.
F1971.P79   1993
972.95—dc20   93-20849
                                                            CIP

Printed in the United States of America.

CONTENTS

Introduction	ix
"Prophecy for the Twentieth Century"	xiii
PART I: DISCOVERY AND CONQUEST	1
Boriquén	3
The Indian Way of Life	4
The First Settlers	15
Queen Isabella's Order	18
"The Grasping Avarice of the White Men"	19
The Indians Rebel	23
PART II: THE COLONIZATION	27
The Costly Colony	29
"Criollos" and "Blancos"	33
The Xivaros	38
Slavery Laws	44
Masters and Slaves	48
PART III: THE SPIRIT OF NATIONHOOD	53
Sailing to San Juan	55
"Arriba, Puerto Ricans!"	59
"You Shall Be Free"	60
The Day Puerto Rico Became a Nation	61
The Abolition of Slavery	67
"The Troubles at Porto Rico"	71
The Autonomist Concept	73
PART IV: MANIFEST DESTINY	77
Puerto Rico as a Permanent Possession	81
"A Dangerous Neighbor"	84

"Have We Not Suffered Long Enough?"   86
"Seize San Juan"   89
Our Flag Raised in Puerto Rico   92
"To the Inhabitants of Porto Rico"   95
Soldier   96
Diary of the War   99

PART V: "CITIZENS OF PORTO RICO"   105

"The Porto Rican Inhumanity"   107
"We Are Becoming Americanized"   110
"They Are Loyal"   112
"Discipline for Porto Rico"   114
Dining With President Taft   119
"Inverted Terms"   121

PART VI: AMERICAN CITIZENSHIP   123

"An Idle Dream"   125
"The Future of My Country"   126
"Treachery and Disenchantment"   135

PART VII: THE GRIM YEARS   141

Ireland in America?   143
Sweatshops on the Spanish Main   147
"The Gentleman's Time Has Expired"   150
Lindbergh's Visit   151
"The Sad Case of Porto Rico"   153
"Joker in the Deck"   162
The Rise of Albizu Campos   167
Rebellion in Puerto Rico   174
Violence and Nationalism   179

PART VIII: "¡JALDA ARRIBA!"   183

"A Time of National Crisis"   185
"Puerto Rico Is the Center"   188
"We Had Better Wait"   190
The Bard of Politics   195
"I Love My Country"   204
Worker in the Cane   207
Don Abelardo   214
The Status Dilemma   217
A Yankee from Massachusetts   220
"The Conscience of His People"   223

PART IX: Exodus   227

The Early Days   229
"What Is Prejudice?"   233
Long Night's Journey   234
"I'm Freezing to Death"   241
American-born "Foreigners"   245
"Hispanos" and "Marine Tigers"   250
Down These Mean Streets   252
Harlem Sí, Tammany No   258
"My Parents, They Cry with Joy"   263
"El Barrio's Worst Block"   267
Bilingualism in El Barrio   272
Neo-Rican Jetliner   276

PART X: The Divided Nation   283

"Nation and Homeland"   285
"From a Jail in Puerto Rico"   289
"Cancio and Compassion"   292
The Cuban Invasion of Puerto Rico   295
A Day at the Bodega   298
"They Lose Heart"   307
The Young Lords   311
The Year 2000   315
Trade or Treason   323
A Complex Reality   325

Bibliography   329

Index   337

SECTIONS OF ILLUSTRATIONS FOLLOW PAGES 112 AND 240

INTRODUCTION

In the summer of 1898, when American troops first raised the Stars and Stripes on Puerto Rico's southern shore, their commanding general promised the natives the "advantages and blessings of enlightened civilization."

Three decades later, American historian Hubert Herring observed, "We were not invited by the Puerto Ricans, nor did we ask their consent. . . . Viewed in the light of the rosy promises made by those who took the island . . . our record has not been brilliant."

Subsequent years have confirmed the emptiness of the general's promises. The invasion of Puerto Rico ended four centuries of oppressive Spanish colonial rule, only to replace it with a more subtle brand of colonialism that still endures.

This book of readings spans nearly five hundred years in the history of the Puerto Rican people, from their ethnic origins to their present dilemma as members of a nation without nationhood—a people whose past and present are obscured by propaganda and whose collective future is shrouded by uncertainty.

There are, in fact, two Puerto Ricos. The first is a small Caribbean island, densely populated by 2.8 million Spanish-speaking people. The first Puerto Rico, la patria, contains all the ingredients of any nation: There are poverty-ridden peasants and urban slum dwellers, but there are also politicians and poets, teachers and students, bankers and clerks, farmers, doctors, musicians, lawyers, judges, bus drivers, policemen—and enough thieves to keep the police busy.

The second Puerto Rico is a recent offshoot of the first: An amorphous mass of about 1.5 million people, mostly rural folk and their children, who, since the end of World War II, have migrated to the United States to seek jobs that they could not find in la patria. The inhabitants of the second Puerto Rico are scattered throughout the fifty states of the Union, in fragmented, embryonic communities; they belong to a poor, silent, and polychromatic minority, in an affluent nation that is torn by racial strife; they are the heirs to the crumbling tenements of the inner city, and the dirty jobs that pay the lowest wages; they have few leaders to champion their cause; in some U.S. cities, their children can spend twelve years in school without ever hearing Spanish

spoken in a classroom, without ever hearing their names pronounced correctly, without ever knowing that there is such a thing
as a Puerto Rican teacher, doctor, lawyer, or poet. Newspaper
columnist José Torres recently visited Chicago (whose 200,000-plus
Puerto Ricans constitute the second-largest mainland community)
and reported with dismay, "There is not one Puerto Rican in a
political position. Professionals are limited to three or four doctors,
two school teachers, four or five lawyers." In Boston, only nine
high school graduates reportedly emerged from a Puerto Rican
community of about thirty thousand in 1971. Even in New York,
where Puerto Ricans are about 1 million strong, their political
"clout" is feeble.

Of course, Puerto Ricans are not the first ethnic group to suffer
the anguish of migration to America, which is a nation of migrants.
To a great extent, American politics is the story of the struggles
and coalitions of its ethnic groups. (When Harry S. Truman became
President in 1945, he complained to a friend, "You know, I've
been in office only a few weeks and already the Swedish-Americans,
the Irish-Americans, and the Polish-Americans have been in to
see me. When are the Americans coming to see me?") Puerto
Ricans are just now learning this "game" of ethnic lobbying, but
they are far down in the pecking order, well below the more
numerous, more militant blacks, who have learned that American
institutions apparently respond only to crisis. (There is a grim
but undeniable link between black militancy and the growth of
new opportunities for blacks in all areas of American society;
in effect, every burning garbage can or shattered store window in
the ghettos, every clenched fist raised in defiance has led to the
"magical" appearance of black-studies programs on college campuses, of black actors in once lily-white advertisements, of black
executives in "blue chip" WASP corporations, and of clusters of
new jobs in myriad fields.)

While Puerto Ricans share a great deal with earlier European
immigrants, and with blacks, they are unique in several respects.
To begin with, the political status of their homeland is in limbo,
and its destiny is still very much in doubt. Thus, one often sees
the bewildering phenomenon of Puerto Rican activists on the
mainland demanding their full rights as U.S. citizens and moments
later shouting vivas for the island's independence. This tug-of-war
of apparently contradictory goals is just one of several factors that
slow the impetus of Puerto Rican entry into the mainstream of
American life. Another factor is the "tentative" status of many
immigrants, who dream of returning to Puerto Rico as soon as
they have enough money to buy a home; this dream is far more
realistic today, when a Puerto Rican can hop a jet and be in
San Juan three hours later, than it was among the European
immigrants earlier in the century, who severed their ancient bonds,
and spent days packed together in the holds of ships.

But—before I get carried away—this is not a book about the Puerto Rican migration, the history of which is still being acted out in America's streets. In this book, I have tried to offer a collection of readings that describe the history and social culture of Puerto Rico, with marked emphasis on this century, a period largely neglected by historians. My main purposes have been to make available in English a substantial body of knowledge for the benefit of the thousands of Puerto Rican students on the mainland, who have been cut off from their national heritage, and to help North American readers to appreciate this important ethnic group. The idea for this book emerged shortly after I finished writing *Puerto Rico: A Profile* (Praeger, 1971), an introductory survey of the island. I realized then that the book's brief chapter on history barely scratched the surface of so vast a subject, and I hoped that a companion volume of readings, such as this one, would enable the interested reader to probe more deeply.

Even this book, in its attempt to cover five hundred years of history, is little more than a collage of events and impressions. But, in providing this kaleidoscopic view of the island's past, I have chosen carefully from a broad variety of sources: Spanish clergy and colonial governors, men of letters, farmers, slum dwellers, politicians (Puerto Rican and American), and journalists of varying opinion. Whenever possible, I have used contemporary accounts, to capture the heat and flavor of the moment. Also, I have given preference to the writings of Puerto Ricans, who have too often been spoken for by others. In most cases where I have used the writings of Americans, I have done so because they treat a vital topic in a unique way or illustrate the cultural bias of a foreigner (I leave to the reader the fun of deciding which does which).

I have no doubt that a book such as this—and others like it—is necessary. During a recent visit to a small Puerto Rican community in Syracuse, New York, I was impressed by the intense curiosity of Puerto Rican students toward their island's history, and I was saddened to see how desperately they were searching for their own identity. My memory of one college student is especially vivid. After struggling to speak Spanish, he lost patience and said, in perfect English, "Look, we know that we Puerto Ricans are a colonial, exploited people. We don't have to study to know that. We see it every day in the lives of our parents, in our homes, on the streets. Now we want the lowdown; it's like walking backwards, to learn the 'why' of what we already know."

Today, the two Puerto Ricos are connected by only tenuous strands. The immigrants in America are largely insulated from the nutrient source of their heritage, and residents of the first Puerto Rico regard them as sons and daughters, sisters and brothers who have left—rarely as the pioneers of a sibling nation-in-exile. Hopefully, this book will, in a small but positive way, strengthen the bonds between the two.

Puerto Rican scholar Frank Bonilla has said:

If we choose to go beyond survival as a community, then our creativity must be fed by a collective vision that reaches out to Puerto Ricans everywhere. When people ask in what way Puerto Ricans differ from earlier migrants, we must be ready with the true answer, which is that we are a displaced offshoot of a people and a land that have yet to be liberated, and whose freedom is our own.

★ ★ ★

For their help with this book, I offer special thanks to Pedro Juan Soto (the noted Puerto Rican novelist whose diligence and generosity have always been an example and an inspiration to me), to Leon King (my editor when this book was first published in 1973 and still my valued friend), and, above all, to my wife—and colleague—Olga Jiménez de Wagenheim.

It is most gratifying to see that this book remains of interest two decades after its original publication. Since that time, some things have changed in Puerto Rico, but much remains the same. The reasons for change and continuity can be found in a careful study of the island's history. I hope that the reader will find some of the answers among these pages.

Maplewood, New Jersey
July 1993

"PROPHECY FOR THE TWENTIETH CENTURY"

The struggle for freedom shall probably be more complicated than ever before. The Anglo-Saxon peoples shall struggle for human freedom, but, having achieved it for themselves, they shall ignore it for others. During the struggle, it shall be questioned whether the mere creation of civil government means true freedom, if that government is exclusively created by Anglo-Saxons for Anglo-Saxons, and not by men for all men. Millions of colored people, armed, shall demand their right to the fruits of civil government, which for them shall begin with the freedom to be colored.

—Translated from "Prophecy for the Century," written in 1900 by Puerto Rican educator-philosopher EUGENIO MARIA DE HOSTOS.*

* Contained in *Obras Completas de Eugenio María de Hostos* (San Juan: Government of Puerto Rico, 1939) (20 vols.). The above excerpt also appears in Carlos N. Carreras, *Ideario de Hostos* (San Juan, Editorial Cordillera, 1966), pp. 241–42.

Part I

DISCOVERY AND CONQUEST

We proceeded along the coast the greater part of that day, and on the evening of the next we discovered another island called Boriquén. . . . All the islands are very beautiful and possess a most luxuriant soil, but this last island appeared to exceed all others in beauty.

—Translated from a letter by DR. DIEGO ALVAREZ CHANCA, who accompanied Christopher Columbus on his second voyage to the New World in 1493.

In 1493, during his second voyage to the New World, Christopher Columbus discovered a "very beautiful" island that possessed a "most luxuriant soil." He named the island San Juan, in honor of Saint John the Baptist. A few years later, the island would be renamed Puerto Rico—meaning "rich port"—because of its great potential, and the capital city would come to be known as San Juan.

Not long after Spain's settlers established themselves in Puerto Rico and the nearby Caribbean islands, they overwhelmed the weaker Indian societies that had lived there since earliest times. The following selections describe those first few years. They include an account of the sighting of Puerto Rico from Columbus's ship in 1493; a description of the way of life of the Taíno Indians who inhabited the island; Juan Ponce de León's official report on how he founded the first European settlement in Puerto Rico; an edict from Spain's Queen Isabella that established the *encomienda* system, which was a thinly disguised form of Indian slavery; an outraged account by Washington Irving of how the greedy Spanish settlers oppressed the Indians; and a history of the brief, abortive Indian rebellion in Puerto Rico—the last struggle of a vanquished people.

1

BORIQUEN

[Because the existence
of the New World was already a certainty, Columbus's second voyage
in 1493 was ambitious and well supported. Seventeen ships bore 1,200
men, including astronomers, cartographers, soldiers, artisans, laborers,
and pardoned criminals. The fleet left Cádiz on September 25 and
reached the Caribbean on November 3. Although Columbus kept diaries
of his first trip, the best-known eyewitness account of Puerto Rico's
discovery is that by Diego Alvarez Chanca, the Admiral's physician. The
doctor's brief notes were soon augmented by historians of the period;
one of the best accounts of that brief first glimpse of Puerto Rico is the
following, written by Fray Bartolomé de las Casas in 1527.]

The next Sunday,
the 10th of November, he [Columbus] ordered the anchor raised
and the sails spread, and he cruised the coast of the island of
Guadeloupe . . . in search of Hispaniola, and he reached a very high
island, which he called Monserrate, because it seemed to have the
shape of the boulders of Monserrate, and from there he discovered
a certain island which was very round, and very steep everywhere, and without ladders or ropes appeared impossible to scale,
which is why he gave it the name of Sancta María la Redonda
(Saint Mary the Round); another island he called Sancta María
del Antigua, which had a coastline of some 15 or 20 leagues; there
appeared many other islands to the North, all very high and
heavily forested; he stopped at one which he called Sant Martin,
and, when they raised anchor, pieces of coral were stuck to the
anchor, it seemed. . . .

On Thursday, the 14th of November, the Admiral stopped at
another island which he called Sancta Cruz [St. Croix, today];
and he sent men ashore to capture some natives, and thus learn
their language. They seized four women and two children, and,
as they were returning in the rowboat, they encountered a canoe,
which contained four Indians and an Indian woman; when the
Indians realized that they could not flee, they, including the woman,
began to defend themselves; they began to fire arrows, and they
wounded two Christians, and the woman even pierced a shield
with her arrow; the sailors crashed their boat into the canoe
and overturned it; one of the Indians, who had not lost his bow,

---

Translated from Fray Bartolomé de las Casas, *Historia de las Indias* (Mexico:
Fondo de Cultura Económica, 1951), pp. 352–55.

swam and fired his arrows with almost the same vigor as if he had been ashore. They saw that one of the Indians had his generative instrument cut off; the Christians believed it was so that he would grow fatter, like a capon, and then the Caribs would eat him. From there, the Admiral continued his voyage towards Hispaniola, and saw many islands grouped together; they seemed to be beyond counting; the largest of them he called Sancta Ursula, and all the others he called the Eleven Thousand Virgins; from there, he reached another large island, which he called Sant Juan Baptista, which we now call Sant Juan, and which, as we mentioned before, was called Boriquén by the Indians, in a bay of this island toward the west, where all the ships caught many kinds of fish. . . .

Several Christians went ashore, and walked to some houses that were very artfully made, although all were of straw and wood; and there was a plaza, with a road reaching from it to the sea, very clean and straight, made like a street; and the walls were of crossed or woven cane; and above, beautiful gardens, as if they were vineyards or orchards of orange or citron trees, such as there are in Valencia or in Barcelona; and next to the sea there was a high watchtower, where ten or twelve people could fit, also well made; it was probably the pleasure house of the lord of that island, or of that part of that island. The Admiral does not mention having seen any people there; they must have fled in fright when they saw the ships.

THE INDIAN WAY OF LIFE

[Ramón Pané was a Catalonian friar who, by order of Christopher Columbus, came to the New World to learn the language and customs of the Indians and to convert them to Christianity. His famous *Relación Sobre Las Antigüedades de los Indios (Account of the Antiquities—or Customs—of the Indians)*, written in 1505, is probably the first anthropological study made in the New World.

Pané wrote of Hispaniola, just across the narrow Mona Passage from Puerto Rico. Early historians, such as Gonzalo Fernández de Oviedo and Fray Bartolomé de las Casas, affirm that there was no substantial difference between the Indians of Hispaniola and those of Puerto Rico,

---

The Spanish version appears in Eugenio Fernández Méndez (Ed.), *Crónicas de Puerto Rico: 1493–1797*, (San Juan: Ediciones Estado Libre Asociado, 1957), Vol. I, pp. 13–32. English version appears in Edward Gaylord Bourne, "Columbus, Ramón Pané, and the Beginnings of American Anthropology," *American Antiquarian Society*, April, 1906, pp. 318–39.

except—as Oviedo points out—the Puerto Rican tribes "were skilled bowmen and more warlike." Eugenio Fernández Méndez, one of Puerto Rico's leading present-day historians, includes Fray Ramón's account in his historical anthology on these grounds, and because "archeological evidence also confirms the fundamental unity of religion and beliefs" of both groups. The original Latin manuscript of this account has been lost. An admittedly marred Italian translation was later rendered into Spanish. The following segment has been translated by the editor, from the Spanish, after referring to a previous English translation.

Through the mist of translation, of Fray Ramón's pro-Christian bias, and of his obvious disdain for the Indians' religion, there emerges a fascinating portrait of their religious mythology; with more time, he might well have been able to construct an Indian counterpart of the Christian Bible, for his spare story has all the ingredients: a supreme being, saint figures (*cemíes*), an account of the creation of the sea (a great flood), a belief in the afterlife of the dead and a place where they reside, and so forth.

His is one of the first accounts of the use of tobacco [*cogioba*] for mystical and medicinal purposes. The friar also passes along to us the ominous prediction made by one of the Indian chieftains, who had learned from a *cemí* idol that one day their tribes would be vanquished and enslaved by a "clothed race"; this prediction accounts, at least partially, for the awe and the respect with which the Indians regarded Columbus and his men.

Finally, there is Fray Ramón's determination—surely reflecting that of all the conquerors—to "convert" the Indians, to Christianize them, to devalue the Indians' long-cherished life-styles, and, when necessary, to accomplish this by force.]

I, Fray Ramón, a poor hermit of the Order of Saint Jerome, by command of the illustrious lord, the Admiral and Viceroy and governor of the Islands and of the mainland of the Indies, write this, which I have been able to learn and know of the belief and idolatry of the Indians and how they worship their gods. . . .

Each one, in praying to the idols that he has in his house, which are called by them *cemíes*, worships in his own fashion and superstition.

They hold that he is immortal in heaven, and that no one can see him, and that he has a mother, but he had no beginning. This god they call Yocahu Vagua Maorocotí, and his mother they call by four names: Atabex, Yermaoguacar, Apito, and Zuimaco. . . .

Likewise, they know from where they came, and whence the sun and the moon had their origins, and how the sea was made, and where the dead go. And they believe that the dead appear on the trails when one walks alone, and that when many go together they do not appear. All this those who have gone before have made them believe, because these people know not how to read or to count beyond ten.

Chapter I

From what direction the Indians came, and in what manner: Española has a province called Caonao, in which there is a mountain called Canta, with two caves: one called Cacibayagua, the other Amayauba. From the first cave came forth the larger part of the people who settled the island. When they dwelled in these caves, a man named Marocael kept watch by night. One day, he tarried in returning to the door, and the sun carried him off. When the people saw this, they closed the door, and he was converted into stone near the door. Later, they say, others who went off to fish were seized by the sun and became trees, which were called by them *Jobos* [a common fruit tree in the Antilles—ed.]. . . .

Chapter II

How the men were divided from the women: It came to pass that a man named Guaguyona said to another called Yadruvava that he should gather an herb called *digo*, used to cleanse the body when they wash themselves. He left before daybreak, but the sun seized him on the way and he became a bird which sings in the morning like the nightingale, and is called Yahuba Bayael. When Guaguyona saw that the man sent to gather *digo* did not return, he resolved to leave the cave.

Chapter III

. . . he said to the women, "Leave your husbands, and let us go into other lands. Leave your sons, and we will take only the herbs with us, and we will return for them."

Chapter IV

He set forth with all the women, in search of other lands, and came to Matinino [usually identified with Martinique—ed.], where he left the women, and went into another region called Guanín. The women had left the small children near a brook. When hunger began to torment them, they wailed and called upon their absent mothers; and the fathers could not help the children, who made sounds like "mama," as if to speak, but were really asking for the breast. Wailing in this fashion, as one who desires something with great longing, they were changed into little animals, after the fashion of frogs. . . . In this way, all the men were left without women.

Chapter V

. . . When Guaguyona carried away all the women, he likewise took with him the woman of his cacique, whose name was Anacacuya, deceiving him as he deceived the others; and, moreover, a brother-in-law of his went off with him by sea. And Guaguyona said to his brother-in-law, when they were in the canoe, "See what a fine *cobo* [sea snail] there is in the water," and when he peered into the water, Guaguyona seized him by the feet and cast him into the sea, taking all the women for himself, and he left them at Matinino, where it is said there are only women today. . . .

Chapter VI

Guaguyona returned to where he had taken the women. They say he had left one woman in the sea, and that he was greatly pleased with her, and straightway sought to wash himself, being full of those sores which we call the French disease. [This could be syphilis, indicating that this disease may have existed in the West Indies before the Spaniards arrived—ed.] She then put him in a place apart; and so he was healed. Then she asked permission to go on her way, and he granted it. This woman was named Guabonito, and Guaguyona changed his name to Biberoci Guahayona. The woman Guabonito gave him many *guanins* [golden ornaments], and many *cibas* [beads] to wear around his arms. In those countries, *cibas* are of marblelike stone, and they wear them tied on the arms and neck, and they wear the *guanins* in their ears, which they pierce when they are children. . . .

Chapter VII

How there were women again on the island of Aití, which is now called Española:

They say that one day the men went off to bathe, and, while in the water, it rained heavily, and they were very desirous of having women. Oftentimes, when it rained, they went to search for their women, but without success. That day, they saw fall down from some trees, and hiding in the branches, a certain kind of persons who were neither men nor women, nor did they have the natural male or female parts. They tried to seize them, but they fled, as if they were eels. Wherefore, they called upon their cacique . . . for men who were *caracaracol*, men whose hands were rough, and could grasp the slippery creatures. They told the cacique that there were four of them, and he sent four men who were *caracaracoli*. This is a disease that causes scabs, and makes the body very rough. After they had caught the creatures, they gathered to discuss what they could do to make them women, since they did not have the natural parts of male or female.

Chapter VIII

How they found a device to make them women:

They searched for a bird called Inriri, which bores trees, and in our language is called a woodpecker [*pico*]. They took these creatures, and bound their feet and hands, and took the bird, and bound him to the body. Thinking they were logs, the bird began to peck and bore where the natural parts of the women are wont to be. In this fashion, the Indian elders say that they had women. . . .

Chapter IX

How they say the sea was made:
There was a man called Yaya, and his son was called Yayael, which means son of Yaya. Wishing to slay his father, the son sent him into exile, where he remained four months, but then the father slew him and placed his bones in a gourd, and fastened it to the roof of his cabin. One day, Yaya, longing to see his son, said to his wife, "I want to see Yayael." She was pleased at that, and he took down the gourd and turned it over to see the bones of his son, and from it came forth many fishes, large and small. . . . One day, when Yaya went to his fields, there came four sons of a woman whose name was Itiba Tahuvava, all from one womb; when this woman died in labor, they opened her and drew out these four sons, and the first they drew out was Caracaracol, which means scabby [or The Mangy One, or The Syphilitic]. The others had no name.

Chapter X

When the four sons, all born together, went to take hold of the gourd, none of them ventured to lay hands on it except Caracaracol who took it from its place, and all filled themselves with fish. While they were eating, they saw Yaya returning from the fields; trying in haste to replace the gourd, they let it fall to the ground, where it broke open. They say that so great was the mass of water that came from the gourd that it filled the whole earth, and with it issued forth many fish, and from this, they say, the sea had its beginning. . . .

Chapter XI

. . . and further, they say that the sun and the moon came from a cave which is situated in the country of a cacique named Maucia Tivuel, and the name of the cave is Yovovava, and they hold it in great regard; it is all painted in their fashion, without any figures, but with many leaves and other things of that sort, and in this cave there are two small *cemies*, of stone, about a foot high, with their hands tied, and they appear to be sweating. They hold these *cemies* in great regard, and, when it did not rain, they went to visit them, and suddenly it rained. . . .

Chapter XII

What they think as to how the dead wander about, and what manner of folk they are, and what they do:

They believe that there is a place whither the dead go, called Coaybay, which lies in a part of the island called Soraya [which means "west," according to some scholars—ed.]. The first man in Coaybay was, they say, one called Maquetaurie Guayava, who was the lord of the dwelling place of the dead.

Chapter XIII

Of the shape which they say the dead are:

They say that during the . . . night they go out to walk; and they eat of a certain fruit called *guannaba* [perhaps the guanábana —ed.], which has the flavor of the quince, . . . and they have feasts and walk with the living, and to know them one must touch their bellies, and, if one does not find the navel, they say that he is *operito*, which means dead. Because they say the dead have no navel. Sometimes men are deceived, and they lie with women from Coaybay, and when they think they have them in their arms, they have nothing, because they disappear in a trice. If the person is alive, they call the spirit Goeiz, and after death they call it Opia. They say the Goeiz appears often, both in the form of a man and a woman, and that a man once wished to contend with it, and when he clinched it, it disappeared, and the man thrust out his arms in another direction, over some trees, to which he hung. And this they all believe, both small and large, and that the dead appear to them in the form of a father, or mother, or brothers, or parents, and in other forms. . . . These dead do not appear to them in the daytime, but always by night, and with much fear do they venture forth alone at night.

Chapter XIV

Whence they derive this and who keeps it in such credit:

There are some men called *bohutis* who practice among them, and try to make them believe that they converse with spirits, and know their secrets, and that when the Indians are ill they can take away the evil. . . . I have seen some of this with my own eyes, although of the other things I shall relate only what I have heard, especially from the principal men . . . because they believe such fables more firmly than the others; like the Moors, they have their laws reduced to ancient songs, by which they are ruled, as the Moors are, by their scriptures. And, when they wish to sing their songs, they play upon a certain drum instrument called the *mayohavau*, which is hollowed from wood and strongly made, and

very thin, an ell long and half an ell in breadth, and the part
where it is played is made in the shape of the pincers of a
farrier, and the other part is like a club. It looks like a gourd with
a long neck. . . . This instrument . . . has so loud a sound that it
is heard a league and a half. To this sound, they sing the songs
which they know by heart; and the principal men play it; they
have learned from childhood to sound it, and to sing according
to their custom. . . .

Chapter XV

The observances of these Indian *bohutís*, and how they practice
medicine and teach the people, and in their cures, are oftentimes
themselves taken in:
All, or the majority, of the people of Española have many *cemíes*
of different kinds. One has the bones of his father and his mother,
and kindred and ancestors; others are made of stone or wood.
Many have them of both kinds; some which speak, and others
which make the things grow that they eat; and others which bring
rain; and others which make the winds blow. These simple-minded,
ignorant people believe in the idols, or to speak more fittingly, the
devils, since they do not have knowledge of our holy faith. When
one is sick, they take the *bohutí* to him as one would to a physician.
The *bohutí* is obliged to abstain from food, like the sick man
himself, and to play the part of the sick man. He must purge
himself, like the sick man, sniffing a powder called *cogioba*
[tobacco], which intoxicates them, so they do not know what
they are doing, and in this condition they speak incoherently,
and claim that they are talking with the *cemíes*, which tell them
the cause of the sickness.

Chapter XVI

What these *bohutís* do:
Before they set out from their lodging to visit a sick man, they
take soot from pots, or pounded charcoal, and blacken their
faces, to make the sick man believe whatever they feel is his
ailment; then they take small bones and a little flesh, wrap it
together in something so that it won't drop, and put it in their
mouth. The physician then enters the lodging of the sick man—who
has already been purged with the powder—and sits down, and all
are silent; if there are children, they put them out, so that they
may not hinder the *bohutí* in his duties; nor does anyone remain
in the cabin, except one or two of the principal men.
And thus, being alone, they take some leaves of the *gueyo*, which
are broad; and another plant, wrapped in an onion skin; and,
crumbling it with their hands, they make a paste of it, and put
it in their mouths at night to vomit up what they have eaten,

in order that it may not harm them; then they begin to sing. And, lighting a torch, they drink that juice. After waiting somewhat, the *bohuti* rises and goes to the sick man, who is seated in the middle of his dwelling, and turns him over twice. Then he stands before him, and takes him by the legs, feeling his thighs, and running his hands down to his feet; then he tugs him hard, as if he wished to pull something out of him; then he goes to the door of the dwelling, closes it, and says, "Begone to the mountains, or to the sea, or whither thou wilt," and blows as though he were blowing away a straw. He turns around again, and puts his hands together, and closes his mouth; his hands shake, as if he were very cold, and he blows on his hands, and then draws his breath in again, like one who sucks the marrow from a bone; and he sucks the sick man's neck, stomach, shoulders, jaws, breasts, belly, and many other parts of his body. This done, he begins to cough and grimace, as if he had eaten something bitter, and he spits into his hand and draws out that which he had put in his mouth before coming there, either a stone, or meat, or a bone. And if it is anything edible, he says to the sick man, "Take notice! You have eaten something which has brought on this illness from which you suffer. See how I have taken from your body what your *cemi* had put there, because you did not pray to him, or did not build him some temple, or give him something of your possessions." And, if it is a stone, he says, "Keep it safe." Sometimes they are convinced that these stones are good, and that they help women in labor, and they keep it very carefully wrapped in cotton in little baskets, and give them of their own food to eat, and they do the same to the *cemies* which they keep in their lodgings. On holy days, when they bring out much to eat—either fish, meat, or bread, or anything else—they put everything in the lodging of the *cemi*, so that the idol may eat.

The next day, they take all this food to their own lodgings, after the *cemi* has eaten. And so may God help them if the *cemi* eats of that, or of anything else, since it is a dead thing made of stone or wood.

Chapter XVII

How sometimes these physicians are deceived:

When they have done what was described, and still the sick man dies, if the dead man has many relatives, or was lord of a village, and can resist the *bohuti* (because those with little power do not venture to contend with these physicians), he who wishes to harm him does so. Wanting to know if the sick man died through the fault of the physician, or whether he did not do what was prescribed, they take an herb called *gueyo*, which has leaves like basil. . . . They take the juice of this leaf, and cut the nails of the dead man, and cut hair from his forehead, and they make a powder

between two stones, mixing it with the juice. They pour it into the
dead man's mouth or nose, and ask him if the physician was the
cause of his death, and if he had followed the regimen. They ask
him this several times, until he speaks as plainly as if he were
alive, . . . and the physician asks him if he is alive, or how it is
that he speaks so plainly; and he replies that he is dead. When they
have learned what they want, they return him to his grave. They
also proceed in another way. . . . They take the dead man and build
a big fire . . . and, when the wood has become live coals, they place
the body into this great fiery mass, and then cover it with earth . . .
and here they let it lie as long as they please. As it lies there, they
ask questions, and the dead man replies that he knows nothing,
and they ask him this ten times, and then he speaks no more.

Chapter XVIII

How the relatives of the dead man take vengeance:

The relatives of the dead man get together and wait for the
bohuti, and beat him with clubs till they break his legs, his arms,
and his head, so that they fairly pulverize him, as in a mortar,
and they leave him in that condition, believing that they have killed
him. They say that, by night, there come many snakes of different
kinds, which lick the face and body of this physician, who has
been left for dead, and who remains so for two or three days.
While he stays there, they say that the bones of his legs and arms
unite and knit together, and he arises and walks leisurely in the
direction of his lodging. Those who see him ask, "Were you not
dead?" and he answers that the *cemíes* came to his aid, in the form
of snakes. The relatives of the dead man, greatly enraged, because
they thought they had avenged his death, grow desperate, and try
to lay hands on him; if they do, they gouge out his eyes and crush
his testicles, because they say that the *bohutís* will not die, no
matter how much they are beaten, unless their testicles are
destroyed. . . .

Chapter XIX

How they make and house *cemíes* of wood or stone:

When someone is going along on a journey, and he sees a tree
with moving roots, the man, in a great fright, stops and asks, "Who
is it?" It replies, "Call the *bohutí*, and he will tell you who I am."
The Indian goes to the physician, who runs immediately to see the
tree, and sits down by it. The wizard goes to the tree, prepares
cogioba, and tells the tree all his titles, as though he were some
great lord, and he asks, "Tell me who you are, what you are doing
here, and what you want of me, and why you have had me called.
Tell me if you want me to cut you down, or if you want to come
with me, and how you want me to carry you, and I will build you

a house with land around it." Then the tree, or *cemi*, becomes an idol or devil, and replies to him. The wizard cuts it in the shape it has directed; builds a house for it; and many times a year makes *cogioba* for it. This *cogioba* is to pray to it, and please it, and to ask and learn things from the *cemi*, either evil or good, and to ask it for wealth. And, when they want to know if they will be victorious over their enemies, they go into a lodging where only the principal men of the tribe may enter; and their chief is the first to make *cogioba*, and none of them speak until the chief is finished; but when he has concluded his prayer, he stands a while with his head bowed and his arms on his knees; then he lifts his head towards the sky, and speaks. Then they all answer him in a loud voice, and, when they have given thanks, he relates the vision he has seen with the *cogioba*, which he has inhaled through his nose into his head. He says that he has talked with the *cemies*, and that they are to enjoy a victory, that their enemies shall flee; or that there shall be great loss of life, or wars, or famine, or other things which occur to him. Consider what a state their brains are in, because they say the lodging seems to be turned upside down, and that the men seem to be walking with their feet in the air. . . .

Chapter XXV

Of the things they say were uttered by two of the leading caciques of Española: one named Cazivaquel, father of Guarionel; the other Gamanacoel:

And that great lord, who they say is in heaven, commanded Cazivaquel to make a fast which all of them keep together; they are shut up six or seven days without eating anything, except the juice of herbs, with which they also wash themselves. Then they eat something which gives them nourishment. In the time that they have been without food, through the weakness which they feel in the body and in the head, they say they have seen something, perhaps desired by them, for they all keep this fast in honor of the *cemi*. . . . And they say that this cacique affirmed he had spoken with the *cemi* Yiocavugama, who told him that whoever remained alive after his death would rule over them only a short time, because they would see in their country a clothed people who were to rule them, and slay them, and they would die of hunger. At first, they thought these would be the Caribs, but reflecting that the Caribs only plundered and fled, they believed that it must be another people. Wherefore, they now believe it was the Admiral [Columbus] and the people he brought with him. . . .

In the province of Magdalena, it pleased God to enlighten with the light of the Holy Catholic Faith a whole household of the principal people. This province was [formerly] called Macorix, and the lord of it was called Guavaoconel. In the aforesaid house were his servants and favorites. . . . They were, in all, sixteen persons,

all relatives, and among them five brothers. Of these, one died, and
the other four received the water of holy baptism. I believe that
they died martyrs, for so it appeared in their death and in their
constancy. The first who received the water of holy baptism was an
Indian called Guaticavá, who then received the name of Juan. This
was the first Christian who suffered a cruel death; and, surely, it
seems to me that he died the death of a martyr. I have heard from
some who were present at his death that he said *"Dios naboria
daca,"* which is to say, "I am a servant of God." And, in like manner,
died his brother Antony, and with him another, saying the same
thing. . . . Those that were left alive, and are living today, are
Christians . . . and now, the Christians are many more in number
through the grace of God. . . .

The Lord Admiral [then] told me that . . . I should go and reside
with another principal cacique named Guarionex, lord of a numerous
people, whose language was understood everywhere in the land
[there was a cacique Guarionex in Hispaniola, and another of the
same name in Puerto Rico—ed.]. . . .

We were with cacique Guarionex for almost two years, giving him
instruction all the time in our holy faith, and the customs of
Christians. In the beginning, he showed a good will and gave us
hopes that he would do everything we wished, and of desiring
to be a Christian, asking us to teach him the Lord's Prayer, the
Ave María, and the Credo, and all the other prayers . . . and many
of his household learned the same. Every morning, he said his
prayers, and made his household recite them twice a day. But, later,
he became offended and gave up that good plan, through the fault of
some other principal men of that country, who blamed him, because
he was willing to give heed to the Christian law, since the Christians
were bad men and took possession of their land by force. They
advised him . . . to conspire together to slay the Christians. For this
reason, he broke off from his good intention, and we resolved to
depart thence and go where we might be more successful in
teaching the Indians, and instructing them in the matters of our
faith. And so, we went to another principal cacique called
Mauiatue, who showed us good will, saying he wished to become a
Christian. . . .

The day after we departed, Guarionex . . . ordered six of his
servants to carry off the holy images we had left in a house, where
the Christians were to kneel, and pray, and console themselves. . . .

Chapter XXVI

What became of the images, and the miracle God wrought to
show his power:

When they came out of the house of prayer, these Indians threw
the images down to the ground, and covered them with dirt, and
urinated upon them, saying, "Now your fruits shall be good and

great." In mockery, they buried the images in a tilled field. When
the boys in charge of the house of prayer saw this, they ran to
their elders and told them that the men of Guarionex had torn
the images to tatters and mocked them. . . . The elders left their
work, and ran crying out to give an account to Don Bartholomew
Columbus, who was then governor, in place of the Admiral, his
brother, who had gone to Castile. The offenders were tried, and, the
truth being known, they were publicly burnt. This did not deter
Guarionex and his subjects from their evil design of slaying the
Christians, on the day appointed for bringing in the tribute. Their
conspiracy was discovered, but . . . still they persisted, and killed
four men, and Juan Mateo, chief clerk and his brother, Antonio,
who had received Holy Baptism. Then they ran to where they had
hidden the images, and broke them in pieces. Some days later, the
owner of that field went to dig *ajíes,* which are roots like turnips
or radishes, and in the place where the images had been buried,
two or three *ajíes* * had grown, one through the middle of the
other, in the form of a cross. It was not likely that anyone would
find this cross, but the mother of Guarionex found it, and said,
"This miracle has been shown by God where the images were
found. God knows why." . . .

Truly, the island has great need of people to punish the chiefs
when they will not urge their people to hear the things of the
Holy Catholic Faith. . . . The first Christians . . . converted as soon as
they understood that there is one God, who has made all things,
and created heaven and earth, without any further arguments or
controversy, because they easily believe. But, with others, both force
and intelligence must be used, because we are not all alike. Because,
if some begin well and end even better, others will begin well and
later will laugh at what has been taught them. For these, force
and punishment are necessary. . . .

THE FIRST SETTLERS

[Boriquén was ignored
for fifteen years after its discovery, as Columbus crossed the Mona
Passage westward and founded the seat of Spain's New World government in nearby Hispaniola. It was not until the middle of 1508, when

---

* Fray Ramón seems to have confused the *ají*—a chili pepper that grows
above ground—with either the *ñame,* the yucca, or some other starchy root.

Translated from "Report to Fray Nicolás de Ovando," Juan Ponce de León,
May 1, 1509, Cayetano Coll y Toste, ed., *Boletín Histórico de Puerto Rico,*
Vol. I, 1914, pp. 119–21.

Nicolás de Ovando, Governor General of the Indies, agreed that Juan Ponce de León should found the first European settlement on nearby Boriquén. Ponce de León had fought in Europe against the Moors, and he had helped Columbus to quell Indian uprisings in Hispaniola during the Admiral's second voyage to America.

Ponce de León founded the first Spanish settlement in Puerto Rico at Caparra, near the southern shore of San Juan Bay, where he lived with his wife and children. Although he left a few years later and discovered Florida during his quest for the fabled Fountain of Youth, Ponce de León was Puerto Rico's first governor. Today, his remains lie beneath a marble slab in San Juan Cathedral, across the bay from the tiny settlement that he founded more than four centuries ago. The following account, a formal report to Governor de Ovando, details his first trip, in 1509, to the island of San Juan, which came to be known as Puerto Rico in 1521.]

Señor: What I, Juan Ponce de León, have done on my voyage to the island of San Juan, where I went to comply with the orders that your grace, in the name of His Royal Highness, sent me to do, is as follows:

First, I left the villa of Santo Domingo to go to San Juan on the twelfth day of July, year one thousand five hundred and eight: I went to Salvaleón in the caravel to seek supplies and the people who accompanied me, who were forty-two persons and eight sailors, fifty in all, and while we were in the port of Yuma, on the third of August, there was such a storm that the caravel ran aground on some reefs, whereupon I freed it, but lost a good part of our supplies.

Item: After the storm, I continued my voyage and reached the island of Mona, where I found the caciques and Indians of the southern part of said island of San Juan, on the twelfth day of August. I landed near the beach that is in the land of the chief Agüeybana, and I went to his house and spoke to him on behalf of your grace, and told him to plant a field for His Royal Highness, and he said he would. Afterwards, they told me he had done it, but I have not been able to learn its size, nor have I been able to go see it, due to the many tasks which occupy me. While the caravel was anchored, on the sixteenth of August, there came another storm, which pulled the vessel aground, and it cost me great effort to free it.

Item: After the caravel was freed, I traveled around the island, talking with the caciques along the coast, and with the Caribs whom I found there, and giving them jewels [or presents] in order to win their confidence. Then I reached the bay, near which is now the house and site [of government]. From the sea, the port and island looked exceedingly good; I entered the bay and circled it, thinking that I would find water and a site, but I did not. From there, I sailed eight leagues down the coast, where I found a river called the Ana. The vessel was able to enter, and there I anchored and unloaded on land all that we carried, and I had *bohíos* [Indian style huts] built, and I sent the ship to Mona island in search of cassava bread.

Item: After one month, being displeased with the port and the water, I went by land in search of a large river, called the Toa, where I stopped with all the people, and the ship brought all our supplies. But, due to some difficulties, I returned to the bay and sought another site, and since I could not find it, I went back to the River Ana.

At the River Ana, I built a site, and a dock, and roads, and sent the vessel for supplies, but then the sea grew rough and flooded the port, and I was forced to leave with fifteen men in search of the bay, to build a site there. I had all the people and supplies brought there by ship, and there I built the site, and made a large *bohío*, a road, and a pavement to the seaside dock; afterwards, since the site was so humid, and for other difficulties, I moved from there half a league inland, where the house is now located, which is closer to the mining areas.

Item: I built a medium-sized house with its terrace, and railing, and tall battlements, and barricade before the gate, all metal within and without. . . .

Item: I had a crew gather some gold, but could not get more since I had no food to give to the people, and since none of the Indians of this island would help me; but the crew gathered eight hundred thirty six pesos worth of gold.

Item: I had two pieces of land prepared, one of them next to the town . . . for the colonizers; the other, four leagues from the River Toa, was for me, and in these lands we shall work for His Royal Highness, because, until now, we have been only able to tell the Indian caciques to work their own lands for His Royal Highness; there are five caciques whom I have ordered to work their lands for His Royal Highness. This is all I have been able to do so far, because I have been required to move the settlement so many times, and for lack of food, and because I have not been able to take advantage of the labor of the Indians, as should be done. . . .

QUEEN ISABELLA'S ORDER

[The Spaniards who settled the West Indies were greedy for gold, and direly in need of food to sustain themselves. But they lacked the men to perform such arduous tasks as mining and farming, and the Indians were unwilling to volunteer assistance. This prompted an edict from Queen Isabella to resolve the problem. As Benjamin Keen comments in *Readings in Latin-American Civilization* (Boston: Houghton Mifflin, 1955), "The Indians were to be forced to labor, but as free men." Isabella's order of December 20, 1503, which follows, set the foundation for the *encomienda* system.]

. . . We are informed that because of the excessive liberty enjoyed by said Indians they avoid contact . . . with the Spaniards to such an extent that they will not even work for wages, but wander about idle, and cannot be had by the Christians to convert to the Holy Catholic Faith; and in order that the Christians of said island . . . may not lack people to work their holdings for their maintenance, and may be able to take out what gold there is on the island . . . and because we desire that the said Indians be converted to our Holy Catholic Faith and taught its doctrines; and because this can better be done by having the Indians living in community with the Christians of the island, and by having them go among them and associate with them, by which means they will help each other to cultivate and settle and increase the fruits of the island and take the gold which may be there and bring profit to my kingdom and subjects:

. . . I command you, our said Governor, that beginning from the day you receive my letter you will *compel* and *force* the said Indians to associate with the Christians of the island and to work on their buildings, and to gather and mine the gold and other metals, and to till the fields and produce food for the Christian inhabitants and dwellers of the said island; and you are to have each one paid on the day he works the wage and maintenance which you think he should have . . . and you are to order each cacique to take charge of a certain number of Indians so that you may make them work wherever necessary, and so that on feast days and such days as you think proper they may be gathered together to hear and be

Cited in Lesley B. Simpson, *The Encomienda in New Spain* (Berkeley: University of California Press, 1929), pp. 30–31. Reprinted by permission of the University of California Press.

taught in matters of the Faith. . . . This the Indians shall perform
as free people, which they are, and not as slaves. And see to it
that the said Indians are well treated, those who become Christians
better than the others, and do not consent or allow that any person
do them any harm or oppress them.

I, THE QUEEN.

"THE GRASPING AVARICE OF THE WHITE MEN"

[Queen Isabella's order
gave official sanction to the Spanish settlers to force the Indians to
labor under a thinly veiled system of slavery that lent itself to many
abuses. Washington Irving, born in New York City in 1783, is best known
for his stories, notably "Rip Van Winkle" and "The Legend of Sleepy
Hollow," but he was also an accomplished historian. In 1826, while
attached to the American embassy in Madrid, he worked on a biography
of Columbus. His account of the oppression of the Indians, which often
cites Fray Bartolomé de las Casas, describes events in Hispaniola, which
was the seat of government. But, as Las Casas himself relates in his
famous *Brevísima Relación de la Destrucción de las Indias*, the same
tragic situation prevailed in the islands of San Juan and Jamaica:
"[They] look'd like fruitful gardens, [but, in the year 1509,] they were
possessed by the Spaniards, with the same bloody intentions as the
others were: for there they also exercised their accustomed cruelties,
killing, burning, roasting men, and throwing them to the dogs, as also
by oppressing them with sundry and various torments in the Gold Mines
as if they had come to rid the earth of these innocent and harmless
creatures. . . . So lavish were the Spanish swords of the blood of these
poor souls, scarce two hundred more remaining; the rest perished
without the least knowledge of God."]

Before relating the
return of Columbus to Hispaniola, it is proper to notice some of
the principal occurrences which took place in that island under
the government of Ovando. A great crowd of adventurers of various
ranks had thronged his fleet—eager speculators, credulous dreamers,
and broken-down gentlemen of desperate fortunes; all expecting
to enrich themselves suddenly in an island where gold was to be

From Washington Irving, *The Life and Voyages of Christopher Columbus*
(New York: United States Book Co., 1828, Vol. II), pp. 586–90.

picked up from the surface of the soil or gathered from the mountain brooks. They had scarcely landed, says Las Casas, who accompanied the expedition, when they all hurried off to the mines, about eight leagues' distance. The roads swarmed like ant-hills, with adventurers of all classes. Every one had his knapsack stored with biscuit or flour, and his mining implements on his shoulders. Those hidalgos, or gentlemen, who had no servants to carry their burdens, bore them on their own backs, and lucky was he who had a horse for the journey; he would be able to bring back the greater load of treasure. They all set out in high spirits, eager who should first reach the golden land; thinking they had but to arrive at the mines and collect riches; "for they fancied," says Las Casas, "that gold was to be gathered as easily and readily as fruit from the trees." When they arrived, however, they discovered, to their dismay, that it was necessary to dig painfully into the bowels of the earth—a labor to which most of them had never been accustomed; that it required experience and sagacity to detect the veins of ore; that, in fact, the whole process of mining was exceedingly toilsome, demanded vast patience and much experience, and, after all, was full of uncertainty. They digged eagerly for a time, but found no ore. They grew hungry, threw by their implements, sat down to eat, and then returned to work. It was all in vain. "Their labor," says Las Casas, "gave them a keen appetite and quick digestion, but no gold." They soon consumed their provisions, exhausted their patience, cursed their infatuation, and in eight days set off drearily on their return along the roads they had lately trod so exultingly. They arrived at San Domingo without an ounce of gold, half-famished, downcast, and despairing. . . .

Poverty soon fell upon these misguided men. They exhausted the little property brought from Spain. Many suffered extremely from hunger, and were obliged to exchange even their apparel for bread. Some formed connections with the old settlers of the island; but the greater part were like men lost and bewildered, and just awakened from a dream. The miseries of the mind, as usual, heightened the sufferings of the body. Some wasted away and died broken-hearted; others were hurried off by raging fevers, so that there soon perished upward of a thousand men. . . .

It will be recollected that when Columbus was in a manner compelled to assign lands to the rebellious followers of Francisco Roldán, in 1499, he had made an arrangement that the caciques in their vicinity should, in lieu of tribute, furnish a number of their subjects to assist them in cultivating their estates. This, as has been observed, was the commencement of the disastrous system of repartimientos, or distributions of Indians. When Bobadilla administered the government, he constrained the caciques to furnish a certain number of Indians to each Spaniard, for the purpose of working the mines, where they were employed like beasts of burden. He made an enumeration of the natives, to prevent evasion; reduced them into classes, and distributed them among the Spanish inhabitants. The enormous oppressions which ensued have been noticed. They roused the indignation of Isabella; and when Ovando was sent out to supersede Bobadilla, in 1502, the natives were pronounced free; they immediately refused to labor in the mines.

Ovando represented to the Spanish sovereigns, in 1503, that ruinous consequences resulted to the colony from this entire liberty granted to the Indians. He stated that the tribute could not be collected, for the Indians were lazy and improvident; that they could only be kept from vices and irregularities by occupation; that they now kept aloof from the Spaniards, and from all instruction in the Christian faith.

The last representation had an influence with Isabella, and drew a letter from the sovereigns to Ovando, in 1503, in which he was ordered to spare no pains to attach the natives to the Spanish nation and the Catholic religion. To make them labor moderately, if absolutely essential to their own good; but to temper authority with persuasion and kindness. To pay them regularly and fairly for their labor, and to have them instructed in religion on certain days.

Ovando availed himself of the powers given him by this letter to their fullest extent. He assigned to each Castilian a certain number of Indians, according to the quality of the applicant, the nature of the application, or his own pleasure. It was arranged in the form of an order on a cacique for a certain number of Indians, who were to be paid by their employer, and instructed in the Catholic faith. The pay was so small as to be little better than nominal; the instruction was little more than the mere ceremony of baptism; and the term of labor was at first six months, and then eight months in the year. Under cover of this hired labor, intended for the good both of their bodies and their souls, more intolerable toil was exacted from them, and more horrible cruelties were inflicted, than in the worst days of Bobadilla. They were separated often the distance of several days' journey from their wives and children, and doomed to intolerable labor of all kinds, extorted by the cruel infliction of the lash. For food they had the cassava bread, an unsubstantial support for men obliged to labor; sometimes a scanty portion of pork was distributed among a great number of them, scarce a mouthful to each. When the Spaniards who superintended the mines were at their repast, says Las Casas, the famished Indians scrambled under the table, like dogs, for any bone thrown to them. After they had gnawed and sucked it, they pounded it between stones and mixed it with their cassava bread, that nothing of so precious a morsel might be lost. As to those who labored in the fields, they never tasted either flesh or fish; a little cassava bread and a few roots were their support.

While the Spaniards thus withheld the nourishment necessary to sustain their health and strength, they exacted a degree of labor sufficient to break down the most vigorous man. If the Indians fled from this incessant toil and barbarous coercion, and took refuge in the mountains, they were hunted out like wild beasts, scourged in the most inhuman manner, and laden with chains to prevent a second escape. Many perished long before their term of labor had expired. Those who survived their term of six or eight months were permitted to return to their homes until the next term commenced. But their homes were often forty, sixty, and eighty leagues distant. They had nothing to sustain them through the journey but a few roots or agi peppers, or a little cassava bread. Worn down by long toil and cruel hardships, which their feeble constitutions were incapable of sustaining, many had not strength to perform the journey, but sank down and died by the way; some by the side of a brook, others under the shade of a tree, where they had crawled for shelter from the sun. "I have found many dead in the road," says Las Casas, "others gasping under the trees, and others in the pangs of death, faintly crying Hunger! Hunger!" Those who reached their homes most commonly found them desolate. During the eight months they had been absent, their wives and children had either perished or wandered away; the fields on which they depended for food were overrun with weeds, and nothing was left them but to lie down, exhausted and despair- ing, and die at the threshold of their habitations.

It is impossible to pursue any farther the picture drawn by the venerable Las Casas, not of what he had heard, but of what he had seen; nature and humanity revolt at the details. Suffice it to say, that, so intolerable were the toils and sufferings inflicted upon this weak and unoffending race, that they sank under them, dissolving, as it were, from the face of the earth. Many killed themselves in despair, and even mothers overcame the powerful instinct of nature, and destroyed the infants at their breasts, to spare them a life of wretchedness. Twelve years had not elapsed since the discovery of the island, and several hundred thousand of its native inhabitants had perished, miserable victims to the grasping avarice of the white men.

THE INDIANS REBEL

[By the time the
Indians of Puerto Rico and other Caribbean islands realized that it was
impossible to coexist peacefully with the Spaniards, it was too late.
Some of the Indian chieftains tried to resist the Spanish conquerors,
but they were soon overcome. The final major Spanish-Indian battle in
Puerto Rico is described here by Ricardo E. Alegría, executive director
of the Institute of Puerto Rican Culture in San Juan. His text is based
on earlier works by Puerto Rican historians, particularly Salvador Brau
and Cayetano Coll y Toste. This battle marked the final chapter of
Indian civilization on the island. From then on, the Indians would constitute a tiny, isolated minority, whose way of life would soon fade.
Remnants of the Indian culture have survived, however, in many important ways: Numerous Indian words were absorbed by the Spanish
language; the Europeans learned many lessons of survival that enabled
them to live in the New World; and intermarriage between Spaniards
and Indians left a striking racial imprint that is still visible on many
of the people of the Caribbean.]

As each day passed,
the Indians of Puerto Rico felt unhappier with the treatment
accorded them by the Spaniards, who had stolen their lands and
their women, and deprived them of their freedom.

When the elder cacique Agueybana died, and he was replaced by
his nephew Agueybana II (or Agueybana the Brave), Indian-
Spanish relations worsened. The younger Agueybana,* a valiant
warrior, had been assigned under the *encomienda* system to Cristobal de Sotomayor, and the treatment afforded the Indian chieftain
by the young Spanish nobleman soured relations even further.
Only the naive belief prevailing among the Indians that the Spaniards were immortal prevented them from taking up arms. Finally,
in desperation, they decided to test the Spaniards' immortality.

An old cacique named Urayoán, whose village was on the island's
west coast near the Guaorabo River, † decided to make the test.
The opportunity arose in November, 1510, when Diego Salcedo, a

---

Translated from Ricardo E. Alegría, *Descubrimiento, Conquista y Coloniza-
ción de Puerto Rico: 1493–1599* (San Juan: Colección de Estudios Puertorriqueños, 1969), pp. 51–69. Reprinted by permission.

* All subsequent mentions of Agueybana refer to the young chief, not his
uncle.

† Near the present site of the town of Añasco.

young Spaniard, who was passing through the region, asked
Urayoán to provide him with some Indians to carry his baggage
across the river. Urayoán appeared willing to comply with the
request, but secretly told the Indians what they must do. Upon
reaching the river, the unsuspecting Salcedo allowed the Indians
to carry him. When they reached the deepest part, they halted,
dropped him in the water, and held him submerged for several
hours. They carried him ashore and, still fearing that he might
be alive, begged his pardon. After watching over him for a day,
and convincing themselves beyond doubt that the Spaniard was
indeed dead, they hastened to give the news to their cacique,
Urayoán.

Finally, the Indians knew that the Spaniards, like themselves,
were mortal. The news spread quickly, and was received with joy
by the Indians.

Soon, the acts of rebellion began. Indians of cacique Aymamón,
who reigned in the region of Aymaco [today Aguadilla], captured
young Diego Suárez and took him to their chieftain, who offered
him up as a trophy in a ballgame. Luckily for Suárez, a young
Indian who served as a scout ran with the news to the Spaniards.
En route, he met Captain Diego de Salazar. Guided by the Indian
youth, Salazar reached Aymamón's village just as the Indians
were watching the ballgame. He untied young Suárez from a tree,
handed him a sword, and told him, "Do as you will." Then he
commenced to slash at the Indians with his own sword. The Indians were astonished at Salazar's sudden brave attack. Aymamón
himself confronted Salazar, but he was disabled by a swipe of
the Spaniard's sword. Taking advantage of the confusion, Salazar,
young Suárez, and their Indian aide fled the village and went to
Sotomayor's settlement. They had not gone far when a group of
Indians caught up to them and called to Salazar, begging him to
stop because the cacique, Aymamón, wished to speak to him.
Believing it was a trap, Suárez implored Salazar not to return.
But Salazar did not want the Indians to think him a coward.
When he returned to the village, he found a badly wounded
cacique Aymamón, who praised him for his valor and begged that
he be permitted to use his name. The cacique, like all the Indians,
believed that names had magical powers, and that by taking on
the brave Spaniard's name he would acquire his skill and valor
in combat. Salazar agreed, but said that first he would have to be
baptized by a priest. The captain returned with Suárez to Sotomayor's settlement, and Salazar's name was from that day on a
source of fear among the Indians, since they considered him to
be the bravest warrior on the island.

Young Agueybana, tired of the humiliations and abuses suffered
by his people, and heartened by the news of the Spaniard's
mortality, decided to convene the principal caciques of the island
in an *areyto* [meeting] at his village. . . . There, the caciques agreed

to wage a war to the death. But the accord reached at the *areyto* was witnessed by Juan González, a young Spanish scout, who had painted his body like an Indian, and knew their language. He hurried to Sotomayor's plantation near Guánica, to warn him. Sotomayor had already been told of impending danger by Guanina, cacique Agueybana's sister, who was the concubine of the Spanish conquistador.

Sotomayor decided to return to his village, accompanied by his nephew, his Spanish servants, and by the interpreter, Juan González. However, he recklessly asked Agueybana to send him some Indians to help carry the baggage. The cacique did so, but had already decided not to allow his hated nemesis to escape. Suspecting an attack, Juan González straggled behind, but he was surprised by a group of Indians who were commanded by Agueybana himself.

Severely wounded, González saved his life when he offered to become the cacique's slave. Agueybana left him there, and led an attack against Sotomayor's group, killing them all. They headed back to finish off González, but the interpreter hid in a treetop. At night, when the Indians returned to their village to celebrate Sotomayor's death, González climbed down from the tree and —despite his many wounds—began a long painful trek, crossing the island's central mountain range, until he reached the plantations of Toa, where he asked that the news of the Indian uprising be forwarded to Ponce de León in Caparra.

Meanwhile . . . Guarionex, cacique of the Otuao region, led his warriors in an attack upon Sotomayor's settlement, burning it, and killing several of its inhabitants. Only the courage of Captain Salazar, who directed the retreat, saved the Spanish families, who reached Caparra safely, although many were wounded.

Other colonizers, who lived on isolated plantations near the mines, were also slaughtered by the Indians, who were now engaged in an islandwide revolt to regain their freedom.

In Caparra, when Ponce de León heard the news, he organized his forces, and decided to attack. With the 120 men that remained, he formed three companies, under the command of Captains Diego de Salazar, Luis de Añasco, and Miguel de Toro. The defense of Caparra was assigned to Salazar and his men, almost all of whom had been wounded in combat at Sotomayor's village. With the remaining men, and without waiting for the reinforcements he had requested from Hispaniola, Ponce de León set out to fight Agueybana II on his own territory.

After crossing the mountains, and reaching the Coayuco River, Ponce de León learned that the Indians in Agueybana's village were celebrating their victories with a huge *areyto*. Knowing that it was their custom to celebrate, and drink a strong liquor fermented with maize, Ponce de León decided to wait until nightfall. When the Indians were drunk and exhausted, Ponce de León and his men launched a surprise attack. The Indians believed that all the slain Spaniards had risen from the dead, and they offered little resistance. Brandishing swords and spears, the Spaniards killed hundreds of Indians, and took others as prisoners, whereupon they returned to Caparra before the Indians could regroup.

Days later, the Indians renewed their attacks upon the Spanish plantations. Ponce de León decided to attack Agueybana once more. He was told that in the region of Yagueca, cacique Mabodamaca, commanding 600 warriors, was seeking combat, and daring Salazar to fight with him. When Salazar learned of this, he received Ponce de León's permission to fight the cacique; in the ensuing struggle, the Spaniards defeated the cacique and his men.

Soon afterwards, Ponce de León received warnings that Agueybana was approaching to attack, with a large contingent of Indians. An experienced soldier, Ponce de León decided to choose the battle site; he deployed his men in a protected area, where they could only be attacked frontally. Using tree trunks, stones, and earth, he fashioned a parapet to protect his men from Indian arrows, and then he waited. Among Ponce de León's men were Juan de León, armed with an harquebus, as well as two soldiers with cross-bows. Each time the Indians attacked the parapet, the harquebus and crossbows inflicted many wounds. When the Indians attacked once more, the harquebusier noticed an Indian chief marching at the front, who wore around his neck a golden disc—or *guanín*—the emblem of the caciques. He took aim and fired, killing the man instantly. It was Agueybana himself. The warriors ran to recover him and retreated in disorder. . . .

Taking advantage of the Indians' confusion, Ponce de León returned to Caparra with his men. Knowing that the Indian resistance had received a fatal blow, he offered amnesty to those caciques who would make peace. Only two accepted the offer: Caguax, cacique of the Turabo region; and another cacique from the Utuao area, who would later be called *don* Alonso, when he was baptized by Bishop Alonso Manso.

The other caciques continued to resist. Many of them fell back to the mountains of the Sierra Luquillo, while others fled to neighboring islands, where they joined with their old enemies, the Caribs, in the common struggle against the Spaniards. The native rebellion had been squashed: the Indians' primitive weapons were no match for the steel swords, crossbows, and firearms of the Spaniards.

Concerned over the Indian emigration to the Lesser Antilles, Ponce de León asked the King for a brigantine to pursue and capture them, to prevent the island of San Juan from being left without people to work the mines. From then on, the struggle moved to those islands, and was directed mainly against the Caribs. . . .

Part II

THE COLONIZATION

The population of the island is so scattered that we find houses everywhere we go. There is a great abundance of bananas, and fish are plentiful in the rivers and along the coast; there is a great supply of fruits, sweet potatoes, beans, corn, and rice in the hills. Cow's milk is abundant. Household furniture . . . usually consists of only a hammock and a kettle. . . . A machete is the only instrument used in their work. With it, they cut the sticks, vines, and palm leaves to build their houses, and also clear the ground and plant and cultivate their crops.

—Translated from FRAY INIGO ABBAD, *Noticias de la Historia Geográfica, Civil y Política de Puerto Rico*, Madrid, 1788.

During the first three centuries of Spanish rule, Puerto Rico was a stagnant, sparsely populated colony. The mother country held absolute control over the political, economic, and religious life of its Caribbean possession. The island seemed rich in natural resources—its soil was fertile, and its mountains promised gold and other minerals—but the Indians had fled or were killed, and the fortune-seeking settlers were not fit for arduous labor. In 1579, the Bishop of San Juan, Fray Diego de Salamanca, reported to the king that

The main reason for the deterioration and stagnation of this island is the lack of slaves, for planting the sugar and mining the gold as before, when it was in such great abundance. . . . There is no lack of gold, but there are no slaves to mine it, and if a number of them were brought here it would do much good for the Royal Treasury, and this poor island would truly recover the title of Puerto Rico [Rich Port].*

* Translated from Luis M. Díaz Soler, *Historia de la Esclavitud Negra en Puerto Rico* (San Juan: University of Puerto Rico, 1965), p. 69.

But the gold mines had little more to give, and a small boom in sugar cane cultivation soon waned. Spain's fortune seekers shifted their eyes to other, more promising, regions of the vast New World.

For military and commercial reasons, however, the island had strategic value; it was one of the relay ports for the treasure fleets that sailed between Europe and the Western Hemisphere. To. protect this port, Spain converted the island into a military stronghold. By 1539, slaves and convicts were building El Morro fortress at the mouth of San Juan Bay. Because the island economy produced too little to underwrite this military enterprise, the *situado*, a subsidy fund, was sent from Mexico.

With its central location, Puerto Rico was viewed enviously by other European powers. Sir Francis Drake attacked the island in 1595 and was driven back in a hard-fought battle. George Clifford, Earl of Cumberland, took San Juan two years later, but tropical disease decimated his troops, and he retreated. The Dutch briefly seized and burned the capital two decades later, but also withdrew. The last major attack—by the British—was repelled in 1797. There had been sustained British interest. In 1706, Daniel Parke, Governor of the Windward Islands, reported, "If we had Porto Rico, the land is so good . . . in seven years we would make sugar so cheap as to be able to undersell the French . . . if we had that island, we should draw numbers of people from the barren land of New England."

At that time, the inhabitants of Puerto Rico lived in small, scattered settlements, where they farmed just enough to keep their stomachs full. Because Spain had outlawed trade with foreign countries, some islanders turned to smuggling with the nearby Dutch, French, and English colonies. Pirate ships roamed the waters of the Caribbean and nested near Puerto Rico's deserted beaches. In San Juan, there was a tiny governing elite that consisted of the military, the church, and a few well-to-do Spanish merchants.

But, as the nineteenth century began, Puerto Rico was stirred by new currents of change. It was not until 1807 that the first printing press came to the island. In the first two decades of the century, wealthy merchants and planters sought asylum from the wars of independence in South America and the slave rebellions in Haiti.

The *criollos* (native-born Puerto Ricans) soon came to resent the immigrants, and this feeling, together with Spain's inflexible system of rule, prompted demands for independence or autonomy. Many of the immigrants received land grants via a Spanish royal decree known as the *cédula de gracia*.

But most of the newcomers were Spanish loyalists, and their conservative influence dampened much of the "nativist" sentiment. Spain, having lost its foothold in South America, focused its strength on the liberal elements in Cuba and Puerto Rico and often used these islands as bases from which it harassed the new Latin American republics.

To maintain the *status quo*, Spain prohibited non-Catholics from settling in Puerto Rico, censured books with the slightest liberal bent, and restricted travel between the island's small, isolated communities.

Within these limits, the islanders were neglected, and allowed to pursue their own innocuous interests; the rural peasantry was free to prosper, or to perish.

THE COSTLY COLONY

[With its meager gold deposits long depleted, and after a short-lived prosperity from sugar cane, Puerto Rico's small farmers raised cattle, ginger, tobacco, and subsistence crops. Spain's strict trade laws discouraged commerce between Europe and San Juan, so the enterprising *criollos* developed a flourishing contraband trade with nearby islands. Government officials looked the other way, or shared in the smuggling business, and precious little revenue found its way into the royal treasury. Governor Juan José Colomo, in 1744, referred to "public scandals without number . . . minor offices sold to the highest bidders; and soldiers . . . two-thirds of whom are married to *mulatas*, which explains why there is no need of barracks at present." Actually, Puerto Rico was enjoying one of the few periods in its history when the colonial power derived little or no benefit from its Caribbean possession. The people were poor and neglected but lived independently and in peace. There were many small farmers, and freemen outnumbered slaves by eight to one. Spain's apathy had permitted the growth of a type of blissful anarchy: Puerto Ricans, left to their own devices, were pursuing their own interests. This, of course, meant that virtually no profits or taxes flowed to the seat of empire in Spain. During the reign of Carlos III (1759–88), officials were sent to all of Spain's colonies to prepare reports that would lead to a thorough administrative reform of the empire. The King, in 1765, sent to Puerto Rico a no-nonsense "efficiency expert," Field Marshal Alejandro O'Reilly. Puerto Rico's governor at the time was a hedonistic fellow named Ambrosio de Benavides, who was known to invite the pretty *mulatas* of the region to frolic in La Fortaleza palace, after discreetly removing the King's somber portrait from the wall. O'Reilly undertook a major fact-finding study, when it turned out that Benavides knew little of the island he supposedly governed. His report launched a number of reforms designed to generate more revenue for the Spanish crown.]

The conquest, population, spiritual guidance, administration of justice, fortification . . . and troops for the defense of the island of Puerto Rico have cost the

---

Translated from *Memoria de D. Alejandro O'Reylly, Sobre la Isla de Puerto Rico, Año 1765.* From A. Tapia, *Biblioteca Histórica de Puerto Rico* (San Juan: Ed. Instituto de Literatura, 1945), pp. 526–55. Also in Eugenio Fernández Méndez, ed., *Crónicas de Puerto Rico, 1493–1797* (San Juan: Ediciones del Gobierno, Estado Libre Asociado de Puerto Rico, 1957), Vol. I, pp. 239–69.

King, in the 255 years of his possession, many people and an immense fortune. Expenses from the Royal Exchequer still continue; more than 80,000 pesos per year come from Mexico for the costs of this island, and the amount must be increased considerably in the near future.

Who could predict that after so many years, and so much money squandered, that the yearly tribute would amount to only 10,804 pesos and 3 *reales*? Especially when one realizes that this island has 39,846 free persons and 5,037 slaves, that the climate is mild, and as healthy for Europeans as it is for the natives, that the island is bathed by many rivers, where good fish abound, and there is never lack of water in the hills, that the flatlands have beautiful plains, that one can harvest corn, rice, tobacco, and other fruits from two to three times a year; that the sugar cane is the thickest, juiciest and sweetest in the Americas; that cotton, indigo, coffee . . . cacao, nutmeg . . . are found in good quality; that the only reason for the poor quality of tobacco is the avarice of the planters, who pick it before it is ripe, in order that it have more juice and weigh more; that except for coffee, tobacco, and sugar cane, the other fruits grow wild in the mountains; that the *palo de Mora*—very much in demand by foreigners, for its yellow dye—is abundant, as is the *Guayacán*, a very good wood for blocks, furniture, and medicinal teas. The Dutch and British take a considerable amount of both each year . . . the island has a great abundance of excellent wood for buildings, ships, and charcoal. Near Guayama, I have seen saltpeter. There are enough salt beds to satisfy all needs; and an infinite number of herbs, roots, and medicinal plants, which could represent a considerable sector of commerce. . . .

The principal reason for the minuscule progress in Puerto Rico is that there is no governmental policy conducive to it. It was populated by soldiers far too accustomed to bearing arms to lower themselves to field work; add to these a number of stowaways, cabin boys, and sailors who deserted from each ship that touched port there. These people, quite indolent by nature, and undisciplined by government regulation, spread out into the fields and forests, where they built miserable shacks. With the few plantains that they planted, the fruits they found growing wild, and the cows that soon abounded in the mountains, they had milk, vegetables, fruit, and some meat; thus, they survived, and they still do. These lazy, aimless men, without tools or aptness in agriculture, nor anyone to help them clear the fields—what could be expected of them? The gentle climate encouraged their casual manner, since no formal attire was needed. They settled for a simple linen shirt, and long trousers. And since all lived alike, there was no cause for envy among them; also contributing were the fertility of the earth, and the abundance of wild fruits. With five days of work, a family has plantains for the entire year. With these, milk from the cows, yucca, and fruit, they are extremely content. For beds, they fashion hammocks from the bark of a tree called the *majagua*. For the bit of clothing they require, they trade with foreigners: cows, wood, horses, mules, coffee, tobacco, or some other item whose cultivation requires little toil. . . . I must add, however, that the inhabitants are very loyal to the King, and display an innocence and candor which I have neither seen nor heard of elsewhere in America. . . .

In all the island, there are only two schools for children; outside of Puerto Rico [San Juan] and the villa of San Germán, few know how to read. They count time by epochs of government, hurricanes, visits of the Bishop, arrivals of ships, or of funds from Mexico. They do not understand what a league's measure is; each man counts distance according to the length or speed of his stride. They walk barefoot in the countryside. Whites feel no repugnance when they mix with the darks. All of the towns, except for Puerto Rico [San Juan], have no more permanent population than that of the priest. The others are always in the countryside, except on Sundays, when those near the church come to mass, or during the three days of Easter, when almost all the parishioners attend. For those days, they erect houses which appear to be palm groves, made upon wooden piles; these houses consist of a pair of rooms; they are open day and night, and have neither windows nor doors. So little furniture have they, that they can move in an instant; the houses in the countryside are built the same way, and are barely more sturdy.

The distinguished persons of the island are few, the only difference among them being that they have a bit more fortune, or they may be officers in the militia.

The governors who knew of these problems tried to solve them by allotting land to the poor, who made enthusiastic offers to cultivate the land. The governors, full of zeal, believed them, without realizing that they could never comply with their promises. *La corte* [the Royal Court in Madrid], unable, at such a great distance, to discern anything except the optimistic picture painted by the island's governors, embraced the system. The result was to spread out the population, which gravely damaged the spiritual and physical development of the people, made schooling impossible, made it difficult to maintain a strong defense, and created less and less incentives for work and culture. . . .

What advantages have resulted? None. Before the allotment of lands, there was more than enough for the people's sustenance; today, they produce the same amount. All the citizens are laborers, and since each possesses the same crops, there is no market, or interior commerce, or reciprocal dependence; not one-twentieth of the land that was distributed has been cleared. . . .

Thus far, there is not even a market in the plaza of Puerto Rico [San Juan]; at times, canoes used to come to the docks with vegetables, eggs, and chickens; some days they sold little, others nothing. . . .

There is an open contraband trade throughout the island; foreign ships come most often to the south and west coasts; without even bothering to disguise their intentions, they drop anchor at any port, send their launch or canoe ashore, the inhabitants flock to the beach, and there the business is done. . . . The illicit trade is carried out with the Dutch of Curaçao and St. Eustatius, the Danes of St. Thomas and St. Croix, and the English of the nearby islands. . . . The Dutch take most of the tobacco, the British take the wood, and the Danes take the foodstuff and coffee. All of them take cattle, and as many mules as they can get.

Via this contraband traffic, the citizens can order any item they want from England or Holland, and those involved in the business are very punctual. . . .

There are, on this island, 4,579 small farms, and 269 ranches for cattle. A number of mills supply all the island's needs for sugar and honey; some is used for making *aguardiente* [cheap rum], but that of the foreigners is even cheaper, and they supply the entire south coast; a profit they would lose entirely, if more sugar mills were developed. . . .

The soldiers of the permanent battalion of Puerto Rico [San Juan] are almost all of them married, with many children. [They] . . . live apart in their own, or rented, huts. . . . The captains would advance the soldiers the money they needed to maintain themselves and their families, and receive in return a good part of their salaries, . . . charging 10 to 15 per cent interest. The two companies sent to Puerto Rico when the last war broke out, to reinforce the garrison, soon followed this example. They had barracks, but each soldier went off to live with some negress or *mulata*, whom he called his housekeeper; he gave her all four of the pesos he received monthly; and, from this money, the soldier, the woman, and their children—if they had any—maintained themselves. What strength can such a poorly fed soldier have? . . . How much honor, zeal, or application to serve can one expect from someone who lives in such spiritual and temporal abandon?

All the veteran troops of Puerto Rico were without any uniforms whatsoever: each man bought and wore what he wanted; many, when not on duty, wore straw sombreros on the streets, and almost all wore broad trousers that reached to their shins. Drills were equally ignored; no one knew how to drill. . . . This was the only defense Your Majesty had for the conservation of the loveliest island in America, upon whose fortification, troops, and other obligations many millions have already been spent. . . .

The importance of the situation of Puerto Rico, the goodness of its port, the fertility, rich products, and population, the advantages that it should produce for our commerce, and the irreparable harm that would occur if foreigners possessed it, demand, it seems to me, the most serious and prompt attention by the King and his ministers. . . . In a few years, with proper regulation, it could be of relief to the Royal Treasury, and one of the finest jewels of the Crown. . . .

"CRIOLLOS" AND "BLANCOS"

[Nearly two decades after O'Reilly's report, Fray Iñigo Abbad y Lasierra published the first comprehensive history of Puerto Rico, offering a rich chronicle of the people and their way of life. By this time, there was a distinct Puerto Rican identity. The *criollos*, or native-born Puerto Ricans, were neither Spaniards nor the children of Spaniards; their family lineage went back for several generations on the island. In this excerpt from his work, Fray Iñigo testifies to the creation of a new nationality: the Puerto Rican.]

The Europeans of different nations who have settled on this island, the mixture of these with Indians and Negroes, and the effects of the climate, have produced different kinds of people, who are different in color, physiognomy, and personality. . . .

The first Spaniards who settled here partly changed the nature of the Indians, but, at the same time, they acquired the Indians' way of life, and habits of food and dwelling. . . .

Those who are born here, no matter from what breed or mixture, are called *criollos*. The Europeans are called *blancos* [whites], or *hombres de la otra banda* [men of the other band]. These cannot avoid the effect of the climate; they commonly fall sick, lose some of the liveliness of their color, and of their blood. With all this, they generally maintain their nature, and are more industrious than the *criollos*. The *criollos* are well-built; one barely ever sees a cripple. Their constitution is delicate, and their limbs are loose and slender, which is proper for a warm climate; but they are also lazy, and the climate makes them look so pale as to appear sick; they are deliberate, taciturn, and always observant; but they have a lively talent for imitating whatever they see; they love freedom, are

Translated from Fray Iñigo Abbad y Lasierra, *Noticias de la Historia Geográfica, Civil y Política de la Isla de San Juan Bautista de Puerto Rico* (Madrid: 1788). A large excerpt is contained in the more recent Eugenio Fernández Méndez, ed., *Crónicas de Puerto Rico: 1493–1797*, Vol. I, pp. 313–25.

unselfish, and very hospitable to strangers; but they are also vain
and inconstant in their tastes.

They have an inclination for feats of honor and brilliancy: They
have proved brave in war, and are good soldiers for short cam-
paigns, since they are accustomed to a sedentary life, and dislike
leaving it for long; they are more inclined to naval expeditions, and
devote themselves to piracy and contraband with zeal and valor;
they know how to resist hunger. . . .

They are wearied by the ardor and liveliness of the Europeans,
but they receive them openly in their homes, feed them with
pleasure, and glory in the fact that they descend from them. The
women love the Spaniards more than the *criollos*; they are of good
disposition, but the salty air of the sea consumes their teeth and
deprives them of the agreeable color found in women of other
countries; the heat makes them indolent and slovenly; they marry
very young, and are fecund; they love dancing and horse racing,
which they perform with extraordinary skill and abandon.

The *mulatos*, who form the largest part of the population, are the
children of white men and negresses. Their color is dark, disagree-
able, . . . they are tall and well formed, stronger, and more accustomed to work than the white *criollos*, who treat them with
disdain. Among this class of people are many . . . who have distinguished themselves for their actions, and they are ambitious
for honor.

Of the *Negros* on this island, some were brought from the coasts
of Africa, others are *criollos*; the former are sold as slaves; of the
latter, many are free. With all this, there is nothing more igno-
minious on this island than to be black, or to be descended from
them; a white man insults any of them, with impunity, and in the
most contemptible language; some masters treat them with unjust
rigor, . . . resulting in disloyalty, desertion, and suicide. Others regard the slaves with great affection . . . employing them only in
household service, but the slaves suffer the rigors of slavery when
the master dies and they pass to another. . . .

Since the slaves come from different provinces, they are also of
different inclinations; nevertheless, one can say that their ways are
formed to a great degree by their masters; if the slaves are loved
and treated with affection, they respond, even with heroism; but if
masters are too harsh, the slave knows how to suffer and hide his
feelings until the time for revenge, which is performed by poisoning
the cattle, or other slaves, or the master himself. Some slaves, especially those from *Mina*, take their own lives, since they are convinced that they shall be reborn in their homeland, which they
believe to be the best in the world. . . .

There is no doubt that the enslavement and lowliness of the
blacks, and other colored people, creates in the Spaniards of America a certain fantasy: From infancy, they are surrounded by servants who are supposed to guess their every whim. . . . On the

other hand, unaccustomed to finding any obstacles or resistance to their whims, or to receiving any form of punishment, they are raised with a presumptuous spirit. They are raised without work and without contradiction, somewhat like Princes who have never known adversity. They are generally frugal, lively, and clear-sighted, but they are also ambitious for glory, which could be useful in terms of politics, if this fact can be utilized by the governors, to whom they display complete submission and respect. . . .

The favorite diversion of these *isleños* [islanders] is dancing: They organize a dance for no other reason than to pass the time. . . . When someone gives a dance, the news travels throughout the territory, and hundreds of persons come from everywhere, without being invited. Since the houses are small, most guests stay outside, until they wish to dance. To begin the dance, the guests stand at the foot of the stairs with their timbrels, gourds, maracas, and small guitars; and sing a song honoring the owner of the house. When the owner appears at the entrance, he welcomes the guests, and urges them to come up; then they embrace and exchange greetings, as though they had not seen each other for years. The women sit on benches or hammocks; the men remain standing, or crouch down upon their heels. . . .

They come out to dance one by one, or two by two; when a man invites a woman to dance, if she has no slippers—as most of them do not—she borrows a pair, and begins to dance around the parlor with exceptional speed. . . . The man who dances remains in a corner of the parlor, his sombrero tipped sideways on his head, holding his cutlass behind his back; he does not move from this spot, but raises and lowers his feet with much speed and force. . . . When a man wishes to show affection for a woman who is dancing, he removes his hat and puts it on her head. Sometimes she has so many that she must carry them in her hands and under her arms; when she tires of dancing, she returns the hats to the men, each of whom gives her half a *real*; this is called *dar la gala* [giving the prize]. If one of the bystanders wishes to dance with a woman who is already dancing with someone else, he must ask the man's permission. This has caused some strong feuds, and, since all of them believe that might makes right, the dance usually ends in a clash of knives.

During the dance, a few slave women [he is obviously describing a dance on a farm large enough to have slaves, not that of subsistence farmers—ed.] serve bowls of breadstuffs with milk and honey, bottles of *aguardiente*, and cigars. Those who grow tired go to sleep in the hammocks, or enter the inner room to rest. . . . others retire to their homes, and return the next day, because these dances tend to last for a whole week. . . .

These dances are more common at Easter time, or before Ash Wednesday [*Carnestolandas*], or at the time of a wedding, whose celebration begins two months previous. The birth or death of a child is also celebrated with a dance, which lasts until the guests can no longer stand the foul odor of the corpse. . . .

Being a *compadre* to these islanders is a very important relationship. Nothing is denied a *compadre*; he enjoys full satisfaction and liberty in the home of his *compadres*, and makes use of their friendship, and comforts, as though he were in his own home. If a man accompanies a brother or sister to their wedding, or attends the confirmation or baptism of a child, he is no longer considered a brother; the treatment between *compadres* is always preferred, because it is more affectionate and expressive of intimate friendship.

Important fiestas are also celebrated with horse races. . . . No one misses these, not even the tiniest child, who is carried in the saddle. In each town, there are races for the most solemn holidays. In the capital, there are the days of San Juan, San Pedro, and San Mateo. The day before San Juan, at sunrise, a great multitude of riders arrive from all the towns of the island to show their horses; at the stroke of noon, men and women of all ages and classes emerge from their homes, all mounted on horses that are decorated to the utmost. Many have saddles that are lined with velvet or trimmed with gold, with spurs of silver, and some add breastplates with bells of the same metal. . . . Those who cannot spend so much adorn their horses with a great variety of ribbons and laces, and do not hesitate to pawn or sell the best items in their household to look good for the *corrida* [race].

There is no order at all: At the stroke of twelve, they race along the streets, generally in groups of friends or relatives; they gallop around the city, without stopping or resting the entire night, until the horses give out. Then, they take other horses, and continue with such vehemence that the entire population of the town seems to be on horseback, riding frantically in every direction.

Despite the confusion, there is rarely an accident, and if there is, the victim is usually some Spaniard who has turned the corner and, faced by a platoon of riders, cannot avoid the horses with the same skill as the *criollos*. Even when the horse is racing full speed, the *criollos* leave the reins loose upon the saddle, cross their arms, and while smoking a cigar, voice their compliments to the ladies in the windows, and to those who are racing. . . .

The entire *corrida* is not so tumultuous. At nine in the morning, out comes the banner of the city, accompanied by the municipal officials, the noblemen, and the officers, two companies of cavalry, and the troops, all presided over by the Governor. This *paseo* is performed with great pomp and order. . . . It proceeds through the main streets of the city, after which the banner is carried to the Cathedral. . . . After mass, it is returned to the city hall, with all the ostentation possible, while in the other streets, there are races, shouting, and merry-making, as the people express their joy and wild passion, which reign that day.

The many rivers, channels, lagoons, and swamps of the island,

and the distance the people live from each other and from the churches, cause them to use their horses frequently. If they must go to mass, or a dance, or to visit a friend, or on any other errand, it is indispensable to travel by horse; when it rains, they would not go by foot for even a hundred paces. ; . . . This custom makes all of them fine horsemen, who travel by day or night, full speed, crossing rivers or swamps . . . without tiring. . . .

With the same facility, they travel by canoe to islands 40 or 50 leagues distant, taking with them a cluster of plantains for food. They go to deserted islands, catch shellfish, make a fire, gather water, and then proceed to another island, until they reach their destination. There is not a single inn throughout the island, but travelers are received in any household; they only seek shelter in case of rain. If it rains while they are en route, a large *yagua* leaf protects them from any shower. If they must cross a deep river, they remove their shirt and trousers and proceed without hesitation. . . . Wherever the night catches them, they dismount, and allow the horse to feed, since there is pasture everywhere. They then hang up their hammock, and fall asleep. The next day, they continue their trip, eat some provision, or satisfy their hunger in any plantain grove. They are not great hunters, nor are there many four-legged animals on the island, except for wild or runaway dogs, which cause great damage to the livestock, but the thickness of the woods makes it impossible to kill them with a rifle. For the same reason, they take little advantage of the hens, guineas, parrots, parrakeets, ravens, and other good-tasting birds; but, in recompense, they fish in the rivers and sea with great skill.

They have an abundance of domestic birds; common hens, guineas, turkeys, and ducks of many kinds; but they only kill them when in need; they usually keep them to sell in the capital city, or in the ports, to the ships that arrive, and this is the industry they most apply themselves to, without any cost or work. . . .

Although the towns are generally deserted, except for the priest, on Sundays and holidays they come to hear mass. They usually arrive at eight in the morning, mounted on horseback, . . . and then return to their haciendas, leaving the town as solitary as before. When they are sick, they advise the priest, who mounts a horse. . . . He confesses the patient, administers the holy sacraments, and returns to town. . . .

They bring the dead to be buried by the church, unless the man has died of some epidemic; then he is buried on his own hacienda, at the foot of a tree. A year or two later, his bones are removed from the earth and taken to the church, where all honors are paid, according to the stature of the person.

These islanders are very devoted to Our Lord: All carry the rosary around their necks, and pray to it at least twice a day. All families begin with this saintly exercise, some repeat it at noon, without forgetting the evening; but the youth are a cause of great ignorance, since most of them are not very well acquainted with Christian Doctrine, because they do not live close to the towns. . . . . Without doubt, this would be one of the happiest places, if its inhabitants were more industrious. Until they are, they shall live in poverty and obscurity, . . . although this island could be one of the richest possessions of the Spanish Monarchy.

THE XIVAROS

[By the early nineteenth century, Puerto Rico's economy was thriving, and the island's population had soared to nearly 400,000—including 45,000 slaves. In those days, it was widely assumed that only African slaves could withstand the rigors of tropical weather in the fields, but the case of Puerto Rico showed that this was not true.

Colonel George Dawson Flinter, son-in-law of one of the wealthiest landed proprietors of Caracas, came to Puerto Rico after Venezuela gained its independence, and for several years he commanded the island's Spanish regiment. He later produced a book—*An Account of the Present State of the Island of Porto Rico* (London: Longman Press, 1834).

The following book review includes the author's compelling description of Puerto Rico's "Xivaro"—an archaic way of spelling *jíbaro*—the white rural peasantry who "are proverbial for their hospitality, and . . . ever ready to fight on the slightest provocation." The reviewer also compares Puerto Rico with its neighboring islands, where slavery was more predominant. Free men, he pointed out, produce far more than slaves, and the "vice" and "tyranny" of slavery are avoided. The fact that the great majority of Puerto Rico's workers, whether white or black, were free made for a more desirable society than those on islands such as Cuba or Jamaica, where a large part of the population was in bondage. Most impressive is the reviewer's prediction that the social fabric of the island would erode once the small family farms were conglomerated into vast sugar estates. This would occur not during the era of slavery but later, in the early years of the U.S. occupation.]

. . . The early history of Puerto Rico affords few features of interest. Although one of the oldest colonies of the Spanish crown, it served for three centuries only as a convict station; and its free population presented, until a few years ago, a marked specimen of the besotted indolence

From *The Edinburgh Review*, LX (1835), p. 328.

which characterized a Spanish settlement of the old times. The military and civil expenses were defrayed by remittances from Mexico; and it was not until the revolution caused these remittances to cease in 1810, that the island, owing to the extreme embarrassment of its financial condition, began to attract the notice of the mother country. In 1815 a decree was published in its behalf . . . [which] whilst it greatly encouraged free industry, unfortunately at the same time gave an impulse to the employment of slave labour, which had hitherto been unused, rather from indolence and want of capital than from motives of humanity. Colonists were invited to the island on the most liberal terms—lands were allotted gratis—the settlers were freed from direct taxes, and, for a certain number of years, from the tithes and alcabala; as well as from the exportation duties, which formed one of the most impolitic features of the old Spanish system.

From the period of this decree, the advance of Puerto Rico in wealth and population has been unexampled, even in the virgin regions of America. A great additional impulse was given by the arrival of capitalists, driven by civil war from the Spanish Main; —men distinguished in the more prosperous times of South America for their steady regularity and probity in the transaction of business. . . . [Puerto Rico is] next to Brazil and Cuba the most formidable rival with which our colonies have to contend in the production of their staple articles, and at the same time a granary competent to supply all the ordinary wants of her abundant population.

The island appears to be one of the most lovely of all those regions of loveliness which are washed by the Caribbean Sea. . . . The sugar-cane, notwithstanding the drought, thrives abundantly, and most of the chief plantations of the island are formed on this [the south] coast. This inestimable benefit of moisture Puerto Rico derives from its forests, which as yet clothe a large portion of the interior; the thick cover at once attracting the rain and preventing evaporation. . . .

[Puerto Rico's] inhabitants . . . seem to enjoy a more than ordinary exemption from the evils which afflict humanity in these sickly regions. The mortality, according to our author's tables, does not exceed that which prevails in some of the healthier countries of Europe. A still more singular characteristic appears to distinguish this island from its neighbors, namely, the great deficiency of native animals of every sort; and especially the entire absence . . . of those noxious reptiles and insects which seem to inhabit the rest of the West Indies as their peculiar possession. . . .

The population of Puerto Rico amounted, according to the Spanish census of 1830, to 323,858; of which 127,287 were free people of colour, and 34,240 only, slaves. But . . . our author calculates, apparently on good grounds, the whole number at 400,000, and the slaves at 45,000; or nearly 180 inhabitants to the square mile.

Here, then, we have a free white population of 200,000 souls, or half the entire amount of inhabitants. What causes can have produced a result so utterly different from that which exists in all the West India islands, except those of Spain? Whence arises this numerous and prosperous Creole yeomanry, (for we shall see that a great proportion of them are owners or occupiers of land), whilst other colonies are divided between a few white proprietors, and a degraded multitude of slaves, with hardly a vestige of an intermediate class? Such was not always the state of our own islands. . . . We have abundant evidence that Antigua, St. Kitts, Dominica, and other colonies, possessed, a hundred years ago, a multitude of English settlers; who have gradually dwindled away, by intemperance, by their own misconduct, and above all through the extension of the sugar cultivation, and of its companion the slave trade, to the small remnant which now exists. We believe, that if any causes should arise to give a sudden impulse to the colonial industry of this now happy Spanish island, it would soon follow—as Cuba is already following—the baneful course of our own settlements, and purchase wealth at the expense of happiness. . . .

Of the free inhabitants of Puerto Rico, a very small proportion is settled in the towns: indeed, the capital, San Juan, with about 8000 souls, is the only place which seems to merit such a title. Some of the best, in point of connexions and respectability, are the descendants of military men, who, during the long period when the island was a mere garrison, formed alliances and settled within it. These people maintain the pride of their descent with all the stateliness of grandees; and some of them are opulent. Wealthy merchants and planters (many of whom are foreigners) form the next class; but the latter, fortunately for the happiness if not for the riches of the island, form altogether but a small, and not now a very thriving class. The number of sugar estates is about 300; chiefly situated on the southern coast. They hardly pay at present, according to our author, the expenses of cultivation. But there are, in addition, some 1,300 small plantations belonging to poor cultivators, who, growing only an acre or two of cane, devote their attention chiefly to the raising of provisions. There are 148 coffee estates; but in this branch of cultivation, as well as that of sugar, the larger capitalists have been gradually losing money and abandoning their estates; whilst the small farmer who pursues various lines of industry on his little tract of land, has been able, in this way, to increase his comforts.

It is this class which forms the distinctive feature of the population. A numerous race of cultivators—brave, for their courage was largely tried in the exigencies of the South American wars—of white blood, and Spanish feelings, opinions, and prejudices,—is something so widely different from what is to be found in our own islands or those of France—that we are almost tempted to abandon

the principles of political economy, and to feel grateful for the
want of enterprise, and slothful contentment, which undoubtedly
have prevented the conversion of the island into one wide sugar
factory, with white overseers and negro labourers. Our author
gives the extraordinary number of 19,000 proprietors of land in
perpetuity: nearly 18,000 of these are small occupiers, raising
provisions and herding cattle. The Xivaros—as the white country
population are called—are, it cannot be denied, an indolent race;
who seem to multiply under an easy condition of existence, without
adding much to the commercial wealth or social refinement of their
country.

"Like the peasantry of Ireland, they are proverbial for their
hospitality: and, like them, they are ever ready to fight on the
slightest provocation. They swing themselves to and fro in their
hammocks all day long, smoking their cigars, and scraping a guitar.
The plantain grove which surrounds their houses, and the coffee-
tree, which grows almost without cultivation, afford them a frugal
subsistence. . . . The cabins are thatched with the leaves of the
palm-tree; the sides are often open, or merely constructed of the
same sort of leaves as tne roof—such is the mildness of the climate.
Some cabins have doors, others have none. There is nothing to
dread from robbers, and if there were banditti, their poverty would
protect them from violence. A few calabash shells, and earthen
pots—one or two hammocks made of the bark of the palm-tree—
two or three game-cocks, and a *machete*—form the extent of their
moveable property. A few coffee-trees and plantains, a cow and a
horse, an acre of land in corn or sweet potatoes, constitute the
property of what would be denominated a comfortable Xivaro
—who, mounted on his meagre and hardworked horse, with his
long sword protruding from his baskets, dressed in a broad-
brimmed straw-hat, cotton jacket, clean shirt, and check pantaloons,
sallies forth from his cabin to mass, to a cockfight, or to a dance,
thinking himself the most independent and happy being in existence."—pp. 76–78.

"Riding out one afternoon in the country, I was overtaken by
one of those sudden showers of rain so common in tropical
climates. I fled for shelter to the nearest house, which happened
to be the cottage of a poor Xivaro. It was on the slope of a little
hill, surrounded by plantain trees, which did not appear to be
carefully cultivated, and a large patch of potatoes was close by.
I placed my horse without ceremony under the projecting roof.
I entered the humble dwelling with the usual salute, which is
the same as in Ireland, 'God save all here,' which was courteously
answered by the man of the house, who seemed to be about forty
years of age. He was dressed in a check shirt and wide linen
drawers. He was coiled up in a hammock of such small dimensions,
that his body was actually doubled in two; one foot rested on the
ground, with which he propelled the hammock to and fro; and

at intervals with his great toe he turned a large sweet potato, which was roasting on a few embers, placed on a flag on the ground close to him, and which no doubt was intended for his evening meal. He had a guitar in his hand, from which he produced sounds which appeared to me discordant, but seemed to please him exceedingly. On my entrance he turned on his side, and offered me the hammock, which of course I refused to accept. Two small children, perfectly naked, were swinging to and fro in another small hammock, and greedily devouring large roasted plantains. The woman of the house was squatted on the floor, feeding four game-cocks, which were lodged in the best part of the house, while the husband every now and then would warn her not to give them too much corn or too much water. They received me with an urbanity unknown to the peasantry of Northern Europe. They placed a large leaf of the palm-tree over my saddle to protect it from the rain; and pressed me to sit down in the kindest manner. The host was very communicative; he gave me the whole pedigree of his game-cocks, and enumerated the battles they had won. He pointed out one to me which he said was 'a most delicate bird,' an expression made use of by the Xivaros to denote its great value; and he concluded by offering it to me as a present. Indeed a Xivaro would form a very poor opinion of a person who could not discuss the merits of a game-cock. In going away they offered me their cabin with as much politeness as if it had been a palace, and hoped to see me again. I was forcibly struck with the native courtesy of these people, and it gratified me to observe the content and happiness they enjoy, without a thought for the present or a care for the future—without wants, without wishes, without ambition."—p. 80.

. . . It is quite clear, that the spread of these tropical back-woodsmen over the virgin soil of the island, has prevented it thus far from falling into the hands of the sugar monopolist; and it furnishes a sufficient answer to those who imagine that a European race, living by its own labour, cannot exist, where 80 degrees is the average height of Fahrenheit's thermometer. With the gradual diffusion of education, of which our author admits that there is a lamentable deficiency, much of the grosser parts of their character may be progressively removed. . . .

The free coloured inhabitants of Puerto Rico are by far more numerous than in any other West India island; and this fact alone,—when we consider the ineradicable prejudice attaching to colour, which has brought such infinite misery, and social discomfort, over a great part of the world,—speaks more than any eulogy in favor of its people and their government. The whole British West Indies contained, before 1834, not more than 80,000 free coloured inhabitants, in a population of ten times that amount; of these, sixteen thousand were to be found in Trinidad alone,—an island which had long been governed by Spanish laws. Although white blood is, in Puerto Rico, as everywhere else beyond the Atlantic, a patent of nobility, yet the Xivaro no more treats with contempt and contumely his inferior in caste than the grandee of Old Spain, his inferior in station. . . .

In 1823, Jamaica, with 340,000 slaves, exported 1,400,000 quintals of sugar. Puerto Rico, with 45,000 slaves, produces about 410,000. The French colony of Guadaloupe, with twice as many slaves as Puerto Rico, produces an equal crop of sugar. The soil of the latter is far more fertile than that of the other islands, already in great measure exhausted. But, on the other hand, capital and industry form essential elements of the manufacture, in the British and French isles, while the Spaniards are far behind in all pursuits requiring either. From these premises our author concludes, not unreasonably, that a large proportion (which elsewhere, however, he calculates at one-fifth only) of this crop of sugar is raised by free labour.

But it must be remembered, that, besides the greater estates, there are in Puerto Rico some 1,200 or 1,300 small sugar plantations, the property of the Xivaros of the interior, who live cheaply and work lazily, but who contrive to raise a small quantity of this valuable article, together with provisions and cattle. If such rough cultivation as this succeeds at all, it can only be in consequence of the vast productiveness of the soil, cleared of its forests only within the last twenty years, which gives the planter the same advantage over his brethren to windward and leeward, as the settler of Illinois has over the cultivator of the worn out "old fields" of the Atlantic coast. Such production can in the nature of things be only temporary. On the other hand, the great sugar estates, which must form the main sources of this commodity, are evidently cultivated here as elsewhere by slaves; and although at present the cultivation of sugar on a large scale is extremely unprofitable, a rise in its price would undoubtedly cause at once an increased importation of slaves, and the application of more capital and ingenuity to the business, until the small farmers would be driven from the market by the slave-owning capitalists. . . .

At present the question of the future destiny of this beautiful and happy island may be said to remain undecided. But it soon must call for a final adjustment. Slave labour, reinforced by the slave trade, cannot long coexist with the industry of a free race of cultivators. Puerto Rico, long neglected and unknown, now called into unexampled prosperity by the same causes which once raised cities and established small commonwealths in the windward islands, is fast reaching the same crisis in her fate which they reached; and it is in the power of the Spanish Government, by abolishing the slave trade, to enable her to pass that crisis in safety. The island is only preserved from presenting a spectacle similar to theirs, by a concurrence of circumstances which render the cultivation of sugar at present a disadvantageous investment of capital; and by its yet unexhausted soil, which affords an ample return of other colonial produce to such labour as her free husbandmen are inclined to bestow upon it. Remove that obstacle, and let capital flow into the island, together with an unrestricted slave trade, and Puerto Rico will follow the fortunes of Cuba. That island, when visited by Humboldt, thirty years ago, was chiefly tilled by the labour of freemen. But at the close of the war, the baleful influence of African importation began. One hundred and eighty-five thousand slaves were landed at Havana alone in fourteen years; a peaceful and industrious people became contaminated with vice and disorder of every kind; the slaves already exceed in numbers the white free population; and the old Spanish kindness and loyalty between master and slave has so far disappeared, and tyranny has so far begun its usual work, that the planters openly confess that one of the reasons for the importation of fresh slaves is, to supply the masters with a guard of mamelukes against the discontented negroes of the colony. If the colonists of Puerto Rico will not follow the example, which Antigua alone of all the West Indian Islands has yet proclaimed, by setting her negroes free on the day when statutory emancipation began, without apprenticeship, or education from freedom of any kind, it is at least in the power of the crown of Spain, without injustice to any one, to cause the greater evil of the slave trade to cease; and to rescue one fair island,—one loyal and gallant people,—from the insidious advances of ruin. . . .

SLAVERY LAWS

[As in the case of the Indians—who were exterminated—Spain promulgated laws to guarantee decent treatment of the African slaves. But the laws were often broken. Historian Luis M. Díaz Soler describes how "for the master, the negro represented an investment and a valuable instrument of production, but for the overseer he was a poor soul who must obey blindly, and who would be punished rigorously if he did not obey orders. Little did it matter to the overseer if the slave were killed or crippled."

Selections in this chapter:
1. Translated from Cayetano Coll y Toste, ed., *Historia de la Esclavitud en Puerto Rico*, compiled by Isabel Cuchí Coll (San Juan: Sociedad de Autores Puertorriqueños, 1969), pp. 27–40.
2. Ibid, pp. 79–82.
3. Ibid, pp. 90–91.

Some masters had little regard for the investment value of their slaves. In his autobiography * (Alejandro Tapia y Rivera, *Mis Memorias, 1826–1882* [New York: Laisne & Rossboro, 1928], pp. 15–17, 76–84) nineteenth-century playwright Alejandro Tapia y Rivera—a militant abolitionist—recalls how some slaves grew so desperate over their plight that they "agreed to kill each other, including mothers and children." He recounts the case of one hacienda owner "who had the teeth yanked out from one of his servants, who used to chew on the sugar cane"; another, who "buried a slave woman alive"; and a third, "who once frankly complained that he had been unable to prevent the escape of his slave, despite the fact that he had forced him to eat human excrement."

The following is an excerpt from the "Regulation on Education, Treatment and Occupations Which the Masters of This Island Should Give to Their Slaves," issued in 1826 by Governor don Miguel de la Torre. The regulation reflects some degree of concern for the treatment of the slaves but also—to perhaps a greater degree—a fear of possible uprising if vigilance were relaxed.]

Chapter II

Of the Christian and Civil Education the Masters Should Give their Slaves. . . . they should instruct them in the principles of the Catholic religion, and in those truths needed for them to be baptized within one year of their residence. . . . this instruction will be every night, after prayer hour. . . . On Sundays and holidays, those slaves already baptized should hear Mass. . . . Unbaptized negroes who are ill should be administered the Holy Sacraments of Baptism . . . so that they do not perish as Pagans. . . . the masters shall make every effort to make the slaves understand the obedience they must lend to established authority; the obligation they owe to revere the priests; to respect whites; to behave moderately with free coloreds, and affably with their equals. . . .

Chapter IV

Of the work and occupations of the slaves. . . . they shall work nine useful hours a day . . . but during harvest-time . . . they shall work thirteen hours, so that the slave has at least 11 hours of rest daily. . . .

Chapter V

On where the tools shall be kept: On all the haciendas there shall be a room, with a good lock, where the tools are kept. This shall be in the exclusive care of the master, or his foreman.

* Translated from Luis M. Díaz Soler, *Historia de la Esclavitud Negra en Puerto Rico* (San Juan: University of Puerto Rico, 1965), p. 153.

and not entrusted to any slave. . . . at the beginning of work, each slave shall be given the tool that he will use, and it shall be returned when he has stopped working. . . . no slave shall ever leave the hacienda with any tool, much less any type of arms, unless he is accompanied by his master, foreman, or their families, whereupon he may carry his work machete. . . .

Chapter VI

Prohibition of slaves meeting with those of other haciendas. . . . No slave will be permitted to receive visits of slaves from other haciendas; and when they must leave their own hacienda, they should carry a written permission, with the date, saying where they are going, and why. . . .

Chapter VII

On Diversion. Masters will permit their slaves to have honest enjoyment and recreation on holidays (after hearing Mass, and attending the explanation of the Christian Doctrine) inside the hacienda, without mixing with slaves from other haciendas, and in a place open to the view of their owners, or foremen. . . . These diversions shall last from three in the afternoon until sunset, or the prayer hour, no more. . . . Owners and foremen are particularly warned not to permit mixing of the two sexes, excess drinking, nor the introduction of slaves or freemen from outside. . . .

Chapter VIII

Masters shall be sure to build rooms for the slaves that are spacious, dry, airy, strong, with separate parts for both sexes, and with a strong lock and key. . . .

At eight o'clock, a roll call will be made, to insure that no slave is left outside, except those entrusted with keeping watch over the hacienda.

A light will be kept on all night in the slaves' quarters, and one or two keepers will insure that the slaves remain quiet in their beds, and report immediately anything out of the ordinary. . . .

Chapter IX

On the marriage of slaves. . . . The masters shall try to avoid any illicit contact between the two sexes, and try to promote marriage among the slaves . . . so that they may live together under the same roof. . . .

Chapter X

. . . a slave shall win his liberty if he reveals any conspiracy by persons of his class, or free persons, to disturb public order, kill a master, his wife, child, or parent. . . .

Chapter XII

Rewards for good service . . . The slave who serves faithfully on a hacienda for thirty-five years shall earn the reward of no work during the first quarter of the day. He who continues for ten years more shall work only half a day, and he who reaches sixty-five years of age shall be given full freedom, but the master shall be responsible for helping and feeding him if he lacks the means of sustenance. . . .

[There is no record of a large slave insurrection in Puerto Rico. The presence of a Spanish military garrison was one deterrent, as was the fact that free men easily outnumbered slaves. In fact, many slave conspiracies were betrayed by slaves, who confessed to their masters, in exchange for their freedom. Small-scale revolts were attempted in 1527, 1821, 1822, 1825, 1843, and 1848. These caused scarcely a ripple. Of more concern was the turmoil in nearby islands, where slaves were in open revolt against governing white elites. This situation, in 1848, prompted an "Edict Against the African Race," by Governor Juan Prim, issued May 31, 1848, and published in the *Gaceta Oficial*, No. 67, June 3, 1848. The edict was designed to "prevent these calamities on our peaceful, loyal soil"].

INHABITANTS OF PUERTO RICO: Via the French ship Argus, which reached port today from Martinique, I have learned of the serious incidents in the French colonies of Martinique and Guadeloupe, due to the latest decrees of the French provisional government, emancipating the slaves in its colonies. The unfortunate immigrants aboard the Argus, who abandoned their families and interests, and came to this island in search of the security and protection they could not find in their own country, are the most evident testimony of the lamentable conditions in those colonies, and of the stupid ferocity of the African race, which—unable to appreciate the blessings conceded by their government—reacts with sentiments that are natural to them: arson, murder, and destruction. Happily, circumstances are quite different on this island. . . .

It is my duty to persuade you to ignore the fears that such news might instill in your spirits, and to assure you that your Captain General keeps constant vigil over the maintenance of order and tranquility. . . .

The critical circumstances of the times . . . oblige me to dictate measures that will prevent these calamities from occurring on our peaceful, loyal soil, and to establish quick punishment for all infractions:

Article 1—Infractions of any kind committed by individuals of the African race—be they free or slave—shall be judged by a Military Council of War. . . .

Article 2—Any African, free or slave, who takes up arms against whites, no matter how justified the aggression, shall—if slave—

be executed by the firing squad, and—if free—have his right hand cut off; but, if he should have caused wounds, he, too, shall be brought before the firing squad. . . .

Article 3—If an individual of the African race insults, mistreats, or threatens with stick, stone, or in any way convinces his master that he plans to offend the person of a white, the aggressor shall be condemned to five years prison, if slave, and, if free, to punishment corresponding to the circumstances.

Article 4—Masters of slaves are authorized to correct and punish them for the slight infractions they commit, without need of consulting any military or civil official. . . .

Article 5—If . . . any slave rebels against his lord and master, the latter is empowered to kill him immediately, to set an example for the other slaves. . . .

[As racial tension eased in the French islands, Governor Prim's successor—Captain General Juan de la Pezuela—rescinded the harsh edict of June 3, and reestablished the regulations previously in force. Part of his proclamation of November 28, 1848 said:]

It is my duty, sons of the African race, to express my gratitude for your peaceful submission to your labors, and to warn you also to ignore the treacherous ideas which may perturb your spirits. . . . Via the law, you have the means to obtain your freedom. Your liberty is in your own hands, by purchasing it with savings from your own activity, and laborious work.* Resign yourselves, therefore, that man can only find happiness in this world by harnessing his desires, and by accepting his destiny.

MASTERS AND SLAVES

[The institution of slavery began in Puerto Rico in the early 1500's, but slaves never formed as large a part of the island's population as they did on the British, French, and Dutch islands of the Caribbean. This, of course, was little consolation to the minority in bondage in Puerto Rico. Advertisements for runaways, so common in the United States, also appeared frequently in the island's Gaceta Oficial. The notice that follows appeared there in 1833.

* Coll y Toste notes the "cruel sarcasm" of General de la Pezuela's remark, since the slaves were not paid wages for their daily labor.

From George Coggeshall, Thirty-six Voyages to Various Parts of the World, Made Between the Years 1791 and 1841 (New York: 1858). An excerpt is contained in Luis M. Díaz Soler, Historia de la Esclavitud Negra en Puerto Rico (San Juan: University of Puerto Rico, 1965), pp. 114–16.

On the night of Holy Week, the second of this month, a slave named Lorenzo fled from the Hacienda Los Cuatro Hermanos, Mayagüez District. He was wearing a tailcoat, straw hat, a new red wool shirt, and a three-pronged iron collar around his neck. He is crafty, short, not very black, good looking, and well built, from twenty-five to thirty years old. He previously belonged to the Hacienda San José, Bayamón, of the widow Vassallo. His owner, Dr. Felix García de Latorre, will pay the cost of his capture and return.

Except for the intensive scholarship of Puerto Rican professor Luis M. Díaz Soler and a few scattered research efforts, the history of slavery on the island has been largely neglected. A few contemporary accounts, however, have been discovered. One of these is a vivid description by a visitor to the island in 1831. He describes first the slave ship *Sultana* and its captain, then a disembarking of slaves on Puerto Rico's west coast, and finally a visit to Ponce, on the south coast, where he conversed with the captain and supercargo of the ship.]

[The Captain] was a native of Paris, then about forty years old, rather above middle size, stout, strong and athletic, a good seaman, and of a bold and daring disposition. He spoke fluently four or five languages, and was altogether an original character. He seemed neither to fear God nor regard man, and appeared to be just fitted for the desperate business in which he was engaged. . . . And though so much is said in condemnation of these men who prosecute the slave-trade, still, they are merely instruments in the hands of capitalists, who in the end, reap the greatest portion of the gain.

Where do the capitalists reside? My answer is, I do not know; they may live sumptuously in England, France, the United States, elsewhere. One thing is certain, that very few of the planters in these islands have very much ready money to invest in this business, and but few merchants who reside in the West Indies can spare means to be employed in the slave-trade; still the business goes on from year to year, and no one knows who owns the ships engaged in the trade. For the information of those who have never seen a slave ship, I will just add that they were armed with great guns . . . they have a strong bulkhead to serve as a barricade, built athwart the after part of the vessel, through which are loopholes; and as all the muskets and pistols are kept in the cabin, the captain and the officers can fire from these holes and put down a revolt, should there be one among the slaves, without endangering their own lives. . . .

There have been imported, into the little bays of this part of Porto Rico within the last two months, three small cargoes of African slaves, say about 500 in number, men, women and children. I saw the remnant of these cargoes for sale in three enclosures. The best looking and most healthy of these miserable beings had been sold to the planters and removed to their estates; the remainder were extremely thin and sickly, and were selling at very reduced prices. There was a little stream of fresh water near where these slaves were kept, and in this little river they were made to bathe daily; if they showed any reluctance to go into the water, they were driven in like cattle. They had some rude instruments of music, such as banjoes and large gourd shells with strings, which made a rude, tinkling noise; on these instruments they were encouraged to play, singing and dancing at the same time to keep up their spirits. The venders of these negroes told me it was absolutely necessary to keep them in a good-natured mood, otherwise they would get the sulke, refuse all kind of food, and die with starvation.

Although the sight of these poor, unfortunate beings creates a melancholy feeling in the breast of a stranger, still there were circumstances connected with it that are so ludicrous, that they produce an involuntary smile even in the midst of this dark scene of degraded humanity. For example, at these depots, two large and healthy-looking negroes are selected, and made to stand erect outside the gate as a sign to indicate to the planters that slaves are sold here. The price of negroes at this time was about as follows: children of five or six years old, 100 dollars each; and what are here called prime slaves, that is, stout, healthy men or women, from eighteen to twenty-five years old, were worth 250 to 350 dollars each. They were generally retailed to the planters, and taken in small or large numbers as the case may be. At the time I visited this island, there were so many obstructions to the African slave-trade that the owners of large vessels dared not risk sending them, and were therefore in the habit of employing small, fast-sailing pilotboat schooners, to elude the vigilance of the men-of-war of different nations who were striving to prevent this inhuman traffic. These pilotboats carried from 150 to 200 of these poor creatures, and when chased by men-of-war, they crammed them all below deck to avoid detection; so also in bad weather they were all forced below to escape being washed overboard.

In hot climates like those between Africa and this island, to confine human beings under deck, where all must suffer, and many of them die with suffocation, is barbarous in the extreme. . . .

While I was here at Ponce, on the 18th. of February 1831, a large brig, under Spanish colors, arrived at a small port about a league to the eastward of this place, with 350 negro slaves from the coast of Africa. They were all landed under the direction of the government officers, and I was told their owners paid a duty to the government of 25 dollars per head. I went with my friend G. (Garrus) to see them landed; they were all taken to a neighboring plantation, and there exposed for sale. They were marched up from the vessel in parties of fifty; the men and women were all naked, except an apron which they wore about their loins; the children, both boys and girls, were in a perfect state of nudity, and, as far as I could judge, they all, both men and women, appeared utterly unconscious of any impropriety in their want of clothing. They were healthy, sleek, and in good condition, appeared pleased to get on shore and seemed to me an inoffensive, docile race of human beings. A large quantity of boiled plantains and salted herring was prepared for them. They all seemed to eat with a good appetite and enjoy their food. The planters from all this part of the island, soon came to this depot to purchase according to their wants or ability to pay; and here they were sold singly, in pairs, or in larger numbers, as was agreed upon by the parties.

During my stay at Ponce, I dined at a planter's house in company with the captain and supercargo of the slave brig; they were intelligent, sociable men, and when conversing on the slave trade, said it was a humane and most benevolent traffic; that in many parts of Africa the negroes were cannibals and extremely indolent; that the different tribes were constantly at war with each other, and if there were no purchases for their prisoners, they would be all put to death; that they were in the lowest state of degradation, and of no service to the world. On the contrary, when they were transported to the West Indies, they soon became civilized and useful to mankind. As a proof of what they had stated, they said that the boys and girls that were allowed to run about the vessel and mix with the seamen, soon learned English and Spanish, and acquired considerable intelligence in the course of a few months, and concluded by affirming that the African traders were benevolent and beneficial to mankind. The above was the substance of their conversation, and shows that a good deal may be said in favor of any system, however absurd it may appear to those who are opposed to it. After this conversation I remarked to these gentlemen that if the negroes were transported from Africa to these islands in large, comfortable ships, and sold to humane and benevolent masters, perhaps in many cases it would be better for the slaves themselves; but unfortunately, at present, this was not the case—on the contrary, they were crammed into small craft, and often perished with suffocation, while those who survived were liable to be sold to brutal masters, and receive inhuman treatment. Their reply was, that those who were engaged in the trade had been driven to adopt every expedient, in consequence of the persecutions they had received from short-sighted and ill-informed philanthropists. . . .

Part III

THE SPIRIT OF NATIONHOOD

> Puerto Ricans . . . your brothers in exile
> have conspired—and they ought to con-
> spire—because the colonial regime must
> some day be ended in our island; because
> Puerto Rico in the long run must be free,
> like the nations of the continent. . . .
>
> —Proclamation signed by
> El Comité Revolucionario and
> circulated in July 1867; attributed
> to R. Emeterio Betances

After 300 years as a small, neglected Spanish colony, Puerto Rico "came of age" during the nineteenth century. The U.S. War of Independence, the French Revolution, the revolt of Haitian slaves in 1791, and the Latin American wars of independence in 1808–24—all had their impact upon the island.

Between 1800 and 1900, Puerto Rico's population exploded from 150,000 to nearly a million. Many of the new arrivals were Spanish royalists—soldiers, merchants, and landowners—fleeing from turmoil elsewhere. In addition to the large populations of creole whites, Africans, mulattoes and resident Spaniards, there were also small French, English, North American, Danish, German, Dutch, and Italian colonies.

As early as 1809, Puerto Ricans were referring to the island as their *amada patria* (beloved homeland), although, politically, it was an overseas possession of Spain. That year, when Napoleon invaded Spain, the Spanish provinces rebelled and formed juntas under the Supreme Junta of Cádiz. The Junta declared Spain's colonies to be integral parts of the mother country. Puerto Rico's leaders rejoiced because this converted them from colonial subjects to citizens, with substantially increased civil rights. One of the delegates elected by the Puerto Rican leadership to represent the island in Spain's Cortes was Ramón Power y Giralt. He took with him a list of demands: for free trade with foreign nations, for a university, for equal job opportunities for natives in government posts and the like. There was also the significant request that, if Spain was conquered, Puerto Rico should be granted the liberty "to choose its own destiny."

Some reforms were granted in 1812, when the Spanish constitution was extended to Puerto Rico and the island became an integral part of the monarchy. All free men were granted Spanish citizenship, and Puerto Rican deputies sat in the Spanish Cortes, with voting power. In fact, Power y Giralt rose to the vice presidency of the Cortes. Limited local power was also granted in the island's towns, where municipal assemblies were created, with nine government appointees and seven landowners.

But Puerto Rico's fortunes rose and fell in accord with changes in Europe, and civil rights were withdrawn as often as they were granted.

The first strong movement to secure a permanent working relationship with Spain and remove the stigma of colonialism began in 1887, in Ponce, when Román Baldorioty de Castro presided over the new Partido Autonomista Puertorriqueño.

The efforts of this movement bore fruit ten years later. In 1897, when Spain was fearful of losing its last grip in the Western Hemisphere, autonomy was granted to Cuba and Puerto Rico. It was too late in Cuba, where rebel patriots continued their battle for independence, but the royal decree of November 28, 1897, proclaiming autonomy for Puerto Rico, was well received. The cabinet of the new government was installed in February, 1898, and general elections for legislators were held in March. In July, however, American troops landed, drastically altering the course of Puerto Rican history.

The Autonomous Charter was not a grant of independence, but it promised more freedom than ever before. The crown named a Spanish Governor General, who was to be commander-in-chief of the armed forces and "supreme authority" on the island. The Insular Parliament consisted of an Administrative Council and a House of Representatives. The Council had fifteen members, eight elected by the people and seven appointed by the Governor General. All thirty-five members of the House were to be elected.

The Parliament was subject to the veto powers of Spain, but it could propose and approve its own laws, impose taxes, and enter into treaties with foreign nations. This was still colonialism, but with a very long leash—longer, in some respects, than the one that now binds Puerto Rico's commonwealth government to the United States.

SAILING TO SAN JUAN

[As early as 1822,
a visitor to Puerto Rico noted "some alarm" over "an intended insurrection of the slave population" and also learned of an expedition "that was about to sail from New York for the purpose of revolutionizing the island." Both of these attempts—to achieve freedom for the slaves and independence for Puerto Rico—failed. But they indicated considerable unrest simmering just beneath the otherwise placid surface of the Caribbean colony. The visitor was Joel Roberts Poinsett, a U.S. diplomat —long active and much resented in Latin America—who gained a certain immortality when he introduced into his country a Mexican flower, which was named the "Poinsettia" in his honor. At the time, Poinsett had been sent on a special mission to Mexico by President James Monroe, but en route he stopped briefly in Puerto Rico. His brief sketch also touches upon the island's social structure and housing conditions, as well as the piracy in Puerto Rico's coastal waters.]

Beating to windward
against wind and current—on the 20th, passed the Islands of Mona and Monica, and on the 21st, made the western extremity of Puerto Rico. We are now near enough to the land to distinguish the plantations of palms and bananas, and all the luxuriant vegetation of the tropics.

26th.—After passing one day in sight of the Moro Castle, we are at length anchored in the port of San Juan. The town is situated on the south side of the hills, and did not come in view until we had passed the Moro, and were within the harbour. Although closely built up, it does not appear capable of containing so many as twenty thousand inhabitants, the reported amount of the population.

We have just received the visit of the captain of the port, who informs us that some alarm has lately been excited by the discovery of an intended insurrection of the slave population. Although the slaves are not numerous, the vicinity of the republic of Hayti renders such a movement a probable event.

27th.—On landing this morning I was agreeably surprised to find the town very clean and tolerably well built. It is situated on the declivity of a steep hill, and at first I was inclined to attribute its

From Joel Roberts Poinsett, *Notes on Mexico Made in the Autumn of 1822, Accompanied by an Historical Sketch of the Revolution and Translations of Official Reports on the Present State of that Country. With a Map. By a Citizen of the United States* (Philadelphia: H. C. Carey and I. Lea, 1824). (Facsimile reprint—New York: Praeger Publishers, 1969), pp. 3–8.

cleanliness to the torrents of rain, so frequent in this climate; but I find, on inquiry, that the police regulations are excellent, and are rigidly enforced. We strolled round the fortifications, which are well constructed and judiciously situated. They occupy a narrow island, about two miles long, on which the town stands, and which is connected with the main by a bridge strongly fortified with a tête de pont. This is united by a chain of small forts which the castle of San Christopher, a very strong fortress, situated so as to defend the eastern entrance of the town, and commanding all the works towards the north and east. . . .

For some time past our trade has been much harassed by privateers fitted out in the different ports of this island. The principal object of our touching here is to remonstrate with the governor against these depredations. Under the absurd pretext of blockading the whole coast of the Spanish main, a few small privateers cruise in the Mona and Sombrero passages, and capture all vessels bound to or from any port on that extensive coast. The prizes are carried into the small ports on the south and west of the island, where they are at the mercy of courts notoriously corrupt. The governor assured us that he had warned the commanders of privateers not to capture vessels sailing under the flag of the United States, and that he should in future exact a bond to a large amount from the Armateurs, in order to indemnify those who might sustain losses from illegal captures; that he had no authority to suppress privateering, as the commissions were issued by the government of Spain, but he promised to exert his influence to prevent their being fitted out. I look upon these professions as words of course, and am of opinion that these acts of piracy ought to be restrained by the strong hand of power, and the government of the island be made responsible for the illegal acts of its inhabitants. The dominion exercised by the mother country over these colonies is too remote and inconsiderable to enable her to control the lawless banditti that inhabit the coast of Puerto Rico and Cuba. The authorities of the islands can alone keep them within bounds, and they ought to be compelled to do so.

Desirous of obtaining an insight into the civil government and institutions of the island, of which I had received very contradictory accounts, I requested the commercial agent to introduce me to a *letrado;* we passed through several clean but narrow streets, the houses two and three stories high, with flat roofs, and latticed windows without glass, the shops neatly set off with French and English goods, and the lazy shop-keepers, with their coats off, sitting on chairs in the street, under the shade of the houses; and still lazier house-keepers swinging in hammocks suspended in the passage of their house, gazing listlessly at the passengers, and drawling away their existence. I found the man of the law wrapped in a loose morning gown, and swinging in a cotton hammock hung within a foot of the floor, with a client sitting by his side. He flung himself out of the hammock on perceiving us enter the room, and received us with great courtesy. He listened to my questions with exemplary patience, and answered them promptly and satisfactorily. Frequently, however, in his turn asking, "But why do you want to know that?" Nor could he comprehend that curiosity alone prompted my enquiries. . . .

By a census made about a year ago, the whole population of the island is stated to be two hundred and twenty-five thousand souls, of which twenty-five thousand, or thereabouts, are slaves. The greater part of the free inhabitants are coloured persons—the whites and free negroes bearing but a small proportion to the whole. Within a few years past the emigration from Europe has been very great, amounting it is said to between six and eight thousand persons. The inhabitants are divided into two classes—the nobles and the people. All the whites may be considered as forming part of the nobility; as custom extends to them an exemption from serving in the militia, and some other privileges that by law belong only to the *noblesse*. The laws know no difference between the white *roturier* and the coloured man; and this circumstance, as well as the Spaniard's being in the habit of mixing with the people of colour without those prejudices so common in the other West India colonies, prevents any jealousy or bad feeling towards him on their part, and forms a great security against the slave population and their neighbours of San Domingo. . . .

The authorities of the island have received information that an expedition was about to sail from New York for the purpose of revolutionizing the island, and are prepared to defeat the project, whatever it may be. It is much to be lamented that these expeditions could not always be arrested where they are fitted out. The object is so palpably plunder—for the pretended motive, the love of liberty, is too puerile to gain credit with the most credulous—and they involve so many innocent men in ruin and misery, and are so dishonourable to our country, that we ought to exercise a more vigilant police, and if possible prevent adventurers from disgracing us.

The rumour of an intended insurrection is confirmed. Sixty negroes, part free and part slaves, have been brought from the west side of the island, and are to be tried by a court martial. In the course of my walk this morning I saw several companies of the garrison on parade. They were of all colours, from the fairest European to the blackest son of Africa.

Dined with the American commercial agent, where I met the Marquis del Norte, a very intelligent and accomplished gentleman, from whom I have derived a great deal of information.

The young officers have this instant returned from a ball, delighted with the charming faces, delicate figures, and graceful movements of the Creole ladies. Those I saw in the streets had good persons, and delicate and well formed features, but very sallow complexions.

29th.—Set out this morning to make an excursion into the country. We crossed the bay in a small sail-boat, and on landing, found horses waiting for us. For saddles, they were furnished with straw pads, with baskets suspended on both sides, intended to support the legs. I found the seat not very commodious or secure, but the horse was quiet, and our feet and legs were elevated above being splashed. The road was a continued quagmire, and our horses frequently plunged up to the saddle girths.

The road, for about a mile from the shore, passes along a narrow valley, the hills on each side being steep and wooded to the summit. It then winds gradually up a chain of hills, passing near two large plantations with extensive buildings, dwelling houses, chapels, sugar mills and store houses. The summit of the ridge commands a view of a charming and highly cultivated plain, clothed with the richest verdure and with the most luxuriant vegetation. Lofty cocoa and date-palms, and plantations of coffee trees and bananas, cover the rising grounds, which skirt a plain cultivated in fields of Indian corn, sugar and cassava, and spotted with neat farm houses. A short ride from this enchanting spot, brought us to the habitation of a French gentleman, who received us with great urbanity and politeness. The house is large, and although it consists of only one floor, is commodious, and looked cool and clean. In front is a small garden, neatly laid out, exhibiting a great variety of flowers, and exhaling a profusion of sweets. We were introduced to a German Baron and to his lady, a fair Parisian; the latter, happy to meet with any one who had been in Paris, and who could understand her, overwhelmed me with her regrets and comparisons between the dull life of an Islander and the delightful life of Paris. . . .

After passing an hour very pleasantly, we set forth on our return. In the course of our ride, I had bought hogs, turkeys and ducks; for they were not to be found in market, and our conductor contrived to cram some into the baskets, and to sling the rest before his pack saddle: so that, on our march, we were accompanied by such a noise, that the folks ran out of their huts to look at us. If they were surprised at our appearance, I was equally so to see such crowds of men, women and children, issuing from habitations so small. The gable-end of every cottage projects about ten feet, with a rude portico, where they must sleep, for the interior cannot contain them all.

In the course of this ride, I met two whites only, but a great many people of different shades of colour. We reached the ship time enough for a late dinner, and all my hogs, turkeys and ducks arrived in safety, to the great consolation of the mess. The market is so badly provided, that we expected to be under the necessity of going to sea without fresh provisions. Limes, oranges, bananas, and other fruits are abundant and cheap, and we laid in a good store of them.

"ARRIBA, PUERTO RICANS!"

[The spiritual leader of Puerto Rico's small pro-independence movement during the nineteenth century was Ramón Emeterio Betances, born in the coastal village of Cabo Rojo in 1827. A graduate in medicine from the University of Paris, he was well known in both the Caribbean region and Europe. Betances spent his lifetime trying to free Puerto Rico from Spanish colonialism. Also a militant opponent of slavery, he, at one time, purchased young slave children from their masters and gave them their freedom. Because of his controversial activities, Betances was forced to live part of his life in exile. In early 1864, the following proclamation was circulated on the island; it is believed to be the work of Betances. Its text, a call to arms against Spain, makes clear many of the islanders' grievances against their colonial condition.]

Puerto Ricans, for more than three centuries, Spanish despotism has oppressed us. Until now, not a single son of this country has occupied a post of any distinction. On the contrary, any man who has dared to speak for the well-being of his countrymen has been persecuted, banished into exile, or ruined.

For more than three centuries, we have been paying immense taxes, and still we have no roads, railways, telegraph systems, or steamships.

The rabble of Spain—its soldiers and clerks—come to the island without a *peseta*, and, after they have squeezed us dry, return to their homeland with millions that belong to us, who have worked for it.

The *gíbaros* are poor and ignorant because of the Government, which prohibits schools, newspapers, and books, and not long ago refused to found a university, so that the poor, who cannot send their children abroad, shall never see them with the titles of doctor, lawyer, etc.

The Government insists that the *gíbaros* should remain nothing more than lowly day laborers with *libretas.** And, lately, to exploit

* Each worker had to carry a *libreta*, or notebook, which severely restricted his activities. This is explained by Juan Antonio Corretjer's article, later in this section.

Translated from Lidio Cruz Monclova, *Historia de Puerto Rico, Siglo XIX, Tomo I, 1808-1868* (San Juan: Editorial Universitaria, Universidad de Puerto Rico, 1958), pp. 477–78.

us even more, it tries to make us hate our brothers, the sons of
Santo Domingo, forcing us to take arms and fight against them. . . .
   Puerto Ricans, let us not be fools, let us not be deceived by the
promises and falsehoods of the Government; we know from experience that Spain never fulfills its promises. Let us not sleep; the
occasion is magnificent; there are no soldiers on the Island, and
even if there were, the war in Santo Domingo must have convinced
us that one *gíbaro* with his machete in hand is worth a hundred
Spaniards.
   Arriba Puerto Ricans! Let us show the rabble, who rob and insult
us, that the *gíbaros* of Puerto Rico are neither cowards against
their executioners, nor assassins against their brothers.
   Let us join together, and rise en masse against the oppressors of
our land, of our women and children. Our *grito* of Independence
shall be heard, and supported, by all friends of Liberty; and there
shall be no lack of arms and money to crush the despots of Cuba,
Puerto Rico, and Santo Domingo into the dust.

"YOU SHALL BE FREE"

[After the previous
proclamation, General Felix María de Messina, the island's Spanish
colonial governor, ordered Betances to appear before him in La Fortaleza, the governor's palace. As Betances told Messina of the need for
independence, the governor interrupted and said, "If you continue this,
I shall be obliged to hang you from one of the battlements of El Morro."
Betances replied, "Well, keep in mind, General Messina, that the night
of that day I shall sleep far more peacefully than Your Excellency."
Betances was exiled, but he continued to support independence from
abroad. The following proclamation, reproduced in leaflet form, was
signed by Betances in November, 1867, and distributed on the island.
He was still in exile, this time on nearby Saint Thomas. The proclamation sets forth "Ten Commandments," listing the conditions under which
Puerto Rico would retain its association with Spain. It is virtually a
declaration of independence.]

PUERTO RICANS!

   The government of Queen Isabella is making a terrible accusation
against us:

Translated from photographic reproduction in *Lecturas Básicas Sobre Historia
de Puerto Rico*, First Part, Curriculum Division, Social Studies Program (San
Juan: Dept. of Public Education, Commonwealth of Puerto Rico, 1967), p. 174.

It says that we are bad Spaniards. The government is spreading falsehoods.

We do not want separation; we want peace and union with Spain; but it is only fair that we should also specify the conditions in the contract. They are very simple:

ABOLITION OF SLAVERY
THE RIGHT TO REJECT ALL TAXES
FREEDOM OF RELIGION
FREEDOM OF SPEECH
FREEDOM OF THE PRESS
FREEDOM OF COMMERCE
THE RIGHT TO ASSEMBLE
THE RIGHT TO BEAR ARMS
THE INVIOLABILITY OF THE CITIZEN
THE RIGHT TO ELECT OUR AUTHORITIES

These are the
TEN COMMANDMENTS
of Free Men

If Spain feels capable of giving us these rights and freedoms, and does so, then it may send us a captain general or governor . . . made of straw, and we shall hang him, and have him burned during the days of *carnestolandas* [three carnival days before Ash Wednesday—ed.], to commemorate all the Judases who, until today, have sold us out.

THUS, we shall be Spaniards. If not, NO.

If not, Puerto Ricans, PATIENCE! You shall be free.

DR. BETANCES
St. Thomas, November 1867

THE DAY PUERTO RICO BECAME A NATION

["Spaniard became Spaniard and the Puerto Rican, Puerto Rican" on September 23, 1868, when a pro-independence insurrection broke out in Lares. The revolt lasted scarcely a day, but it was the first time that the island's sons had mustered an armed uprising of such dimensions, and it served notice to Spain that the days of colonialism were numbered. Lares was followed

Juan Antonio Corretjer, "The Day Puerto Rico Became a Nation," *San Juan Star Sunday Magazine*, September 22, 1968. Reprinted by permission.

by Spanish efforts at reform, and—just five years later—by the abolition
of slavery. As the author of the following essay notes, "The abolitionist
movement had reached a point where its connection with the independence movement could only result in igniting a revolution."

Juan Antonio Corretjer, born in 1908, is an accomplished poet and
journalist, and a lifelong activist for Puerto Rican independence. A former member of the Nationalist Party—he was a close associate of the
late Pedro Albizu Campos—Corretjer is now president of the island's
Socialist League. His essay was written to commemorate the one hun-
dredth anniversary—in 1968—of the Grito de Lares, which is now celebrated as an occasion for the island's pro-independence groups to rally
thousands of followers to that historic mountain town.]

The centennial of the
Grito de Lares tomorrow is a commemoration not so much of a
short-lived insurrection against Spain as of the culmination of
Puerto Rico's 19th Century revolutionary process. It is also the
observance of an event which finally succeeded in forging a true
Puerto Rican identity.

This does not mean that attempts to free Puerto Rico from
Spanish colonial oppression had not occurred before or after. The
red flag that waved under fire during the three attempts to take San
Sebastián by assault the day after Lares was stormed, had appeared 30 years before in Carolina. The same bold spirit of Lares,
with equal political intention, warmed the hearts of Fidel Vélez
and his followers in Yauco, March 24, 1897.

Just two years after Lares, in 1870, Captain General Laureano
Sanz was forced to move to Ciales, where a serious insurrectionist
organization had reached full development. Repression was severe
—as was to be expected from the iron hand of General Sanz.

The Lares insurrection has been pointed out as the historical
moment in which Puerto Rico's nationhood was defined. Our nationalist leaders and theoreticians have maintained that that is the
deep meaning of the Lares insurrection. National thought had developed enough to see independence as a necessary condition to
solve Puerto Rico's social and economic problems, and national
will sufficiently developed to carry this understanding to what
some consider its logical conclusion of separation by force of arms.

History, Puerto Rican life itself, shows nothing was again the
same in Puerto Rico after Lares. The Spaniard became Spaniard
and the Puerto Rican, Puerto Rican. In the 1890's, commenting on a
servile reference to the Lares Revolt made by Luis Muñoz Rivera,
Ramón Betances who led the revolt, wrote to a friend: "Without
Lares, *La Democracia* (Muñoz' newspaper) would not be published
now in Ponce." Betances's clear words were a reflection of a well-
guarded colonial opinion that all reform obtained from the Spanish
crown after the Lares revolt originated from the Spanish fear of
an independence insurrection in Puerto Rico at the time when the

Spanish Army was fighting the Cuban war. That is to say, they feared a repetition of Lares.

In the 1930s, Tomás Blanco in "Prontuario Historico" wrote that the Lares insurrection was responsible for the abolition of slavery in Puerto Rico. He said just that. No more. But one must bear in mind the fact that the abolitionist movement had reached a point where its connection with the independence movement could only result in igniting a revolution.

The provisional government formed in Lares by the successful revolutionists immediately proclaimed that every slave that took arms in defense of a free and independent Puerto Rico would become a free man. Shortly after the military defeat of the revolution, the Spanish Government decreed the gradual abolition of slavery, making the decree effective on a date previous to the Lares uprising. Five years after, in 1873, slavery came to an end.

It was not only slavery that was solved at Lares. The so-called "free" laborer of the time was in reality a feudal serf. By decree of a General Pezuela, the "free" laborer, who lived as an "agregado" (something like a sharecropper) on a plantation could not leave the plantation limits without the owner's permission. Even his Sundays were spent as his master decided. He had to write his time of departure and return in a notebook that was always to be on his person and in this book he had to make note of every act of his life: work, expenses, morality. He was, in reality, a feudal serf.

And so the Liberation Army was joined not only by the Negro slaves but the laborers as well. And it was the laborers who piled up those notebooks and set them on fire in the center of Lares Plaza on Sept. 23, 1868. Shortly after, the Spanish government abolished the notebook system.

It is obvious that nations are not made with slaves and serfs. Nations themselves are part of the historical development of society. Slavery and serfdom come to a point, historically, when they chain the development of society. The slave owner's acquiescence to abolition had no altruistic motive. It was an economic, historical compulsion, idealistically phrased by their intellectuals in the resounding words of 19th Century liberalism. That is why we say that the Grito de Lares brought Puerto Rico to its definition as a nation.

The social contradictions steaming within the colonial society worked themselves to the point of what Marxism calls the highest form of struggle: insurrection. The property owner's protest against Spanish taxation and restrictions on trade; the general hunger for education; the call for freedom and a cultural consciousness on the part of the intellectuals—all this came to coincide with what many consider a logical revolt against imperialistic oppression. In Puerto Rico's history, its name is Lares.

The abolition of slavery and of the labor-notebook system put the colonial landed aristocracy on the road in a long march toward greater wealth. These beneficiaries of the crown's abolition of communal property now entered into a time of new prosperity. (In 1775 Charles III had abolished communal property on the recommendation of Alejandro O'Reilly, a Spanish general he had sent to the island to make a report of its progress. Up to then, all land was owned by the crown which could deed it to individuals but it reverted to the crown again after the second generation.) If the O'Reilly reform had permitted them to monopolize the land, the abolition of slaves and the labor-notebook system now gave them the benefit of a new working class, more willing to work and learn now that it was "free."

Results were seen immediately. Coffee production entered a time of unprecedented growth. Sugar and tobacco production multiplied. The Juntas de Agricultura, Industria y Comercio were formed and shortly after unified into a government bureau. The Junta Provincial de Estadísticas y Evaluación de la Riqueza came into being. Two agricultural experimental stations were founded, one of them in Río Piedras where the present station is located. The Asociación de Agricultores was organized and the Banco Territorial y Agrícola was founded. Agricultural "colonies" were established by law and a system of tax exemption was created to help their development. The Sociedad Anónima Para El Fomento de la Cría Caballar, the Liga Económica and the Negociado de Montes y Terrenos Baldíos; the Banco Crédito y Ahorro Ponceño, the Banco de San Germán and the Banco Popular, are all institutions born of this great surge of the economy as a consequence of the social forces freed by the abolition of slavery and the notebook system.

But there was also a shadowy side. After the revolutionary recession, colonialism as a way of life dug deep into the Puerto Rican upper and middle classes. Defeatism was politically systemized. It became, indeed, the very center of institutional life.

In 1870 the political parties were organized. With their coming into being duplicity came to reign in a colonial kingdom that has known no democratic overthrow. The reactionary elements barricaded themselves in religion, tradition, paper nobility and other forms of social simulation, and the Partido Conservador, Incondicionalmente Español. A large section of the independence forces hid within these parties, where consequently they were castrated. In time, their leaders became the masters of this game. Wrapped in the Spanish flag, kowtowing to María Cristina, they used independence and revolution as a source of prestige before the people and of blackmail against Spain. This forced them into partisan leadership and government positions. Thus the bombing of San Juan by American guns found them ready to kneel before a new god.

The leader of the nationalist movement was Ramón Emeterio Betances. . . .

Twice ordered to exile in Spain by the colonial authorities, he first fled to St. Thomas, then to New York, then to Santo Domingo. From exile, he organized the insurrection of 1868. He put into it all he had: his prestige, his fortune, his dreams of freedom and happiness for Puerto Rico. He was not, however, to be at Lares. His plans were discovered. The Dominican government seized the arms that were to be shipped to Puerto Rico. "El Telégrafo," the steamer he had bought to take him and his closest comrades to Puerto Rico, was confiscated.

What happened to Betances in Santo Domingo happened also to the conspiracy in Puerto Rico. The secret societies did their work well, but an indiscretion caused the arrest of Manuel María González, a distinguished member of the "Lanzador del Norte," the secret society in Arecibo. The Arecibo military found incriminating documents in González's Camuy residence which led to further arrests.

Gonzalez's arrest precipitated the insurrection. The news was received by Manuel Rojas at his coffee hacienda in Lares. Rojas put the conspiratorial apparatus into immediate action. His call to the Mayagüez patriots brought 100 men to Roja's hacienda under the command of Juan Terreforte. At the suggestion of Mathias Brugman, Rojas was named commander of the Liberation army, over 400 men strong. The night of Sept. 23, at 9 o'clock, Rojas riding at the head of the cavalry, they set off for Lares. Without meeting any resistance, a little before midnight, he took the town.

A meeting was held at the Ayuntamiento (city hall) which was located where the plaza del mercado (market place) stands now. Spanish functionaries were arrested and the Spanish symbols replaced by those of the revolution. A provisional government was formed. Francisco Ramírez Medina was elected president; Fedcrico Valencia, minister of the treasury; Aurelio Méndez Martínez, minister of government; Clemente Millán, minister of justice; Manuel Ramírez, minister of state; and Bernabé Pol, secretary to the cabinet. Rojas was confirmed as military head.

Four decrees were immediately issued. One declared that all Puerto Ricans wcrc duty bound to fight for the revolution; another that every foreigner who voluntarily took arms on the side of independence was to be considered a patriot; that every slave who joined the revolution would automatically cease to be a slave; and another abolished the labor-notebook system. Comments historian Lidio Cruz Monclova: "It is obvious that the revolution was affirming with facts, from its very beginning, its decision to make a reality of the beautiful trilogy of its supreme ideals of political, economic and social freedom."

Three flags flew at Lares. Two of them—a red flag, used 30 years before by Vizcarrondo in Carolina and a white flag one ending in two points on which Capt. Manuel Cebollero Aguilar, president of the revolutionary committee, Junta Porvenir of San Sebastián, wrote with his cigar: Death or Liberty! Long Live Puerto Rico

Libre! Year of 1868—came under fire during the three attacks on San Sebastián next day.

The other, a flag created by Betances and made by Mariana Bracetti, was placed at the altar for a Te Deum celebrated by the Catholic Church and sung in a small wooden hermitage near a corner of the plaza. It was the flag we know as the flag of Lares. This was to be the official flag of the republic.

As the revolutionaries entered Lares, they say, cries were heard of "Down with the taxes! Down with the Spaniards! Down with Spain. *Viva Puerto Rico Libre.*"

Tomorrow, Sept. 23, what we celebrate is, of course, not a defeat. It is the military success of an action that took place 100 years ago. That military success enabled the leaders of the Lares insurrection to gather at the town hall, proclaim Puerto Rico free of the Spanish crown, and organize a provisional government based on the principles of democracy. This government, sovereign in its moment, decreed the abolition of slavery and of the labor-notebook system. In doing so, Lares forced the Spanish government to free the slaves and put an end to the labor notebooks. . . .

Yet it is true that the Liberation Army was routed and disbanded at San Sebastián the day after; that this defeat put Puerto Rico under a reformist counter-revolutionary political preponderance that paved the way to both the autonomous constitution of 1897 and the American invasion of 1898.

So Puerto Rico did not become a national state independent of Spain and did become a colony of the United States. Lares failed, from this point of view. Why?

Let us go back to Sept. 23, 1868.

Was the revolution not popular? Was Puerto Rico not ready for revolution?

Betances was not a daydreamer. The whole of his life, and the whole of his activities, the testimony of his contemporaries, show him as a well-balanced, extremely intelligent, widely read person whose scientific mind and apostolic zeal in no way carried him away from reality. He loved his people and knew them well. Yet Betances to the last day of his life repeated that in 1868 the country was ripe for revolution. His testimony is worthy of respect and consideration. It is well to remember, too, that he did not say the same of subsequent uprisings. . . .

Cruz Monclova believed all the factors so far mentioned were present and adds others: bad training of the military; no help from the outside world (due to the seizure in Santo Domingo of Betances's arms and ship): disorientation because of González's sudden, unexpected arrest; 30 years of consistent anti-independence propaganda.

It is well known that the insurrection was planned on a national scale and as Pérez Moris (the best informed and most anti-Lares historian of them all) suggests, it involved a section of the most influential people in the country. And, to a degree, it was politically convenient for the government to ignore that fact. It is equally known, that, because of the moving up of the date of the uprising caused by González's arrest, practically all the revolutionary committees never received Rojas's call to arms.

I give credit to Betances, on one side and to his most bitter enemy, Pérez Moris, on the other. Betances said that the country was ready and that it was the haste that caused the revolutionary abortion. Pérez Moris, a Spaniard, so near to the Spanish General Staff, said it was lack of armament, and implicitly, not a lack of popular support.

Now, why did Rojas concentrate on attacking San Sebastián? Why his apparently stubborn attacks on that city?

There were arms in the Spanish headquarters there. That fact is known. No student of history—military, revolutionary history—ignores what an effect a resounding victory has in fortifying a people's will to fight. Or, on the contrary, the depressive effect of a confrontation with defeat. Rojas was right to try to seize San Sebastián because the weapons were there that he needed to go on to Arecibo.

He could not wait to be attacked at Lares. He was right in fighting with all he had to seize San Sebastián. If he had succeeded, the call to revolt he had issued to all the committees could have reached them on the wings of victory. Possibly, Puerto Rico's history could have been more similar to Venezuela's than to Saint Thomas's.

THE ABOLITION OF SLAVERY

[The abolition movement in Puerto Rico was closely linked with the cause in Cuba. Both islands also linked the issue of slavery with that of political emancipation—of blacks and whites—from Spain. Eric Williams, Prime Minister of Trinidad and Tobago since 1956, is a distinguished historian and a specialist in West Indian politics. In this excerpt from a recent book, he puts the issue of Puerto Rican–Cuban abolition in a world perspective and shows how "the Puerto Rican situation was unique."]

The slave system was abolished at different times during the nineteenth century throughout the Caribbean. The slave trade, abolished finally by Denmark

Eric Williams, *From Columbus to Castro: The History of the Caribbean, 1492–1969* (New York: Harper & Row, 1970), pp. 280, 290–95, 303. Copyright © by Eric Williams. Reprinted by permission of Harper & Row, Publishers, Inc.

in 1803, was abolished by Great Britain in 1807. Restored by Bonaparte in 1802, it was abolished by the French Government in 1817. In the same year the Spanish Government signed a treaty with Great Britain whereby it pledged itself to abolition in 1820. Holland proclaimed abolition in 1818, Sweden in 1824. Slavery was abolished in the British colonies in 1833. Sweden followed suit in 1846, France in 1848, Holland in 1863. Slavery was abolished in Puerto Rico in 1873 and in Cuba in 1880. . . .

Whereas the abolition of the slave system in the British, French, Dutch and Danish colonies in the Caribbean area was a metropolitan measure imposed on recalcitrant colonials, in the Spanish colonies, Cuba and Puerto Rico, it was the metropolitan government which insisted on the system in the face of powerful colonial opposition. The colonials rested their case chiefly on the economic ground that white, free labor was cheaper than the black slave. In Cuba it was estimated in 1862 that the sugar production from 490 acres and 74 free workers was equivalent to that from 635 acres worked by 142 slaves. . . .

The Puerto Rico situation was unique in the Caribbean, in that not only did the white population outnumber the people of color, but the slaves constituted an infinitesimal part of the total population and free labor predominated during the regime of slavery. The following table has no counterpart in Caribbean history:

Population	1827	1834	1860	1872
Total	323,838	357,086	583,181	618,150
Whites	162,311	188,869	300,430	328,806
Mulattoes	100,430	101,275	>241,015	>257,709
Free Negroes	26,857	25,124		
Slaves	32,240	41,818	41,736	31,635
Slaves as % of total	10	12	14	5
Slaves as % of coloured	21	33	16	11

These 31,635 slaves were divided among nearly two thousand owners. Few owners owned more than fifty slaves. Of the total there were only 21,000 between the ages of 15 and 50. Many were domestics; male laborers numbered 11,748. The explanation is that Puerto Rico's was a small farming and diversified economy, based on the cultivation of minor crops rather than plantation staples. In 1830 the total acreage under cultivation amounted to 120,721 cuerdas, divided as follows: starchy vegetables, 40,955; coffee, 17,247; maize, 16,674; rice, 15,290; sugar, 15,242; fruits, 8,301; cotton, 3,170; tobacco, 2,676; other crops, 1,166. . . .

Essentially a food-producing colony, with a birth rate of 56 per thousand in 1824, and a density of population of 180 per square mile in 1872, Puerto Rico did not need slavery, had an adequate supply of free labour, and could anticipate no shortage. The island sent delegates to Spain in 1866 to demand the abolition of slavery, not only as a moral necessity, but also as an economic necessity. "No really acceptable reason," they stated in their official memorandum, "can be given for its continuation in Puerto Rico. The general wealth of the island does not need it: its disappearance will not affect any productive element, and the self-interest of the owners must demand the overthrow of that institution."

Their arguments for the superiority of free labour over slave would have done credit to Adam Smith himself. They deserve to be quoted:

Let all the disadvantages of the one and all the advantages of the other be weighed; let the greater intelligence and interest with which free men work be appreciated, the fidelity and personal responsibility they display, the cheapness of their wages, the stimulus which is awakened in them, let all this be appreciated on the one hand, and then on the other consider the sickness, flights, captures, baptisms, marriages and burials of the slaves, all the expenses which fall on the owner; the thefts and the judicial proceedings to which they give rise; the absenteeism resulting from punishments, sickness and sometimes also indolence; finally, let the endless and continuous expenses of maintenance, medical care and so many others be added, and it will be seen that, in order to make slave labour cheaper than free, it is necessary for the master to dismiss from his mind every generous sentiment, every notion of justice, and to consider the Negro only and exclusively as a machine for production which, with a minimum of subsistence, can function fourteen hours a day, for four or five years at most.

If Puerto Rico, by the conventional standards of the final quarter of the nineteenth century, ranked as one of the most backward sectors of Caribbean economy, in intellectual perspective it was head and shoulders above its neighbours. . . .

From the standpoint of the Spanish colonials, the abolition of the slave system was an integral part of the struggle for independence in Cuba and autonomy in Puerto Rico. The first war of independence broke out in Cuba in 1868. Céspedes, who raised the standard of revolt, immediately freed the slaves. . . .

Like Lincoln before him, Céspedes understood that no nation could survive half slave and half free. Also like Lincoln, he used emancipation as a powerful political weapon in the struggle. According to the decree, the slaves were freed and drafted into the service of the country. Owners who supported the revolution would be eligible for compensation for their slaves if they so desired; those who opposed it would be ineligible. . . .

In Puerto Rico, also, the white population, openly bracketing together dictatorship, monopoly and slavery, placed the rights of the slaves before its own civil liberty. Rafael de Labra, one of the island's representatives in the *Cortes*, quoting Figaro's phrase that "liberty is not an overseas commodity," challenged the men of the 1868 (Spanish) revolution who had revolted for the imprescriptible rights of men to say that what was truth on one side of the Pyrenees was a lie on the other. "What example," asked another representative, Emilio Castelar, "can we give to Latin America, independent, republican, democratic, when it sees existing in Spanish territories white slavery and Negro slavery, the colonial regime and the slave regime, which the human conscience rejects in indignation?" Referring to the abolition of slavery by the Convention of France in 1794, Castelar, with a knowledge and appreciation of history rare in the protagonists of emancipation, asserted:

> Even though the Convention had committed more crimes than it did, the tears of the pariah redeemed, of the eternal Spartacus emancipated, of the slave made man; those tears which condensed the gratitude of all the future generations and the blessings of all the past generations trampled under the vile heel of slavery, those tears sufficed to wipe out all the stains of blood.

It was widely suggested in Spain that the settlement of the slavery issue in Puerto Rico should await the outcome of events in Cuba, where the war of independence was in full swing. This was anathema to the Puerto Ricans. Sanromá replied to the *Cortes* in 1873:

> To subordinate the interests of Puerto Rico to those of Cuba . . . is a signal iniquity. I do not admit it; neither from the legal point of view, nor from the political, nor from the historical, nor from the economic can the interests of Puerto Rican be subordinated to those of Cuba. . . . When on earth will they leave us of Puerto Rico in peace with their eternal Cuba?

. . . . The establishment of the Spanish Anti-Slavery society in 1865 did not materially alter the situation. The government followed the beaten path of gradualism, though the Society itself stood committed to immediate emancipation. In the very years of Céspedes' emancipation proclamation, the Spanish republican government castigated slavery as an outrage to humanity and an affront to Spain; their humanitarianism was limited, however, to the modest proposal that all children born thereafter should be declared free. This so-called "law of the free stomach" was promulgated in 1870; in addition, freedom was decreed for slaves who had helped the Spanish troops in the civil war in Cuba, for slaves of the State, and for slaves who had reached the age of sixty. Eventually, emancipation was proclaimed [in Cuba] in 1880. But gradualism triumphed; a period of apprenticeship was instituted which lasted until October 7, 1886.

Spanish paternalism was best illustrated by the case of Puerto Rico. The planters to a man demanded immediate emancipation with or without compensation. The metropolitan government decreed otherwise. On March 22, 1873, slavery was abolished. But the 31,635 slaves were required to enter into contracts with their owners for a period of not less than three years. If their owners refused to enter into such contracts, they were entered into contracts with other persons or with the government. Three funcionaries were appointed protectors of the freedmen. After five years the freedmen were to receive political rights. It was like using a sledge-hammer to kill a fly. . . .

"THE TROUBLES AT PORTO RICO"

[The Lares revolt in 1868 was just a symptom of widespread distaste for Spain's absolutist rule. Despite strict press censorship, word of the growing schism between native Puerto Ricans and Spanish officials filtered abroad. In this article, a journalist, signing the pseudonym of "Quasimodo," described, in 1871, how the worried Spaniards had formed volunteer self-defense companies. The unpopularity of these loyalist volunteers is indicated by the fact that they were ordered "not to appear in the streets in uniform, so as to avoid complications." The article is also significant in that it contains an account of what is described as "the first time that the hitherto peaceful capital, San Juan de Puerto Rico, has witnessed a riot."]

. . . The revolutionary spirit has been on the eve of breaking out for a long time past, and has only been kept within bounds by the leaders of the radical party, who were determined to wrest the island from Spain without fighting for it. . . . Some hot blooded spirits have long fretted over the apparent slowness of emancipation, and the outbreak of Lara [Lares?] was the first fruit of their untimely action. Flushed with their success at the recent elections, their numerical superiority over the Spaniards, and the tacit aid of many Spaniards themselves, these hot headed radicals have again preached and abetted open rebellion and instigated the colored population to begin the row, which the latter, many of whom are still held as slaves, are nothing loth to inaugurate. These extreme radicals also act under the impression that any disturbance in Porto Rico, no matter how small, will aid the revolutionary cause in Cuba, both morally and materially, and in this they are right; it is positively known that since

"The Troubles at Porto Rico," *New York Times*, August 11, 1871.

the outbreak of the revolution in Cuba more natives from Porto Rico have joined the Cuban rebels than from many a place in Cuba itself, but this is foreign to the subject, and only tends to illustrate the propensities of the Porto Ricans to become an independent Spanish American country.

The Spaniards in Porto Rico . . . began to form volunteer companies, and about one thousand volunteers are at the present time organized and armed in the island. The islanders saw this movement with disgust, and feared that a part of their countrymen might become tainted with *Españolism,* as so many hundreds of Cubans are; that they might even take up arms against their countrymen in case of an outbreak, and, as in Cuba, . . . organize those terrible counter-guerrillas, who, composed of natives of the island, commit such havoc among their revolutionary countrymen. But whatever the motive may have been, the ultra radicals refused to have any person dressed in volunteer uniform parade the streets, either singly or collectively. Wherever a volunteer appeared he was hooted by the populace, and threatened with violence in some cases. No demonstrations of hostility had been made against the regular troops until the eve of the 25th, during the music on the Plaza de Armas in front of the Captain-General's palace, when several stones were flung from the neighboring jail, striking a couple of soldiers. The volunteers had received that same morning an order from the Captain-General not to appear on the streets in uniform so as to avoid complications. Another soldier who was walking along remarked: "This is getting unbearable. I advise nobody to fling stones at me else they'll suffer for it." He had hardly spoken these words when a stone struck him in the face. Seeing a dandified negro close by, he suspected him to be the author, and drawing his sword began the attack. Another negro, probably the one who flung the stone, saw the affair, and rushing up to the soldier stabbed him in the back. This enabled the first one to escape, the soldier cutting down the negro who had stabbed him. Negroes and soldiers flocked together, houses were barricaded, and a scene of indescribable confusion ensued, the cries of the combatants in the street, and the women and children inside of their houses, forming a strange contrast, this being the first time that the hitherto peaceable capital, San Juan de Puerto Rico, has witnessed a riot. The fighting continued in the streets wherever a negro met a soldier or a soldier a negro, until armed patrols appeared, and at 11 PM quiet was restored. The Captain-General immediately proclaimed martial law throughout the island and the capital itself in a state of siege. The result of the riot is stated to be three soldiers and one officer killed, nineteen men wounded, and five negroes killed and a very large number wounded. The police and armed patrols arrested a number of negroes during the night, and searched several houses for hidden arms. The Spanish party accuses the radicals of having hired the negroes to commit these excesses, and the natives say that the Spaniards purposely provoked the conflict. Either story is improbable, and the true explanation of the occurrence may be summed up in the fact that the natives, black and white, hate and execrate the Spaniards, and that the feeling is mutual. Until the morning of the 28th, the tranquility of the capital had remained unaltered, but reports were in circulation that outbreaks had occurred at Mayagüez and other points. . . .

THE AUTONOMIST CONCEPT

[Despite the widespread dislike for Spain, all of the armed might was in the hands of the military government, a substantial portion of the upper class was loyal to Madrid, and the illiterate peasants, who comprised the mass of the population, were too concerned with daily survival—and too isolated from each other—to join in an effective pro-independence conspiracy. Thus, most of the island's liberal leaders were discouraged by the prospects for armed insurrection, and sought a compromise. The spirit of their pessimistic views is captured in the following statements, by various leaders. In 1869, Román Baldorioty de Castro favored a Canadian-style autonomy as a means to resolve colonialism in Puerto Rico. He advocated free trade and the abolition of slavery, in accordance with the position taken by the Puerto Rican liberals who formed part of a commission in Madrid.]

In the question of the public interest, as in an issue of private interests, compromises are frequently necessary. We seek solutions which are both practical and possible. However, we will never accept the colonial system, which places the province in humiliating conditions of inferiority, in contrast with the harmony of equality enjoyed by

Selections in this chapter:
1. Translated from Lidio Cruz Monclova, *Historia de Puerto Rico*, Vol. II (Río Piedras: University of Puerto Rico, 1958), pp. 34–35.
2. Translated from Pilar Barbosa de Rosario, ed., *La Obra de José Celso Barbosa* (San Juan: 1957), pp. 167–88.
3. Translated from *Barbosa*, pp. 167–88.
4. Translated from Luis Muñoz Rivera, *Campañas Políticas*, part of "*Obras Completas*," Luis Muñoz Marín, ed. (Madrid: Editorial Puerto Rico, 1925), pp. 34–37.
5. Translated from Luis Muñoz Rivera, *Campañas Políticas*.
6. Translated from *Barbosa*, pp. 294–95.
7. From Edward J. Berbusse, *The United States in Puerto Rico, 1898–1900* (Chapel Hill: University of North Carolina, 1966), p. 50.
8. From a letter to Antonio V. Alvarado, February 16, 1892.

other provinces of the nation; nor will we accept a system based on slavery, whether overt or veiled, nor one which can permit, as has been the case up to now, the ruinous abuses of an irresponsible administration.

Such is and continues to be the colonial system which reigns in Puerto Rico; contrary to the true interests of the nation, this traditional regime represents blind opposition to the cultural, economic, and political progress of the island. We have protested against the colonial system, and we will continue to do so, accepting as an honor the calumny and vicious rumors perpetrated against our cause.

[In 1890, Baldorioty was leader of the Autonomist Liberal party. Here, he compares Puerto Rico with Cuba—then engaged in a bloody war for independence.]

The difference between Puerto Rico and Cuba is immense. Here, we have no man of stature, and they have many. Here, we would agree to a municipal life that is fairly reasonable, while they aspire or are driven on to the life of Canada or Australia. They desire a Cuban country within or without the national unity; we would agree to desire the life of a secondary province. . . . [Puerto Rico] will be reduced by misery or emigration; or it will, by entreaty, gain better conditions of government. Cuba will be an autonomic colony, or it will be lost through the war.

[In 1890, Julio Vizcarrondo, Puerto Rican deputy for Ponce in the Spanish Cortes, opposed the idea that Puerto Rico should join with Cuba in a revolt against Spain.]

I do not believe it fitting that Puerto Rico should follow the good or bad fate of Cuba . . . We have different inclinations . . . and other aspirations. . . . Let us live in friendly separation. I, who do not wish to see my island a colony of Spain, but rather a Spanish province, would never want to see it a colony of Cuba. The unhappiest slave is the slave of a freedman.

[Also pessimistic about independence was Luis Muñoz Rivera, the journalist who became the autonomy movement's *líder máximo*. Here, in 1890, he says:]

[Puerto Rico] is absolutely dependent upon the Castilian metropolis; and from it—or from annexation to a foreign country, which is a crime—we must hope for all. . . . [Compared with Cuba] we are lacking in the strength of the people, because of the ignorance of the country population. We are without a militant youth, because of the apathy and laissez-faire attitude of our youth. We are

wanting in leaders, because they greatly fear creative statesmanship; and are motivated by an unpardonable selfishness. It is
necessary to educate the first group, to stimulate the second, and
to attract the third. . . .

[In 1891, Muñoz Rivera, writing in his newspaper *La Democracia*,
urged a pact between his Puerto Rican Autonomist Party and the
the Spanish Liberal Fusionist Party, led by Práxedes Mateo Sagasta.
Six years later, when Sagasta gained control of the Spanish government, autonomy was granted to the island.]

We are not bent on fighting useless battles or pursuing the
impossible. For those who cherish beautiful ideals, let us inquire
whether the ideal is possible, and then make haste to follow its
luminous path. If it cannot become a reality, let us limit our desire
to the dictates of reason, rather than waste our energies in fruit-
less combat. We are men of our times, eminently practical in the
noble and generous sense of that phrase. Today's world is not one
of dreams and mirages. Platonism leads nowhere in our era.

[A year before the granting of autonomy to Puerto Rico, small
revolutionary groups in exile were trying to join Puerto Rico with
Cuba in the battle for independence. Here, Muñoz Rivera cites an
interview in July, 1896 with Gerardo Forrest, of the Puerto Rican
Revolutionary Junta of New York.]

My position is this, Mr. Forrest: I am a partisan of independence as an ideal. All have to be free. Nevertheless, I consider
that the independence of my country is absolutely impossible. Our
masses are even lacking in a complete civic education. They never
fought, and will not fight, with the power of the Cuban masses. To
attempt force is the equivalent of making a useless sacrifice.
After twenty-five years of titanic struggle, Cuba has not been able
to succeed. Puerto Rico would succumb without success and
without glory . . .

[The exiled revolutionaries soon became frustrated over the in-
ability of the island's leaders to aid the cause of independence.
Claims were made that the Autonomists had become instruments
of the Spanish colonial government. In a letter dated Jan. 23, 1896,
Dr. José C. Barbosa wrote to Roberto Todd of the Revolutionary
Junta in New York, replying that. "From New York all seems
very easy, but it is necessary to be here in order to be able to
judge the situation." Those favoring independence remained ada-
ment. An example of this unyielding position is contained in a
letter by Ramón Emeterio Betances in 1892, after he was asked to
write an article honoring the memory of the late autonomist leader

Román Baldorioty de Castro. In refusing, Betances explained:]

You know that in our country the separatists have been in disfavor for some time; and I do not feel capable of writing something which agrees with the thinking of the autonomists, neither those of today or yesterday. I know I have been defeated, but I harbor the hope that our people some day will say that if any party in Puerto Rico showed proof of its virility, it was the separatist party of Lares. The Spanish government has been able to calm down most of those who were with us by granting them the insignificant concessions which they now possess; but it is good to remember that all despotic governments throughout history have followed the same policy, whenever they have realized that the people are ready to claim their rights, with weapons in hand. Let us not forget that Lares means something in the Hispano-Puerto Rican struggle for obtaining freedom; and I, who have been, am, and shall die a separatist, believe that without a revolution, and without independence, we will never be anything but the eternal colony of Spain.

Part IV

MANIFEST DESTINY

> I spent all of yesterday with the spyglass in my hands; from Desecheo to Ataud, from Punta Borinquen to Punta Ponce, I saw all of her, I looked and looked at her, I admired her, and blessed her, and grieved for her . . . I grieved for her, and with her, for her beauty and misfortune. I thought how noble it would have been to see her free by her own efforts, and how sad, and crushing, and shameful it was to see her change from one master to another, without ever being her own . . .
>
> —EUGENIO MARIA DE HOSTOS, writing in his diary, September 13, 1898, while aboard the steamer "Philadelphia" as it left Puerto Rico.

As Carl Sandburg observes later in this section, the Spanish-American War was "a small war, edging towards immense consequences."

The war marked new eras for both the United States and Puerto Rico. It was America's first major step as an imperialist power; the first on a long road that led to the quagmire in Southeast Asia.

The United States had, for some years, contemplated expansion beyond its continental borders. The administration of President Franklin Pierce made overtures in Hawaii, Alaska, and Nicaragua. Perhaps the most brazen move was the Ostend Manifesto of 1853, which called for the annexation of Cuba (and probably Puerto Rico). If Spain did not accept a price for Cuba, said Pierce, "we shall be justified in wresting it from Spain."

In 1885, historian John Fiske wrote, in an article entitled "Manifest Destiny," * that, "The work which the English race began when it colonized North America is destined to go on until every land on the earth's surface that is not already the seat of an old civilization shall

* *Harper's New Monthly Magazine*, LXX, pp. 578–90.

become English in its language, in its religion, in its political habits and traditions . . ." He was not alone among influential Americans who believed in the inherent superiority of Anglo-Saxon culture.

That same year, Congregationalist clergyman Josiah Strong mirrored the growing "Darwinian" surge in America when he wrote: "This powerful race will move down upon Mexico, down upon Central and South America, out upon the islands of the sea. . . . And can anyone doubt that the result of this competition of races shall be the 'survival of the fittest'?" *

Alfred Thayer Mahan, Captain in the U.S. Navy, and one of the nation's most influential "sea power" advocates, wrote in 1890, that "At present the positions of the Caribbean are occupied by foreign powers . . . a distinct advance will have been made when public opinion is convinced that we need them." †

In the same mood of expansion, U.S. Secretary of State James G. Blaine wrote to President Benjamin Harrison the next year: "I think there are only three places that are of value enough to be taken; one is Hawaii and the others are Cuba and Puerto Rico."

"From the Rio Grande to the Arctic Ocean, there should be one flag and one country," wrote U.S. Senator Henry Cabot Lodge, just three years before the Spanish-American War. England, he concluded, "has studded the West Indies with strong places which are a standing menace to our Atlantic seaboard. We should have among these islands at least one strong naval station . . ." ‡

In Boston's exclusive Middlesex Club, on April 27, 1898, Senator Albert J. Beveridge voiced the concern that "American factories are making more than the American people can use. . . . We will establish trading posts throughout the world as distributing points for American products." He went on to speak of "great colonies, governing themselves, flying our flag, and trading with us . . ." §

A few days later, the *New York Journal of Commerce* editorialized that it was necessary to have Puerto Rico or Cuba, and that, "Whatever territory of that nature falls into our hands must never be parted with." || At the same time, letters from American businessmen to the U.S. State Department urged the annexation of Puerto Rico as a "garden spot" that would boost American commerce.

There were, to be sure, some dissenters. Governor William O. Bradley of Kentucky, for example, spoke out against "troublesome entanglements and complications" abroad, and the danger of converting Americans into "an aggressive and war-waging people." #

Recalling the withered empires of Rome and Spain, Bradley warned that "the acquisition of one piece of territory begets a desire for another, and in the end an effort to take by force that which justly belongs to others will lead to the loss of all we have."

* Josiah Strong, *Our Country: Its Possible Future and its Present Crisis*, Harvard University, Cambridge: Belknap Press, 1963, pp. 208–27 (facsimile of 1891 editorial).
† "The United States Looking Outward," *Atlantic Monthly*, December, 1890.
‡ "Our Blundering Foreign Policy," *Forum*, March, 1895.
§ Mr. Beveridge may have been clairvoyant, since Puerto Rico today is a "self-governing commonwealth" which flies the U.S. flag next to its own, and is America's fourth largest offshore trading partner.
|| *New York Journal of Commerce*, May 11, 1898.
New York Times, July 3, 1898, p. 3.

But he was in the minority. Even God, it seemed, was on the side of imperialism. On July 4, 1898, in the Central Presbyterian Church of Brooklyn, which was "ablaze with American, British and Cuban flags," The Rev. J. F. Carson read from the Holy Bible: "And Joshua took the whole land, and the land rested from war." He sermonized that "the high, the supreme business of this Republic is to end Spanish rule in America, and if to do that it is necessary to plant the Stars and Stripes on Cuba, Puerto Rico, the Philippines, or Spain itself, America will do it." *

Another clergyman foresaw a "widespread religious revival" because "the defeat of Spain will be the death knell of the Latin races. The Anglo-Saxons now hold the purest type of divinity." †

On the same night, in the Presbyterian Church of New York's Fifth Avenue, the Rev. Robert Mackenzie told parishioners that "God is calling a new power to the front. The race of which this nation is the crown . . . is now divinely thrust out to take its place as a world power." ‡

But terrestrial liberty and eternal salvation for the oppressed were only marginal reasons for America's entry into war with Spain. The so-called good old days of "the gay nineties" were neither so good, nor so gay. The period of 1893 through 1897, for example, was one of savage depression in America. Businesses failed, hungry tramps roamed the country, and Coxey's Army of the Jobless marched on Washington, demanding public works projects. In Chicago, federal troops battled against striking rail workers.

Unemployment, low wages, and strikes bred resentment toward the waves of alien workers from Europe, who worked for less, and were often trucked in under guard as strikebreakers.

The aliens were regarded as subhuman brutes, or as dangerous political radicals. In Chicago, an anarchist newspaper told its readers how to make dynamite. In Buffalo, in 1901, an anarchist would murder President McKinley.

Domestic turmoil engendered an upsurge of "nativism," and some states passed laws to exclude aliens from jobs. "Nativism" also bred "jingoism," a belligerent feeling towards not only aliens, but foreign lands.

It was not hard, then, for government leaders, aided by a sensationalist press that was engaged in its own little war to peddle papers, to divert the attention of the American people away from their domestic concerns, and towards Cuba, where a cruel, bloody war for independence was being waged.

Americans were urged to intervene in this war, to help free Cuba from the oppression of Spain. Fantastic stories of Spanish atrocities in Cuba abounded in the U.S. press. And, in early 1898, when the U.S. battleship *Maine* sank suddenly in Havana Harbor (although no one yet knows why), cries for war drowned out all appeals to reason.

Puerto Rico was a mere pawn in this power struggle. Spain, which had lost almost all of her Latin American colonies earlier in the century, was now embroiled in the Cuban conflict. In 1897, she granted a charter of autonomy to Puerto Rico. This charter gave Puerto Rico a substantial

* *New York Times*, July 4, 1898, p. 4.
† *Ibid.*
‡ *Ibid.*

degree of home rule, and was the most liberal political status ever attained by the island until that time.

But the new autonomous government—which convened for the first time on February 11, 1898—never was able to flex its muscles. War was declared on April 25. Six days later, Admiral George Dewey crushed the Spanish fleet at Manila. On July 3, Santiago, in Cuba, was surrendered to American troops. On July 25, Americans landed on Puerto Rico's southern shore, and, on October 18, the island was formally surrendered by Spain.

On December 10, the Treaty of Paris released Cuba from Spain, surrendered the Philippines to the United States for $20 million, and ceded Guam and Puerto Rico to the United States "as compensation for the losses and expenses occasioned . . . by the war."

No Puerto Ricans took part in the Treaty of Paris negotiations. The fledgling autonomous government was stripped of its powers, and the island came under U.S. military rule.

PUERTO RICO AS A PERMANENT POSSESSION

[From the United States, Puerto Rico was not viewed as the *patria* of nearly one million people with a distinct culture and nationality, but as a tract of tropical real estate: a fine naval station with a "commanding position between the two continents"; the "real gem of the Antilles," with "prolific" soil and an "exceptionally salubrious climate"; and a "charming winter resort."

These enthusiastic remarks were made by an influential business writer on the editorial page of one of America's largest daily newspapers. If he did not speak with official government sanction, subsequent events proved him to be uncannily accurate. As he says, Puerto Rico "is an island well worth having." If his article rankles the sensibilities of those who abhor colonialism, it is at least refreshing for its candor, compared with the bland double-talk issued by today's power brokers. Some passages have been italicized here for emphasis.]

There can be no question to perplex any reasonable mind about the wisdom of taking possession of the Island of Puerto Rico and keeping it for all time. There has been the same depressing misrule there as in Cuba, and the only reason why there has not been the same revolt against it is that the case was hopeless. The comparatively small and compact territory and the military weakness of the population have enabled Spain to crush out any attempt with merciless promptitude. At the same time she has taxed the little colony to help put down insurrection in Cuba as well as to enrich the Spanish officials. There can be no doubt that the people of the island, very few of whom are Spanish by birth, would rejoice to be relieved of the oppressive and exhausting rule of Spain, although they have been powerless to resist it, and have hardly dared to give vent to a desire to be rid of it.

There is the same reason for driving the corrupt despotism of Spain out of Puerto Rico as for driving it out of Cuba, save for the melancholy difference between a hopeless submission to wrong and a hopeless struggle against it.

The former condition is, indeed, the worse, for the cruelties practiced in trying to suppress chronic revolt excite sympathy and provoke interference from which rescue may come, while the deadening misery of hopeless submission may be allowed to go on

From Amos K. Fiske, *New York Times*, July 11, 1898, p. 6.

forever. It is fortunate for Puerto Rico that Spanish outrages in Cuba have brought about an intervention which will rescue both islands at once. We are under a pledge to leave the fate of Cuba in the keeping of her own people when the Spanish sovereignty over them shall have been destroyed. They have created a claim to this by their own long and costly struggles for independence and by their own part in achieving it, and they have only to justify the claim by proving themselves capable of self-government and worthy of their heritage in order to become a free and prosperous nation. If they find themselves unable to do this, they may yet call upon the United States to take charge of their future destiny, and *that may in the long run be better for them.*

But we shall free Puerto Rico from Spanish rule practically without any effort on the part of its own people, and at our own proper cost as an incident of the contest to expel it from Cuba. This result is necessary to make that expulsion complete and lasting, for to be rid of the Spanish disturbance to civilization in the Western World, Spain must be thrust from her last foothold on American soil. *We are not pledged to give Puerto Rico independence, and she will have done nothing to entitle her to it at our hands.* Besides, it would be much better for her to come at once under the beneficent sway of the United States than to engage in *doubtful experiments at self-government,* and there is reason to believe that her people would prefer it. It would be in accordance with the genius of our institutions to accord them self-government in local affairs as soon and as far as they showed themselves capable of it, and experience would soon teach them how much they had gained by their providential escape from the cruel stepmother country.

The circumstances of the conflict for the enfranchisement of Cuba and Puerto Rico fully entitle us to retain the latter as a permanent possession. Our need of a foothold in the West Indies for naval purposes has long been recognized, and it is now more obvious than ever before. We have made efforts to secure it on the island of San Domingo which were rendered futile by circumstances that we need not now recall. Once we secured it, so far as negotiation and agreement went, in the Danish Island of St. Thomas, and lost it again by the fatuous conduct of Congress in refusing to ratify the bargain, to the just resentment of Denmark and the humiliation of our Government in the eyes of its own people and of the world. *Now we have it within our grasp in a far better form, with Congress and the people in a mood for taking and keeping it, and with every just and proper consideration in favor of our doing so.*

As a naval station, the Harbor of San Juan de Puerto Rico is preferable in location to the Bay of Samaná, Mole St. Nicholas, or any other place on the island of San Domingo, and to Charlotte Amalia, the port of St. Thomas. Of the advantage of possessing all the land to which a naval station is appurtenant there can be no doubt. Puerto Rico occupies the central place on the eastern frontier of the great American archipelago, the outpost of the Greater Antilles, and the watch tower between the Bahamas and the Caribbees. The Mona Passage on the west and the Virgin Passage on the east are pathways to the South American coast. It is a commanding position between the two continents of the west, and upon the island rampart between the Atlantic Ocean and the Caribbean Sea. The most deliberate choice of a naval station in the West Indies could not have placed it better than the course of events, which has put the Island of Puerto Rico at our disposal.

And it is an island well worth having—the real gem of the Antilles. . . . In spite of misrule, exhausting taxation, and a backward state of industry, it is a populous island, having more than 800,000 inhabitants, or about as many as Connecticut. This is because the soil is most prolific and the climate exceptionally salubrious; and twice as many people could live there in ease and comfort. . . .

Of the commercial value of Puerto Rico as a possession there is no possibility of doubt. Under a government that discouraged enterprise and prevented improvement, with an almost complete lack of roads and bridges in the interior to make communication and transportation economical, with primitive methods of cultivation and practically no manufactures, and with a stifling system of taxation and official corruption, it has supported a relatively large population and had a foreign trade of $35,000,000 a year. What is it not capable of under an enlightened policy and with a systematic application of enterprise and industry?

. . . . There is nothing in the tropical climate of Puerto Rico to prevent our people from going thither, but the labor force already there has never been half utilized. The real Spanish element is small even in the cities. The white population is mainly like the native element of Cuba—creole descendants of European colonists alienated from the Spanish stock. There are many blacks, possibly a third of all the people, and much mixed blood, but the population is not ignorant or indolent or in any way degraded. It is not turbulent or intractable, and there is every reason to believe that under encouraging conditions it would become industrious, thrifty and prosperous. It is certain that a great advance could be made upon the present state of things, and the island could be rendered of no small commercial value to us and to its own people.

There is no reason why it should not become a veritable garden of the tropics and an especially charming winter resort for denizens of the North. Apart from the attractions of climate and scenery, there is a quaint picturesqueness in the old Spanish towns, and many interesting associations with the infancy of America. . . .

Whatever may be said or thought of keeping the Philippines or acquiring the Hawaiians, there can be no question of the wisdom of taking and holding Puerto Rico without any reference to a policy of expansion. We need it as a station in the great American archipelago misnamed the West Indies, and Providence has decreed that it shall be ours as a recompense for smiting the last withering clutch of Spain from the domain which Columbus brought to light and the fairest part of which has long been our own heritage.

"A DANGEROUS NEIGHBOR"

[Mr. Fiske's views in the preceding article were not shared by Puerto Ricans. Members of the island's small elite were aware of growing U.S. influence in the Caribbean, and a few of them favored annexation by their North American neighbor. Others were steadfastly loyal to Spain, while others demanded outright independence. The party in power, however, supported a compromise position of autonomy, under loose Spanish rule. All, to some extent, were afraid that a change of sovereignty would bring a tidal wave of change that might overwhelm them. Even in 1892, six years before the outbreak of the Spanish-American War, journalist Mariano Abril could write:]

To believe that the *yankees* will grant us all their freedoms and all their progress just for our pretty face is nonsense. Yes, they would grant us those liberties which they judged to be adequate, in exchange for guaranteed and ample exploitation.

Yes, we would have elevated trains crossing our streets; big, beautiful ports, with jetties and docks; bigger factories and commerce than ever before; but all of this in their hands; taken over and exploited by them; because all those things are not achieved without large amounts of capital, which would be *yankee* capital, because there is nothing here to support such enterprises. And,

---

Selections in this chapter:
1. Translated from Lidio Cruz Monclova, *Historia de Puerto Rico* (Río Piedras: University of Puerto Rico, 1952), Vol. III, p. 386.
2. Translated from *La Democracia*, 1894, no. 1030.
3. Translated from *La Democracia*, May 4, 1898.

after a few years, industry, commerce, and even our agriculture, would be monopolized by the *yankees*, and the Antillean would be reduced to the condition of a miserable tenant farmer, without a homeland, without a home, and without fortune. . . .

And, as for liberties, we would have a *yankee* army, a *yankee* navy, a *yankee* police, and *yankee* courts, because they would need all of this to protect their interests. And this rich and beautiful Castilian would disappear from our lips, to be substituted for by the cold, barren English language. . . .

[In 1894, an editorial in the newspaper *La Democracia* said:]

The American nation is a dangerous neighbor, especially for Cuba, the Dominican Republic, and Puerto Rico. We must trust very little in her statements. We must not fall asleep, and must keep watchful eyes on the Florida Channel. Anglo-American traditions are not the most reassuring.

There you have Mexico, invaded and dismembered, due to the greed of the Colossus. There you have Nicaragua, where they arrived one day, stirring troubles and difficulties. The North American Republic is too powerful to relax her pressure on the weak Latin American Republics.

On the alert, then. . . . the United States urgently needs to establish a position in the Antilles. In 1891, they talked and acted in this direction, without beating about the bush.

[As the war touched Cuba and the Philippines, and the invasion of Puerto Rico seemed imminent, an editorial expressed concern over the expected clash of cultural values.]

This war is the continuation of the terrible clash between two races, that started in the ancient times of the Roman decadence, and which sooner or later will shake the world. . . . We do admire the Yankee people for their gigantic activity, for their industrial power, for their extraordinary prosperity. But we prefer to be Spanish. We prefer death, rather than lose our nationality.

We do not wish to disown our blood, nor the sweet tongue with which our mothers lulled our sleep in the cradle.

"HAVE WE NOT SUFFERED LONG ENOUGH?"

[While the American invasion force sailed to Puerto Rico, Eugenio María de Hostos, the eminent writer and educator, arrived in the United States. He sought an audience with President McKinley, to ask that Puerto Ricans be allowed to decide their political future by popular vote. A brief audience was later granted, but McKinley ignored the request. De Hostos was well known in several Latin American nations, where he had been awarded prizes for his literary works, and also founded institutions to help the Cuban revolutionary movement against Spain. He was held in particularly high esteem in the Dominican Republic, where he founded schools to train teachers, and in Chile, where he was commissioned by the government to direct the reform of that country's educational system. De Hostos also organized chapters of what he called The Puerto Rican League of Patriots, a pro-independence group. It was on behalf of the League of Patriots that he visited President McKinley.]

Referring to his mission to this country, Señor Hostos said:

"It is my intention to ascertain as far as possible the plans of the United States Government relative to the disposition of Puerto Rico when that island becomes by right of capture its possession. It looks now as if my native land is destined to become American territory whether the inhabitants desire it or not, and to this I as well as many of my associates interpose serious objections. I wish, however, at the beginning to deny any reports to the effect that several Puerto Rican Juntas in foreign countries or in this country have advised their compatriots to offer any resistance to the United States troops in any manner. I fully realize that an expression of that character made on American soil would be treason, and I am quite sure that no sane person would ever utter it.

"Should I succeed in obtaining the desired interview with President McKinley I shall endeavor to impress upon him the fact that if Puerto Rico is to be annexed to the United States it should be with the consent of its population expressed through a regular plebiscite. If the majority of the people desire it we shall all bow to the majority and accept the inevitable.

"But neither I nor any other Puerto Rican patriot and repub-

"Señor E. M. Hostos Talks," *New York Times*, July 22, 1898, p. 2.

lican would like to see the American people violate their mission
as a great democratic nation by forcing our native island to
become a dependency of the United States, instead of assisting
it to shake off the yoke of its Spanish oppressors and then leave
it to build up its own independent government and work out its
own destiny.

"We should be only too glad to have the American people act
in the capacity of our mentors, our teachers in the art of enjoying
and making use of our liberty, which to the masses of the people
who have lived for so many years under the ban of Spanish tyranny
is a new feeling.

"As soon as I learn something of the readiness of the President
and other high functionaries of the United States Government to
receive me, I shall proceed to Washington and lay my mission
before the President.

"To prepare the way for my coming and to ascertain the
feeling in the White House with regard to my errand, Dr. [Julio]
Henna, the President of the Puerto Rican Junta of this city, has
sent Secretary [Roberto] Todd of our organization in Washington.
I expect an answer in a few days, and in the meantime a meeting
of all our people in this city will be held next Friday, and the
situation will be thoroughly gone over.

Suggestions to be Offered

"If I shall be allowed to offer any suggestions to the President,
I shall make it my object to point out to him the cause which
in my opinion is the only one worthy of the dignity and high aim
of the American people. I am certainly entirely in sympathy with
the course pursued in sending an expedition to Puerto Rico, as
this is absolutely necessary to carry out the joint resolution of
Congress on the merits of which the war was begun.

"Spain must be driven from the Western Hemisphere, and
to do this requires men and arms; but there is another provision to
this joint resolution which I think should not be left entirely out
of sight. I refer to the declaration which says emphatically that
this is not a war of conquest, but for the sake of humanity and
the independence and liberty of a people entitled to both.

"If Cuba is to be free and its people their own masters, are not
Puerto Ricans entitled to the same privilege? Have we not suffered
long enough under the yoke of an oppressive government and
should we not have an opportunity to show our capability of
governing ourselves?"

Señor Hostos was asked to give his opinion of the strained
relations said to exist between the Cubans and the Americans at
Santiago. "It grieves me very much to learn of the unfortunate
affair, but it should not, in my opinion, create surprise, after the

conditions under which the Cubans have been living are looked into. Suffering for many, many years under a tyranny which drove them to extreme despair, is it at all to be wondered at that at the first opportunity that offers itself they should desire in some measure to avenge the wrongs they have endured? It but carries out the idea I have expressed, that all these peoples who have been buried in the thraldom of slavery do not appreciate the responsibilities of liberty, and for that reason must have mentors, teachers, to show them how to act and what to do for their own good. In this role I am sure the Americans, who have demonstrated so well their ability to govern themselves, will be accepted with gratitude and will receive the heartiest cooperation.

"Let them establish over all their conquered territory not a protectorate, that is too much on the order of sovereignty, but rather a mentorate, backed by a show of actual interest, and let them reward themselves in whichever manner they may see fit for their trouble, retaining if need be such control of the independent government as will insure their own interests and at the same time guarantee the rights of their proteges."

Señor Hostos is about fifty-five years old, short and slender, and bears a likeness to the portraits of Premier Sagasta. He knows the head of the present Spanish Ministry well, as they were both exiles in paris in 1867. Señor Hostos is a Puerto Rican by birth, but received his education in Madrid and took part in the September revolution of 1868.* After the revolution he came back to America, living for the most part in Venezuela and Chile. He is well known in South America and among Republicans in Spain as the author of several works on political economy, with a decided leaning toward republicanism.

He speaks French excellently, in addition to Spanish, and while he understands English, it is difficult for him to speak the language. Since 1868 he has visited his native land but once, and that was shortly after the treaty of Zanjón, but after becoming convinced that the concessions supposed to have been granted the Puerto Ricans were such in name only, he decided to leave the island and devote himself to the cause of its emancipation, from a distance, where he would be free from prosecution.

* The year of "The Grito de Lares."

"SEIZE SAN JUAN"

[The invasion of Puerto Rico, at the south coast town of Guánica on July 25, 1898, came at a time when Spain was clearly beaten, and was pleading for peace. But America meant to have the island before the war's conclusion, in order to avoid disputes over its possession. In May, 1898, Assistant Secretary of the Navy Theodore Roosevelt, in a personal letter to Senator Henry Cabot Lodge, wrote: "give my best love to Nannie, and *do not make peace until we get Porto Rico.*" * Lodge replied: "Porto Rico is not forgotten and we mean to have it. Unless I am utterly . . . mistaken, the administration is now fully committed to the large policy that we both desire." †

On May 25, Washington correspondents observed great activity in the War and Navy Departments, and strong rumors indicated that President McKinley had decided to "seize San Juan de Puerto Rico and establish a permanent colonial government in the island." Influential congressmen explained that "the United States Government has awakened to the necessity of actually possessing Porto Rico before the end came. That island and the Philippines had come to be looked on as an essential recompense to the United States for its expensive intervention," while unless these territories were secured "before Cuba fell, embarrassing complications, leading possibly to grave international complications with European powers, might not be avoided." ‡ These feelings were reinforced by millionaire industrialist Andrew Carnegie, who cabled from Europe, "Take Porto Rico first, for its effect on Europe." §

In early July of 1898, a worried Dr. Ramón Emeterio Betances, exiled in Paris, wrote to Dr. Julio J. Henna, president of the Puerto Rican wing of the Cuban Revolutionary Party in New York:

"What are the Puerto Ricans doing? Why don't they take advantage of the blockade to rise en masse? It's extremely important that when the first troops of the United States reach shore, they should be received by Puerto Rican troops, waving the flag of independence, and greeting them.

"Let the North Americans cooperate in the achievement of our freedom; but not push the country to annexation. If Puerto Rico does not move quickly, it will be an American colony forever."

* *Selections from the Correspondence of Theodore Roosevelt and H. C. Lodge, 1884–1918* (New York: Scribner's, 1925), Vol. I, p. 299.
† *Ibid.*
‡ Millis, Walter, *The Martial Spirit: A Study of Our War With Spain* (Boston: Houghton Mifflin), pp. 226–27. 1931.
§ *Ibid.* It should be noted that Mr. Carnegie later established a library in San Juan, as a "philanthropic gift."

On July 21, a "practically official" statement by the U.S. Government was released to the press, saying that "Puerto Rico will be kept. . . . That is settled, and has been the plan from the first. Once taken it will never be released. It will pass forever into the hands of the United States. . . . Its possession will go towards making up the heavy expense of the war to the United States. Our flag, once run up there, will float over the island permanently." *

The United States expected little trouble in the occupation of Puerto Rico, where there had been no war (unlike Cuba), and no large, organized movement for independence.

As the time for the U.S. invasion of the island grew near, Antonio Mattei Lluveras, head of a Puerto Rican commission aboard the auxiliary U.S. cruiser *St. Louis*, wrote a letter to Washington. In it, he explained that some of his colleagues favored annexation to the United States, and others believed in independence, but "the main object . . . was to drive the Spaniards from the island."]

The Puerto Rican annexationists have formed a secret organization . . . and in nearly every city and village in the island they have established a branch. Every member of the society has been pledged to use his utmost endeavors to bring one or more friends or acquaintances into the society, which has annexation *or independence* [italics added] for its object. . . . A circular issued by the society, which has adopted for its name "Justicia" (Justice) explains to the ignorant native population of the island the injustice and tyranny of the Spanish government, and calls attention to the treatment which has been accorded a number of Puerto Ricans who have fallen into the hands of the Spaniards after openly favoring annexation. These prisoners were tried by court-martial and shot without ceremony. At their trials they were tortured to make them reveal the names of their fellow-conspirators but the organization of "La Justicia" is so excellent that no one man knows another man by name, but only by signs.

All of the members of the society are not in favor of annexation to the United States. Their main object is to drive the Spaniards from the island. After that has been accomplished they are willing to take the best they can get from the United States Government, knowing that it will be *fair and equitable* [italics added].

Puerto Ricans opposed to Spanish misrule are firmly convinced that the United States, once the island has been rescued from Spanish control, will give them *independence to some extent* [italics added]. Even if the island is annexed, they believe that the

---

* "Diary of the War," *Harper's Weekly*, July 30, 1898, p. 754.

Selections in this chapter:
1. From *New York Times*, July 30, 1898, p. 1.
2. From *Harper's Weekly*, August 13, 1898, p. 801.

United States will allow them the same home rule which is now accorded every State in the Union, and will not by military or moral force place Americans only at the head of affairs in the island.

Over 2,000 native Puerto Ricans, from different cities and villages in the interior, have assembled among the mountains on the southern coast to await the landing of the American army of invasion. They will immediately offer themselves, and thousands more will flock to the American standard. These people are a motley crew, armed with pistols, Remingtons, and old-fashioned guns, but they depend upon the American army to supply them with the necessary weapons. They are enthusiastic and will make excellent fighters.

[Sr. Mattei Lluveras's views in the previous article should be compared with those below, in a U.S. magazine. It notes that the Puerto Rican Junta in New York "has advocated independence," but those commissioners allowed to board the U.S. cruiser were annexationists. The glib final paragraph reveals how seriously the Puerto Rican views were received.]

On the opposite page is a picture * of the group of Puerto Rican commissioners who were selected, under direction of General Miles, by former Consul-General Warner P. Sutton and Captain Whitney of General Miles' staff, to land in Puerto Rico with our army and apprise the people of their several localities of the present status of the war between the United States and Spain, and of the intention of the United States to annex Puerto Rico.

They are to give their former neighbors a general idea of our institutions, and of the advantages to Puerto Rico which will follow annexation. They went to the island (from Newport News, Va.) on the cruiser *St. Louis.*

Their intention, as set forth by General Mattei and Mr. Fajardo, is to establish newspapers at once in Puerto Rico, through which, as well as by circulars, the announcements of General Miles may be circulated in the island. The Puerto Rican Junta in New York has advocated independence rather than annexation, but these commissioners have all along been annexationists, and were chosen for their present duty largely on that ground. Mr. Sutton has a large acquaintance in Puerto Rico, and understands the people there, and being on terms of warm friendship with the annexationist leaders is likely to be very useful in promoting good feeling between the people of the island and our forces.

* Photo showed Rafael Muñoz, Rafael Marxuach, José Budet, Mateo Fajardo, Emilio González, Domingo Collazo, P. J. Besoso, and General Antonio Mattei Lluveras, together with former U.S. Consul-General Sutton.

The fact that the commissioners seem to have got their flag
upside down indicates that they are not quite used to it yet;
but the American flag is already much more familiar to the
Puerto Ricans than it was when the picture was made.

OUR FLAG RAISED
IN PUERTO RICO

Four Spaniards Fall in the
First Fight of the Invasion

Americans Escape Unhurt

Guánica, on the Southern Coast,
the Scene of the Landing

Enemy is Surprised

Excellent Military Road Leads to
San Juan, 85 Miles Distant—Good
Work Done by the Gloucester

Copyright, 1898, by The Associated Press

GUANICA, Island of
Puerto Rico, July 25—Via St. Thomas, D.W.I., July 26—The United
States Military expedition, under the command of Major Gen.
Nelson A. Miles, which left Guantánamo Bay (Cuba) during the
evening of Thursday last, was landed here successfully to-day,
after a skirmish with a detachment of the Spanish troops and a
crew of thirty belonging to the launch boat of the United States
auxiliary gunboat Gloucester.

Four of the Spaniards were killed, but no Americans were hurt.

The American troops will be pushed forward promptly, in order
to capture the railroad leading to Ponce, which is only about ten
miles east of this place. From Ponce there is an excellent military
road, running eighty-five miles north to San Juan de Puerto Rico,
the capital of the island.

The ships left Guantánamo Bay Thursday evening, with the
Massachusetts . . . leading. Capt. F. J. Higginson was in charge of

From *New York Times,* July 27, 1898, p. 1.

the naval expedition, which consisted of the Columbia, Dixie, Gloucester, and Yale. Gen. Miles was on board the last-named vessel. The troops were on board the transports Nueves, Lampasas, Comanche, Rita, Unionist, Stillwater, City of Macon, and Specialist. This was the order in which the transports entered the harbor here. . . .

At noon yesterday Gen. Miles called for a consultation, announcing that he was determined not to go by San Juan Cape, but to go by the Mona Passage instead, land here, surprise the Spaniards, and deceive their military authorities. The course was then changed, and the Dixie was sent to warn Gen. Brooke at Cape San Juan.

Ponce . . . is a harder place to take. In addition, the water at Ponce is too shallow for the transports to be able to get close in shore. . . .

One advantage of this place is that it is situated close to the railroad connecting with Ponce, which means of transportation our troops will secure.

Early this morning the Gloucester, in charge of Lieut. Commander Wainright, formerly of the Maine, and one of the heroes of the naval battle off Santiago de Cuba, steamed into Guánica Harbor, in order to reconnoitre. . . .

The Spaniards were completely taken by surprise. Almost the first they knew of the approach of the army of invasion was in the announcement contained in the firing of a gun from the Gloucester, demanding that the Spaniards haul down the flag of Spain, which was floating from a flagstaff in front of a blockhouse standing to the east of the village. The first two three-pounders were fired into the hills right and left of the bay, in order to scare the enemy. The Gloucester purposely avoided firing into the town, lest the projectiles hurt women and children.

The Gloucester then hove to within about 600 yards of the shore and lowered a launch, having on board a Colt rapid-fire gun and thirty men, under command of Lieut. Huse. The launch was sent ashore without encountering opposition.

Quartermaster Beck thereupon told Yeoman Lace to haul down the Spanish flag, which was done, and they then raised on the flagstaff the first United States flag to float over Puerto Rican soil.

Suddenly about thirty Spaniards opened fire with Mauser rifles on the American party. Lieut. Huse and his men responded, the Colt gun doing effective work. Norman, who received Admiral Cervera's surrender, and Wood, a volunteer Lieutenant, shared the honors with Lieut. Huse.

Almost immediately after the Spaniards fired on the Americans the Gloucester opened fire on the enemy with all her three and six pounders which could be brought to bear, shelling the town and also dropping shells into the hills to the west of Guánica, where a number of Spanish cavalry were to be seen hastening toward the spot where the Americans had landed.

Lieut. Huse then threw up some intrenchments, which he named Fort Wainright. Barbed wire was laid in the street in front of it in order to repel the expected cavalry attack. The Lieutenant also mounted the Colt gun and signaled for reinforcements, which were sent from the Gloucester.

The Associated Press dispatch boat Cynthia II was the only boat in the harbor except the Gloucester. While the Mausers were peppering all around, Lieut. Commander Wainright called out to the Cynthia:

"They fired on us after their flag was down and ours was up, and after I had spared the town for the sake of the women and children. The next town I strike I will blow up."

Presently, a few of the Spanish cavalry joined those who were fighting in the streets of Guánica, but the Colt gun killed four of them.

By that time the Gloucester had the range of the town and of the blockhouse, and all her guns were spitting fire, the doctor and the Paymaster helping to serve the guns.

Soon afterward white-coated galloping cavalrymen were seen climbing the hills to the westward, and the foot soldiers were scurrying along the fences from the town. By 9:45, with the exception of a few guerrilla shots, the town was won and the enemy was driven out of its neighborhood.

The Red Cross nurses on the Lampasas and a detachment of regulars were the first to land from the transports. . . .

Gen. Miles . . . went ashore about noon . . . and said:

"Guánica and Cinga [?] are in the disinfected portion of the island. Matteo, the insurgent leader, lives at Yauco, a few miles inland. Had we landed at Cape San Juan, a line of rifle pits might have stopped our advance."

. . . Guánica is the most delightful spot yet occupied by our forces. It is a centre for the coffee and sugar industry and large herds of cattle are pasturing in the meadows, which are bordered by cocoanut palms. Many head of cattle and a large number of horses have been driven into the mountains by their owners. Some of them will be captured.

Ponce is the second city of the island, has a splendid harbor, and will make a good base of operations . . . [it] is sure to fall shortly before the combined attack of our army and navy. The main fighting until San Juan is reached will be along the line of a splendid military road leading from Ponce to San Juan. Street shields, of which a supply was brought with the expedition, will be used to protect the troops. . . .

At 9 o'clock to-night the commander of the Dixie said he had been almost around the Island of Puerto Rico and had not seen any men-of-war or transports, except the New Orleans, which was blockading the port of San Juan.

A heavy gale was blowing, causing the dispatch boat to consume nineteen hours in making the 125 miles to St. Thomas.

"TO THE INHABITANTS OF PORTO RICO"

[On July 29, four days after the landing of American troops, Major General Nelson A. Miles, commander of the invasion force, issued a general proclamation from his military headquarters in Ponce. This was the first official public statement from the U.S. Government to explain its plans for Puerto Rico.]

In the prosecution of the war against the Kingdom of Spain, the people of the United States in the cause of liberty, justice, and humanity, its military forces have come to occupy the Island of Porto Rico. They come bearing the banner of freedom, inspired by noble purpose to seek the enemies of our country and yours, and to destroy or capture those who are in armed resistance. They bring you the fostering arm of a nation of free people, whose greatest power is in justice and humanity to all those living within its fold. Hence, the first effect of this occupation will be the immediate release from your former political relations, and it is hoped, a cheerful acceptance of the Government of the United States. The chief object of the American military forces will be to overthrow the armed authority of Spain and to give to the people of your beautiful island the largest measure of liberties consistent with this military occupation. We have not come to make war against a people of a country that for centuries has been oppressed, but, on the contrary, to bring you protection, not only to yourselves but to your property, to promote your prosperity, and to bestow upon you the immunities and blessings of the liberal institutions of our government. It is not our purpose to interfere with any existing laws and customs that are wholesome and beneficial to your people, as long

---

From U.S. War Department, *Military Government of Puerto Rico from October 18, 1898 to April 30, 1900*. Government Printing Office, Washington, 1902.

as they conform to the rules of military administration, of order and justice. This is not a war of devastation, but one to give all within the control of its military and naval forces the advantages and blessings of enlightened civilization.

SOLDIER

[Carl Sandburg, the famed poet and Lincoln biographer, was twenty years old when the Spanish-American War began. He enlisted and saw active service in Puerto Rico. This excerpt is from his autobiography.]

We sailed out of Guantánamo Bay, three thousand troops on the transports. Rumors ran that we were going to Porto Rico. . . . Soon after daylight on July twenty-fifth we sighted a harbor and moved into it. Ahead we saw gunfire from a ship and landing boats filled with bluejackets moving toward shore. We were ordered to put on our cartridge belts and with rifles get into full marching outfits. We heard shooting, glanced toward shore once in a while and saw white puffs of smoke while we stood waiting our turns to climb down rope ladders into long boats called lighters. We were rowed to a shallow beach where we dropped into water above our hips. Holding rifles above our heads, we waded ashore. We were in Guánica, a one-street town with palm and coconut trees new to us. We expected to be ordered into action against Spanish troops somewhere in the town or near-by hills. So our talk ran. We were marched to a field near the town where we waited over noon and afternoon. We ate our supper of cold canned beans and hardtack and soon after were ordered to march.

When we came to a halt we waited in the dark and heard shots that seemed not far away. This was the one time on that island when most of us expected to go into battle, to shoot and be shot at. And it didn't happen. We waited and marched back to our fields near Guánica. A story arose that Sixth Illinois troops that night did some wild firing, some of their bullets hitting the transport on which General Miles was sleeping, others of their bullets hitting a ship carrying Red Cross nurses. . . . It could have

From Carl Sandburg, *Always the Young Strangers* (New York: Harcourt, Brace, 1953), pp. 403–24. Reprinted by permission.

been that the shots we heard sounding to us like enemy fire were from the Krag-Jorgensens of Sixth Illinois boys aiming at random at an unseen enemy. Some of us had been "shaking in our boots" and it would have been a relief to shoot at anything in any direction. We heard in the morning that bluejackets from the ship *Gloucester* and regulars with artillery had killed four Spanish soldiers, driven a troop of cavalry to the hills, and there was no enemy in sight or hearing. . . .

We marched to Yauco and on to Ponce, finding those towns surrendered. . . . On roads and streets as we marched were barefooted men and women smiling and calling to us *"Puerto Rico Americano."* For four hundred years this island had been run by a Spanish government at Madrid. Now it was to be American and it was plain that the island common people liked the idea and had more hope of it. More than once we saw on the roadside a barefoot man wearing only pants, shirt, and hat, eating away at an ear of parched corn. We saw kneehigh children wearing only a ragged shirt and their little swollen bellies told of something wrong with their food, not enough food and not the right kind. . . .

We camped at Ponce a few days and then began a march up mountain roads. The August tropic heat was on. We carried cartridge belt, rifle, bayonet, blanket roll, half a canvas pup tent, haversack with rations, a coat. We still wore the heavy blue-wool pants of the Army of the Potomac in '65 and thick canvas leggings laced from ankles to knees. On one halt after another there were men tearing their blankets in two so as to lessen weight to carry. I tore a third of mine away. Some let the whole blanket go. Men fell out, worn-out, and there were sunstroke cases. We passed more than one on the ground raving about the heat. It was an eight-mile march upgrade. . . .

We camped on a slope on the edge of Adjuntas, where we saw the American flag run up. Cook Metcalf over a long afternoon had boiled a tinned beef we named "Red Horse." For all the boiling it was stringy and tasteless, "like boiled shoestrings flavored with wallpaper." . . . About three o'clock in the morning a heavy downpour of rain kept coming. We were on a slope and the downhill water soaked our blankets. We got out of our tents, wrung our blankets as dry as we could and threw them with ponchos over our shoulders. Then a thousand men stood around waiting for daylight and hoping the rain would let down. . . . Midmorning the sun did come out and we dried and marched on to Utuado.

There at Utuado came news, "The protocol has been signed and peace is declared and we are ordered back to Ponce." Marching down the mountain roads we had climbed came easy along with rumors that we would take transports home from Ponce and replacements were on the way. Rains beat down and we were lighthearted and cried, "Hurrah for the Protocol!" It was a new funny word we liked. Instead of "Good morning," we said, "How's your old protocol?" We slept a night in a building used for drying coffee. Each man fitted nicely into a dry bin enclosure rich with a coffee smell.

At Ponce many of us weighed to see what we had sweated and groaned out. . . . My one hundred and fifty-two pounds in April had gone down to one hundred and thirty pounds in August. Many were gaunt and thin, with a slightly yellow tint on the skin of hands and faces. Uniforms were fading, here and there ragged and torn. Hats had holes in them. On some hats the fellows had written in purple with indelible pencils the names of the places we'd been. . . .

As for history, Theodore Roosevelt summed it up in a speech at the Stockyards Pavilion in Chicago which I (years later) covered for a newspaper. He happened to mention the Spanish-American War and added with a chuckle and a flash of his teeth, "It wasn't much of a war but it was all the war there was."

. . . . And the Mayor of Yauco, Francisco Mejía, whom we saw on a balcony, wasn't all wrong in his proclamation words: "Porto Ricans, we are, by the miraculous intervention of the God of the just, given back to the bosom of our mother America, in whose waters nature placed us as people of America."

The war, though a small one, was the first in which the United States sent troops on ocean transports to fight on foreign soil and acquire island possessions. At a banquet in Paris American citizens celebrated and offered toasts, the first one, "Here's to the United States, bounded on the north by Canada, on the south by Mexico, on the east by the Atlantic Ocean, on the west by the Pacific." The second speaker: "In view of what President McKinley has termed manifest destiny and in consideration of the vast new responsibilities that loom before our country, I offer the toast: To the United States, bounded on the north by the North Pole, on the south by the South Pole, on the east by the rising sun, on the west by the setting sun." The third speaker: "With all due humility in view of the staggering tasks our country faces across the future, I would offer the toast: To the United States, bounded on the north by the Aurora Borealis, on the south by the Precession of the Equinoxes, on the east by Primeval Chaos, on the west by the Day of Judgment." It was a small war edging toward immense consequences.

DIARY OF THE WAR

[Angel Rivero, born in Trujillo Alto, Puerto Rico, in 1864, was captain in charge of a Spanish artillery garrison which defended Fort San Cristóbal in San Juan. His book about the Spanish-American War in Puerto Rico is probably the most complete account of the conflict ever written. Excerpts from the section called "Diary of the War" follow.]

From the very day that I climbed the ramp of San Cristóbal castle to take command of its batteries, I began this diary. As my readers will see, they are spontaneous, disconnected, at times puerile. Upon looking over this document I've decided against adding or removing a single word; my desire is that it conserve its truthful *flavor* of the time. . . .

July 27—Today's *Gaceta* publishes an account of the enemy landing at the port of Guánica. . . .

July 29—Yauco captured. . . .

July 30—General alarm; it's advised that the enemy is landing at Boca de Cangrejos; the 3rd Provision marches there with all speed. They return a bit later . . . false alarm. . . . Since yesterday there have been two enemy ships in front of the [San Juan] port maintaining the blockade. . . .

July 31—Yesterday two coaches from the funeral parlor of Adrián López left for Caguas. This businessman, like the others, follows the scent of his clients. . . .

. . . Last night I went down from the castle and stopped for some time at a refreshment kiosk owned by a fellow named Domingo in the Plaza de Colón. There, seated upon a bench, I found Luis Muñoz Rivera and José de Diego. We spoke . . . discussing for quite some time the alarm displayed by all of the residents who were passing before us en route to Santurce. As I left I said to them: "Perhaps we won't see each other again, because if the enemy squadron attacks . . . I could lose my life from one moment to the next, since my batteries are the most exposed of the fort and without protection. Since you are authorized by the Governor to live outside of the city, I advise you to leave as soon as possible

Translated from Angel Rivero, *Crónica de la guerra hispánoamericana en Puerto Rico* (Madrid: Sucesores de Rivadeneyra Artes Gráficas, 1922).

and reunite with your families." Then, Luis Muñoz Rivera, getting
to his feet and taking my hand, answered me: "It's true that
they've given us permission, but we won't use it; as officials of the
insular government, we have duties just as you do . . . and if our
time comes, it, too, will find us at our posts . . . ; de Diego made
a similiar declaration, the three of us embraced, I returned to
my castle and they headed up Calle San Francisco towards the
Plaza of Alfonso XII. . . .

August 2—News arrives that the Americans have captured
Arroyo . . .

August 4—Last night a man from my battery, in a moment of
madness, threw himself into the sea from the top of wall . . . we
were able to recover him alive . . . ; two days before, another man
from San Gerónimo tried to commit suicide also, hanging himself
with a rope. The continuous nervous tension in which we live is
the cause. . . .

August 6—Headquarters publishes a notice saying that in the
combat sustained in Guayama against the invaders, the force led
by Captain Acha had 17 dead and wounded, representing casualties
of 20 percent. . . .

August 13—I think peace is very imminent, because censorship
has been relaxed. Today's *La Prensa* publishes a few articles extol-
ling the American flag, Old Glory. Signs of the times. . . .

. . . At one-thirty in the morning artillery Captain Aureliano
Esteban, who has just reached the castle, said that he was in a
meeting with the Captain of the Port, Eduardo Fernández, who
claims to have seen a cable saying that the protocol of peace has
been signed. General Ortega becomes furious and orders Esteban
and me to go, immediately, to speak with Captain Fernández. We
reach the Marina and, after waking him up, he tells us that the
cable has been received, adding that among the conditions agreed
so as to terminate the war, Spain renounces its sovereignty of
Cuba and, furthermore, cedes Puerto Rico to the United States. . . .

. . . Such a sad night! I spend it, all of it, seated upon a cannon;
as the sun comes out I affirm my resolution, taken before the
war; as soon as the peace is signed I will leave the Spanish army
and return to civilian life so as to share in whatever fortunes
befall my country. . . .

August 14—I am sad. It seems as though someone very beloved
to me has died; and yet many officers in the garrison do nothing
to hide their joy. "At last the war has ended," they say. "And we'll
be going home; Puerto Rico means nothing to us, and in the
future we'll no longer dream of yellow fever and other tropical
diseases. . . ." The conduct of these men contrasts with that of my
artillerymen who looked extremely sad for not having had the
chance to fight against the army advancing to occupy the fort. . . .

August 15—An American ship, one of the four in front of El Morro, has raised a white flag and after certain formalities some American officers disembarked by the arsenal docks. . . .

August 18—The *Gaceta* publishes an extra edition including the cable by the Minister of War, offering the news that the American government has lifted the blockade from Cuba, Puerto Rico and the Philippines, reestablishing commercial and postal communications.

August 22—Eugenio Deschamps in Ponce has commenced to edit the first newspaper written in English. It's called *The Porto Rico Mail*.

August 27—They tell me that signs have been placed upon many of the businesses in Mayagücz belonging to Spaniards. They say: *Don't enter you in here because it is a worst Spaniard.* The Spaniards may not be any good, but the English on the signs is much worse.

August 28—There is a great interest in learning English; men, women and children walk about the streets with a vocabulary that's just been put on sale and that's titled: *Idioma inglés en siete lecciones.*

August 29—A North American warship, the *New Orleans*, entered port today. Two officers disembarked, and one of them . . . was in the arsenal.

September 5—General Brooke, his escort and Chiefs of Staff arrived in Caguas today . . . ; at one in the afternoon he reached Río Piedras . . . ; at four the general and his staff came to San Juan . . . to greet General Macías, who awaited them in the Palacio accompanied by General Ortega . . . , the visit was very brief, purely a courtesy call, and then General Brooke and his companions went to the Hotel Inglaterra where they conferenced with Commodore Schley and General Gordon, returning soon afterwards to Río Piedras. . . .

September 11—General Wilson in Ponce made the following public declaration: "Puerto Rico will at first be governed by a military regime; then it will be declared an American territory, and later it will achieve the category of sovereign state within the Union. The duration of these periods will depend more or less upon the merits of the country."

September 12—In Río Piedras American and Spanish soldiers get along well together; they walk arm in arm down the streets, go to cafés and public places, as though nothing had ever happened. . . .

September 14—Today is the beginning of the evacuation of the Spanish forces. At eleven in the morning, the ships *Isabel II, Concha, Terror* and *Ponce de León* sailed for Spain. A great crowd followed the troops to the docks, offering them an affectionate farewell.

September 21—The surrender of the island has begun, town by town . . .

September 22—A seditious band of 40 men entered Fajardo last night, sacking three stores. . . .

September 23—Bands of arsonists are marauding through Garrochales, Factor and Hato Arriba, *barrios* of Arecibo, and also in Camuy. From Quebradillas one could see the flames last night. . . .

October 4—Today labor leader Santiago Iglesias has been freed after a long imprisonment resulting from political differences. . . .

October 9—Bands of robbers are spreading terror in the *barrios* of Adjuntas. . . .

October 11—A commission of American officers has visited the school established in Arroyo by professor Enrique Huyke, and they left highly satisfied over the English language examination given to the students. . . .

October 16—A daughter of Dr. Arrastia has flown the first American flag in Cataño; there was no objection on the part of the police . . . The Volunteer Regiment of Kentucky is aboard the Mississippi, anchored in port. . . . The Red Cross still shows sign of life. D. Dolores Aybar de Acuña, president of the women's section, is tireless; she distributes clean clothes and many other articles to all the repatriated troops and administers medicine to all the sick and wounded. . . .

October 17—Some soldiers from the Kentucky regiment have left their ship without permission, and their presence causes some disorder. A patrol lands immediately and obliges them to get back aboard. . . . Press censorship has ceased as of today. . . .

October 18—Today is the day for the official surrender of San Juan. There's not a single Spanish flag in the town . . . since yesterday they'd been put away in a cedar chest expressly made for that purpose. . . . Pairs of soldiers with bayonets mounted have been stationed at the street corners . . . all businesses have closed their doors, fearful of what might happen.

. . . Today is a sad day, yet I take notes for my *Chronicle of the Spanish American War in Puerto Rico*. . . .

. . . This very afternoon the American forces took possession of Customs, allowing all employees to remain at their posts. *The Gaceta de Puerto Rico* has been published today, displaying on its front page the American eagle instead of the Spanish coat of arms.

. . . General Brooke has sent letters to all the secretaries of the insular government and the foreign consuls, inviting them to the official surrender of the city, which took place today at noon in the Palacio de Santa Catalina. . . .

. . . During the night there were serious disorders in the café La Mallorquina, incited by the American soldiers. . . .

October 21—Today an official commission arrived from Washington to study our laws, customs, commerce, agriculture and finance, with the purpose of proposing the best form of government for the country.

October 22—Boarding the ship *Montevideo* today were General Ortega, my battalion and some other forces; the only ones who have not yet been repatriated.

October 23—The *Montevideo* sailed this afternoon. Happy voyage!

Part V

"CITIZENS OF PORTO RICO"

> Now, when I look into the depth of my
> soul, I can only perceive a portion of blue
> sea, and far away a white Latin sail, as a
> wing in flight. Where will it go? Where?
> Where?
>
> —Translated from Eugenio Astol,
> *La Democracia*, February 19, 1907.

The United States had
no clear plan for governing Puerto Rico, but one thing was clear: it
would not relinquish the island. American newspapers clucked content-
edly over the new prize—"a highly productive island . . . yielding coffee,
sugar, fruits, nuts and tobacco"—and remarked that "the business of the
country is in an unusually sound and healthy condition." * As for allowing Puerto Ricans some measure of self-rule, an editorial doubted the
wisdom of "putting votes into the hands of men who can make no intelligent use of them. A few years of experimenting with the natives will
instruct them in the duties of freemen and ourselves in regard to their
capacities." †

Some Puerto Rican leaders welcomed the invasion, as did the pro-
Republican newspaper *La Correspondencia*, which was not concerned
"about the disappearance of the customs of this country . . . because if
our people's customs are to continue being a matter of our peasants
and workers walking with bare feet and legs, badly dressed and poorly
nourished . . . it is better that such customs be substituted by others." ‡
Two months later, the same paper applauded the material benefits expected under American rule, but warned: "Let us have the good sons
of the North come and transform our minds, but let them not pretend
to transform our hearts." § By 1912, the same paper would favor independence for Puerto Rico.

There was criticism of the American takeover, but mostly from pow-

* Editorial, *New York Times*, July 28, 1898, p. 6.
† Editorial, *New York Times*, July 27, 1898, p. 6.
‡ Translated from *La Correpondencia*, August 22, 1898.
§ Translated from *La Correspondencia*, October 10, 1898.

erless sources. A small, liberal U.S. magazine editorialized that "Porto Rico is entitled to decide her own destiny by a fair vote of her people, and that she ought not to be forcibly annexed . . . without the consent of the inhabitants." *

As the months passed, it became evident that Puerto Ricans would not be allowed to vote upon their political destiny. The question then became: How would the United States govern the island? President McKinley assigned Dr. H. K. Carroll, a Protestant clergyman, to prepare a detailed report on conditions in Puerto Rico. Carroll concluded with a plea: "Let Porto Rico have local self-government . . . and she will gain by her blunders, just as cities and States in our own glorious Republic are constantly learning." He described Puerto Ricans as "industrious, law-abiding . . . and temperate." †

Robert E. Pattison, a former Governor of Pennsylvania, toured the island, and said that charges about ignorance prevailing in Puerto Rico were "not justified." He was favorably impressed by "merchants from San Juan and Ponce, tobacco planters from Cayey, doctors and businessmen from Coamo, the shopkeepers of Aibonito . . . the mayor and schoolteachers from Barranquitas . . . the municipal emyloyees of Utuado," and described Federal Party leader Luis Muñoz Rivera as "one of the most capable and forceful men that I have ever met." ‡

And the powerful Senator J. B. Foraker of Ohio said that Puerto Ricans "have had no experience that would qualify them . . . for the great task of organizing a government, with all the important bureaus and departments needed by the people of Puerto Rico." §

The imperious attitude in Washington soon created resentment in San Juan. In February, 1899, Governor-General Henry abolished the Autonomous Council of the island government, on the grounds that its members were uncooperative. A few days later, an editorial in a Puerto Rican paper demanded more local participation in government and warned: "Let the generals from the North remember that they were greeted as friends; they should not labor in a way that tomorrow will cause the Germans or Russians to be so welcomed." ‖

There was little help from liberal circles in America. At its 1900 national convention, the U.S. Democratic Party denounced Congress's treatment of Puerto Rico, saying, "In this, the first act of its imperialistic programme, the Republican party seeks to commit the United States to a colonial policy." #

But inaction by the Democrats in subsequent years suggests that they were merely using Puerto Rico as a political campaign issue. In fact, the Democratic Presidential candidate, William Jennings Bryan, who was running on a platform of "anti-imperialism," eventually voted to ratify the Treaty of Paris, which legitimized the U.S. takeover of Puerto Rico.

* Translated from *The Nation*, July 28, 1898, pp. 65–66.
† *The Independent*, January 4, 1900. Vol. 52, pp. 57–77.
‡ *The New York Journal*, October 7, 1900.
§ U.S. Congress, Senate, *Congressional Record*, March 8, 1900.
‖ Translated from *La Democracia*, February 20, 1899.
Official Proceedings, Democratic National Convention, Kansas City, Missouri, July 4–6, 1900, p. 114.

"THE PORTO RICAN INHUMANITY"

[In 1899, as the
United States prepared to remove its military governor from Puerto
Rico, and establish a civilian government, a strong controversy emerged
as the Republican administration in Washington proposed a temporary
tax on Puerto Rican imports and exports. Supporters of the measure,
such as Senator J. B. Foraker of Ohio, argued that the tax monies were
needed to support the island's administration; in other words, Puerto
Rico was expected to pay its own way from the start. Critics of the tax,
such as the author of the following article, felt that it would cripple
the already impoverished island.]

The humane people
of the United States cannot too soon be aroused to the fact that the
Republicans in Congress are proposing to commit, in the name of
this nation, an act of unparalleled and shameful cruelty. We refer
to the bill taxing Porto Rican exports and imports to the extent of
25 per cent of the Dingley rates. There are strong reasons for thinking this bill unconstitutional. They are set forth in the minority report, and also in the individual report of Mr. McCall of Massachusetts, a Republican who has the courage of his convictions, and, what
his Republican colleagues apparently have not, a sense of humanity.
But we do not now insist upon the illegality of the measure. Cha-
tham indignantly cried in Parliament: "I come not here armed at
all points with law cases and acts of Parliament, with the statute-
book doubled down in dog-ears, to defend the cause of liberty."
So we say to-day, be the constitutional right what it may; let the
Supreme Court reverse itself if it choose; rule out all questions of
fiscal need and policy—the fact remains that this proposed legislation is so cruel, so heartless, so charged with disaster and starvation
for 900,000 human beings, that to adopt it would entitle Spain or
Russia or even Turkey to send missionaries to us.

What are the facts? They are set forth in voluminous detail and
with overwhelming force in the reports of our own officials.
Governor-General Davis, Consul Hanna, Secretary Root, Commissioner Carroll, the President himself, have all shown how the
immediate necessities of Porto Rico cry out for freedom of trade
with this country. The inhabitants had practically a free market

From *The Nation*, LXX, No. 1807 (1899), p. 122.

in Spain and Cuba. We destroyed that. Then we double-locked
our own against them. The result is, as Secretary Root declared,
that two crops of tobacco lie rotting in the warehouses of Porto
Rico; that her coffee and her sugar are practically unsalable.
This was true even before the hurricane of last August came to
complete the ruin we had done our best to bring about by neglect.
The hurricane was "an act of God." What can we call our deliberate
attempt to prevent the Porto Ricans from living by honest labor
but an act of the devil?

The tax on their exports is flagrant enough; but to make them
pay one-quarter the Dingley rates on the necessaries of life would
argue a perfectly fiendish ingenuity of malevolence. People do not
generally understand this. The Dingley Schedule G, "Agricultural
Products and Provisions," is a section full of "fake" duties, so far
as we are concerned. These are the hoary old tariff taxes put in to
fool the American farmer, and make him think that he, too, is
"protected." But every one knows that the high duties dangled
before his innocent eyes are not operative. They do not affect the
cost of the prime necessaries in this country, for practically none
are imported. In Porto Rico, however, these Dingley duties would
take effect in crushing fashion. The island has long imported a
vast amount of food products, paying for them with tobacco and
coffee and sugar. Now the Republican plan is, on the one hand
to refuse the Porto Ricans a market for what they raise, and on
the other to tax them exorbitantly for the food they must have
or starve.

Take a few sample figures. Commissioner Carroll returns the
Porto Rican imports of rice in 1897 at 77,994,122 pounds. Here is
a necessary of life, now free. We propose to clap on 25 per cent
of the Dingley rate of 2 cents per pound. In other words, we
propose to tax a ruined and starving people $389,000 on a single
and necessary article of food! Did a Borgia or a Bajazet ever
condemn his subjects to death with a more refined cruelty? The
case will be very much the same with the other leading imports
of Porto Rico—kerosene oil, pork, lard, flour, fish. Salt fish is
taxed three-fourths of a cent a pound in the Dingley tariff; flour,
25 per cent ad valorem; lard, two cents a pound; pork, two cents
a pound, and so on. In other words, all these sleeping Dingley
duties on food, which are only a joke to us, are to be wakened
by the bill before Congress, and set to clutching the throats
of the unhappy Porto Ricans, whom we rescued from the tyranny of
Spain in order to fling them into the jaws of our Moloch of protection.

This, we say, is an act of stark inhumanity, to which we do
not believe the American people will ever consent. Certainly they
will not if its monstrous nature is brought home to them. Why,
we might as well turn our soldiers loose in the island to butcher the

inhabitants as to decree their death by act of Congress. When Russia annexed the Crimea in the last century, she put 30,000 Tartars, men, women, and, children, to the sword. Is our proposed course a whit less unfeeling and bloody? Here are 900,000 fellow-men; if not fellow-citizens, they are at least our subjects, as even the Imperialists must admit. Their lives and fortunes are in our hands. We propose to rob them of both. And the leaders in the crime are the Senators from Connecticut—the State of schools and universities and churches! That State has no more inhabitants than Porto Rico; yet its representatives in Congress, some of them lights in the religious world, coolly urge a bill to extinguish the right of nearly a million men under our flag to life, liberty, and the pursuit of happiness.

The whole thing seems a ghastly joke—like Swift's proposal to kill and eat the babies in Ireland. But if this law is pushed in dead earnest, there will be need of Swift's *sæva indignatio* against its authors and abettors. Is this to be a final demonstration of the inhuman nature of protection? When the McKinley tariff worked distress in Vienna, its author exulted over the misery he had wrought. Will he now sit idly by and see a protective tariff made an instrument of torture for men and women and children under the American flag? We cannot believe it; nor can we believe that the religious and educated opinion of this country will tolerate the crime which the Republicans in Congress are intending to commit in the name of protection. The American people are not cruel. They do not want the blood of Porto Ricans or Cubans or Filipinos on their heads. But, if they would be guiltless, they must lose not a moment in letting their selfish and besotted representatives at Washington know what they think of this attempt to make the United States synonymous with greed and cruelty.

"WE ARE BECOMING AMERICANIZED"

[The early years of the U.S. occupation were years of harsh adjustment. Change burrowed its way into every corner, even causing the island's name to be anglicized to "Porto Rico." New institutions sprang up to deal with health, education, and other central affairs. The island's traditional export markets were severed. U.S. investors came southward, buying up choice land for corporate farms that were gigantic by local standards.

The greatest strain was caused by the cultural impact, as a powerful English-speaking nation sought to mold a small Spanish-speaking colony into a more compatible entity. This was often a cruel, abrasive process.

The island's leaders had, for centuries, dealt with Spanish colonial administrators, sharing the same language and basic customs. Now—in their own homeland—they were forced to communicate in English with foreigners who held the reins of government.

Many despaired. In 1902, Luis Muñoz Rivera would write to a friend: "In the future there will be prosperity . . . but there will be no fatherland. And if there is, it will belong to Americans and their children and grandchildren. Within half a century, it will be a disgrace to bear a Spanish surname."

The brief U.S. military rule in Puerto Rico ended on April 12, 1900, when Congress passed a bill known as The Foraker Act. It provided for a governor, to be appointed by the President of the United States,* an Executive Council (with eleven Presidentially-appointed members, only five of whom had to be Puerto Ricans), and a Chamber of Delegates, with thirty-five members, all elected by the people. With this law, real power was in the hands of the American Governor and the six American members of the Executive Council. The power of the Chamber was restricted to minor local affairs. A Resident Commissioner in Washington, elected by the people, had a voice, but no vote, in Congress. Puerto Ricans were made "Citizens of Porto Rico." Congress reserved all powers to legislate on Puerto Rican affairs. A reaction to this situation appeared in an island newspaper editorial.]

* In theory, the President could have chosen a Puerto Rican, but appointed American governors held office for nearly half a century, until after World War II.

Selections in this chapter:
1. Translated from *La Democracia*, October 29, 1900.
2. From *U.S. Congressional Record*, 56th Congress, 1st session, Feb. 26, 1900, p. 2231.
3. From *The Puerto Rican Papers of Victor S. Clark*, Manuscript Division, Library of Congress, Washington, D.C.
4 - 6. Translated from *La Democracia*, Aug. 16, 1900.

Yes, we are becoming Americanized; . . . but not by the Constitution that is so wise, nor through freedom that is so great, nor through the law that is so magnificent; we are becoming Americanized through privilege, through monopoly, through injustice, through despotism. We are being Americanized the wrong way, and from this wrong Americanization the dealers who put on sale the honor of the country are to blame; not the American people, who have not yet come to know us, but the adventurers who fall upon the fields of Puerto Rico like swarms of ravenous locusts.

[Puerto Rican leaders also sent messages to Congress, such as this one:]

The United States has not been fair to those who gave their hand to their redeemer . . . who turned their backs upon the old conditions and accepted the new, only to discover themselves cut off from all the world—a people without a country, a flag, almost without a name, orphans without a father. . . . Who are we? What are we? . . . Are we citizens or are we subjects? Are we brothers and our property territory, or are we bondmen of a war and our islands a crown colony?

[One of the first acts of the United States was to establish a system of education, with the clear political goal of "Americanizing" the populace. This was attempted by organizing a highly centralized, islandwide school system, under an American Commissioner of Education. The first commissioner felt that:]

[Puerto Ricans do not have] the same devotion to their native tongue or to any national ideal that animates the Frenchmen, for instance, in Canada or the Rhine Provinces. . . . A majority of the people . . . do not speak pure Spanish. Their language is a patois almost unintelligible to the natives of Barcelona and Madrid. It possesses no literature and little value as an intellectual medium. There is a bare possibility that it will be nearly as easy to educate these people out of their patois into English as it will be to educate them into the elegant tongue of Castile. Only from the very small intellectual minority in Puerto Rico, trained in Europe and imbued with European ideals of education and government, have we to anticipate any active resistance to the introduction of the American school system and the English language.

[The following statement was attributed to U.S. Senator Teller of Colorado, and reported in the July 9, 1900 issue of La Democracia:]

I do not like the Puerto Ricans, they are not fighters as the Cubans, they remained subdued by Spanish tyranny for hundreds

of years without showing themselves to be men in opposition. Such
a race does not deserve citizenship.

[The next day, an angry editorial in *La Democracia* replied:]

Few, very few, are the Americans living in Puerto Rico who
sympathize with the people of our country, believing themselves
superior to us, when most of them do not attain the degree of
culture and understanding of that large number of Puerto Ricans
educated in Europe, and who constitute our intellectual circles. . . .
If that senator from Colorado, whose country [region] still is
half savage, were not an ignoramus, he would know Puerto Rico
never found itself in the same circumstances as Cuba did. . . .

[*La Democracia* continued its attacks, taking aim at racial prejudice in the United States.]

The extremely unfair treatment taking place in a country that
calls itself free and democratic, cannot do less than dampen faith
among those who believe that liberty and equality in the laws must
govern the social world.
Since we don't want to see such a spectacle in our country, we
defend our identity in every respect, since under its protection,
Negros live here intermingled with Whites, enjoying the same
rights and freedom, taking part in the administration of the country, something they have not attained in the United States, and
exercising together with the Whites the right to vote.
Nevertheless, we observe with sadness that in Puerto Rico . . .
the men of the colored race seem happy and satisfied with the
absorption [by United States] menacing us all, without reflecting
that they, more than anyone else, will suffer the consequences,
the day when our island forfeits its personality.

"THEY ARE LOYAL"

[Six years after the
U.S. occupation, at a banquet in Washington for the local Yale alumni
association, those gathered sang proudly of alumnus "Billy Hunt," who,
as "Governor, he's steering Porto Rico's ship of State." The journalist
who covered the banquet noted that "the people of Porto Rico are full
of gratitude to the Americans" and earnestly desired Americanization."
He observed that a new word had been coined: "spigotty"—later short-

From *New York Times*, December 12, 1906, p. 7.

A view of San Juan in early Spanish colonial times.

Statue of Ponce de León, Puerto Rico's first governor, in the San José Plaza, Old San Juan.
Puerto Rico Information Service

El Morro castle in Old San Juan. For 350 years, the fortress served as a New World bastion for Spain.

José Campeche, the first important Puerto Rican painter, who lived in San Juan when it was a small village surrounded by thick fortress walls.

Ramón Emeterio Betances, who inspired the 1868 Lares revolt for independence.

Eugenio Maria de Hostos, writer, abolitionist, and one of Puerto Rico's foremost educators.

Market scene in Ponce in the late 1890's.

Ramón Baldorioty de Castro, political leader and journalist, who fought for autonomy from Spain.

*Institute of
Puerto Rican Culture*

Lola Rodríguez de Tió, poetess, who wrote the words to Puerto Rico's hymn, *"La Borinqueña."*

José de Diego, lawyer, orator, and writer, who was Secretary of Justice in the autonomous government in 1897. After the U.S. occupation, he became the first President of the Puerto Rican House of Representatives. In later years, he devoted himself to Puerto Rican independence.

Spanish shore battery at Fort San Cristobal, Old San Juan, at the time of the U.S. invasion in 1898.

Landing of American troops at Arroyo in July, 1898.

ened to "spic"—which was a "new synonym for the Porto Rican native" who "delightedly" greeted American soldiers with the exclamation, "I speak de Inglish." The journalist acknowledged widespread poverty, but also remarked that "the native, while lying in his hammock, can pick a banana with one hand and at the same time dig a sweet potato with one foot." *

In 1906, after President Theodore Roosevelt visited the island, he reported to Congress that the people of Porto Rico "are glad to be under our flag" and recommended the granting of U.S. citizenship.]

To the Senate and House of Representatives:

On Nov. 21 I visited the Island of Porto Rico, landing at Ponce, crossing by the old Spanish road by Cayey to San Juan, and returning next morning over the new American road from Arecibo to Ponce. The scenery was wonderfully beautiful, especially among the mountains of the interior, which constitute a veritable tropic Switzerland. . . .

I doubt whether our people as a whole realize the beauty and fertility of Porto Rico and the progress that has been made under its admirable government. We have just cause for pride in the character of our representatives who have administered the tropic islands which came under our flag as a result of the war with Spain. . . .

I am very much struck by the excellent character both of the insular police and of the Porto Rican Regiment. . . . The insular police are under the local Porto Rican Government. The Porto Rican Regiment of troops must be appropriated for by Congress. I earnestly hope that this body will be kept permanent. There should certainly be troops in the island, and it is wise that these troops should be native Porto Ricans. It would be from every standpoint a mistake not to perpetuate this regiment.

In traversing the island even the most cursory survey leaves the beholder struck with the evident rapid growth in the culture of both sugar cane and tobacco. The fruit industry is also growing. . . .

Unfortunately, what used to be Porto Rico's prime crop—coffee— has not shared this prosperity. It has never recovered from the disaster of the hurricane, and, moreover, the benefit of throwing open our market to it has not compensated for the loss inflicted by the closing of the markets to it abroad. . . .

There is a matter to which I wish to call your special attention, and that is the desirability of conferring full American citizenship upon the people of Porto Rico. I most earnestly hope that this will be done. I cannot see how any harm can possibly result from it, and it seems to me a matter of right and justice to the People

* John Ball Osborne, *World's Work*, VIII (1904), pp. 4759–66.

of Porto Rico. They are loyal, they are glad to be under our flag, they are making rapid progress along the path of orderly liberty. Surely, we should show our appreciation of them, our pride in what they have done, and our pleasure in extending recognition for what has thus been done, by granting them full American citizenship.

Under the wise administration of the present Governor and the Council, marked progress has been made in the difficult matter of granting to the people of the island the largest measure of self-government that can *with safety* be given at the present time. It would have been a very serious mistake to have gone any faster than we have already gone in this direction. . . .

In short, the Governor and the Council are co-operating with all of the most enlightened and most patriotic of the people of Porto Rico in educating the citizens of the island in the principles of orderly liberty. . . . It has not been easy to instill into the minds of people unaccustomed to the exercise of freedom the two basic principles of our American system—the principle that the majority must rule, and the principle that the minority has rights which must not be disregarded or trampled upon. Yet real progress has been made. . . .

THEODORE ROOSEVELT
The White House
December 11, 1906

"DISCIPLINE FOR PORTO RICO"

[The first rebellion against American rule in Puerto Rico, albeit a peaceful one, occurred in 1909, when the insular House of Delegates refused to pass the appropriations bill for the next year's budget, on the grounds that appointed U.S. leaders wielded excessive power over island affairs. President William Howard Taft lost little time in rebuking the Puerto Ricans, in a message to Congress on May 10, 1909. "In the desire of certain of their leaders for political power, Porto Ricans have forgotten the generosity of the United States in its dealings with them," said Taft. He concluded that "the present development is only an indication that we have gone somewhat too fast in the extension of political power to them for their own good." *

Quite a different view of America's generosity was offered two years later by Tulio Larrinaga, Puerto Rico's elected Resident Commissioner in Washington.]

* *The Independent*, LXVI (May 20, 1909) 1050–51.

From *The Independent*, LXX (February 16, 1911) 356–59.

That Porto Rico has been prospering for the last eight years—prospering from one viewpoint—is a fact which no one will deny. . . . Porto Rico has been exploited for eight years to develop her wealth-producing qualities, for the benefit of large money interests. Porto Rico has prospered, from that viewpoint. Under the protective tariff of the United States the sugar and tobacco interests have been greatly enlarged. From 69,000 tons of sugar exported in 1901 the production increased to 284,000 tons in 1910. It is a suggestive fact, however, that whereas there were then 345 sugar planters, the number is now reduced to less than 200, showing a concentration which is very undesirable in any country. And the increase in the production of sugar marked a corresponding decrease in the production of coffee, then the most important production of the island—still more important because the coffee farms, like the sugar farms at the start, were all comparatively small holdings owned and managed by the local planters, to their own profit and the benefit of Porto Rico. If it were not for the little money from sugar making which remains in the island today there would be great suffering among the poor. For with the advent of America and the tariff, there being no protective duty on coffee, the small farmers found it impossible to live, and their little farms were sold by the hundreds for taxes amounting to no more than ten or twenty dollars, and were bought up by the large interests. There was a law limiting the amount of land which could be bought by single interests, but there was no penalty affixed for disobedience, so no one cared.

No one denies the material prosperity, but the Porto Ricans are keenly alive to the fact that their political status, which should have kept pace with material progress, has been going down and that more and more they are losing their rights and losing their hold upon their island. In this connection one should not forget that Porto Rico has 1,100,000 inhabitants; that 100,000 children attend the public schools; that there are high schools, normal schools and a university in Porto Rico; that last year the exports of Porto Rico reached $30,000,000; that Porto Rico is more densely populated than any State of the Union; that we have a history and a Christian civilization centuries old.

During the past century, under the Spanish regime, the one aim of the Porto Ricans was to obtain political advancement toward their ultimate desire of self-government. Canada was their model. The English system in Canada was the goal of their aspirations. Toward this they made no mean progress. Several times during the past century they took real steps in advance—the promulgation of the Spanish Constitution, for example. In the first part of the nineteenth century they were granted representation in the Spanish Congress; a representation which made a brilliant record, in 1812,

in the framing of the Spanish Constitution. In 1870 this representation was made permanent. Sixteen representatives and four senators were then allowed under the Spanish apportionment law.
And with this as a fighting base they obtained several liberal
reforms; such as an insular legislative body elected by a moderately
restricted suffrage; in 1869 the abolition of slavery, and later the
authority to make a loan to pay the slave owners; then the gradual
suppression of the tariff was begun, which eventually was fully
carried out, deducting every year one-tenth part of the duties on
all goods exchanged between the colony and the mother country.

In 1887 the Autonomist party was formed and finally declared
to be a legal party and admitted to an understanding with the
Liberal party, then controlling in Spain. At last, in 1897, as a
preparatory measure to the final establishment of self-government,
the island was divided into two districts, and natives as well as
Spaniards were appointed governors both of the North and of the
South districts. In December, 1897, local self-government was at
last granted, and besides there went with it the right to concur in
treaty making with other nations thru special delegates chosen by
the island for the purpose.

This was the status of Porto Rico at the time of the American
occupation, and the arrangement was continued by General Brooke,
the first military governor of the island, as established by his
general order No. 1. But in December, 1898, General Brooke was
succeeded by General Guy S. Henry, U. S. V., who began to introduce changes, and finally did away entirely with the autonomic
organization. In April, 1900, an act of Congress established a civil
government in Porto Rico, fashioned after the English system for
their partially civilized colonies, such as the Fiji Islands. The act,
commonly known as "The Foraker Act," granted a legislature
composed of two houses. The lower house was to be elected by
the people. The upper house, called the Executive Council, was
formed mainly by the heads of the various departments appointed
by the President.

This organization of an appointed, foreign body to make the laws
of the country—a body whose members were at the same time
the executive heads of departments—was naturally a great disappointment to the Porto Ricans. With the governor retaining the
veto power and the Congress the right to amend or annul all
acts of the local legislature, there could not have been any danger
in leaving both houses in the hands of the people; nor could a
better system have been furnished as a school for self-government
training, if the advocates of the act were in good faith, in 1900,
in their claim that we were not capable of self-government. Under
the autonomic constitution which was taken away from us we had
the right to name the major part of the upper house. They were
simply to be citizens of Spain—and for thirty years previous we

had been citizens of Spain; ever since the Spanish Constitution was extended to Porto Rico, when the colony was abolished and the island became a province of Spain. Now, after ten years of the Foraker Act, depriving us of the upper house appointments, why should we find ourselves given a legislature bereft of all power whatsoever, except that of amending criminal and civil laws already made? There was also added to the bill the provision that the legislature should not meet as often as it had. This was wise and, in the judgment of many, under such conditions it would have been still wiser to provide that the legislature should not meet at all.

Just a lower house, with practically no power at all, is a strange sop to hand to people who were enjoying almost complete home government, after they had been waiting ten years for the fulfillment of the early promises made upon American occupation. There are inconveniences, evils, injustices, wrongs inherent to a foreign executive council appointed by a foreign executive and responsible to no one in Porto Rico. Take the matter of granting franchises in the island, for example, The Porto Ricans have suffered several serious losses and great wrong in the granting of franchises to irresponsible people, for wildcat schemes known to be technically and economically impossible; to a bankrupt company, a company that was in the hands of a receiver. All these failures to protect the people of Porto Rico—the unjust and unwise franchises, the failure to keep the land from absorption by large foreign interests, and the rest—would never have occurred if the upper house had been elected by the people and responsible to the people. Members of the Executive Council now only await removal to go back to the United States, caring very little for what they leave behind. Some of them, indeed, have drawn salaries for long periods and have not been there half the time. There were members of the council in Washington for three or four months, their salaries being paid by the people of Porto Rico, while they carried on the campaign which resulted in Congress deciding to take away from the people of Porto Rico the right to concur in appropriation bills for the expenditure of their own taxes, for the benefit of their own island. Now we have no power whatsoever. The Executive Council may go on from year to year, appropriating the money of previous years, and they can dispose of this as they please. There is something which the Porto Rican cannot fully understand in this persistent tendency to reduce his rights instead of fulfilling any of the assurances given him in the past.

The chief open contention of those who claim that the people of Porto Rico cannot as yet be trusted with self-government is that they are not prepared for the duties and responsibilities of the status. But every one knows that, in the first place, they have already proven their capacity, when, in 1870, the Republican

form of government was established in Spain as well as in Porto
Rico, and when they organized their insular machinery by popular
vote; also in the organization of their autonomic government in
1898. But suppose such experience was not conclusive of fitness
for self-government; how are they ever to gain or prove that
fitness without a limited opportunity? It is true that Porto Rico
has prospered in a material sense in the past ten years. But it is
also true that Porto Rico would have escaped several serious
wrongs from which she has suffered, and who can say that her
material prosperity would not have been still greater had she
been allowed a voice in the conduct of her own affairs and the
expenditures of her own resources. Would the new States which
were admitted to the Union several years ago have made the rapid
strides which have marked their progress if they had been kept
down, under the arbitrary rule of a limited number of men sent
there from outside, with the sole authority to make their laws
and administer their material wealth and resources? Many of the
territories did not have at the time of their admission to the Union
anything like the favorable conditions which Porto Rico presents,
in simply asking for the right of home jurisdiction.

Porto Rico has a civilization centuries old; has a larger population than eighteen States of the Union; has a greater commerce
and wealth than several of them; has a larger trade with the continental United States than many of the nations with which they
interchange commerce.

Those who demand colonial government for Porto Rico, and who
realize that this first argument is absurdly weak, advance another
which seems to be the only thing left upon which they can spread
false accusations and incorrect impressions giving any apparent
ground for depriving Porto Rico of the right of local jurisdiction.
It is illiteracy. But even this cannot be taken seriously by one
who knows anything at all about Porto Rico and is honestly
trying to decide impartially in the matter. The proportion of
illiteracy really existing is not really known. The only data upon
which the argument is based are those quite inaccurately obtained
and given out as the result of the first hurried census of ten
or eleven years ago. But even supposing that the illiteracy of today
is as high as 60 per cent, this, in the 1,100,000 inhabitants, will
still represent a number of persons *not* illiterate, several times
larger than there were inhabitants—with a degree of education
or without it—in some of the territories admitted to the self-
government of statehood in the United States several years ago.

Failing this, another, yet more absurd, argument is advanced.
The large number of schools established and the many miles of
good roads built in the last ten years—at the expense of Porto
Rico—is used as an argument against any change in the present
system of governing the colony. The Porto Rican feels that this

progress is due mainly to his initiative and would direct attention to the fact that while the lower house retained the right of concurring in appropriations it readily agreed to every effort at progress. And if this co-operation and universal energy, under the present system, is to be used as an effective argument against improvement in their political status, then the Porto Ricans, with their industry and energy, are every day digging deeper into the grave of political oblivion. Why, upon this basis, they would be better fitted for home government if they deliberately combatted every effort at progress.

Now, if the partisans and advocates of the *status quo* are honest, and so sure of the incompetency of the people of Porto Rico to take care of themselves, let them accept this challenge and settle the controversy by putting it to the test. The governor of the island will always retain the veto power and the Congress of the United Staes will always have the right to amend or annul whatever vicious legislation may be enacted. There could be no possible danger either to the United States or to the island. Indeed, there could be no question raised unless with some sinister motive by money interests profitably exploiting Porto Rico. And this constant refusal to give them a chance in self-government has created a sentiment among the people that the partisans of the *status quo* really attach more importance to their control of the island and the benefit derived from it by outside interests than they do to the people of Porto Rico and their welfare.

Even the bill passed by the House of Representatives last year —which was meager enough in favorable provisions for Porto Rico—has already been shorn of its more liberal points by the Senate Committee and was so reported to the Senate, to be acted on, the other day, to the great chagrin and disappointment of the Porto Ricans, who are at this moment in grave excitement and distress, despairing of ever seeing fulfilled the promises made to them at the time of the occupation of the island, or of redress in harmony with the American claims of justice and democracy.

DINING WITH PRESIDENT TAFT

[Perhaps the most ridiculous incident in U.S.–Puerto Rican affairs, and the one most frankly indicative of America's attitude towards its Caribbean colony, occurred in 1912. A group of insular leaders, together with Puerto Rico's Governor,

Translated from Roberto H. Todd, *Patriotas Puertorriqueñas* (Madrid: Ediciones Iberoamericanas, 1965), pp. 178–80.

George R. Colton, went to Washington, to seek more local participation
in government affairs. The narrator is a former Mayor of San Juan.]

The night arrived
of our invitation to the White House, and the table was located on
the roof of the smallest edifice of the White House. Gathered
there were President Taft, the Secretary of War, the President of
the Puerto Rico Commission in the House, Governor Colton, and the
delegates from Puerto Rico. The meal was splendid, and afterwards
the President invited us to pass into his office to discuss the affairs
which I had suggested.

The Puerto Rican Republican Party, in those days, was trying
to get the appointment of a sixth member of the Executive Council
of Puerto Rico. . . . Thus, the island would have a majority of
Puerto Ricans on the Council (North American appointees were
in the majority). Governor Colton had promised me that he would
advise the President in favor of this measure, so long as he had
a free hand in choosing the candidate for the post. . . .

Seated around the President's great desk, I had to begin the
conversation, telling Taft about the matter which we wanted to
bring before his consideration. I then referred to Governor Colton,
so that he could offer his views. Colton did not say a word, and
then Behn and Fajardo (two members of the Puerto Rican delegation) intervened, saying that Puerto Rico was prepared to assume
the responsibilities of a majority in the Executive Council of Puerto
Rico. For every answer, the President said that whenever the Governor, through the Secretary of War, recommended such a measure,
he would immediately follow through. Puerto Rico, in 1912, was
under the jurisdiction of the War Department.

We continued talking, when suddenly we heard a loud snore,
and everyone fell silent. It was President Taft, a man with an
enormous abdomen, who had dozed off. The only one who dared
say anything was *don* Mateo Fajardo, who commented in Spanish:
"*Ajo!* The rascal's fallen asleep on us."

And the meeting was over.

"INVERTED TERMS"

[As the impact of American rule upon Puerto Rico spread, confusion—cultural and political—prompted different solutions to the dilemma.]

Some wish to be Americans without ceasing to be Puerto Ricans; others want to be Puerto Ricans without ceasing to be Americans. It is a matter of inverted terms. Some of us want independence, but with the American protectorate, because it would be of great worth, because in that solution we glimpse the true bond of Union of feelings and interests between the small nation of the Caribbean and the big nation of the North. The others want annexation, where the State is free inside the Nation. They believe assured, in that way, the Independence of the country. But those countrymen . . . do not understand that, if it is true that we would achieve a personality in the Nation, we would lose it before the world. . . .

[Pleas for more home rule continued to receive little sympathy in the United States.]

The American residents in Puerto Rico have the same point of view that I have: it would not be the part of wisdom for us to surrender the government entirely into their hands, since they are of a different civilization, not looking upon matters of government in the same light as the Anglo-Saxons: They really have no conception of the true meaning of equality and liberty.

[Racial prejudice among some American leaders also helped to shape attitudes in Washington.]

Selections in this chapter:
1. Translated from *La Democracia*, July 2, 1914.
2. From William D. Boyce, *United States Colonies and Dependencies* (Chicago: Rand McNally, 1914), pp. 414–15.
3. From letters of April 18 and July 21, 1913, to President Woodrow Wilson, from his friend, Judge Peter A. Hamilton.
4. Translated from an interview with poet Doña Trina Padilla de Sanz, known as "La Hija del Caribe," in *La Democracia*, February 20, 1915.
5. Translated from a column by poet-journalist Luis Llorens Torres, *La Democracia*, March 30, 1915.

. . . they have the Latin-American excitability, and I think America should go slow in granting them anything like autonomy. Their civilization is not at all like ours yet. . . . The mixture of black and white in Porto Rico threatens to create a race of mongrels of no use to anyone, a race of Spanish-American talkers. A governor from the South, or with knowledge of Southern remedies for that trouble, could, if a wise man, do much. . . .

[As English became the first language of the schools, and its usage quickly multiplied in commercial life, there were concerns about the survival of the mother tongue.]

The Castilian language cannot be banished from the country without the loss of the Puerto Rican personality. . . . Therefore, to relegate the Spanish language to a secondary position in our schools, not only because of the honor of the race that is so important, but because of the disaster that arbitrary action would bring, is a grave danger to the Puerto Rican people.

English must be taught in our schools, since it can be stated that it is the universal language. . . .

Let us struggle, not just today, but always, so that our tongue be the Castilian . . . since a people who know how to preserve their language and their customs can never be crushed or swallowed up.

[Some Puerto Ricans resented the impact of American culture on the island, and others tried to ignore it. But others zealously adopted every new fad and wrinkle that reached Puerto Rico's shores. The new word *pitiyanqui*—which literally means "tiny yankee"—came into vogue, to describe in contemptuous terms the individual who casts aside his own culture, and becomes a 200 per cent American.]

. . . *pitiyanquis* are the Johns, the Peters, and the Williams, born in sweet potato fields, who sign themselves "Junior" and say that they are from Comerío or from Manatí; they are the snobbish "boricuas" who smoke a pipe, who coil up their pants, who spit through their eyeteeth, and eat their avocadoes with a spoon. They are the native sons . . . who, aping truckdrivers, in the belief that they are imitating American "gentlemen," unhinge themselves dancing the native *danza*, to the style of the "turkey trot" and the "one step"!

And *pitiyanquis* are, finally, those hundreds of Puerto Rican insular government employees, who preach Americanization of the country, led by the sole self-interest of their greedy stomachs. . . .

Part VI

AMERICAN CITIZENSHIP

> We request American citizenship with all
> the rights inherent to the great title of
> American citizens. This is citizenship with
> autonomy. And if one of these two, one
> independent of the other, which is absurd,
> is offered to us, we prefer self-government
> to American citizenship, rather than citi-
> zenship without self-government.
>
> —JOSE DE DIEGO, July 1, 1907.

It is no mere coincidence
that, one year before the United States entered World War I, it purchased the Virgin Islands from Denmark for $25 million, and, just one
month before hostilities began, granted U.S. citizenship to Puerto Ricans.

It was a time when German ships prowled the Atlantic; when Herr
Arthur Zimmermann, the German foreign secretary, sent the now famous telegram to his minister in Mexico, that Mexico and Germany
should "make war together and together make peace," promising financial rewards, so that Mexico might "reconquer the lost territory in New
Mexico, Texas and Arizona."

When a nation goes to war, it takes no chances. And America wished
to take no chances in the Caribbean, a key strategic zone. Puerto Rico—
unhappy with its colonial government and limbolike civil status—and
the Virgin Islands were needed to shore up the U.S. presence in the
West Indies.

This was not the first time that Americans or Puerto Ricans had discussed citizenship. The topic was born the moment that U.S. troops
landed at Guánica in 1898.

But there was little sentiment in Congress to admit the Caribbean
island as a full member of the Union. In Puerto Rico, some viewed citizenship as a means to achieve equal rights with Americans. The island's
principal elected leaders, however, preferred self-government to Americanization.

José de Diego, for example, at a conference on the U.S. mainland in
1910, said:

The entry of our island in your brotherhood of states—let us be frank—is impossible; neither you nor we wish it, or believe in it. With that path closed, there remains only the explicit recognition of the Republic of Puerto Rico, under the protectorship of the United States.

At the same conference, Luis Muñoz Rivera said:

Our problem has three solutions: the proclamation of Statehood, which would blend us with you in national life; the concession of home rule, which would join us with you in a sentimental link of gratitude and would be a real bind for the exchange of commercial products; and the concession of Independence, by law of Congress, which would make us the sole masters of our destiny. Of these three solutions, we would prefer the first, we propose the second, and we reserve the third as the last refuge of our right and honor.

But Congress would grant no solution. It would merely impose citizenship upon Puerto Ricans, without allowing them to vote upon the question. Those who refused citizenship would become "citizens of Porto Rico," and be denied certain civil rights, including the right to hold public office in their own homeland.

"AN IDLE DREAM"

[As the first decade of the twentieth century rolled by, the U.S. War Department continued to control Puerto Rican affairs, and Congress took no steps to resolve the colonial condition. By 1911, even the pro-statehood party had abandoned its ideal, and was courting the idea of independence. An American magazine, in describing the dilemma, said: "Our readers will remember Edward Everett Hale's famous story, 'The Man Without a Country'; the Porto Ricans are all men without a country."* Pressure to allow more self-government for the island culminated in proposed legislation that came to be known as the Jones-Shafroth Bill of 1917. When Congress began to discuss the bill, Muñoz Rivera, the resident commissioner in Washington, supported it, because extra powers would be transferred to the island. But two clauses were added to the bill; one granted American citizenship; the other gave absolute veto power to the Governor—an American—over all insular legislation. In 1914, Congressman John F. Shafroth of Colorado spoke with Muñoz Rivera at the Senate hearings in Washington.]

CHAIRMAN (speaking to Muñoz Rivera): Your party's position is as follows, if I understand correctly: you want the part about citizenship to be left aside, because you believe that if you are declared citizens now, this will hurt your cause, and will preclude the chance in the future for obtaining complete independence, or independence as an American protectorate. Is that correct?

MUNOZ RIVERA: That is my position, exactly.

CHAIRMAN: Now, it seems to me, on the other hand, that the people of the United States desire that Puerto Rico remain as a permanent possession of the United States, but that it should be granted the most liberal form of government that it is capable of having. . . . The bill is already based on the idea that Puerto Rico should be a permanent possession of the United States. The idea is to resolve this question, and thus remove it from Puerto Rican politics. What do you say to that, Mr. Rivera?

MUNOZ RIVERA: That is a very difficult question for me, because as you know, the final aspiration of my party is nationalism, with

* *The Outlook*, XCIX (November 18, 1911), pp. 643–44.

From Hearings Before the Committee on Insular Affairs, House of Representatives, 63d Congress, 2d Session, on H.R. 138118, p. 61.

or without an American protectorate, and according to the understanding of the Puerto Rican people, the concession of citizenship would interfere with their ambitions for independence.

CHAIRMAN: I don't think that changes the feeling of the United States, and I can say, speaking for myself, that this talk of independence is an idle dream of the Unionist Party, and it would be much better to resolve the affair right now, much better for the people of Puerto Rico themselves.

"THE FUTURE OF MY COUNTRY"

[Soon afterward, Muñoz Rivera wrote to José de Diego, then president of the House of Delegates, to tell him of his "agonies and anguish" in Washington. "They are imposing citizenship upon us because they want to tie us to the Republic forever," he wrote, adding that, despite his tireless efforts,

No one helps us. No one supports us. Not one of the four Democrats who visited the island will speak out for our freedom. No senator, no representative, is with us. No newspaper is concerned about us, or responds to our propaganda, or will respond to our protest. The machine functions, and the machine is omnipotent.*

On May 5, 1916, Muñoz Rivera—realizing that his cause was lost—rose in the U.S. House of Representatives to discuss the Jones Act, and the issue of American citizenship. His statement reveals the complexity of the man, and the dilemma of a small island, seeking to retain its identity within the realm of a giant.]

On the 18th day of October, 1898, when the flag of this great Republic was unfurled over the fortresses of San Juan, if anyone had said to my countrymen that the United States, the land of liberty, was going to deny their right to form a government of the people, by the people, and for the people of Puerto Rico, my countrymen would have refused to believe such a prophecy, considering it sheer madness. The Porto Ricans were living at that time under a regime of ample self-government, discussed and voted by the Spanish Cortes, on the basis of the parliamentary system in use among all the nations of Europe. Spain sent to the islands a governor, whose power,

* Translated from *Revista del Instituto de Cultura Puertorriqueña*. No. 4 (July-September, 1959), San Juan, pp. 35-36. Reprinted by permission.

From *Congressional Record*, 64th Congress, 1st Session, 1916. LIII, pp. 7470-73.

strictly limited by law, made him the equivalent of those constitutional sovereigns who reign but do not govern. The members of the cabinet, without whose signature no executive order was valid, were natives of the island; the representatives in the senate and in the house were natives of the island; and the administration in its entirety was in the hands of natives of the island. The Spanish Cortes, it is true, retained the power to make statutory laws for Porto Rico, but in the Cortes were 16 Porto Rican representatives and 3 Porto Rican senators having voice and vote. And all the insular laws were made by the insular parliament.

Two years later, in 1900, after a long period of military rule, the Congress of the United States approved the Foraker Act. Under this act all of the 11 members of the executive council were appointed by the President of the United States; 6 of them were the heads of departments; 5 exercised legislative functions only. And this executive council, or in practice, the bureaucratic majority of the council, was, and is in reality, with the. governor, the supreme arbiter of the island and of its interests. It represents the most absolute contradiction of republican principles.

For 16 years we have endured this system of government, protesting and struggling against it, with energy and without result. We did not lose hope, because if one national party, the Republican, was forcibly enforcing this system upon us, the other national party, the Democratic, was encouraging us by its declarations in the platforms of Kansas City, St. Louis, and Denver. Porto Rico waited, election after election, for the Democratic Party to triumph at the polls and fulfill its promises. At last the Democratic Party did triumph. It is here. It has a controlling majority at this end of the Capitol and at the other end; it is in possession of the White House. On the Democratic Party rests the sole and undivided responsibility for the progress of events at this juncture. It can, by a legislative act, keep alive the hopes of the people of Porto Rico or it can deal these hopes their death blow.

The Republican Party decreed independence for Cuba and thereby covered itself with glory; the Democratic Party is bound by the priniciples written into its platforms and by the recorded speeches of its leaders to decree liberty for Porto Rico. The legislation you are about to enact will prove whether the platforms of the Democratic Party are more than useless paper, whether the words of its leaders are more than soap bubbles, dissolved by the breath of triumph. Here is the dilemma with its two unescapable horns: You must proceed in accordance with the fundamental principles of your party or you must be untrue to them. The monarchies of the Old World, envious of American success and the republics of the New World, anxious to see clearly the direction in which the American initiative is tending, are watching and studying the Democratic administration. Something more is at stake than the fate of Porto Rico—poor, isolated, and defenseless as she is—the prestige and the good name of the United States are at stake. England learned the hard lessons of Saratoga and Yorktown in the eighteenth century. And in the nineteenth century she established self-government, complete, sincere, and honorable, in Canada, Australia, and New Zealand. Then in the twentieth century, immediately after the Anglo-Boer War, she established self-government, complete, sincere, and honorable, for the Orange Free State and the Transvaal, her enemies of the day before. She turned over the reins of power to insurgents who were still wearing uniforms stained with British blood.

In Porto Rico no blood will be shed. Such a thing is impossible in an island of 3,600 square miles. Its narrow confines never permitted and never will permit armed resistance. For this very reason Porto Rico is a field of experiment unique on the globe. And if Spain, the reactionary monarchy, gave Porto Rico the home rule which she was enjoying in 1898, what should the United States, the progressive Republic, grant her? This is the mute question which Europe and America are writing today in the solitudes of the Atlantic and on the waters of the Panama Canal. The reply is the bill which is now under discussion. This bill can not meet the earnest aspirations of my country. It is not a measure of self-government ample enough to solve definitely our political problem or to match your national reputation, established by a successful championship for liberty and justice throughout the world since the very beginning of your national life. But, meager and conservative as the bill appears when we look at its provision from our own point of view, we sincerely recognize its noble purposes and willingly accept it as a step in the right direction and as a reform paving the way for others more acceptable and satisfactory which shall come a little later, provided that my countrymen will be able to demonstrate their capacity, the capacity they possess, to govern themselves. In regard to such capacity, it is my duty, no doubt, a pleasant duty, to assure Congress that the Porto Ricans will endeavor to prove their intelligence, their patriotism, and their full preparation to enjoy and to exercise a democratic regime. [Applause.]

Our behavior during the past is a sufficient guaranty for our behavior in the future. Never a revolution there, in spite of our Latin blood; never an attempt to commercialize our political influence; never an attack against the majesty of law. The ever-reigning peace was not at any time disturbed by the illiterate masses, which bear their suffering with such stoic fortitude and only seek comfort in their bitter servitude, confiding in the supreme protection of God. [Applause.]

There is no reason which justifies American statesmen in denying self-government to my country and erasing from their programs the principles of popular sovereignty. Is illiteracy the reason? Because if in Porto Rico 60 per cent of the electorate can not read, in the United States in the early days of the Republic 80 per cent of the population were unable to read; and even today there are 20 Republics and twenty monarchies which acknowledge a higher percentage of illiteracy than Porto Rico. It is not the coexistence of two races on the island, because here in North America more than 10 States show a higher proportion of Negro population than Porto Rico, and the District of Columbia has precisely the same proportion, 67 white to 33 per cent colored. It is not our small territorial extent, because two States have a smaller area than Porto Rico. It is not a question of population, for by the last census there were 18 States with a smaller population than Porto Rico. Nor is it a matter of real and personal property, for the taxable property in New Mexico is only one-third that of Porto Rico. There is a reason and only one reason—the same sad reason of war and conquest which let loose over the South after the fall of Richmond thousands and thousands of office seekers, hungry for power and authority, and determined to report to their superiors that the rebels of the South were unprepared for self-government. [Laughter.] We are the southerners of the twentieth century.

The House of Representatives has never been influenced by this class of motives. The House of Representatives has very high motives, and, if they are studied thoroughly, very grave reasons for redeeming my country from bureaucratic greed and confiding to it at once the responsibility for its own destinies and the power to fix and determine them. They are reasons of an international character which affect the policy of the United States in the rest of America. Porto Rico, the only one of the former colonies of Spain in this hemisphere which does not fly its own flag or figure in the family of nations, is being closely observed with assiduous vigilance by the Republics of the Caribbean Sea and the Gulf of Mexico. Cuba, Santo Domingo, Venezuela, Colombia, Costa Rica, Honduras, Nicaragua, Salvador, Guatemala maintain with us a constant interchange of ideas and never lose sight of the experiment in the colonial government which is being carried on in Porto Rico. If they see that the Porto Ricans are living happily, that they are not treated with disdain, that their aspirations are being fulfilled, that their character is being respected, that they are not being subjected to an imperialistic tutelage, and that the right to govern their own country is not being usurped, these nations will recognize the superiority of American methods and will feel the influence of the American Government. This will smooth the way to the moral hegemony which you are called by your greatness, by your wealth, by your traditions, and your institutions to exercise in the New World. [Applause.] On the other hand, if these communities, Latin like Porto Rico, speaking the same language as

Porto Rico, branches of the same ancestral trunk that produced Porto Rico, bound to Porto Rico by so many roots striking deep in a common past, if these communities observe that your insular experiment is a failure and that you have not been able to keep the affections of a people who awaited from you their redemption and their happiness, they will be convinced that they must look, not to Washington but to London, Paris, or Berlin when they seek markets for their products, sympathy for their misfortunes, and guarantees for their liberty.

What do you gain along with the discontent of my countrymen? You as Members of Congress? Nothing. And the Nation loses a part of its prestige, difficulties are created in the path of its policies, its democratic ideals are violated, and it must abdicate its position as leader in every progressive movement on the planet. Therefore if you undertake a reform, do it sincerely. A policy of subterfuge and shadows might be expected in the Italy of the Medicis, in the France of the Valois, in the England of the Stuarts, or the Spain of the Bourbons, but it is hard to explain in the United States of Cleveland, McKinley, Roosevelt, and Wilson. [Applause.]

The bill I am commenting on provides for a full elective legislature. Well, that is a splendid concession you will make to your own principles and to our own rights. But now, after such a magnificent advance, do not permit, gentlemen, do not permit the local powers of the legislature to be diminished in matters so important for us as the education of the children. We are citizens jealous of this dignity; we are fathers anxious to foster our sons toward the future, teaching them how to struggle for life and how to reach the highest standard of honesty, intelligence, and energy. We accept one of your compatriots, a capable American, as head of the department of education, though we have in the island many men capable of filling this high office with distinction. We welcomed his appointment by the President of the United States. In this way the island will have the guaranty to find such a man as Dr. Brumbaugh, the first commissioner of education, who deserves all our confidence. But let the legislature regulate the courses of study, cooperating in that manner with the general development of educational work throughout our native country.

I come now to treat of a problem which is really not a problem for Porto Rico, as my constituents look at it, because it has been solved already in the Foraker Act. The Foraker Act recognizes the Porto Rican citizenship of the inhabitants of Porto Rico. We are satisfied with this citizenship and desire to prolong and maintain it—our natural citizenship, founded not on the conventionalism of law but on the fact that we were born on an island and love that island above all else, and would not exchange our country for any other country, though it were one as great and as free as the

United States. If Porto Rico were to disappear in a geological catastrophe and there survived a thousand or ten thousand or a hundred thousand Porto Ricans, and they were given the choice of all the citizenships of the world, they would choose without a moment's hesitation that of the United States. But so long as Porto Rico exists on the surface of the ocean, poor and small as she is, and even if she were poorer and smaller, Porto Ricans will always choose Porto Rican citizenship. And the Congress of the United States will have performed an indefensible act if it tries to destroy so legitimate a sentiment and to annul through a law of its own making a law of the oldest and wisest legislators of all time—a law of nature.

It is true that my countrymen have asked many times, unanimously, for American citizenship. They asked for it when through the promise of Gen. Miles on his disembarkation in Ponce, and when through the promises of the Democratic Party when it adopted the Kansas City platform—they believed it not only possible but probable, not only probable but certain, that American citizenship was the door by which to enter, not after a period of 100 years nor of 10, but immediately into the fellowship of the American people as a State of the Union. Today they no longer believe it. From this floor the most eminent statesmen have made it clear to them that they must not believe it. And my countrymen, who, precisely the same as yours, have their dignity and self-respect to maintain, refuse to accept a citizenship of an inferior order, a citizenship of the second class, which does not permit them to dispose of their own resources nor to live their own lives nor to send to this Capitol their proportional representation. To obtain benefits of such magnitude they were disposed to sacrifice their sentiments of filial love for the motherland. These advantages have vanished, and the people of Porto Rico have decided to continue to be Porto Ricans; to be so each day with increasing enthusiasm, to retain their own name, claiming for it the same consideration, the same respect, which they accord to the names of other countries, above all to the name of the United States. Give us statehood and your glorious citizenship will be welcome to us and to our children. If you deny us statehood, we decline your citizenship, frankly, proudly, as befits a people who can be deprived of their civil liberties but who, although deprived of their civil liberties, will preserve their conception of honor, which none can take from them, because they bear it in their souls, a moral heritage from their forefathers.

This bill which I am speaking of grants American citizenship to all my compatriots on page 5. On page 6 it authorizes those who do not accept American citizenship to so declare before a court of justice, and thus retain their Porto Rican citizenship. On page 28 it provides that—

No person shall be allowed to register as a voter in Porto Rico who is not a citizen of the United States.

My compatriots are generously permitted to be citizens of the only country they possess, but they are eliminated from the body politic; the exercise of political rights is forbidden them and by a single stroke of the pen they are converted into pariahs and there is established in America, on American soil, protected by the Monroe doctrine, a division into castes like the Brahmans and Sudras of India. The Democratic platform of Kansas City declared 14 years ago, "A nation can not long endure half empire and half republic," and "Imperialism abroad will lead rapidly and irreparably to despotism at home." These are not Porto Rican phrases reflecting our Latin impressionability; they are American phrases, reflecting the Anglo-Saxon spirit, calm in its attitude and jealous— very jealous—of its privileges.

We have a profound consideration for your national ideas; you must treat our local ideas with a similar consideration. As the representative of Porto Rico, I propose that you convoke the people of the island to express themselves in full plebiscite on the question of citizenship and that you permit the people of Porto Rico to decide by their votes whether they wish the citizenship of the United States or whether they prefer their own natural citizenship. It would be strange if, having refused it so long as the majority of people asked for it, you should decide to impose it by force now that the majority of the people decline it.

Someone recently stated that we desire the benefits but shirk the responsibilities and burdens of citizenship. I affirm in reply that we were never consulted as to our status, and that in the treaty of Paris the people of Porto Rico were disposed of as were the serfs of ancient times, fixtures of the land, who were transferred by force to the service of new masters and subject to new servitudes. The fault is not ours, though ours are the grief and humiliation; the fault lies with our bitter destiny which made us weak and left us an easy prey between the warring interests of mighty powers. If we had our choice, we would be a free and isolated people in the liberty and the solitude of the seas, without other advantages than those won by our exertions in industry and in peace, without other responsibilities and burdens than those of our own conduct and our duty toward one another and toward the civilization which surrounds us.

The bill under consideration, liberal and generous in some of its sections, as those creating an elective insular senate; a cabinet, a majority of whose members shall be confirmed by the senate; and a public-service commission, two members of which shall be elected by the people, is exceedingly conservative in other sections, most of all in that which restricts the popular vote, enjoining that the right of registering as electors be limited to those who are able to read and write or who pay taxes to the Porto Rican Treasury. By means of this restriction 165,000 citizens who vote at present and who have been voting since the Spanish days would be barred from the polls.

Here are the facts: There exist at present 250,000 registered electors. Seventy percent of the electoral population is illiterate. There will remain, then, 75,000 registered electors. Adding 10,000 illiterate taxpayers, there will be a total of 85,000 citizens within the electoral register and 165,000 outside of it. I can not figure out, hard as I have tried, how those 165,000 Porto Ricans are considered incapable of participating in the elections of their representatives in the legislature and municipalities, while on the other hand they are judged perfectly capable of possessing with dignity American citizenship. This is an inconsistency which I can not explain, unless the principle is upheld that he who incurs the greatest misfortune—not by his own fault—of living in the shadow of ignorance is not worthy of the honor of being an American citizen. In the case of this being the principle on which the clause is based, it would seem necessary to uphold such principle, by depriving 3,000,000 Americans of their citizenship, for this is the number of illiterates in the United States according to the census of 1910. There is no reason that justifies this measure, anyway. Since civil government was established in Porto Rico, superseding military government—that is, 16 years ago—eight general elections have been staged. Each time the people, with a most ample suffrage law, have elected their legislative bodies, their municipal councils, their municipal courts, and school boards. These various bodies have cooperated to the betterment and progress of the country, which gives evidence that they were prudently chosen.

Perhaps one or a hundred or a thousand electors tried to commercialize their votes, selling them to the highest bidders.

For the sake of argument I will accept that hypothesis, though it was never proved. But even supposing that we had not to do with a presumption, but with an accomplished fact, I ask, Were there not and are there not in the rest of this Nation worthless persons who negotiate their constitutional rights? Did not the courts of a great State—the State of Massachusetts—convict four or five thousand men of that offense? Was there not a case in which the majority of a legislature promised to elect and did elect a high Federal officer for a few dollars? I do not think that these infractions of the law and breaches of honor reflect the least discredit on the clean name of the American people. I do not think that such isolated crimes can lead in any State to the restriction of the vote. They are exceptional cases, which can not be helped. The courts of justice punish the guilty ones and the social organization continues its march. In Porto Rico, if such cases occur, they should have and do have the same consequences. But it would be a sad and unjust condition of affairs if, through the fault of one, 1,000 men were to be deprived of their privileges; or, to speak in proportion, if, through the fault of 160 electors, 160,000 were to be deprived of their privileges.

The aforesaid motives are fundamental ones that require careful attention from the House. But there are deeper motives yet, those that refer to the history of the United States and of the American Congress. Never was there a single law passed under the dome of the Capitol restrictive of the individual rights, of the rights of humanity. Quite the contrary, Congress even going to the extreme of amending the Constitution, restrained the initiative of the States for the purpose of making them respect the exercise of those rights without marring it with the least drawback. There is the fourteenth amendment. Congress could not hinder States from making their electoral laws, but it could decree and did decree that in the event of any State decreasing its number of electors it would, ipso facto, decrease its number of Representatives in this House. The United States always gave to the world examples of a profound respect for the ideal of a sincere democracy.

I feel at ease when I think of the future of my country. I read a solemn declaration of the five American commissioners that signed, in 1898, the treaty of Paris. When the five Spanish delegates, no less distinguished than the Americans, asked for a guaranty as to the future of Porto Rico, your compatriots answered thus:

> The Congress of a country which never enacted laws to oppress or abridge the rights of residents within its domains, and whose laws permit the largest liberty consistent with the preservation of order and the protection of property, may safely be trusted not to depart from its well-settled practice in dealing with the inhabitants of these islands.

Congress needs not be reminded of its sacred obligations, the obligations which those words impose upon it. Porto Rico had nothing to do with the declaration of war. The Cubans were assured of their national independence. The Porto Ricans were acquired for $20,000,000, and my country, innocent and blameless, paid with its territory the expenses of the campaign.

The treaty of Paris says:

As compensation for the losses and expenses occasioned the United States by the war and for the claims of its citizens by reason of the injuries and damages they may have suffered in their persons and property during the last insurrection in Cuba, Her Catholic Majesty, in the name and representation of Spain, and thereunto constitutionally authorized by the Cortes of the Kingdom, cedes to the United States of America, and the latter accept for themselves, the island of Porto Rico and the other islands now under Spanish sovereignty in the West Indies, as also the island of Guam, in the Marianas or Ladrones Archipelago, which island was selected by the United States of America in virtue of the provisions of article 11 of the protocol signed in Washington on August 12 last.

You, citizens of a free fatherland, with its own laws, its own institutions, and its own flag, can appreciate the unhappiness of the small and solitary people that must await its laws from your authority, that lacks institutions created by their will, and who does not feel the pride of having the colors of a national emblem to cover the homes of its families and the tombs of its ancestors.

Give us now the field of experiment which we ask of you, that we may show that it is easy for us to constitute a stable republican government with all possible guarantees for all possible interests. And afterwards, when you acquire the certainty that you can found in Porto Rico a republic like that founded in Cuba and Panama, like the one you will found at some future day in the Philippines, give us our independence and you will stand before humanity as the greatest of the great; that which neither Greece nor Rome nor England ever were, a great creator of new nationalities and a great liberator of oppressed peoples. [Applause.]

"TREACHERY AND DISENCHANTMENT"

[On May 23, 1916, the House of Representatives passed the Jones Bill—with the provision for U.S. citizenship intact. In August, Muñoz Rivera—tired, disillusioned, yearning to go home—wrote from Washington to Mariano Abril, his old friend and fellow journalist in Puerto Rico: "Those mountains, that brook, those starry nights in Barranquitas always bring to my spirit a sweet, dreamy melancholy. . . . And politics? If you knew how tired I am,

Selections in this chapter:
1. Translated from *El plebiscito puertorriqueño* (San Juan: Tipografía Boletín Mercantil, 1917), pp. 75–76.
2–3. From *New York Times*, August 15, 1917, p. 4.
4. From *New York Times*, August 27, 1917, p. 8. © 1917 by the New York Times. Reprinted by permission.
5. From Woodrow Wilson, *The State: Elements of Historical and Practical Politics* (Boston: D. C. Heath, 1918), p. 357.
6. Translated from editorial in *El Mundo*, February 1, 1919.
7. From *New York Times*, March 2, 1919, p. 10. © 1919 by the New York Times. Reprinted by permission.

knowing that I keep to myself such treachery and disenchantment. We shall talk about it soon; not in San Juan, but up there, in the shadow of a tree, in the peace of a cool afternoon." *

On September 19, 1916, Muñoz Rivera sailed to San Juan, where he was greeted warmly by a large crowd of his followers. Two days later he fell ill, and, by the afternoon of November 15, he was dead. A few days before his death, he had dictated his "political testament" to Antonio R. Barceló, his young successor. Calling the Jones Bill "the first step in our evolution," Muñoz said, "The path is firmly outlined. . . . Although the final end to the problem is the independence of our homeland, we must have great confidence and absolute faith in the great people under whose influence and under whose protection our destiny must be determined." He called upon his people to "decide their destiny, according to the circumstances that the future may determine." †

On February 20, 1917, the U.S. Senate approved the Jones Bill, and, on March 2, President Woodrow Wilson signed it, making Puerto Ricans American citizens.

Before Wilson signed the bill, however, the Congressional Union for Women's Suffrage called a mass meeting at New York City's 48th Street Theatre, to protest against self-government for Puerto Rico "so long as it is denied the women of the United States." A spokesman said: "The President has announced his desire for immediate action in the bill giving self-government to Porto Ricans *as a war measure. The imminence of war makes it wise, the President thinks, to insure the loyalty of the Porto Ricans.*" ‡

The passage of the citizenship bill created more confusion and dissent than before. Ostensibly designed to grant more self-government, it allowed the American Governor to retain final veto power. On its way through Congress, the bill was tinkered with by several legislators. A Senator from North Dakota, for example, added an amendment that imposed the prohibition of liquor, despite the fact that the island's impoverished economy derived great revenues from rum sales. This, too, was accepted by the powerless Puerto Ricans, who had no political "clout" in Washington. Above all, the Jones Act did nothing to resolve the long-range issue of political status. One of its most eloquent critics was José de Diego, who was then the leader of the. insular House of Representatives.]

Never before in the realm of international law has such a thing been seen in the democratic nations of the world: 1,200,000 human beings, who by the law of the Congress of a Republic . . . are stripped of their natural citizenship, but under the menace and coercion of losing their right to vote or be eligible for public office, in the country where they are obliged to respect all the laws of the State, and

* Translated from *Revista del Instituto de Cultura Puertorriqueña*, No. 4 (July–September, 1959), San Juan, pp. 35–36.
† Translated from *La Democracia*, January 5, 1917.
‡ *New York Times*, February 22, 1917, p. 20. Italics added by the editor.

pay military tribute to the dominant nation; in the country of their birth and life, where they aspire to be buried, Puerto Ricans who for some heretofore unknown crime—the love of their own citizenship—are reduced to the condition of being foreigners in their homeland; they are exiled from their land, and thus, out of fear, and due to the harshness of the punishment, only a tiny number of Puerto Ricans renounce the citizenship imposed upon them; almost all of them accept, and thus present—before the world—this unusual fact, the false demonstration that the Puerto Ricans did voluntarily and joyfully accept the citizenship of the United States, and with it abandoned the ideal of joining their country with the other free and sovereign nations of America.

[Six months after U.S. citizenship was granted, both houses of the Puerto Rican legislature sent resolutions to President Wilson, respectfully demanding complete self-government for the island. José De Diego sent the following telegram to Wilson and the Congress:]

. . . The House of Representatives has resolved unanimously to offer, through you, to the American people, a message of gratitude for the law which has caused a realization *in part* of the legitimate aspirations of the people of Porto Rico. The House also resolved to express to the people of the United States that the people of Porto Rico were ready to contribute with their blood, under the glorious flag of the United States, to the triumph of democracy throughout the world, and demand from the United States the completion of its work in Porto Rico by granting to our people the full right of self-government.

[Antonio R. Barceló, president of the insular Senate, also telegraphed the President:]

The first Porto Rican Senate greets President Wilson and relies on him and the American Congress for a greater development of the system establishing in Porto Rico a Government of and by the people to its fullest extent and purity.

[A few days later, a Puerto Rican in New York City wrote to the Editor of the *New York Times*:]

Reading your article under the heading "Texans Protest to President Against Negro Soldiers in the South," I learn that the War Department contemplates the encampment of patriotic Porto Rican soldiers with the negroes in South Carolina. This plan is a great mistake and a revelation. It makes it clear that it will take long for us as a nation to understand the psychology of peoples of alien nationalities who come under our banner, and it teaches us Porto Ricans that our ultimate destiny is to possess one status in which we keep up the most cordial commercial and political relations, but as a distinct entity.

R. M. DELGADO
New York, Aug. 24, 1917

[At about the same time, President Wilson saw little hope for statehood.]

With the acquisition of Porto Rico and the Philippines as a result of the war with Spain, the United States acquired noncontiguous lands, already inhabited by peoples differing from ourselves in language, customs and institutions. Unlike the territory previously acquired—with the exception of Alaska and Hawaii—the insular possessions are not adapted for the progressive development from territories to states. They are dependencies, and will remain as such until they reach the stage when they may become independent or self-governing.

[It was not strange, then, that Puerto Ricans should be confused. One of the island's major newspapers wrote:]

We have come to the conclusion that the political program of the United States for Puerto Rico, in the final analysis, is *to have no program*. They send us diverse pieces to make a dress that does not correspond to a model or to a definite style. Congress decides that Puerto Rico is not even an incorporated territory. Evident it is that we enjoy rights, but they have not patterned a clearly defined status; they are beautiful frames for the structure, and with yearning, intelligence, and patriotism we will toil in order to select the best materials to organize them; not worrying about its outward appearance nor about the names under which the field of political architecture identifies it; but always looking toward Washington, whose Capitol is a lighthouse whose rays shine over the whole earth.

[The Puerto Rican legislature several times urged Washington to move in one direction or the other, to indicate a reasonable, sure road to end the political status dilemma. In early 1919, a headline in the *New York Times* said; "Porto Rican parties demand statehood. If that be denied, they want complete independence."]

SAN JUAN, Porto Rico, March 1—After a debate of more than two days in both houses of the Insular Legislature, the Unionists and Republicans today reached an agreement that now is the time to join forces on insisting that the American Congress make known what the future of Porto Rico is to be. It was agreed that if there can be no assurance that statehood is possible, the parties should work for independence.

The debate came after the receipt here of the full text of the speech made in the House of Representatives in Washington on Feb. 11 by the Resident Commissioner, Felix Córdova Davila, in which he urged Congress to state definitely whether statehood and complete self-government for Porto Rico were possible. If it was not possible, the commissioner told the House he would insist on complete independence. . . .

Part VII

THE GRIM YEARS

> As we look back . . . we find that by 1936
> we had hit a new low. . . . [We] were
> puzzled, distressed and angered by the sad
> and unacceptable plight of our society.
> We oscillated between frustration and re-
> vulsion. At times, incensed by our own
> helplessness, we felt the compulsion to
> close our eyes and charge. Some of the
> best among us did. . . .
>
> —JAIME BENITEZ, President,
> University of Puerto Rico, in 1968.

The years between
World Wars I and II were grim ones; thousands of Puerto Ricans were
ravaged by starvation and disease. Absentee investors continued to acquire control of the economy, and some of them used their dollars to
manipulate the elections. It was almost inevitable that, under such conditions, militant anti-American political forces should emerge.

In 1920, while Republican Presidential candidate Warren G. Harding
was on the campaign trail, he spoke out against Puerto Rican independence; after his election, a number of anti-American cablegrams and
letters from the island arrived in the White House. In March, 1921, Antonio Barceló, President of the Puerto Rican Senate, received a letter
from Horace M. Towner, Chairman of the Committee on Insular Affairs
of the U.S. House of Representatives, warning him that "friends of Porto
Rico will find it difficult to help the island if this propaganda is continued. I assure you there is not now, and there is not likely to be, any considerable sentiment in this country for the independence of Porto
Rico." *

Discord increased when President Harding paid off a political debt by
appointing E. Montgomery Reilly, a Kansas City businessman, as Governor of Puerto Rico. In his inaugural address, Reilly rejected independence, adding "Neither, my friends, is there any room on this island for

* *New York Times*, March 10, 1921, p. 22.

any flag other than the Stars and Stripes. So long as Old Glory waves over the United States, it will continue to wave over Puerto Rico."

Then, in a letter to Barceló, Reilly said, "While discussing appointments, I want you to fully understand that I shall never appoint any man to office who is an advocate of independence. When you publicly renounce independence, and break loose from your pernicious and un-American associates, then I will be glad to have your recommendations." *

Early in 1922, Barceló's Unionist Party, trying to develop a *modus vivendi* with Washington, removed independence from its platform, and proposed an autonomous form of government that resembled the recently established Irish Free State. The proposal asked that the island become an Associated Free State (*Estado Libre Asociado*), the same type of status granted Puerto Rico in 1952. But the proposal was ignored. Nor did Washington offer hopes of independence or statehood. Puerto Rico, it seemed, was doomed to colonialism.

* *New York Times*, August 18, 1927, p. 17.

IRELAND IN AMERICA?

[Cayetano Coll y Cuchí
was a member of the Puerto Rican House of Delegates and of the Unionist Party. He was on record as favoring statehood for Puerto Rico.
Nevertheless, he was so irate at the unwillingness of the United States
to offer a status of political dignity to Puerto Rico that he once said:
"Are we going to be Americans? If so, all right, let us have it [state-
hood]. If not, let us be independent. We would be as much an independent country in the Union as out of it." In the following article, he
traces the development of his views.]

I entered public
life in 1902, together with many other young men, all graduates of
American universities. Almost immediately a phenomenon worthy of
note occurred. The men of my generation had been born at a time
when the radical parties in Porto Rico were engaged in their long
and bitter struggle against our Spanish rulers. We had grown up in
an atmosphere of ardent longing to be free from Spain. We believed
that every patriot should insist that Porto Rico become an independent republic, like her South American neighbors. All our political thinking and theories were based on these assumptions, at the
time when we departed for the United States to study in the
academic halls of the great Republic.

As students in American universities, we read and re-read the
nation's great Declaration of Independence, and studied sedulously
its Constitution and the principles upon which its government was
formed, until we almost forgot the lessons of our earlier years. We
spoke English better than our mother tongue. Our whole intellectual
life was Anglo-Saxon. By the time we returned to Porto Rico, just as
the United States was setting up a civil government in our homeland, we had thoroughly assimilated that nation's political ideals.

Naturally, we were ardent partisans of the Americanization of
Porto Rico. But our old and battle-scarred leaders started an agita-
tion against the new government Washington had imposed upon us,
and when we had leisure to review our past, and to recall our
glorious Castilian origin, we joined and speedily became the leaders
of that movement. It fell to us, the graduates of American uni-

---

First appeared in Spanish in *Repertorio Americano*, a Costa Rican political
weekly, on March 27 and April 3, 1922; later, in English translation, under the
title "American Rule in Porto Rico," in *Living Age*, XXVII (1922), pp. 262–66.

versities, to voice Porto Rico's protest, to give her people a political programme, to show the logic and reason of her demands, and to become the champions of our traditions and our race.

I fancied, when I graduated, that I possessed an immense fund of political wisdom. I was filled with ardent enthusiasm for the great struggles for freedom of thought, for separation of church and state, and for the rights of man. My political standards had been formed in accordance with these doctrines. But I had forgotten my soul, which still retained the memories of my Spanish childhood. The moment that my artificial student personality came into conflict with my true native personality, with the traditions of my race, as soon as I discovered that what I had learned in the United States was repudiated by the spontaneous sentiments of my heart, I realized that it was impossible to change that part of us which God has shaped with his own hand. I still cherished profound respect for all that was great and noble and just in the North American people; but my Spanish soul asserted itself. My fellow students of Spanish ancestry passed through the same experience. It seemed to us abnegation of our rights as men, apostasy to our own higher impulses, to act otherwise than as we did. So we threw ourselves headlong into the battle to rescue our indestructible heritage— our traditions, our race, our language, our religion.

It was clearly an unequal battle. A million and a quarter people, inhabiting thirty-six hundred square miles of territory, defied one hundred and fifteen million people, possessing more than three million miles of territory. But even these figures do not measure adequately the immense power of the United States, which America's leaders so confidently expected would speedily Americanize Porto Rico and demonstrate the ease with which Anglo-Saxon civilization can establish its sway over a Spanish-American people. But we were undaunted. Political delegations from North America, the pressure of North American capital, the political philosophy of that country's thinkers, the efforts of her representatives to deprive us of our civil rights and to rob us of our Spanish civilization—all these things counted as nothing against our enthusiasm, which burned the brighter after every attempt to quench it.

So we accepted the challenge of battle, although we still welcomed, small country that we were, whatever the United States could give us that did not prevent the free development of our Spanish culture. This struggle culminated in 1909. That year an effort was made to abolish the teaching of Spanish in the public schools. Our schoolmasters were ordered to give their instruction exclusively in English.

We knew perfectly well that the soul of a people is incarnated in its language. We would have preferred being without a country, to losing our native tongue. Upon this issue, we joined battle, and spontaneously my friends and I threw ourselves into the thickest of the fight. That was quite natural. But it was the children—children of six, seven, and ten years of age—who really started the revolt. They were the first to rebel. The men at the head of the government were first apprised of the resistance to substituting English for Spanish by a pupils' strike. Children refused to attend their classes unless they might be instructed in the language of their fathers and their country.

A resort to brutal measures followed. Children were expelled from the schools. Those who did not attend English classes, or who refused to be taught in that language were turned into the streets. They could not continue their studies; their future was ruined. Then we got together and founded a Spanish school—the José de Diego Institute—where children expelled from the public schools were received and taught gratuitously.

We next appealed to the authorities at Washington. Immediately after President Wilson assumed office, we sent a commission to that city to describe the evils under which we were laboring. The President and the leaders of his party gave us a cordial welcome. A bill to confer upon us complete autonomy was submitted to Congress. Since that change could not be made immediately, Wilson sent a new Governor to the Island, to whom he gave most liberal instructions. All of the North American cabinet members were replaced by Porto Ricans.

At last we were given an autonomous régime. We elected our first independent legislature. My party, the party that championed a free Porto Rico, won in practically every precinct. The moment they had an opportunity to express their will, the Porto Rican people voted for liberty.

Then came the War. At the instance of the Administration, a bill was brought into Congress establishing compulsory military service, but expressly excluding Porto Ricans from this provision. Porto Rico protested at once, and insisted that her soldiers also should be sent to the battle fields of France, and should share both the sacrifices and glories of our national victory. Her protest was heard. Our Island, with 1,300,000 inhabitants, mobilized 140,000 soldiers, among whom there was not a single deserter. We witnessed the unusual spectacle of a people, not themselves entirely free, ready to die for the freedom of another nation, even though it were under the flag of a Government that refused them their full rights.

After the War was over, and Wilson left office, the new Administration at Washington adopted an absolutely reactionary policy toward Porto Rico. In place of the Governor appointed by President Wilson, we received a man who had previously been a commercial traveler, or something of the sort, in his own country. As soon as he arrived in Porto Rico, he began to denounce, in violent discourses, our national aspirations. Six hours after his inauguration, the Unionist party took up the challenge. The whole Island was aroused. The new Administration started out by dismissing Porto Rican officials, and replacing them with men from the United States.

So at present we are in a most unhappy situation, a situation likely to imperil seriously the good relations between our Island and the United States. The people of Porto Rico are more resolved than ever to resist such a reactionary policy, and are courageously confident that their protest will eventually be heard and their rights respected.

We cannot hold the noble people of North America responsible for the reprehensible deeds of an unjust and incompetent Governor, who has used the powers entrusted to him to serve men that are enriching themselves by oppressing a helpless community. The Porto Rican people rest their hope in a nation whose cemeteries in France are symbols of its love for liberty. We cannot conceive that the people of the United States, after liberating Poland and restoring Bohemia, will refuse freedom to Porto Rico, and thus create an Ireland in America.

What lesson does the recent history of Porto Rico, which we have here so briefly traced, teach to the Spanish-American nations? In the first place, that there are no grounds for fearing the results of the contact of Anglo-Saxon and Spanish civilization. That is the fundamental lesson. Marvelous progress in industry, science, and commerce, and a successful pursuit of riches are not, exclusively, the patrimony of the Anglo-Saxons. But our culture of two thousand years belong to us alone.

By studying Anglo-Saxon methods and accommodating Anglo-Saxon institutions to our own ideals and temperament, we can create Spanish-American communities where all men are equal, where there is no hereditary privilege, where justice is unbought, where every man's home is his castle. But our efforts and sacrifices will amount to naught unless the Spanish-American nations realize that they must work shoulder to shoulder. Such a union of effort, however, means something far more permanent and enduring than our present Latin-American rallies and banquets, and our exuberant floods of sentimental oratory.

We should bear in mind that we are one hundred and ten millions of people, that we dwell in the richest and most fertile territory upon the globe, and that nearly every great modern industry depends upon us for indispensable raw materials. Let us bear these facts steadily in mind as our gaze sweeps over the immense spaces of the American continent. Then we shall comprehend what Spanish-American union may come to mean; what the future of the Spanish race in the Western hemisphere may prove to be.

SWEATSHOPS ON THE SPANISH MAIN

[A high birth rate, the collapse of family farms, and the seasonal nature of sugar cane employment created a huge surplus of workers—so desperately poor that they would toil for the lowest wages. This article describes the "sweatshop" type of business which emerged as a result.]

Imagine yourself turning a corner in the city of Ponce, now four centuries old, and coming face to face with a modern concrete building, one tall story high, from which comes the familiar sound of the power-driven sewing machine, and reading over the door "A. Blaustein & Co., Blouse Manufacturers."

Nothing but the sound and the name is familiar. There are no overshadowing brick walls, no dark windows, no stuffy low-ceiled workrooms. Half-latticed doors and windows admit the bright sunlight from all four sides; trade winds that blow twelve months in the year fan the workers; under the high ceiling a cushion of air as deep as a full story in an ordinary city building deflects the heat of the sun. Fancy if you can palm trees loaded with cocoanuts, bananas lusciously ripe on the stem, spreading guavas bent with their delicate fruit and a wealth of other tropical growth close to the rear of the building, and you will have a picture of surroundings such as palaces—out of the tropics—cannot boast.

The pleasing environment fades from the mind, however, when a local business man at your elbow remarks with unction on the progress manufacturing is making in Porto Rico. You remember the saying that the constitution follows the flag, but listening to the monotonous hum of the machines you are unable to keep back the cynical thought that, where profits invite, the sweatshop follows too.

With the constitution there came to Porto Rico medical science, education, prison reform, law enforcement and social order. But when, after these, there appeared the old, familiar face of the sweatshop, scarred and wrinkled, it seemed young and hopeful to Porto Rico, and now it goes by the name of industrial progress. In the United States, the sweatshop is recognized as a menace to workers and consumers; in Porto Rico it is thought of as the bearer of a

From G. L. Jones, *The Survey*, LI (November 15, 1923), pp. 209–10.

kind of industrial salvation, and is welcomed by the government, business organizations and the unemployed. . . .

Hundreds and thousands are unemployed or find work irregularly, and are eager to work on any terms that will better their living conditions. To Porto Ricans of all classes, craving economic and social advancement, the need for new industries seems imperative, and their welcome to the needle trades is a hearty one. Porto Rican capital is ready to match American dollars, provided the Americans furnish the directing effort. The government backs the invitation strongly, and can point to an educational budget of $12,000,000, which emphasizes this year the addition of 300 new trade schools, as an earnest of its desire to supplement agriculture by new industries. New money in circulation seems to spell prosperity; every town is clamoring for its own row of sewing machines.

Such an invitation has very concrete appeal for the manufacturer who is facing the competition of the clothing-trade centers. Labor costs in Porto Rico may be judged from the fact that housemaids and cooks can be hired at from $4 to $15 a month, day laborers at from $.60 to $1.00 a day. The working day is as long as one chooses to make it. There are 1200 miles of paved roads, motor transportation is excellent, railroads girdle the island, tonnage rates facilitate carriage to and from the United States. It is said that the manufacturer can ship his raw materials to the island, make them up, re-ship the finished product to New York—and cut his manufacturing costs by a full third. There is of course no tariff wall to climb: Porto Rico is on a par with New Jersey or Illinois in that respect. Cheap water power, cheap and abundant labor—and no unions to deal with— give the booster a pretty good case.

Two noteworthy responses have followed these generous encouragements—the sweatshop and contract needlework in the home. In many respects, the general situation resembles that found in the old South immediately following the Civil War, when the cotton mills were introduced. Somewhat the same poverty, the same cheap power and cheap labor, found in the South by the New England mill owners, prevail in Porto Rico, accentuated by the same pressure of necessity created by the desire for higher standards of living. But the sweatshop finds advantages in Porto Rico that the cotton mill owner did not find in the South. The water power is developed and ready for him to throw in the switch, and a still greater advantage is found in the skilled hands of the Porto Rican women ready to be used in the sewing trades. The superior quality of this labor goes directly back to the time when lacemaking, drawnwork, embroidery and kindred arts flourished in the households of Spanish families, and were transmitted by them to their subjects and slaves. If this handwork seems widely separated from the field of the power-driven sewing machine and blouse making, the facts contradict it: the building of sweatshops, and the premium placed on Porto Rican garments by retailers in our American stores. For it is represented that these garments are better made than those manufactured in this country. Moreover, the adaptability of the skilled hand-workers in the sewing trades has become a part of the propaganda for more sweatshops in Porto Rico.

The hand crafts of lacemaking, drawn-work and embroidery are not for the present being sacrificed to the machine. This work is being stimulated by a system of contracts made by New York concerns that market the product. These firms have representatives all over the island who contract with native women in the villages and the hills, on a piecework basis, for fancy work, underwear, and also for dresses supposed to come from Paris. From all reports, these contracts have proved very profitable to the makers and have furnished employment to many hundreds of women, as well as material benefits to their families. The sweatshop and this home contract work have only scratched the surface of the available supply of labor. The one operates in a modern plant located in cities and towns; the other in the unsanitary shacks in which the masses of the people live. As they come into sharper competition for the choice of labor, the advantage would seem to lie with the sweatshop, for labor in Porto Rico, like any other, will sell to the highest bidder, and higher wages can be earned on the power machines than by artistic hand-work.

It took half a century to secure the existing safeguards for workers in the southern cotton mills, and the job is not finished yet. How long it will take to accomplish the same for sweatshop workers in Porto Rico it is hard to say. The proper protection of contract workers in their homes, and of the consumers of their products, is even more difficult. Where labor so greatly exceeds the demand, the workers themselves can accomplish little to improve their condition. And Porto Rico lacks experience, even if it had the desire to establish the rights of the workers. Certainly legislation now proposed in the interest of the workers, or tending to eliminate the Porto Rico manufacturer's advantage over his American competitor, would be interpreted as discouraging new industries. For that reason, if for no other, the proposal must wait upon a popular movement growing out of a more equalized supply and demand of workers. . . .

"THE GENTLEMAN'S TIME HAS EXPIRED"

[In 1926, Felix Córdova Dávila, Puerto Rico's Resident Commissioner in Washington, rose in the House of Representatives to ask that Congress allow the island to elect its own governor. This right would not be granted until twenty-two years later. The *Congressional Record* incorrectly calls him "Mr. Dávila," using his second—maternal—surname.]

THE CHAIRMAN. . . . the gentleman from Porto Rico is recognized for 10 minutes.

MR. DAVILA. . . . We are not asking for independence. We have not lost our faith in the United States of America; and it is our honest opinion that the association of Porto Rico with this country would not only secure freedom to our people but also that happiness which is the main objective of human activities. . . . Our paramount purpose is to make our people happy, and any solution which will mean the realization of this idea will be favored by us.

But it is only fair that the Representative of Porto Rico should state once more on the floor of this House that my country will not be happy and satisfied with anything suggesting inferiority in the solution of our permanent status. We come to you on the basis of equality, always ready to share the national responsibilities and to do our duty in the supreme hour of sacrifice, but claiming the same privileges, rights, and liberties that are enjoyed by American citizens in the continental United States. . . .

Of course, if the granting of statehood is an impossibility, as has been held by prominent American statesmen, and if the right to complete home rule with the election of the executive [island governor] is denied to the island of Porto Rico, then we would be justified in asking for the absolute independence of our country. But it is our belief and hope that the island of Porto Rico can secure her happiness under the guidance of American institutions. We have entire confidence in the American people, and your sense of justice and our faith in the Almighty God incline us to believe that Congress will not unduly delay the recognition of our right to enjoy complete home rule with the executive elected by the people. What we need is a sincere and frank understanding, mutual confidence, and mutual respect. Most of our evils and frictions in life

From *Congressional Record*, House of Representatives, March 24, 1926, pp. 6203–4.

are due to misunderstanding. Have faith in the Porto Ricans, believe them, trust them. They are good and lovable people. They are true to this country. It was proved beyond any doubt during the crisis of the World War. But if you want to apply once more the acid test to the loyalty of the people of Porto Rico, wait till the arrival of a national crisis—God grant it will never come— and pronounce your request of us in only one word: Sacrifice. [Applause.]

Mr. GARRETT of Tennessee. Mr. Chairman, will the gentleman yield?

Mr. DAVILA. Yes.

Mr. GARRETT of Tennessee. The gentleman desires that the people of Porto Rico be given the right to select the governor?

Mr. DAVILA. Yes. We want complete home rule with the election of the governor.

The CHAIRMAN. The time of the gentleman from Porto Rico has expired.

Mr. DAVILA. May I have two minutes more?

The CHAIRMAN. The gentleman from Porto Rico is recognized for two minutes more.

Mr. DAVILA. I have introduced a bill in the House providing for the election of the executive in the year 1932. It is the same bill that unanimously passed the Senate last year and which was favorably reported by the Committee on Insular Affairs. There is no reason in the world to delay the passage of this bill, and I hope that the Committee on Insular Affairs will understand the advisability of enacting this legislation at this time. [Applause.]

The CHAIRMAN. The time of the gentleman from Porto Rico has again expired.

LINDBERGH'S VISIT

[Even nature seemed to be against the luckless colony. In 1928, Hurricane San Felipe swept through, followed four years later by Hurricane San Ciprián—the final toll, 567 dead, hundreds of thousands homeless, and more than $125 million in property damage.

Also in 1928, the island welcomed an eminent visitor, Charles Lindbergh, who was on a goodwill tour a year after his famous nonstop solo flight from New York to Paris. It was February 3, and thousands of children and adults honored the young aviator on the parade grounds of

From *New York Times*, March 16, 1928, pp. 1, 12.

El Morro Castle. Later, at a special session of the legislature, a medal was pinned on Lindbergh's coat by Senator Antonio Barceló. Then, the Speaker of the House, José Tous Soto, read a joint resolution of the legislature, asking Lindbergh to take the following message "to your country and your people":

> You will convey a message of Porto Rico not far different from the cry of Patrick Henry—'Liberty or Death!' It is the same in substance with but a difference imposed by the change of time and conditions. The message is . . . grant us the freedom that you enjoy, for which you struggled and which you worship; which we deserve and you have promised us.*

Barceló and Tous Soto then sent a cablegram to President Calvin Coolidge, stating that:

> Puerto Rico feels humiliated because of the inferior condition she is subjected to in spite of the hopes that the Treaty of Paris awoke in us; in spite of the unfulfilled promises made to our people, and in spite of the repeated legitimate demands in favor of a regime that may enable our island to exercise her own sovereignty over her own internal affairs and to freely solve the grave economic situation she is undergoing. †

President Coolidge's reaction was an angry letter to Governor Towner on February 28, which was made public on March 15.]

. . . The request is made that Porto Rico be constituted as a "free State" and not "a mere subjected colony." Certainly giving Porto Rico greater liberty than it has ever enjoyed and powers of government for the exercise of which its people are barely prepared cannot, with propriety, be said to be establishing therein "a mere subjected colony." . . .

We found the people of Porto Rico poor and distressed, without hope for the future, ignorant, poverty-stricken and diseased, not knowing what constituted a free and democratic government and without the experience of having participated in any government. We have progressed in the relief of poverty and distress, in the eradication of disease, and have attempted with some success to inculcate in the inhabitants the basic ideas of a free, democratic government. We have now in Porto Rico a government in which the participation by Americans from the United States is indeed small. We have given to the Porto Rican practically every right and privilege which we permitted ourselves to exercise. . . .

It is not desired to leave the impression that all progress in

* *New York Times,* February 4, 1928, p. 1.
† U.S. *Congressional Record,* 70th Congress, 1st Session, March, 1928, p. 6,584.

Porto Rico was due to continental Americans. Without the co-operation and assistance of Porto Ricans progress would indeed have been negligble, but the cooperation is largely due to the encouragement of American assistance, American methods and an increase in the reward of efforts made. . . .

Perhaps no Territory in the world has received such considerate treatment in the past thirty years as has Porto Rico, and perhaps nowhere else has progress been so marked and so apparent. . . . We are certainly entitled to a large part of the credit for this situation. . . .

There is no disposition in America, and certainly not on my part, to discourage any reasonable aspiration of the people of Porto Rico . . . but it certainly is not unreasonable to ask that those who speak for Porto Rico limit their petition to those things which may be granted without a denial of such hope. Nor is it unreasonable to suggest that the people of Porto Rico, who are a part of the people of the United States, will progress with the people of the United States rather than isolated from the source from which they have received practically their only hope of progress.*

* In Washington, Resident Commissioner Córdova Dávila replied, "There is not so much as a word in the President's letter to suggest . . . that, in holding Porto Rico, the United States derives benefits of a political and economic character." Complaining of "a point of view of American charity," Córdova Dávila declared "emphatically" that "we are not asking for charity, but for rights."—*New York Times*, April 13, 1928, p. 14.

"THE SAD CASE OF PORTO RICO"

[Luis Muñoz Marín, the son of the late Resident Commissioner Muñoz Rivera, was thirty-one years old when this article was published. Born in San Juan in 1898, the young Muñoz was raised in the United States, and now began to take an active role in island affairs. At the time Muñoz wrote this, he was Economic Commissioner of the Legislature of Porto Rico in the United States. Two decades later, he would become the island's first elected governor.]

I

Two major problems perplex the old Spanish province of Porto Rico, arising out of its enforced relationship to the United States. One deals with

From Luis Muñoz Marín, *The American Mercury*, XVI, No. 62 (February, 1929). Reprinted with permission.

the consequences of American economic development, the other with cultural Americanization. Both go to the root of the drama now being acted on that gorgeous stage; both are portentous in their potentialities.

The importance of the economic problem is obvious to all, whatever their views or interests. Americanization is more insidious. The tendency works while you sleep. It changes the expression of your eyes, the form of your paunch, the tone of your voice, your hopes of Heaven, what your neighbors and your women expect of you—all without giving you a chance to fight back, without even presenting to you the dilemma of fighting back or not. Certainly no two things are more important than to have what you want and to live as spontaneously as you can manage. These two hopes are now in process of being shot to hell in my country.

The American flag found Porto Rico penniless and content. It now flies over a prosperous factory worked by slaves who have lost their land and may soon lose their guitars and their songs. In the old days most Porto Rican peasants owned a few pigs and chickens, maybe a horse or a cow, some goats, and in some way had the use of a patch of soil. Today this modest security has been replaced by a vision of opulence. There are more things that they can't get. The margin between what they have and what they can imagine has widened monstrously. While there are many more schools for their hungry children and many more roads for their bare feet, their destiny is decidedly narrower now than it was when they were part and parcel of one of the most interesting and incompetent nationalities in the world.

In 1898 Porto Rico was a semi-feudal country, typical of the old Spanish provinces in America, willing and capable of assuming with a natural grace and a natural awkwardness its position in the Spanish commonwealth of provinces, or to venture into a simple, old-fashioned Latin-American national form. Its economics were those developed by Spain in the tropical New World: fiscally rotten, socially humble and sound. Culturally, it was a slow, calm place. Racially, it shared with Costa Rica one peculiarity: a predominantly unmixed European peasantry—if Spain be Europe.

Schools were few, roads were fewer; chickens laid eggs under thatched cottages, goats cavorted outside and were corraled for a milking and sometimes killed for a stuffing, the squall of pigs and not of factory whistles woke up the countryside. Pale, wiry, moustached, sleepy-eyed men tumbled out of hammocks pulling up their trousers for the day, and barefooted women in terribly starched dresses of many colors began preparing strong coffee in iron kettles and serving it steaming in polished cocoanut shells. Although Porto Rico was not then one of the great sugar producing centres of the world, there was usually sugar at the bottom of the cocoanut and the sleepy-eyed man stirred it lazily with a wooden spoon, tasting it with his eyes and his nose. Inside the hut the brats wailed; one of them soothed itself by finding five eggs, certified by cackles, under the floor, another by plucking from the wall the image of the Virgin, printed in screaming blue and red. The men left for the field to cut cane, to lead the oxen on their sugar grinding merry-go-round, to prune or pick the coffee bushes in the sloping shade of the tall guavas, to pick and seed the cotton or sift the tobacco leaves or spade in their master's truck field. As they wound their way along the coastal plain or twisted along the precipitous mountain paths a very few pennies jingled in their pockets.

At noon the jíbaro comforted himself, for two cents, with a tumbler of rum bought at the store under the ceiba tree, and went home to a meal of codfish with sweet potatoes and rice mixed with beans. The rice and beans were plentiful; he ate of them until he had enough, and then he slept. After the day's work he loafed in the starlight, sang fantastic songs, usually depicting a topsy-turvy grandeur of some sort, made love to one or two girls, and then went home and made love to his wife.

Of a Sunday, he might with a number of his friends eat a barbecued pig, get drunk in the shade and go to cockfight. If there was sickness in the family, the master of the plantation would send his doctor, and the master's wife might send some quinine or rhubarb or cadillo leaves. I don't believe he ever went to bed hungry or muddled through a spell of sickness without attention.

As he could not read, it was unlikely that he would discover that Porto Rico's total production for the year came to something less than $9,000,000, and that 950,000 human beings were living, sleeping, eating, drinking, feasting, gambling, singing, and loving on that money.

His master, the feudal lord, rose out of an enormous mahogany bed, washed his hands and face in cold water out of an enamelled bowl with a design of roses, and breakfasted on a cup of coffee, rolls, butter, and cheese. Then he shouted for his horse and rode over his land, seeing that everyone was at work, inquiring after those who were sick or lazy, listening to gossip, giving advice on marriages. It was not until later in the morning that, coming upon a secluded bend of the stream where the pomarrosales bent over the water, he took off his clothes and bathed.

He owned his house; his hills and ravines were lightly mortgaged or not at all; he chose out of several horses for his tours of his domain; he bred, bought or swapped roosters to uphold the honor of his judgment; he fathered his men gruffly or kindly, intelligently or stupidly. Perhaps he wanted a house in the nearest town, or, perhaps not in the nearest town but in the capital of the district.

Maybe some day he would even move to San Juan. Someone had a horse or a rooster he coveted. They said that Madrid was a lively place, but it would probably bore him, so far from home, where no one would know him or greet him with deference or seek his advice. His son might be sent across to study, and might receive a visit from his parents during his last year at the university. It was a long trip though.

In San Juan, a city of many colors crowded within thick brown walls, occasional carriages clattered over the cobblestones; high ceilings made cool dark interiors; a rare cocoanut shell mounted in silver gave evidence in certain old houses of the time when glassware was an infrequent importation; the cafés were clubs where politics and women were discussed over ice cream, chocolate, or rum; and a bowlegged mulatto was famous as a procurer. Regional autonomy had been granted by Spain, and a native Cabinet with a native Premier ruled the green fields and polychromatic towns.

If you didn't own a house, you might own one. If you didn't have a carriage, you might have one. If you did have these goods and a little money in the bank for a trip to Madrid or Paris now and then, you were at the top, and peace, romance, or prestige were your remaining goals. Porto Rico was a land of opportunity. Opportunity in a serene Spanish sense. Opportunity within classes. All that a man of a given class could imagine himself as attaining, he could attain. His economic imagination wasn't stimulated by the brash parade of contraptions which were later to become badges of honor and tokens of social superiority. You didn't have much, and you could only want a little more. There was only one millionaire on the island, but there were many lords and masters of the soil.

II

Presto, the flag! The one and only. The magic carpet on which Rotary, benevolence, and interference fly over the crumbling liberties and inefficiencies of the earth. It found a dignified little world, bearing with an easy penury, playing the tiple, and dreaming of a moon which was attainable. Its servitors set to work to transform that little world into a hasty one, pushing great iron wheels, slipping innumerable bills of lading across Grand Rapids desks, and dreaming of automobiles, which are mostly unattainable. "Mother," the troubadours used to sing.

> I bought a toy
> In the market-place of love.
> How pretty it was, oh, how pretty it was,
> But what price I had to pay!

But soon they were singing:

> The automobile, oh, mother, is something
> That surprises all people, oh, mother,
> And is prodigious.

Spain had recently granted Porto Rico an autonomous form of government. The island was run by Porto Ricans under a responsible Cabinet system, and the Governor-General, barring his military command, was as purely ceremonial as his colleague of Canada. Porto Rico had control of her customs, a measure of treaty-making power, sixteen representatives in the Madrid Cortes. She was empowered to develop her economic life as best suited her tastes and interests. Her statesmen and politicians had the future in their hands. Theirs was the responsibility for molding this quiet lovely place into an image of unassuming prosperity and justice. Porto Rico is small, not very complex, and the task was—and is— an easy one, if only it be undertaken in a spirit of objective statesmanship, with no axes to grind.

But there seems to be a feeling in the United States against permitting others to be responsible for their own welfare. Under American rule the native Cabinet, tolerated at first, soon found its existence made unendurable by the encroachments of the Military Governors. It resigned. A mongrel system of government, under the Foraker Act, took the place of the ample autonomy established by Spain. The Lower House was elected by popular suffrage. The Cabinet was the Upper House, blithely combining legislative and executive functions. This Cabinet-Senate was composed of six Porto Ricans and five Americans, all appointed by the American authorities.

It was not difficult to find six adequate Porto Ricans. They were found. But, although a community can be ruled by a few men willing to rule it in a nice way, some kind of supporting majority is demanded by the democratic yen. So a majority was found. To be a member of this majority all you had to do was to proclaim yourself an ardent American in bad English, or in no English at all. If you were a member of the majority, you could become a street-cleaner or a health inspector, or you could recommend some poor henchman for either job.

Then the tariff wall was thrown around the island. Sugar became the chief beneficiary and cane spread over the valleys and up the hillsides like wildfire. The Spanish economy had been somewhat haphazardly predicated on small land-holding. The American economy, introduced by the Guánica, the Aguirre, the Fajardo and other great *centrales* was based on the million-dollar mill and the tight control of the surrounding countryside.

By now the development of large absentee-owned sugar estates, the rapid curtailment in the planting of coffee—the natural crop of the independent farmer—, and the concentration of cigar manufacture into the hands of the American trust, have combined to make Porto Rico a land of beggars and millionaires, of flattering statistics and distressing realities. More and more it becomes a factory worked by peons, fought over by lawyers, bossed by absent industrialists, and clerked by politicians. It is now Uncle Sam's second largest sweat-shop.

It is a sweat-shop that has a company store—the United States. American dollars paid to the peons are so many tokens, redeemable in the American market exclusively, at tariff-inflated prices. The same tariff that protects the prices of sugar and tobacco, controlled by the few, skyrockets the prices of commodities that must be consumed by all. Porto Rico obtains tariff prices and pays tariff prices. The appearance of justice is maintained, but the reality is a pawn-broker's reality.

The favorable trade-balances, so naively emphasized by the official reports, are therefore a choice bit of irony. During the last twenty-eight years of American rule the island has enjoyed an unfavorable trade-balance only twice. In each of the other twenty-six years the exports have exceeded the imports in the same manner that the exports of a burglarized house exceed its imports. In brief, the renowned favorable balance is nothing but the profit of the absentee landlords and industrialists.

Here, as Al Smith would say, is the lowdown. From 1901 to 1927 $228,000,000 was extracted from Porto Rico and reported as a favorable trade-balance. But if the island had been privileged to forego that flattering balance, a reasonable proportion of those millions would have gone into the development of its industrial resources. As the whole island is now valued at about $300,000,000, the effect of such reinvestment on the living standards of its overcrowded population would have been very important. To the American people, on the other hand, that money spread over that number of years, means nothing. Its ingress, even in one single year would have no more appreciable effect on their prosperity than a bucket of water on the tides of the Great Lakes. Yet these life-giving pennies have been filched from the pocket of a pauper by the fingers of an opulent kleptomaniac.

Of course, no such gorgeous dividends could have been declared had not the influence of American enterprise and the actual investment of American capital increased Porto Rico's output of dollars so fabulously. Certainly, the imperialists could argue if they felt compelled to, those millions represent but a small percentage of the increase of wealth brought about by the American regime. In dollars, they represent a profit of 16%. In value they represent incalculably more. The operation of the tariff against the consumer and the expanding land monopoly explain the discrepancy. So far as the bulk of the population is concerned, only an eighty-cent wage paid during six months of the year to the head of each family, and redeemable only in the world's highest market, separates them from the angels.

III

It is close contact with the United States rather than the influence of the small group of resident Americans that has given a decided, if superficial, direction to the institutional life of the island. The Y.M.C.A. has its swimming pool, its basket ball court, its inspirational talks, but I doubt that such implied notions as Christ's disapproval of cigarettes get much serious attention from the local young men. Rotary slaps backs, sings, and hears speeches in a bored and genial way, but when I gave it a somewhat fantastic talk on the culture of light ladies as an index of civilization, the members really had a good time. The Elks and Odd Fellows play with their rituals, charity becomes slightly organized, evangelical preachers thunder in the villages, Holy Rollers roll in the back alleys, three or four prominent citizens become Protestants and are considered funny, women are beginning to be feared as the rolling-pin follows the flag, virginity still abounds and often attains to old age, but is perceptibly on the wane.

It is probably through the women that the largest doses of Americanism are being administered. The Latin-American attitude in this respect is confusing to a narrowly egalitarian world. Certainly we are wont to make a sharp nonsensical distinction between good and bad women—there is hardly any middle ground between chastity and prostitution. But this has not heretofore meant that the mere goodness of good women gave them any appreciable influence on the social point of view. Good women have been powerless and tame among us, and have grown smug in the consciousness of their hard luck. Generally speaking, there were only four things Latin women could be: old maids, wives, mistresses, or prostitutes. Now they can be girls. They can be girls for a long time.

They can also be stenographers, bookkeepers, telephone operators, shop assistants, and feminists. They may speak in public and harass legislators.

Porto Rican politicians may now be publicly accused of keeping mistresses. The charge doesn't come near defeating them, but evidently there is some suggestion in the atmosphere that makes it seem relevant. Twenty years ago it would have seemed preposterous to advance such an argument as in any way affecting a man's fitness for office.

The indications are that we may soon find ourselves adopting a subtly feminized point of view as unsatisfactory to both men and women as the one now prevailing in the United States. The change, in spite of the stupid simplicity of our traditional mores, would seem to be for the worse. We were groping toward adjustment; now we are drifting toward equality.

There are two kinds of Americanized Porto Ricans: the young men freely and spontaneously shaped into the image of whatever happens to be the Young Generation up here, just as young Germans, Italians, and Swedes are shaped in New York or Pittsburgh; and the older fellows who Americanize themselves out of a sense of their inadequacy as Porto Ricans. The former may be as charming and as innocuous as the youths who play tennis in the Saturday Evening Post. The latter are a sight for the gods. Their manner is as unctuous as that of Y.M.C.A. secretaries and quite as unreal. They approve and disapprove of many things. They have Ethics and go in for Service. They emphasize the importance of their smallest actions to the working of the sacred social machinery. They need the crutch of a principle to support their conduct as it hobbles along the straight and narrow path where the primroses grow—and, of course, they always find one.

Whether as a result of American tailoring or of psycho-biological imitation, their paunches no longer grow in the reticent Spanish fashion, but rather in the aggressive. imperialistic, genial American fashion. They are gregarious and dull and oversimian, and try pathetically to find innocent amusements. They immolate the paramount heritage of Spain—individuality—in the altar of regular-fellowship. The girls don't like them, and I maliciously suggest this fact as an issue to the Porto Rican nationalists.

The tone of life in the cities has been speeded up. A certain efficiency is observable. Clerks take shorter siestas after lunch. Telephone connections are quickly achieved, although private messages may still be conveyed through the operators if they like your voice. Transportation is rapid and cheap. Good liquor is delivered within a few minutes—Scotch, $5 a quart; champagne, $7; Holland gin, $8. Soda fountains suffuse the narrow streets with their sweet odor. Cafés are arranged to look more and more like glittering American beaneries, but conversation and not food is still the major inducement for tarrying in them.

The population is about as susceptible to nationalist emotions as to American manners. While the latter grow like a monstrous parasite on the island's Latinity, it remains a fact that whenever a politician of intelligence and prestige has taken up the issue of national independence, he has swayed the island. It is the students at the university, however, who give expression to the most conscious and complex form of nationalism, not only as a sovereign control of the jobs, but as a cultural continuity.

They don't want the local temperament violated by the bayonets of education or by the contagion imminent in close commercial relationships. They want Porto Rico to be Porto Rico, not a lame replica of Ohio or Arizona. They want its spirit to be part of the great Spanish spirit, now in process of saving itself from its political and economic ruin.

IV

The university authorities, under the leadership of Dr. Thomas Benner, who is far from sharing the political viewpoint of the students, follow a policy that is friendly to this end. The university can boast of the most brilliant Spanish department on American territory. It is in fact among the soundest of any to be found in Spanish-speaking countries, having enjoyed at one time or another the services of such men as Vasconcelos, ex-Minister of Education of Mexico; De Onís, head of the Spanish department at Columbia; Amado Alonso, of the Centro de Estudios Históricos of Madrid; Américo Castro of Oxford, and many other first-rate men.

What effect this may have on the destiny of the island is of course doubtful. However, saving a culture, even an inferior one, from becoming the monkey of another, even a superior one, is a good in itself. And in the present case it is by no means certain that the heritage shared by Porto Rico is to be unfavourably compared with the heritage to which the blind forces of production and exchange now seek to hook it up.

The haphazard manner in which the character of the island spars for survival may influence its political future. Whether the island is to be semi-independent, like Cuba, or autonomous under some special dispensation of Congress, is a question to be determined by the interplay of politic and economic interest. But it is certain that it will never be incorporated into the Union as a State save through the operation of cultural forces: that is, not unless, and until, our manner of life and thought has been respectably Americanized.

Will this ever come about? Will the island retain its historical personality? An unqualified answer to either of these questions would necessarily fall short of the possibilities. Perhaps a more absurd fate is in store for us. Perhaps we are destined to be neither Porto Ricans nor Americans, but merely puppets of a mongrel state of mind, susceptible to American thinking and proud of Latin thought, subservient to American living and worshipful of the ancestral way of life. Perhaps we are to discuss Cervantes and eat pork and beans in the Child's restaurant that must be opened sooner or later. Perhaps we will try not to let mother catch us reading the picaresque verses of Quevedo. Perhaps we are going to a singularly fantastic and painless hell in our own sweet way. Perhaps all this is nothing but a foretaste of Pan-Americanism.

"JOKER IN THE DECK"

[In scrutinizing Puerto
Rico's apparently favorable economic trade balance, two American authors reveal the "joker in the deck"—the fact that most of the benefits
accrue to absentee investors. This book excerpt shows in considerable
detail how U.S. corporations quickly monopolized the economy of
Puerto Rico. The authors discuss the impact upon the island worker
who is "forced to work for a wage far below his needs," and ask the
question, "Can we [the United States] govern the island for its own best
interests?"]

After thirty-two
years of American occupation . . . anyone who wishes to face the
truth of the situation must recognize that the progress made
in certain lines has been astounding. No country ever started
nearer the bottom than Porto Rico did and few, if any have ever
set about climbing in any more determined manner. . . .

Among the most prominent changes . . . are those in the realm
of economics. . . . Fruit growing sprang from nothing in 1898 to
occupy the third place in value of the agricultural exports in
recent years. . . . This crop is more nearly dominated by local
men . . . but still the percentage of absentee ownership is large,
and will probably increase. . . .

About one per cent of the cultivated area was in tobacco in
1898 and today the percentage is more than five. . . . Today it is
the second industry in importance, being surpassed only by sugar.

The sugar industry . . . furnishes more than half of the exports
and at least half, if not more, of the wealth is due to this one
business alone. Occupying but 15 per cent of the cultivated area
at the time of the American occupation, it today claims more
than 44 per cent of all the land in cultivation. . . .

The needlework industry, famous for its quality but not for its
quantity in 1898, reversed this and by 1929 showed an export
trade of . . . $15,000,000. The total export trade, made up in the
main of the four industries just named, grew from less than
$5,000,000 gold in [1897] . . . to more than $100,000,000 in 1928.
The apparent trade balance has been in favor of Porto Rican
products almost continuously in the last 32 years, becoming

From Bailey W. Diffie and Justin Whitfield Diffie, *The Broken Pledge* (New
York: The Vanguard Press, 1931), pp. 199–220. Reprinted by permission.

adverse only when some unusual upset like the hurricane of 1928 struck the Island.

But this favorable trade balance has long been proclaimed the "joker in the deck" by the Islanders. . . . In 1928 the apparent excess in favor of the Island was more than $14,000,000. . . . That this was a false balance may be seen . . . in casting up the items resulting in a net outgo from Porto Rico. Freight payments to steamship companies and marine insurance, commissions collected by outside houses, remittances to Porto Ricans abroad, tourist expenses, other types of insurance, motion picture royalties, lottery tickets bought in the lotteries of Spain, Santo Domingo and other nations, interest, dividends, rents and miscellaneous items amounted to more than $25,000,000, leaving a net deficiency for all trade and service operations of something over $10,000,000. . . .

In other words, each year shows a net deficit of several million dollars which has been met so far by handing over Porto Rico, bit by bit, to the absentee. . . .

Let us turn now to what social improvements have been made with this vast new wealth and revenue. . . . Few countries can match the road building achievements of the Porto Ricans in the last generation. Unaided they have built more than 1,500 kilometres of hard-surfaced roads in regions which would defy a mountain goat. . . . Public health, too, has engaged the interest of Porto Rican statesmen . . . As a result, the death rate was lowered from an average of 30 per thousand for the period from 1888 to 1892 to about 23 per thousand for the ten year period ending with 1930.

But it is in the field of education that we find the most decided progress . . . expenditures increased to where they claim more than 38 per cent of the Insular budget. . . . Illiteracy has decreased from around 80 per cent to something less than 50. The number of schools increased from 560 to 2,238. The total registration of pupils was less than 30,000 in 1898 and by 1928 had increased to 230,000. . . .

But what is the American share in Porto Rican progress? There are some who point to every forward step as the work of the United States. . . .

Hundreds of American teachers have gone to Porto Rico to teach English, but they were paid with Porto Rican dollars. None of this came out of the public purse of the United States. Their salaries, along with other expense attached to English instruction, have been a crushing burden on the slender resources of the Island. Why spend millions of dollars to teach English to people who were 80 per cent illiterate, in preference to teaching them their own language? Why teach them English when the majority live and die within twenty miles of the ocean and never see it? Why teach them English when they are ragged, hungry, unskilled and might better have learned a trade or been taught something of scientific agriculture? The last thing that the Porto Rican masses needed was English. . . . And to the teaching of English the American Government has never contributed one penny. Only to the College of Agriculture have we given financial assistance. . . . But in spite of the burden placed on the Insular and Municipal Governments for education there are almost 300,000 children for whom there are no school facilities. . . .

In the field of public health we have been equally as liberal. Outside of a meager amount of work carried on by the Army there has never been any serious effort to stamp out the atrocious health conditions . . . [which] today can be depicted in just about the same language as in 1898. Diphtheria has been increasing constantly since 1915, while in the United States it has decreased 95 per cent since 1900. Typhoid tells the same story. . . . The death rate from tuberculosis is likewise growing. . . . The dreaded hook-worm disease has still the preferred place among the causes of sickness, and though thousands are cured each year the poor cannot afford the necessary shoes to protect them from re-infection.

When we come to our participation in road building, we find a record wholly devoid of anything to which the continental American can point with his accustomed pride. . . . Up to the hurricane of 1928, the United States Government had never contributed one cent for road building in Porto Rico. All of the more than 1,200 miles of hard-surface roads have been built by Porto Rican initiative and with Porto Rican money. . . .

But where the American Government has been neglectful, American capital has not. In every branch of Porto Rican business, American corporations have steadily absorbed the interest once belonging to Spaniards, or natives. The sugar industry, tobacco manufacturing, fruit growing, banks, railroads, public utilities, steamship lines and many lesser businesses are partially or completely dominated by outside capital. . . .

Approximately 60 per cent of the [sugar] crop is ground by American and other absentee companies. Sugar cane growing has absorbed about all of the fertile valley land, and the absentee companies dominate the four chief sugar cane sections. More than 100,000 acres of the most fertile soil are the property of men who seldom or never see the Island and who have no interest in it except to make it pay dividends.

The assets of the four principal companies, all American companies owned by men who for the most part dwell outside Porto Rico, were more than $63,000,000 in 1928. These properties have paid dividends over long periods sufficient to replace their original investment many times over. From 10 to 30 per cent per annum is the rule and dividends exceeding 100 per cent a year have been known.

An examination of the taxes paid on their holdings show them to be at most half and sometimes not even one-fourth of the true value. . . . In 1928, the Aguirre Sugar Company was assessed at less than $4,500,000 and its net income capitalized at 10 per cent was more than $27,000,000! . . . High profits and low assessments have not inspired these companies to be liberal with Porto Rico or the Porto Ricans. The *colono*, the farmer who grows the cane, is receiving his substance from the little end of the funnel. He gets less than 65 per cent of the sugar from his cane, but has to pay 80 to 89 per cent of the cost of production. The cost of financing his crop, the low return he receives, the disadvantage in which he finds himself compared with the owners of the sugar manufacturing Centrals is tending to drive him out of his farm and make of him a day laborer. The result is that his land is passing into the hands of a few large corporations, in opposition to the Organic Law of Porto Rico, which forbids corporate owner-ship of land in excess of 500 acres. The Congress of the United States which passed this provision and placed it in the Organic Law of Porto Rico has never bothered to make it effective. The men who own the sugar companies control both the Bureau of Insular Affairs and the Legislature of Porto Rico. . . .

The effect of this land concentration has been disastrous to the agricultural economy. While sugar acreage was increasing almost four times, crops devoted to food were declining to about two-thirds their former acreage. . . . Porto Rico has only one acre of food crops today for every 15 people, whereas only 30 years ago she had an acre for every six people. . . . After 30 years of sugar economy, during which time millions have been made from Porto Rican soil, Porto Rico is facing the fact that sugar has not paid. . . .

Tobacco may have paid the grower a little better return, but it is the absentee capitalist who has made the real profit. . . . The case of fruit is somewhat different. This crop is owned more largely by residents who live on the land and market their own product. Sugar and tobacco have paid the manufacturer; fruit has paid the owner; but none of them has paid the laborer!

. . . this monopolization . . . is carried into every branch of business. Practically every mile of public carrier railroad in the Island belongs to two companies—the Ponce and Guayama and the American Railroad Company, which are largely absentee owned. . . . The public utility service is likewise the property of those who for the main part live outside Porto Rico. Every trolley ride taken by a Porto Rican pays tribute to a foreign owner, and about half the towns depend on absentee companies for their lights and power, and more than half the telephone calls go over wires owned by outsiders. . . .

. . . the island consumer . . . is buying in the dearest market in the world, or he pays such a high tariff that the resulting price is many times what it would otherwise be. The price of rice, his chief food, is more than doubled. Beans, potatoes, bread—in fact everything he eats—cost him twice what they would in the cheapest market. And this same tariff, while apparently protecting him, is rendering him every day more subservient to the absentee interests.

The native is forced to work for a wage far below his needs. The unemployment situation, like that of many other countries, is a temporary problem that has become permanent. Starting in 1899 with only 17 per cent unemployed, Porto Rico has made such startling progress in this line that she had 36 per cent unemployment in 1929. . . . This good business for the owner has driven the wage down to where the day laborer is compelled to work 33 days to supply himself with rice today, as against 25 in 1898. He spends more than 20 days for flour now, whereas only 10 were formerly necessary, and for his dry vegetables the number of days work rose from three and a half to more than 13. Altogether he must today spend 104 days working to buy imported foods that once cost him only 70 days to work!

. . . the Porto Rican . . . uses more of his income for food than the Oriental laborer does, about 94 per cent being so spent, as compared with only 90 per cent in the Far East. . . . What seems more incredible, he pays in actual money more for the same foods than the New York City laborer! By actual test, 17 articles comprising 65 per cent of the food used by the Porto Rican *jíbaro* cost from eight to 14 per cent more than the same articles in New York City. . . .

The average Continental American will immediately say that Porto Rico's troubles are vestiges of the evil and incompetent Spanish regime. The patriotic Porto Rican nationalist believes just as firmly that the breeze which unfurled the stars and stripes was an evil breath which has since that time cursed the Island. Neither of these opinions can be entirely correct. . . . Porto Rico was a sadly neglected little Island during most of its existence. . . . It was in such condition when it fell into the willing lap of Uncle Sam. Why it is still in about the same condition is a question that should be of interest to every American and a true answer might do something to rectify our present policy of "muddling along" with our possessions. . . .

The injunction of President McKinley to the first governor to "prepare them for statehood as rapidly as possible" was in the mind of the United States the only solution needed. Once they had statehood they would automatically become a 49th section of paradise! . . .

Officially, the United States has been doctoring its patient for thirty-two years without counting the pulse or taking the temperature. The first reason we can assign, then, for American failure to remedy bad conditions, is the failure to diagnose the trouble and to meet the issue squarely once the trouble was known.

The second is a peculiar mixture of "laissez-faire" and mercantilism of the twentieth century type. We are great worshippers of "give business a free rein" and of "rugged individualism." We seem to believe honestly that all a man needs is a chance, to become a president or a Henry Ford, regardless of the fact that we have only one president at a time and only one Henry Ford. . . .

. . . the bitterest complaint against us today is not on political grounds; nor are the main problems political. It is the economic and social condition which draws the shafts of critics, and these are the ones most in need of solving. . . .

The problem of the United States in Porto Rico . . . resolves itself into one question: can we govern the island for its own best interests? As long as the United States Government has the ultimate word in policies, the island will be governed for the good of those interests considered "American." Porto Rico is at once the perfect example of what economic imperialism does for a country and of the attitude of the imperialist towards that country. Ragged, hungry, diseased and dispossessed, Porto Rico has just been examined by the President of the United States and has been given his official approval. Its land owned by absentee capital; its political rights resting in the hands of the United States Government; its people in the depths of deprivation, it has been told to help itself. That is the "remedy" which the President prescribes—imperialism's answer to problems of its own creation! . . . Porto Rico can hope for no relief under the existing system. This is well proved in the fact that the President of the United States visited Porto Rico and "saw that it was good."

THE RISE OF ALBIZU CAMPOS

[The Great Depression in the United States hit Puerto Rico with extra force, tumbling wages from their already miserable level. In 1933, a study on the offshore municipality of Vieques Island showed that its 11,000 inhabitants were surviving on a *total* income of $500 a week—less than seven cents per person, daily.

In the political arena, many of Washington's appointed American officials were inept, and at least one governor misused public funds. The

Translated from *Claridad*, Puerto Rico, November 1, 1970.

U.S. sugar corporations had strong lobbying power in Congress, and in the colonial legislature.

Relief and public works projects, founded after Franklin D. Roosevelt's "New Deal" government took power in 1933, staved off starvation for many, but these programs were—at best—a cosmetic cure for a host of deeply rooted ills.

Four years earlier, Theodore Roosevelt, Jr. was named Governor of Puerto Rico by President Herbert Hoover (he served in the post from April 7, 1929 to January 18, 1932).

Like his father, Roosevelt was an energetic man, who traveled through the island's poverty-stricken countryside and saw "farm after farm where lean, underfed women and sickly men repeated again and again the same story—little food and no opportunity to get more."

"I have seen mothers," he wrote, "carrying babies who were little skeletons, I have watched in a class-room thin, pallid, little boys and girls trying to spur their brains to action when their little bodies were underfed. I have seen them trying to study on only one scanty meal a day, a meal of a few beans and some rice. I have looked into the kitchens of houses where a handful of beans and a few plantains were the fare for the entire family." *

The Nationalist Party, headed by Pedro Albizu Campos, became a focal point for radical protest, and—though few Puerto Ricans would admit it—a loudspeaker for the pent-up anger and frustration of the long-silent, long-abused masses.

Pedro Albizu Campos was a graduate of Harvard Law School and served as a second lieutenant in the U.S. Army during World War I.

He entered politics in the 1920's, and, by 1930, was president of the Puerto Rican Nationalist Party. During the 1932 elections, the party received 5,300 votes; from then on, Albizu preached abstention from "the colonial elections."

"Puerto Rico must create a grave crisis for the colonial administration in order that its demands be heard. . . . A nation like the United States, with enormous national and international problems, has no time to pay attention to submissive, servile men. What is needed is a rebel organization . . . to make a clean break with the colonial regime, and to request recognition of our independence from the free nations of the world," he wrote.

"Nationalism," he wrote later, "is the only salvation, because it causes to be reborn in each of us the conscience of a free man, for whom human dignity is priceless, and who cannot conceive why he should not have the right to direct the destinies of his children or his homeland." †

Although always in the minority during the next two decades, the Nationalists had moments of genuine popular support. Albizu was a fiery, compelling speaker, and a man who did not shrink from his self-appointed role as martyr for the cause of independence. Here are excerpts from one of his speeches, made in 1930 "to mark the first 30 years of *yanqui* intervention." It was a prelude to a long, turbulent career, marked by violence and imprisonment in Federal jails. Albizu died in 1965, after a long illness that left him partially paralyzed. Puerto Rico's

* *Review of Reviews*, January, 1930, which was a condensation of a December 8, 1929, article in the *New York Herald Tribune Magazine*.
† Translated from *El Mundo*, November 16, 1933.

pro-independence militants regard Pedro Albizu as the "apostle" of their cause, and they have adopted as their slogan his statement: *"La patria es valor y sacrificio"* (The homeland is courage and sacrifice).]

Although the sinister purpose of the United States was always to take possession of the Antilles, convert the Caribbean into a *yanqui* lake, and thus exercise strategic influence over Mexico, and Central and South America, the true purpose of the conquest could not be revealed to the North American people. They were told of a war for humanitarian reasons. The case of Cuba and Puerto Rico under Spanish sovereignty was presented as something so intolerable to civilization that it forced a nation, anxious not to disturb the peace, to interfere, so that our right to freedom would be respected. . . .

The *yanqui* invasion in 1898 . . . meant the coming of a regime of liberty, equality, fraternity, and material prosperity, to judge by *yanqui* propaganda. And all that happiness would be generally heaped upon us by North American philanthropy and humanity.

The invaders imposed the Treaty of Paris upon Spain. We were never consulted in the preparation or approval of the treaty. They forced Spain to cede Puerto Rico, as war indemnity.

All this revealed the true face of *yanqui* humanitarianism, but their propaganda did away with Boricuan [Puerto Rican] concern, and with international suspicion.

Puerto Ricans—without distinction of political party—offered to cooperate in this supposed coming of liberty.

No one believed that the invader had decided to profane mankind's most sacred words.

They imposed a regime with absolute powers, to control all taxes and privileges, and to determine the displacement of all native wealth into the hands of the invaders. Thus, agriculture, industry, commerce, and the communications media all practically became theirs.

Today, barely twenty per cent of these [sectors of the economy] are under native control.

Voices of alarm, shouts of patriotism, and imprecations against the invader were heard.

But *yanqui* propaganda again benumbed the Boricuan conscience. With our fears becalmed, we were presented to ourselves and nations abroad as a country enjoying extraordinary prosperity, owing exclusively to the presence of the magical North American flag.

Workers came to believe that their good salaries depended upon the *yanqui* government; many intellectuals pinned their greatest hopes on occupying a high position in the North American Government, especially in the diplomatic and consular service; farm owners were warned against the possible demagoguery of the working class; commerce was attracted by the supposed advantages of tariff-free transportation between Puerto Rico and the United States; businessmen became convinced that they ought to deposit their money in the banks of the invaders, because *yanqui* propaganda subtly accused everyone of lack of honesty; teachers were convinced that they should teach everything in English; in sum, the nation assented to its moral and material dismemberment, anesthetized by so-called good intentions.

The patriotism of some natives was not enough.

The worker could not believe that the *yanqui* government was actually encouraging *latifundismo* and absentee-ownership, and the destruction of all native industries, so that unemployment would grow on a large scale, and so that cheap labor would be available, in order for *yanqui* corporations to accumulate enormous profits.

Commerce lost all sense of accounting. It did not expect its own inevitable bankruptcy, as a result of the tariff-free structure that requires us to sell to the *yanqui* at the price he wishes to pay, and to buy from him at the price he wishes to stipulate.

The naive businessman, attracted by foreign propaganda, believed that the branches of foreign banks were backed by many millions of dollars, and deposited his cash in them, so that the invader could finance his own enterprise; with this money retired from the market, interest rates were raised, making it impossible for native business to survive.

The land owner became a slave of exploitative enterprises, and sooner or later had to hand over his farm to the creditors who hounded him.

The government assessed his farm at the highest price possible. But foreign interests were—and are—permitted to hide all types of wealth; low prices are fixed for their declared wealth, and their nonpayment of taxes is tolerated.

Meanwhile, year after year, native farms are systematically auctioned off, in many cases for less than two dollars.

Still, with the excuse of teaching English, a public education system is maintained that uses the language of the invader as the only vehicle for instruction, at a cost of $4 million a year. In reality, English is not taught, and the only result is to brutalize our young, forcing them to study science, and Latin, in English, and languages in the tongue of the invader.

The invader reached the point where he no longer needed to justify himself. There were paid natives to do it for him. Thus, we have outstanding "pedagogues" in the Department of Education sanctioning the barbarities that we have pointed out.

Lawyers to defend foreign interests are in abundance.

There is a group of pseudointellectuals who have dared to preach the creation of a hybrid type, a monster that is half *yanqui*, half Boricua.

North American propaganda had triumphed. Despite these facts, it insisted that our prosperity was real, and that ours was a most advanced civilization.

Abroad, we were advertised as a prosperous, happy people, enjoying such a good standard of life that we deserved to be emulated.

Then, a nationalist movement arose, that refused to be trapped in colonialism. It sought international cooperation. It pointed out the lie of North American kindness in Puerto Rico. It is painful to confess, but even abroad there were Puerto Ricans who accepted the assignment of the government to continue maintaining its falsehoods.

With public opinion focused upon the nations of our race, the colonial legislature sent a cablegram to the Sixth American Conference, being held in Havana.

Everyone knows how that message produced such anger in the despot [President] Coolidge.

In his reply, although he continues to claim that Puerto Rico's progress is owing exclusively to North American leadership, he outlined the new propaganda of misery. When Puerto Rico was supposed to be prosperous and happy under the American flag, there was no reason to lower it. Now that the island is composed of suffering hungry people, there is no reason to lower the flag, either, because it is needed to help our people.

With the propaganda of prosperity worn out, the propaganda of misery is begun.

Then came the San Felipe hurricane, and colonial Governor Roosevelt, to justify our poverty.

This man, with the sense of a vulgar *barrio* politician, tries to pass as our friend; he goes up into the mountains, and takes photographs of our nudity and our hunger. Propaganda in the United States asks for public and private North American charity, alleging that we have no resources to attend to our needs.

The gullible fall quickly. The servile, as always, grow emotional over the voice of the master. Others fear to fight him. All applaud.

The Nationalist Party raises its voice of protest against this perverse propaganda, which demeans our prestige as a people.

The party says this, in the very legislature of the colony. It points out that there is neither public nor private charity in the United States for Puerto Rico. It affirms, with dignity, that if there were, we do not want it. We only demand justice for our nationhood.

The colonial governor asks for special powers from the legislature to solve the supposed crisis. He walks right into the Capitol building to give orders. No one dares protest against his presence.

He wants all municipal administration to be submitted to his complete authority—which is the only thing that is partially in Puerto Rican hands. There are suspicions. The legislature refuses.

But, he obtains from the legislature the creation of various bureaus that will function under his direct command. They are too important to be located in any department of the cabinet. . . .

He speaks of industrializing the country. Everyone is confounded by such a pleasing hope.

He introduces the party leaders in the legislature to the Davidson Brothers, as our saviors. These newcomers are going to build, Roosevelt says, a great refrigeration plant for native fruits; they have many millions of dollars, and they can distribute many millions.

But the Legislature must give them 6,000 square meters of land on San Juan's waterfront, to build the great docks that will permit the entry of large ships. The solvency of Davidson Brothers is investigated. They are incorporated in Florida with a capital of $25,000.

We have just been informed that these gentlemen are mere agents for the *yanqui* octopus, the United Fruit Company, and now we understand the presence in San Juan of a representative of United Fruit.

We say that we shall not permit our misery to be used as an excuse to rob us. The industrialization gets off to a bad start.

Now, Roosevelt tries to make us believe that the salvation of Puerto Rico depends upon a donation of $3,000,000 from the United States Congress, which has always begrudged the expenditure of a cent. . . .

Three million! What good are three million for solving a national crisis? Let us stop this farce. . . .

And now we have the report of the Brookings Institute. Its publication coincides with the presence of Roosevelt in the United States.

This surprises no one who understands something of the *yanqui* propaganda system.

The "experts" paint a gloomy picture. They recommend drastic measures to solve the crisis. Let us see a few: Eliminate the colonial senate!

In practice, this body has never existed. It has always submitted to the will of the colonial governor. . . .

Since the colonial legislature is a comedy, accepted until now, according to the Institute, it would not be surprising if it accepted bare-faced despotism.

It is dangerous to maintain a comedy, if you give serious actors the opportunity to convert it into a tragedy.

Restrict municipal power, increase the direct central power

emanating from Washington, etc., etc., are measures necessary for our salvation, according to these "experts."

The important thing is to legalize *latifundismo* [they say]. The law restricting land ownership to 500 acres should be eliminated, because it no longer exists. The colonial legislature never enforced it.

Let Puerto Rico be a factory. Peons, foremen, and cheap policemen are needed. A factory needs neither a legislature nor political power.

We must economize. Get rid of superfluous jobs. When all of Puerto Rico's wealth passes to the invaders, they, for the first time, will have to carry the entire weight of the budget. There will no longer be natives to cover up their expenses.

Public power will openly be a department of the administration of the factory.

Puerto Rico will be another Hawaii. Puerto Ricans will be peons, foremen, and policemen, to guarantee the invaders the enjoyment of our riches, and to oppose any complaints that might arise.

And, still, some people dare plead for tolerance of the invader. The time has come to apply sanctions against those who cooperate with the invader.

There is misery, but not for lack of resources.

The monopolizing of these resources must be discouraged. We must distribute them among our people. The legion of landowners that we had in 1898 must rise again.

The Nationalist Party is not surprised by the declarations of the Brookings Institute. We know the maquinations [sic] of *yanqui* propaganda. . . .

The politicians not in our party must be warned that the Puerto Rican nation demands the immediate suppression of this regime, and it will not permit itself to be disoriented in its effort to definitely end this situation.

We shall not tolerate feigned acts of rebelliousness. If there is sincerity—as is to be expected—before this great collective tragedy, why not call together immediately the general assemblies of each party, and resolve to demand recognition of our right to constitute a free, independent nation? The Puerto Rican nation demands definite action from those who pretend to be her representatives.

REBELLION IN PUERTO RICO

[In 1933, an eminent
U.S. historian described the situation in "our one Latin American colony
[which] would without question vote to leave us tomorrow if given a
chance." His article is a strong indictment of the patronage system employed in appointing overseas representatives of the U.S. Government.]

Two of the
smaller Atlantic islands—Manhattan and Puerto Rico—now have a
common bond. President Roosevelt gave both to Postmaster Farley.
Farley picked Joseph McKee to rule Manhattan and Robert Gore
to rule Puerto Rico. Both islands rebelled; Manhattan has achieved
a rousing success, and Puerto Rico will probably soon rid itself
of Gore.

In the long story of American ineptitude in Puerto Rico the last
chapter must be written down as the most melancholy. For thirty-
five years we have extended what General Miles termed in 1898
"the fostering arm of a nation of free people." The governors
bestowed by this fostering arm have usually been gentlemen of
good intentions; they have perhaps been deserving of political
favors; they have rarely been distinguished for their ability. The
worst was Mont Reilly, Harding's gift; the best, Theodore Roosevelt, Hoover's appointee; the dullest and most pathetic, Robert
Gore, lifted from oblivion by Farley and about to be retired to
oblivion by the grace of God, supported by the rage of the Puerto
Rican people.

The case of Robert Gore might be forgotten were there not
danger that the President may absent-mindedly allow his postmaster to repeat the performance. That cannot be, and the record
must contain the entry showing the price which we exact from
our subject people in Puerto Rico in the name of political ex-
pediency. Mr. Gore had made money in Florida and spent large
sums on the Roosevelt cause. He was given Puerto Rico. True, he
had other qualifications—genuine human sympathy and vestigial
traces of a liberalism acquired in the days of Eugene Debs. He
went to Puerto Rico in the sincere hope of translating the ethical
ideals of the New Deal into practical terms for the island. He saw

From Hubert Herring, "Rebellion in Puerto Rico," *The Nation*, CXXXVII
(Nov. 29, 1933), pp. 618–19.

the struggle between the possessors and the dispossessed. He wanted to do something about it. That from the beginning he was unable to obtain results commensurate with his sympathies was because of defects of the head, not the heart.

It is reported that when he was appointed, Mr. Gore was not quite sure where Puerto Rico was. After a talk with him, it is clear to me that he is still confused on that point. Someone in Washington, someone near the Great White Throne, told Mr. Gore that the Puerto Ricans were children, and that the wise governor would treat them as children. The unnamed misinformant should be warned not to make that mistake again. Whatever may be said of the Puerto Ricans, they are not children. For 400 years they served Spain. Other colonies revolted and escaped, but Puerto Rico was peaceful and small. The Puerto Ricans had recourse to politics, and they became expert. They outplayed Spanish governors and cabinets systematically and malevolently. Mr. Gore arrived with his trunkload of colored beads; the politicians took his beads away from him, they took everything from him, and he is returning to the United States, unhappy and sick, with no glimmer of an idea what happened in this island, seemingly so innocent and peaceful. He is, however, obsessed by the conviction that the island is seething with a dreadful thing which he calls "anti-Americanism." Those who oppose him are perforce "anti-Americans."

From the beginning Mr. Gore talked and played politics. His predecessor, Theodore Roosevelt, had escaped that pitfall; he had talked about the suffering children, about the exploited needle-workers, about the plight of the sugar workers. But Gore put his head into the political trap, and it clamped down with a dull crunching of gubernatorial bones. The complicated political picture includes three major parties: first, the Union Republicans, composed of the respectable people who own things or work for people who own things, the lawyers, doctors, and business men; second, the Socialists, of a breed which has forgotten Karl Marx and thinks William Green a labor leader. They are a pathetically ineffective but honest group, sincerely working for the improvement of the lot of the workers. Their greatest spiritual handicap is too long and too close association with the American Federation of Labor. Third, there are the Liberals, a new hopper into which has been gathered a miscellaneous collection of old conservatives and young liberals. For the most part they are the habitual follow-ers of Antonio Barceló, the most picturesque politician of the island, honest, magnetic, an opportunistic patriot. The chief plank in the Liberal platform is insular independence, and it is upheld honestly and tenaciously by the rank and file of the younger leaders in the group. The first two of these parties are at present united against Barceló's Liberals. This coalition received 210,000 votes in the last election, against the Liberals' 175,000, thereby winning control of the Congress. Gore, innocently thinking that things are as they seem, decided to be realistic and to play ball with the coalition. He forgot its complete artificiality and seemed not to realize that while Barceló and his party were for the moment submerged they have an obstinate capacity for rising again. Gore played the coalition game and showed decided animosity toward the Liberals. This animosity was natural to a man of Gore's type. The Liberals were "anti-American." They wished to have Spanish taught as the language of the island, and they proposed at the earliest possible moment to pull down the Stars and Stripes. His distaste was promptly reciprocated. Unfortunately for Gore, the Liberals have several men who know how to express distaste in stirring fashion. One of them is Luis Muñoz Marin. The columns of *La Democracia* have kept Mr. Gore awake nights. Nothing has been left unsaid, and Mr. Gore gave a clever editor plenty of things to say.

The first too astute political move of the new governor was a requirement that all new appointments should be filed with undated resignations. The inevitable storm aroused by this affront to the dignity of appointees was met by a blanket denial of the order from Gore. Whereupon Barceló's *La Democracia* came out with a streaming headline in English. "Governor Gore, you are a damn liar!" Muñoz Marin in his editorial suggested that the Governor bring a libel suit. The Governor didn't.

The patronage question came next. Gore had reason to know that to the victors belong the spoils. He had profited under that accepted principle. The Democratic Party is represented in Puerto Rico by a select group of 175 hopeful Democrats. President Roosevelt owed much to this group. Their six votes in the convention that nominated him were his from the first day. Farley saw to that. The local leaders of this valiant band were quick to press their claims. One Mrs. Whittemore was open-minded on the subject of being appointed governor. Failing in that, she revealed her willingness to serve as commissioner of education. This post was held by José Padín, whom Theodore Roosevelt had persuaded to give up a more lucrative business post in order to take it. Padín had made a conspicuous success, and he was acclaimed wherever educators foregathered. From the beginning Gore showed marked dislike for Padín. Padín, it seemed, spoke Spanish, approved of teaching Spanish, had no interest in politics, refused to allow the politicians to meddle with his schools—obviously he was "anti-American." A cable from Washington requested Padín's resignation. Things looked bright for the Mrs. Whittemore who had helped to elect Roosevelt. Then the storm broke. Almost everyone in Puerto Rico who knew or cared about schools wrote or wired to Washington. American educators entered the lists and told the President in unmistakable words exactly what they thought of paying party debts with the schools of Puerto Rican children. Padín is still commissioner, and Farley had to find other jobs for his staunch Puerto Rican henchmen. Mrs. Whittemore was given the post of collector of internal revenue, Mr. Horton of attorney-general, Mrs. Dooley of chief of immigration—all well-paying jobs which should have gone to more competent Puerto Ricans.

The most spectacular scene—and probably the last in which Gore will play a part—was staged on the campus of the University of Puerto Rico in Río Piedras. The university has been the football of island politics ever since it was founded, but under the able direction of Carlos Chardón, a brilliant scientist and able executive, it has made steady progress. It is the proud center of island culture and is dear to Puerto Rican hearts. It symbolizes the spiritual independence of the people in the face of alien domination. Faculty, students, alumni, and islanders generally have repeatedly demanded that the politicians keep their hands off. The Governor soon gave evidence of suspecting the university. It too was put on the anti-American list. A place on the board of trustees became vacant, and it was the Governor's duty to make an appointment. He has wide latitude under the law, the only requirement being that the nominee must have made a name in the arts, in science, or in letters. Gore appointed Alonso Torres, an active politician, a congressman, a labor leader, a Socialist, an honest and zealous protagonist for the workers of the island. The appointment was inspired by two motives, one political and one emotional. Torres was a leader in the dominant coalition, chairman of the finance committee of the house. Furthermore, he was a recognized leader of labor, and Gore thought that he was striking a blow for the dispossessed by making the appointment. If it had been a clear case of appointing a labor man to a place on the university board, Gore might well have been applauded, but the case was not clear. The appointment was definitely political. The coalition was determined to control the university and to "Americanize" it. Further, Torres did not qualify as competent in the field of arts, science, or letters. He had on numerous occasions expressed his dislike of the university. His literary efforts were brought out to confound him, especially the report of an economic commission of which he had been chairman. Included among the proposals for the betterment of economic conditions in the island was one which suggested the possibility of raising nightingales, these to be trained to sing the Star Spangled Banner and to be sold in the United States for fifty dollars each. The appointment of Torres evoked a cry of rage from students and alumni, parents and friends. It was the *cause célèbre* which solidified the island against the Governor. A delegation of students sought an appointment with the Governor, but was refused. The students paraded with a coffin labeled *Cultura*, and in the shadow of the Governor's home shed tears

over the bier. They sent three girls with a copy of a book of eti-
quette for Mr. Gore. They called an assembly and voted a student
strike. The Governor broke into a cold sweat. Here was anarchy,
insubordination, ingratitude, and—anti-Americanism. He decided
to call out the militia, but was dissuaded by men of calmer mind.
He decided to close the university altogether, but someone reminded him of Machado. In the meantime the students laughed
and marched and sang. They campaigned throughout the island.
Alumni and parents joined forces with them. Chancellor Chardón
kept his head. Commissioner Riggs of the insular police talked
with the boys and suggested that all retain their sense of humor,
and the university voted a recess of two weeks. The Governor
ordered extra guards for his house, and the two weeks went by.
Torres, under orders, or out of his own wisdom, resigned. The
students went back to work. They had captured the respect of
practically all sections of the population, for they had expressed
the stored-up resentment against a man who presumed to ride
rough-shod over the dignity and self-respect of the island. They
won the strike, and more. They made it certain that Governor
Gore must retire.

The most heartening experience one can have in Puerto Rico is a
talk with the leaders of the student directory. I have just talked
for three hours with five of them. They are young men of poise and
idealism. They stand out in welcome contrast to Puerto Rican old-
guard politicians. They are thinking in fundamental economic and
social terms of the island's future. Their minds are not closed.
Many of them believe that Puerto Rico should be allowed to work
out its destiny as a separate nation. They have not been "Americanized," and I hope they will not be. The word has a bad con-
notation in Puerto Rico.

I regret the necessity of writing these words about Robert Gore,
but he represents a political habit which must be rooted out. He
has gone far toward undoing the excellent work of Theodore
Roosevelt in building up relations of mutual respect between the
island and the mainland. Yet the fault is not primarily Gore's.
The real culprit is Postmaster-General Farley together with the
spoils system of which he is belated administrator.

On the eve of the Seventh Pan-American Conference in Montevideo it is fitting that the Administration take swift measures to
make honorable amend to the Puerto Ricans. The Latin American
peoples question our good intentions. Puerto Rico is a test of the
reality of those intentions. We have failed miserably there during
the greater part of thirty-five years. Our one Latin American colony
would without question vote to leave us tomorrow if given a
chance. It is a sorry commentary on our handling of the island's
affairs.

VIOLENCE AND NATIONALISM

[On Sunday, February 23, 1936, Puerto Rico's insular police chief, E. Francis Riggs—an American—was shot to death by two young Nationalists while he walked to church in San Juan. The youths, Elías Beauchamp and Hiram Rosado, were taken to the police station and shot to death but not before one of them posed solemnly for a news photographer outside and proferred a stiff military salute. It was a clearcut political assassination, causing severe repercussions on the island and in Washington.

Soon afterward, legislation was proposed in Congress to grant independence to Puerto Rico. This caused a furor on the island, because the terms of separation were considered punitive, even by many independence advocates. For example, after four decades of colonialism, the island would have to bear the full brunt of U.S. tariffs in four years.

A prominent U.S. magazine called Washington's "offer to free Puerto Rico . . . little more than window trimming for the coming Pan American conference." *

"The best-informed authorities in this country," the article went on to say, "feel confident that Puerto Rico cannot afford to sever its connections with the country under the terms of this proposal."

The article adds that "Our naval base on the island would be all that would remain of American control." That, apparently, was not negotiable.

"Puerto Rico is almost entirely dependent on the United States as a market outlet . . . due to a policy carefully cultivated over the past years. . . . The new bill . . . will . . . give the United States a fresh slate to deal firmly with a terroristic minority without being accused of being an imperialistic oppressor by the rest of Latin America," the article concludes.

Tension continued in Puerto Rico, as the Nationalists pressed their demands for independence, and the island government reacted by taking repressive measures. Perhaps the most infamous moment of this period is the so-called Ponce Massacre, which occurred on Palm Sunday of 1937, when more than twenty persons were killed and 150 wounded on Ponce's Marina Street as the Nationalists began a parade. Many different versions of the carnage were offered, and an official of the American Civil Liberties Union was asked to head a commission that would investigate. Here, he summarizes the results of the inquiry.]

* *Business Week*, May 2, 1936, pp. 41, 43. The reference was to a conference in Buenos Aires, "to prove to the Latin American countries . . . that the United States has no intention of forcing its sovereignty over any territory when the people in those lands no longer wish it."

Arthur Garfield Hays, "Defending Justice in Puerto Rico," *The Nation*, CXLIV (June 5, 1937), p. 647.

In the fall
of 1935 five members of the Nationalist Party of Puerto Rico sought
to make their way to a meeting which students at the Puerto Rico
University were to hold to protest against certain remarks made
by Pedro Albizu Campos, the Nationalist leader. The story is that
the Nationalists were stopped by the police, that they shot at the
police, and that, as a result of the fracas, four of the five Nationalists in the automobile were killed. It was said that they carried bombs and guns.

In February, 1936, Colonel Riggs, head of the insular police, was
assassinated by two Nationalists. The assassins were seized and,
while in the hands of the police, were shot. Although Colonel
Riggs was popular with the Puerto Ricans and was himself a be-
liever in independence, the cold-blooded murder of the two Puerto
Rican "martyrs" aroused not only the Nationalists but great numbers of Puerto Ricans who opposed Nationalist methods. Americans thought of the murder of Colonel Riggs; Puerto Ricans
thought of the murder of the two assassins.

Albizu Campos and other Nationalist leaders were charged with
conspiracy to overthrow the government of the United States and
later, in July, 1936, were convicted and sentenced to six years in
jail. Governor Blanton Winship apparently felt it was necessary to
deal with the Nationalists with a heavy hand and acted to suppress
not only those who were militantly demanding Puerto Rican freedom but also a united front of groups opposed to the conviction of
Albizu Campos. Parades and meetings of Nationalists and other
protesting groups were prohibited. The Puerto Ricans take seriously their Organic Act guaranteeing the rights of free speech and
assemblage, and resentment grew apace.

On March 21, 1937, the Nationalists announced that they would
hold a parade and meeting in the town of Ponce. A permit was
first given by the mayor of the town. At the last moment it was
canceled. The insular police commanded by Colonel Orbeta, who
was acting under orders of the Governor, prohibited the parade
as it was about to start. The national hymn of Puerto Rico was
played, the crowd cheered, the parade advanced. Suddenly there
was shooting, and when it was all over, it appeared that the casualties were 20 killed—including those who died later, among whom
were two police officers—and from 150 to 200 wounded, among,
among whom were 6 police officers.

Governor Winship reported to Washington that several "divisions" of the so-called "Army of Liberation" had arranged a concentration in the town of Ponce; that a parade was forbidden;
that nevertheless the Nationalists insisted upon proceeding; that
when the command "Forward march!" was given, a Nationalist
fired a shot killing a policeman on the left of the chief of police
and another Nationalist fired a shot killing a policeman on the

right of the chief of police; that shooting then broke out from all sides as well as from roofs and balconies where Nationalists were stationed; and that casualties resulted. He ended his report by commending the patience and consideration of the police.

The leading citizens of Ponce formed a committee of prominent citizens of San Juan and asked that they make an investigation. The proposed commission consisted of Emilio Belaval, president of the Athenaeum, who acted as secretary; Mariano Acosta Velarde, president of the Puerto Rican Bar Association; Lorenzo Pineiro, president of the Teachers' Association; Dr. Manuel Díaz García, president of the Puerto Rican Medical Association; Antonio Ayuso, editor of the *Imparciale*; Francisco M. Zeno, editor of the *Correspondencia*; and Davila-Ricci, assistant editor of the *Mondo*. None of the commission were Nationalists. Request was made to the American Civil Liberties Union to appoint the chairman of the commission, and the writer was so appointed. The commission undertook to investigate not only the events in Ponce on March 21 but the general subject of civil rights and liberties in Puerto Rico.

Hearings were held at Ponce beginning Friday, May 14, and were thereafter adjourned to San Juan. Evidence as to what happened on March 21 was adduced not only from disinterested eyewitnesses but from a series of photographs which tell the story in incontestable fashion. Photographs show that the "divisions" of the "Army of Liberation" consisted of about eighty young men wearing black blouses and white trousers, about twelve girls dressed in white as nurses, and a brass band of about six pieces. The Nationalists, known as "cadets," carried no arms; the girls did not even have Red Cross kits.

A photograph shows the scene just before the shooting. About eighteen policemen armed with revolvers, shotguns, and tear-gas bombs, stood in front of the line of these eighty boys and twelve girls; about twenty policemen armed with Thompson submachineguns were in the rear; a number of armed police were on the street along the side; a crowd of men, women, and children stood across the way watching the parade. The Nationalists had brought their wives, mothers, and children along to see the parade. The evidence showed that there was no shooting whatever from any roofs or balconies, and this was confirmed by the district attorney of Ponce, Pérez Marchand, who made the first investigation and who later retired as district attorney because, according to him, he was not given a free hand in his inquiries. One of the photographs shows a policeman actually firing at the crowd and other policemen drawing their guns, all in menacing posture. The police who were wounded or killed seem to have been caught in a cross fire.

The commission unanimously reported that the people of Puerto

Rico have properly described the occurrence as the "massacre of Ponce."

I shall never forget the photograph of those cadets whom newspapers have described as "ruffians" and "gangsters," standing quietly with their hands at their sides waiting to be shot—defenseless but not one of them running away.

Part VIII

"¡JALDA ARRIBA!"

He [Muñoz Marín] is, more and more, a
Puritan in Babylon. He likes to dream of
American capitalism as a non-sacred cow
to be rationally utilized by rational Puerto
Ricans. He fails to see that, in grim reality,
it is a raucous tiger not easily tamed.

—GORDON LEWIS, *San Juan Review*,
October, 1964, p. 47.

Puerto Rico took
a giant leap forward during the two decades that followed World War II.
A poor, rural island transformed itself into a "semideveloped" society;
factories replaced farms as the chief means to earn a living; schools and
medical care were made available to virtually all citizens, a large middle
class emerged, cars clogged new cement highways, and thousands of
tourists streamed in each year, to bask in the Caribbean sun.

There were still awful slums, and long lines of unemployed, but
Puerto Rico had thrust itself into the modern world.

Why all this happened precisely when it did is a complex story. After
World War II, the U.S. economy enjoyed an unheralded boom, and spill-
over profits were used by mainland investors to build factories abroad;
many of them chose Puerto Rico, which offered liberal tax benefits—
under the "Operation Bootstrap" industrialization program—and a plentiful supply of jobless people, willing to work for low wages.

The once dormant economy was also spurred upward by Puerto Rican
GIs returning from the war, who received federal loans for housing, and
grants for education. It was stimulated, too, by the availability of FHA
mortgages for homes, and easy credit plans for consumer purchases.

Puerto Rico was guided through this period of rapid change by the
left-of-center Popular Democratic Party, which took power in the elections of 1940, and ran the government for the next twenty-eight years.
Senator (later Governor) Luis Muñoz Marín and his colleagues, many of
whom favored independence, undertook bold programs designed to provide decent jobs, housing, and education for the island's impoverished
majority. Between 1940 and 1970, personal income per year spiraled from

$118 to $1,200; this was a dramatic improvement, even when one takes into account the rise in living costs, and the fact that income was not distributed on a wholly equitable basis.

It is most interesting to note that Puerto Rico progressed in the same proportion as its powers of home rule increased.

Not until 1941 did the United States appoint a governor—Rexford Guy Tugwell—who was competent, imaginative, and sympathetic to the aims of the elected Puerto Rican leaders in the island government. Not until 1948 was Puerto Rico allowed to elect its own native governor. And it was not until 1952 that Puerto Rico was granted more self-rule, under the Commonwealth form of government.

Puerto Rico made its greatest economic progress in the 1950's and 1960's, at a time when Puerto Ricans—not Americans—directed the island's local affairs.*

There are numerous books and shorter studies that chronicle the Muñoz era. Here, we shall look at a few selections that describe highlights of the time when ¡jalda arriba!—up the hill!—was coined as a battle cry against poverty and social injustice.

* A number of Americans lent their expertise as consultants and aides, but all key cabinet and legislative posts were held by Puerto Ricans.

"A TIME OF NATIONAL CRISIS"

[In 1939, President Franklin D. Roosevelt chose a military man—Admiral William D. Leahy —to govern Puerto Rico; America was readying itself for war with Germany and Japan. Almost immediately, Congress appropriated $30 million to build large air and naval bases on the island, in order to shield the Panama Canal.

The threat of global war dwarfed Puerto Rico's internal problems, which were never of great concern to Washington. Even a liberal U.S. magazine said at the time: "If, in the interest of national defense, Puerto Rico must be turned over to military rule, we can think of no better choice [than Admiral Leahy]. Naturally, we would prefer a world in which such a disposition of Puerto Rico was unnecessary." *

Puerto Rico was well on its way to becoming an island fortress, much as it was during Spain's heyday, by the time Admiral Leahy was reassigned. Soon afterwards, President Roosevelt appointed Rexford Guy Tugwell, a member of his "Brain Trust," to govern the island. At the same time, the zealous, reform-minded "young Turks" of the Popular Democratic Party had taken power in the insular elections. Their leader was Senator Luis Muñoz Marín. Tugwell, who governed from 1941 through 1946, worked closely with Muñoz in laying the groundwork for an ambitious socio-economic reform plan. Tugwell's writings offer perhaps one of the most intimate accounts of relations between Puerto Rico and the federal government. Here, he explains his—and President Roosevelt's—views on the island's strategic importance during wartime, and on its future political development. Italics are added for emphasis.]

Because no Colonial Office existed to assume the complex administrative responsibilities involved in the relationship [with Puerto Rico], the President was quite unable to see to it that Puerto Rican interests were effectively protected. The power to interfere was willfully retained by the Congress and protected by refusal to establish an adequate office in the executive establishment. Actually a Bureau of Insular Affairs was set up in the War Department to look after both Puerto Rico and the Philippines when they were occupied, and military Governors were appointed. That Bureau in the War Department continued, right down to 1934, when President Roose-

* *New Republic*, XCIX (May 24, 1939), p. 58.

From Rexford Guy Tugwell, *The Art of Politics* (New York: Doubleday, 1958), pp. 36, 147–51. Reprinted with permission.

velt moved it to Interior—to be all there was of colonial administration in the executive branch of the federal government. . . .

Before 1934 a certain change had taken place in the formal
relationship—the Jones Act of 1917 had modified the Foraker
Act of 1900. As to this, *it should not escape notice that 1917 was
again a time of national crisis, when certain grudging concessions
could be got from an unwilling Congress on the plea of national
security. There would not be another change until World War II,
when the same arguments would again apply—that the principles
we professed to be fighting for were very poorly observed in our
own dependencies, and that the loyalty of Puerto Ricans was
important.* . . .

I was inclined at first to consider immediate independence, or
at least an announcement of eventual independence, as necessary.
About this I had several talks with the President [Roosevelt]. He
was against it. It was not that he thought the Puerto Rican affilia-
tion of any advantage to the United States, except in a *strategic
sense*, but that he felt we had a serious obligation we had not dis-
charged. The most I could get from him was a willingness to
give way to advance. It seemed to me that unless Puerto Ricans
were to accept independence—which I felt certain Congress would
grant for the asking—they must move toward a more agreeable
status than now existed.

The attitude of President Roosevelt toward Puerto Rico was
partly, then, shaped by misinformation. But partly, also, it came
from the same general impulse that led him to prefer retired
admirals and generals as Governors for all non-self-governing
areas. I had had to join [Harold] Ickes in a fervent plea in 1934
to prevent the President from returning the Virgin Islands to the
Navy administration; and the smaller Pacific possessions never
had a civilian government during his time. The imperialist ideas
in his mind were still warring with more recent ones. When he
had been Assistant Secretary of the Navy he had visited Haiti
and Santo Domingo on a historic occasion and had taken credit
in his 1920 campaign for the vice-presidency—unjustifiably—for
bringing order to these republics by way of the Marines and new
constitutions. There was an admiral concealed somewhere in
Roosevelt and had been, I suppose, ever since his ambition for
a naval career had been thwarted by his father. . . .

. . . . Actually Muñoz's ambitions for Puerto Rico had their
climax in Truman's acquiescence—and, perhaps it should be said,
his ignorance. It would not be fair to say that Muñoz took
advantage of the President's lack of experience; nevertheless,
Truman was willing to have the United States, at that time,
assume the generous posture involved in the Commonwealth status
without many safeguards. *This did not, and could not, have
happened with Roosevelt's consent.*

Looking at Puerto Rico as a problem for the United States, it is well to recall that Muñoz happened to be rising to power when a change of attitude was in process. Until the end of the war in 1945, the dominant consideration had been a *strategic one.* The military dispositions of the decade preceding had naturally been determined by the weapons available, and the source, the objective, and the direction of the possible attack. The source was Germany, the objective was the Panama Canal, and the direction was through the Caribbean island arc from Florida to Trinidad. In this arc *Puerto Rico was central. Bases there were, in the strict sense, strategic and essential. Puerto Rico therefore had to be maintained as a controlled and, if possible, friendly base. As wartime Governor, this was my first responsibility.*

But when the African invasion was established, there was a complete change, somewhat tardily acknowledged by the military bureaucracy, but apparent at'once to one with such a responsibility as mine. There was no longer any possibility of actual invasion, although the submarine blockade was still a serious problem; and the development of new weapons, together with the acceleration in airplane range and speed, made it unlikely that Puerto Rico would ever again be strategically important even if there should be another threat to the United States from the east. The significance of this was that policy could be revised. And it was then that I laid before President Roosevelt my analysis of the change and my proposals for new relationships.

In general I urged that local government should be freed from outside controls. I told the President he was quite wrong to think of the Puerto Ricans as politically immature or incapable of administering their own affairs. They were, in fact, more advanced than many of the states of our Union. We ought to begin successive changes as rapidly as the Congress could be got to grant them. Specifically we ought to begin at once with the elective governorship, proceeding to a status somewhat short of full statehood—it could not be full because for a long time more economic assistance would be needed than the federal government gives to the states. We need not worry about local protection for military bases; they were no longer necessary to our defense. . . .

While I was arguing thus with President Roosevelt, Muñoz was consolidating his political power. . . . He was extremely cautious about encouraging hopes. He had so little faith that anything would happen that he isolated the question of status and for years refused to discuss it. He even had the reluctance I have mentioned to serve on the committee I persuaded the President to set up for making the first recommendations to Congress. He balked badly at my proposals and my timetable. Not only that, he made up his mind that Roosevelt would be defeated in 1944, as he had similarly made up his mind in 1940, and this confused his planning. He succeeded in alienating both Secretary Ickes and President Roosevelt, and neither of them made any energetic effort to implement the committee's recommendations about the governorship.

But President Roosevelt was re-elected. Then, within a few months, he was succeeded by the former Senator from Missouri. . . . [In 1946] Truman showed an active interest. He saw half the problem—the need for autonomy; but he missed the other half—the continuing interest of the nation—thus reversing Roosevelt, who saw the half Truman did not see but missed the rest. . . .

"PUERTO RICO IS THE CENTER"

[President Roosevelt, in 1943, supported an unsuccessful bill to amend the law that defined U.S.-Puerto Rican relations, in order to allow the people to elect their own governor. In his message to a Congressional committee, Roosevelt reaffirmed the importance of Puerto Rico as the "center" of an "island shield" to protect the Panama Canal. "There is no reason why their Governor and other officials should continue to be appointed from without," he said. But he was quick to add that "the ultimate power of Congress" would not be altered. Italics are added for emphasis.]

During the 45 years which have passed since the occupation of the island by the United States the economic situation of the Puerto Rican people, although materially improved in some respects, has not changed in essential character. Instead of development toward economic self-reliance, there has been a steady tendency to become more dependent upon outside markets for disposal of the single great crop—sugar—and upon outside sources for food, clothing, building materials, and most of the other necessities. Partly because of economic and geographical factors and partly because of tariff preferences and shipping laws, these relationships, are, by now, almost wholly with the continental United States. . . .

Selections in this chapter:
1. From U.S. Congress, House, Committee on Insular Affairs. To amend the act to provide a civil government for Puerto Rico. S. 1407. August 26, 1944, pp. 14–15.
2. From U.S. Congress, Senate, Subcommittee of the Committee on Territories and Insular Affairs, Hearings on § 1407, A Bill to Amend the Organic Act of Puerto Rico. 78th Congress, 1st Session, 1943, p. 364.

During the 45 years of our sovereignty, the elements of world military and naval strategy have changed also. When the island was brought under our flag, the Panama Canal had not yet been dug, and the airplane had not yet been invented. The Caribbean was something of a backwater in the broad current of world affairs. When the present war became imminent, however, it was obvious that the chain of islands running in a great arc from Florida to the shoulder of South America, enclosing the Caribbean Sea, formed a vast natural shield for the Panama Canal, suited in distance and conformation to the uses of the military plane. *And of this island shield, Puerto Rico is the center. Its possession or control by any foreign power—or even the remote threat of such possession —would be repugnant to the most elementary principles of national defense.*

It has long been the policy of the Government of the United States progressively to reinforce the machinery of self-government in its territories and island possessions. The principles for which we are now fighting require that we should recognize the right of all our citizens—whether continental or overseas—to the greatest possible degree of home rule and also of participation in the benefits and responsibilities of our Federal system.

Puerto Ricans of all political parties, however divergent their views as to the political future of the island, are united in asking for the right to elect their own Governor. I believe that they are entitled to it. . . . The fiscal relationship of the insular government to the Federal Government would not be altered, nor would the *ultimate power of Congress to legislate for the Territory.* The people of the island would, however, be given assurance of the intention of Congress to obtain the concurrence of the people of the island before imposing upon them any further changes in the Organic Act. . . .

[The question of granting real autonomy to Puerto Rico was never seriously entertained. When the elective governor amendment was discussed in 1943, Federal officials suggested that a U.S. High Commissioner might be appointed to serve as liaison with the Puerto Rican governor. When island officials objected to this, Abe Fortas, Undersecretary of the Interior, and later a U.S. Supreme Court Justice, impatiently shot back:]

The U.S. Government will continue to be supreme in Puerto Rico, and that is that. There just is not any question about it. We might just as well quit if we are not going to proceed on that basis, and you might as well all have that very clearly in mind that the United States, under this scheme, will continue to be supreme in Puerto Rico.

"WE HAD BETTER WAIT"

[In 1943, a bill
providing for Puerto Rican independence was also submitted to Congress. Testimony was heard from many persons, for and against. Vicente
Geigel-Polanco, Floor Leader of the Popular Democratic Party in the
Puerto Rican Senate, called the bill a "just, adequate, democratic, and
historically feasible solution to our problem of sovereignty." The island's
legislature, by unanimous vote, asked that "the colonial system of government be ended," and encouraged "free, democratic elections" so that
the status problem could be solved "by the free will of the people. of
Puerto Rico themselves." Congress, however, was heeding other voices,
such as that of John J. McCloy, U.S. Assistant Secretary of War.]

. . . We do not
consider it to be within our purview to comment on the political
wisdom of the independence of Puerto Rico at this time. We do
have rather strong feelings from a purely military point of view.

The bill . . . provides for . . . a transition of sovereignty during
the period of the war. For military reasons, we believe that to
be unwise. . . . I think perhaps the political disturbance that might
occur in connection with these various steps [of transition] would
be unwise during the war period.

I do not need to dwell upon the military significance of Puerto
Rico. . . . It is an outpost in our Caribbean defense; it is one of
the islands which is farthest removed from the Panama Canal,
and constitutes a bulwark in the defense of that area.

There are likewise some features of the bill that we think should
require elaboration. . . . We think some of the reservations that
are in there providing for the establishment of military installations should be broadened in a substantial degree. . . .

Senator HAYDEN. Mr. Chairman, I think there is considerable
force in what the secretary says, because you will remember that
although we took great care and trouble with respect to the bill
providing for the independence of the Philippines, it was afterwards
discovered that there were certain military installations in the

From U.S. Congress, Senate, Committee on Territories and Insular Affairs.
Puerto Rico. Hearings before the Committee on territories and insular affairs,
United States Senate, 78th Cong., 1st session, on S.952, a bill to provide for
the withdrawal of the sovereignty of the United States over the island of
Puerto Rico and for the recognition of its independence, and so forth. Wash-
ington, U.S. Government printing office, 1943, pp. 9–21.

islands that were transferred to the Government of the [Philippine] Commonwealth that might better have been retained by the United States.

Mr. McCLOY. That is quite true, and the same situation came up in Panama, which embarrassed us very much in this war.

The CHAIRMAN. We do not want to make that mistake the third time, so we are going to look to the War Department to clarify the defense features of this bill in every possible way.

Mr. McCLOY. But I also want to make it clear that even with that improvement in the bill, we think it unwise, from a military point of view, to pass the bill during wartime. . . .

The CHAIRMAN. In other words, your concern is to keep the status quo there during the period of hostilities?

Mr. McCLOY. That is right. I would like to make this suggestion also, that you do not limit it precisely to the date of the armistice. . . . We ought to have a "look-see" in regard to what the Caribbean area is at the end of the war, who occupies the adjacent islands, who is controlling the Atlantic, and so forth.

Senator VANDENBERG. . . . . How do you think our interests would be adversely affected by starting the processes [for independence] during the war? They still have elections there anyhow. They have heated political contests.

Mr. McCLOY. Well, a heated political contest in an area as limited as that is not too advisable in the course of a war, since the entire island is largely a garrison, and a contest on such a substantial issue as this might be most disturbing. . . .

Senator CHAVEZ. People get excited when they talk about independence, and it is liable to interfere with the general [defense] program.

Senator VANDENBERG. They get excited down there, anyway. . . .

The CHAIRMAN. I do not want to bring out military secrets, but I think we could generalize by saying there is a considerable amount of our Army and Air Force there from time to time. Is that true?

Mr. McCLOY. That is true. There is also a very substantial Puerto Rican Army. It is part of the American Army.

The CHAIRMAN. You are familiar, too, with the fact that the conditions in Puerto Rico for the last 10, 15, or 20 years, even going back to 25 years ago, have been—well, more or less in a turmoil?

Mr. McCLOY. Yes; so I understand.

The CHAIRMAN. There is more activity there politically, economically, and otherwise than you find in most places, but the amount of lawlessness, from a governmental standpoint, has been very, very, very small; is not that true?

Mr. McCLOY. That is my impression. . . .

The CHAIRMAN. You would not be opposed to it [independence]

from the standpoint of the War Department after the war period, is that correct?

Mr. McCLOY. With suitable protections, that is right.

Senator BONE. You would have no objection to this Government doing for Puerto Rico what was done for Cuba after the Spanish War?

Mr. McCLOY. With improvements, perhaps, on our military reservations—reservations in a general sense rather than the territory. . . .

Senator TAFT. Mr. Secretary, I do not understand your position exactly, because if it is unwise to have Puerto Rico independent during this war why isn't it unwise to have Puerto Rico independent at any time, as long as war is not insured against in some way? Will not Puerto Rico always occupy the same strategic position that it occupies in this war?

Mr. McCLOY. Well, it will . . . I suppose, speaking in a purely military vein, it would be always easier if we had sovereignty over any area, to make our military dispositions over that area. But those considerations are minor, or can be minor in the face of the general desire or of political considerations.

Senator TAFT. Puerto Rico occupies, does it not, today, a strategic position, a very key position in the defense of the Caribbean?

Mr. McCLOY. Yes.

Senator TAFT. Is there any reason why it will not always occupy that position?

Mr. McCLOY. It will always be a key position in the Caribbean.

Senator TAFT. Puerto Rico is about 35 miles wide by 100 miles long. In order to have an effective military and naval base, will not you require practically that much land to use for that base? For instance, you have the Borinquen Field at one end of the Island . . . you have the base at San Juan. How can you possibly have a military base at San Juan Harbor and still have San Juan the capital that is governed and ruled by an independent nation?

Mr. McCLOY. Well, perhaps I put too much faith in the reservations we write into the bill to give us free access between the two ends of the island. It is, as you say, not too large an area for our military dispositions in the event of war. . . .

Senator TAFT. You have enough troops there to make a large-size city. . . . Borinquen Field [now Ramey Air Force Base] is on the west end of the Island, a large new naval base at the east end of the Island [now Roosevelt Roads], and San Juan in between. . . . What I cannot see is how you can effectively permit an independent nation to be operated in a base so important in which you are using so many parts of the island. . . . I can understand a certain amount of autonomy, but I cannot understand how you can reconcile complete independence of the Island with the effective and necessary use of Puerto Rico for military control of the Caribbean.

Mr. McCLOY. Well, it depends on what you mean by complete independence. I do not think any area as small as that is completely independent if it has any soldiers of any foreign government on it, or if it has military installations of any size on it. . . .

Senator TAFT. . . . There are 25,000 trained Puerto Rico soldiers who are now in the American Army but who would immediately become a Puerto Rican army upon Puerto Rico obtaining independence . . . surrounding and operating between the different Army and Navy posts of the United States. . . .

The CHAIRMAN (to Mr. McCloy). Of course, what you are saying is even if the people of Puerto Rico want independence and even though they give you all the bases that you want, there might still arise a question where you would want a watershed or a valley.

Mr. McCLOY. Yes; or a right of access. . . .

The CHAIRMAN. So that, in the end you would rather have no independence at all. That is a logical conclusion, isn't it?

Mr. McCLOY. Yes; from a purely military point of view. The soldier wants to have a chance, without consulting anybody, to issue his orders. . . .

Mr. TAFT. I think the (War) Department might consider also the question of some kind of autonomous government under which we would retain control of foreign relations and military control of the island. I think the department, in making their general study of this question, might consider whether that condition was not more consistent with the military needs than complete independence when you make your final report.

The CHAIRMAN. I think that is a very good suggestion. . . . I do not mean to say we can get everything we want without hurting the Puerto Ricans somewhat or that they can get everything they want without minimizing our rights somewhat, but I think there is a fair field where the War Department can get substantially what it needs now, and that it thinks it must need in the future, without any impairment of the sovereignty of the Puerto Ricans if they do vote for independence. . . .

Senator BONE. So, if you want to give Puerto Rico independence with certain prescriptions in the bill as to military and naval installations and means of egress and ingress, a reservation of certain rights for the acquisition of watersheds, and the like, control over foreign affairs, and all other things incident to protecting ourselves against the disturbed conditions in the world today, those can be made by prescriptions in the legislative formula that you adopt; there is no doubt about that, is there?

Mr. McCLOY. I think there is no doubt about that.

Senator VANDENBERG. I disagree with that completely. I want

to make that perfectly plain. I think our experience in Panama proves it. There is something inherent in independence; there is something inherent in sovereignty which constantly arises. Any peacetime reservations you make are an infringement on that sovereignty and independence, and slowly but surely you will find, in spite of all the formulae you can write, that your reservations are gradually being eaten away.

Mr. McCLOY. The Senator used the word "status." I said "yes" to status. If he used the word "sovereignty," I think I would have had made a reservation. What the implication of the status that he sets up may be is another question.

Senator BONE. . . . I am not prepared to admit that the lawyers of Congress, together with the assistance they are able to get from the legal departments, are unable to work out a formula. . . . Here you are starting from scratch with a piece of white paper upon which you may write. Whether it is good or bad, I am not trying to say. I do not assume the Congress is capable of writing a prescription, in the event we decide Puerto Rico should have independence, in which I think you can preserve all the rights that the Puerto Rican Government wants. We know what we are likely to meet in the future in the way of air power and sea power, both on the surface and under the surface. I am not prepared to admit we cannot take a fresh sheet of white paper and write on it exactly what Congress wants to write. I think we can write that. I believe Congress would have the power to do it, but if it did, then it would not be independence.

The CHAIRMAN. Well, if they accepted it, then there would be a meeting of the minds. That is what we are after.

Senator VANDENBERG. For the time being.

The CHAIRMAN. I am not one of those . . . who believes you can write an independence bill and that forever after there never will be a dispute arise over the bill, but that, to me, is a minor point. The major objective is to protect America in that area and to give these people the God-given right to govern themselves if they want it.

Senator TAFT. Mr. Secretary, I want to suggest that the problem we meet here may be repeated hundredfold all over the world after the war, in the post-war settlement, and whether it is not better to hold up the determination of it until that time. Many islands throughout the world will have a semi-autonomous status. This is only one phase of the problem, it occurs to me. We had better wait and see what develops out of the treatment of colonies, territories, and islands after the war before we determine exactly what we ought to do with Puerto Rico. . . .

THE BARD OF POLITICS

[Between 1940 and 1968, while the United States was led by a Roosevelt, a Truman, an Eisenhower, a Kennedy, and a Johnson, in Puerto Rico, there was only Luis Muñoz Marín.*

Because Muñoz had been a poet and journalist in his early years, he was popularly referred to as *El Vate* [The Bard]. His literary talent notwithstanding, Muñoz's forte was politics, which he practiced with the flair and discipline of a fine poet. Muñoz had an uncanny rapport with the people, whether it be from the speaker's platform in the dusty plazas of the island's small towns, or in their rustic homes, where he sipped their home-grown coffee and listened sympathetically to their concerns. As a consummate politician, Muñoz gathered together a host of talented colleagues with differing ideologies and sensitive egos, and united them under a single party banner for three decades.

Born in 1898 (the same year of the U.S. invasion), Muñoz spent much of his youth on the American mainland; he was perfectly bilingual. He rose to power as head of the insular Senate in 1940, became Puerto Rico's first elected governor in 1948, and was the guiding spirit behind the establishment of the Commonwealth status in 1952. During his long, eventful career, Muñoz won international fame for his role in Puerto Rico's dramatic transformation.

Muñoz began as an advocate of independence and socialism, but as the years passed these goals were diluted by multiple pressures.

In the early 1940's, Puerto Rico launched "Operation Bootstrap," an ambitious program to create industrial jobs. In the first phase, the island government opened a small nucleus of factories that produced basic products such as cement (for homes and highways), glass (for rum bottles) and boxboard paper (for shipping export products). The government also bought the electric companies and vast tracts of land, set up a central planning agency and a development bank, and adopted a socialist-style approach to numerous other socio-economic problems.

But the obstacles to such a plan were many. It was soon realized that a few factories, even under optimum conditions, would not generate enough profits to build more factories and make a noticeable dent in unemployment. There was a shortage, too, of trained technicians, who are so essential to a large-scale manufacturing network.

Perhaps even more important, leaders in Congress and in the U.S. business world viewed Puerto Rico's "socialist experiment" as inimical to the free enterprise system.

* In the latter four years, 1964 to 1968, Roberto Sánchez Vilella governed the island. But he was hand-picked by Muñoz, who served in the Senate, led the Popular Democratic Party, and played a major role in the 1967 status plebiscite campaign.

San Juan Star, July 25, 1962, p. 18.

An influential American business writer reflected this concern when he described Puerto Rico's cement plant as "an ugly sign of growing bureaucracy and state socialism . . . frightening away investment capital." * In his hostile report, he called Puerto Rico's development plan "a Utopian-Marxist-Soviet dream," and sounded the alarm that "public money is being used to launch a new beef cattle product, and make Porto Rico independent of U.S. meat packers."

Considerable pressure, public and private, was put upon the island, and Puerto Rico soon sold away its factories to private interests. Instead, an aggressive promotion campaign was launched to attract U.S. factories, offering tax exemption and other inducements. (Since then, about 2,000 factories have opened, creating more than 100,000 direct jobs, and earning an average of 20 per cent profit yearly for their investors.)

Thus, Puerto Rico under Muñoz evolved into a hybrid of government welfare statism and laissez-faire capitalism; many essential services remained under public control, but private enterprise (largely absentee-owned) dominated manufacturing and commerce.

In politics, the same pragmatic course was followed. The federal government discouraged independence, and Muñoz felt that Puerto Rico had neither the military nor the economic strength to force the issue. Statehood had little support in Washington or San Juan. Faced by the *status quo* of colonialism, Muñoz, in the late 1940's, began to explore a midway course, a third alternative, that would hopefully achieve a dignified form of self-government for the island.

Muñoz has explained his rationale many times, perhaps best in the following speech, which was given on July 17, 1951, in the mountain town of Barranquitas, the birthplace and resting place of his father, Luis Muñoz Rivera.†

One year and one week later, on July 25, 1952, the Commonwealth status was formally inaugurated, and Puerto Rico became known as an *Estado Libre Asociado:* a "state" that was "free" and yet "associated" with the United States.

Advocates of independence and statehood called the new political formula a "perfumed" type of colonialism. The *independentistas* argued that Puerto Rico's "permanent union" to the United States under Commonwealth would never permit true sovereignty. The statehooders called Commonwealth an insidious trick, a way of allowing independence to sneak in "through the kitchen door."

Muñoz, near the end of his speech, emphasizes that "what we have done is to initiate a process of political creation," which "needs to grow."

How it will grow, and in what direction, is unclear. Muñoz and other spokesmen for Commonwealth believe that the present system can, and should, be perfected, allowing for more autonomy. The final answer, as Muñoz himself has said, rests with future generations.]

Language was given to man to enable him to make himself understood by his fellow man. But one of the frailties of language is that there are

* Emmett Crozier, *New York Herald Tribune,* Dec. 4, 1946.
† July 17 is a holiday in Puerto Rico, marking Muñoz Rivera's birth in 1829.

some words which for a time prevent understanding. In Puerto Rico *patria*—the homeland—has been such a word. At first blush this may seem strange, as there is no people of the earth who love their native land more profoundly than do the people of Puerto Rico.

To the Puerto Rican, *patria* is the colors of the landscape, the change of seasons, the smell of the earth wet with fresh rain, the voice of the streams, the crash of the ocean against the shore, the fruits, the songs, the habits of work and of leisure, the typical dishes for special occasions and the meager ones for everyday, the flowers, the valleys, and the pathways. But even more than these things, *patria* is the people: their way of life, spirit, folkways, customs, their way of getting along with each other. Without these latter things *patria* is only a name, an abstraction, a bit of scenery. But with them it is an integral whole: "the homeland *and* the people." Those who profess to love their country while taking an irresponsible attitude towards the destiny of its people suffer from spiritual confusion. The implication of their attitude is that we must save the country even though we destroy the people!

Love of country must mean love of all of the country—both the *patria* and the people. But some of us confused love of the homeland with the narrow and bitter concept of the national state. We felt that love of Puerto Rico has as a necessary corollary the desire for separate independence. We had not yet comprehended that no law, divine or human, commands that countries must be suspicious, vain, and hostile, that they must live separate from other countries whose peoples are a part of the broad equality which the Lord created on the earth. Because of the rigidity of our thinking, we could not disentangle the concept of love for our country from the fixed idea of separate independence. Anything other than independence seemed to clash with our love for Puerto Rico.

The Dawning Light

The difficult process of clarifying these ideas began when the Tydings bill was introduced in Congress in 1936. On the one hand this bill offered the separate independence for which many of us had asked because of our feeling for the abstract idea of the *patria*. On the other hand, it condemned the people of our homeland to extreme poverty from which they could never hope to escape. Suddenly what had seemed to be an integral idea—the homeland and separate independence—turned out to be two conflicting ideas: one, acceptable as an abstract idea; the other, a mortal enemy of the people. The Tydings bill would have made Puerto Rico independent; but it would have shackled the people with economic misery.

It was not easy to change our views on this subject. Our minds could grasp the point that if we could have separate independence only under the economic conditions of the Tydings bill it would be not independence but a living death of hopeless poverty for Puerto Rico. Yet our emotions led us to search for other economic conditions under which independence would be possible.

At the time, our emotions were stronger than our powers of reasoning. Rationalization works where understanding is the servant, instead of the master, of emotion. Instead of using reasoning objectively to seek the truth, we used it to justify our emotions. Just as one might confuse the glittering uniform of a doorkeeper with that of a king, our powers of reasoning were led astray by rationalization induced by our emotions. We were the victims of wishful thinking in believing that separate independence would be feasible if the economic conditions in the Tydings bill came into effect over a period of ten years instead of immediately. This was also inadequate; but it served for a time to protect, in the minds of many of us, the preconceived idea of separation.

The Untaught Wisdom

We were gripped with this emotional confusion wanting independence but not wanting economic upheaval—when the campaign to found the Popular Democratic party was running its course between 1938 and 1940. At this point, well aware of the great economic needs of our people, and knowing our simple people well, I set out to talk with them. I learned many things from these talks.

I learned that there is a wisdom among the people in the towns and in the countryside which education may lead, but cannot improve, in its magnificent human essence. I taught many of them something, but they taught me more. I learned that the people are wise—wiser than we think. I learned that to them freedom is something deep in the heart, in the conscience, in everyday life, in personal dignity, in the furrow, the plow, and the tools. I learned that among the simple people the nationalistic concept does not exist, because in its place there is a deep understanding of freedom. I learned that in their wisdom they prefer—if they have to choose—one who governs respectfully from a distance to one who governs despotically from nearby. And that understanding is the unequaled basis and root of every great federalist concept, of great unions between countries and between men which cut across climates, races, and languages. The nationalistic concept prefers the despotic government of the nearby to the democratic government of the remote. Naturally, democratic federalism requires respect and liberty in the local as well as in the federal levels of government.

I learned many things, probably many more than I think I learned; for we learn by planting things in the mind which later bear fruit in understanding. And I learned better something I already knew:

that it is unworthy of the conscience, that it is the denial of all ideals, to risk, for abstract concepts, the hope for a better life, the deep belief in the integral freedom of the good and simple people who populate the long paths, which sometimes cross the streets and squares, which are Puerto Rico. I learned all this, and I also learned that the great majority of the people of Puerto Rico prefer close association with their fellow citizens of the American Union and with all men on earth, to the bitter narrowness of separation.

I realized that with a program calling for separate independence we would never obtain the support of the people for economic development—equitable distribution and production—which the people needed so much. The profound intuition of the people was quick to point out the contradiction in a program which on the one hand talked about the struggle to reduce their extreme poverty and on the other hand talked about separate independence which would destroy any hope of ever conquering that extreme poverty —which in fact would rapidly aggravate the seriousness of that poverty.

From the instinct of the people which I observed in my journeys among them, from the doubts in my own mind and the minds of others, and from the compulsion to deal with the great economic and social problems of so many good people in Puerto Rico, there emerged the formula which made possible everything that was to come, the formula that "the political status is not in issue." The votes in favor of the Popular Democratic Party would not be counted either for separate independence or for federated state-hood; they would be votes in favor of an economic and social program. Our political status would be decided by the people on another occasion, wholly apart from the regular elections—pre-sumably in a plebiscite.

This new concept of separating the economic from the political problem of Puerto Rico liberated the Popular Democratic party from a platform which was its own worst enemy—a platform in which the political plank could destroy the economic planks with the devastating fury of a tropical hurricane. This liberated those of us who had suffered from an intolerable perplexity of spirit. It enabled us to tackle the economic problems of Puerto Rico in a way that introduced a new, large movement of reform, creation, and hope. We are still engaged in that great task; in spite of the great deal which we have accomplished, there is much more to be done.

The Either/Or Concept Persists

However, we were free of this perplexity of the spirit for only a short period. We continued to be preoccupied as a collective group with the notion of a plebiscite in which we would be required to choose between separate independence and federated statehood —despite the fact that under either alternative the economic life of our people would be gravely threatened. It must be understood that it was not the people who were insisting on this course. This came from the political assemblies, who in this respect were not so representative of the people as they were in economic questions.

Those of us who participated in these assemblies were not insincere. With more learning and less wisdom, we continued to believe, although assailed by anguished doubts, that the choice must be between separate independence and federated statehood under economic conditions different from those in the Tydings bill and from those which existed for the states of the Union. We persisted in this view without examining closely the question of whether it would be possible to obtain these necessary economic conditions without any deviation from the two rigid alternatives. We were impaled on the horns of the dilemma which seemed to force an inexorable choice between separate independence and federated statehood. Actually, the instinct of the people used the idea of a plebiscite between these two classical forms of government to provide time for a better and autochthonous solution of the problem to appear. We can see this now. It was not easy to see it at that time.

In the 1944 campaign the promise to the people that the political status was not in issue was repeated. However, it was still imperative that we find a solution for that problem. The wisdom of the people, which I have mentioned, does not consist in a belief that the question of political status is of no importance whatsoever. Rather, recognizing that man does not live by bread alone and is in part a political being, the people have wisely refused to be bound by the intellectual straitjacket of rigid and preconceived formulas which stifle the creative will and energy of men. It was this instinct of the people, which at times their leaders must channel into action, which engendered the happy thought that the solution might well lie in some form other than the two inflexible formulas upon which the political assemblies had long focused their attention.

A Third Possibility Recognized

We were thus one step farther along the road to reality: in a request to Congress for a plebiscite we used language which permitted consideration of solutions other than the two rigid classical alternatives. True, we committed the error, at the insistence of some of the members of the political assembly, of inserting a deadline; we asked for a solution of the problem when World War II ended. But we had freed ourselves from the tyranny of the labels, separate independence and federated statehood. We were making progress.

In 1945 I went to Washington for discussions on the question of the political status of Puerto Rico. As a result of this visit, a bill was introduced in the Senate by Senator Tydings and in the House of Representatives by Resident Commissioner Piñero. That bill presented *three* alternatives: separate independence, federated statehood, and dominion status; the economic conditions were completely different from those of the original Tydings bill and from other Tydings bills. Under either of these alternatives, free trade between the United States and Puerto Rico would continue, the internal revenue taxes which now revert to the Treasury of Puerto Rico would continue to be covered into our Treasury, and federal aid for roads, hospitals, school lunchrooms, and many other public works and services would be extended for a long period of time.

During these consultations in Washington I became aware that such a bill could not pass. However, it did serve to present graphically to Congress and to the people of Puerto Rico the minimum economic conditions we needed in order to survive, irrespective of our political status.

The Object Lesson of the Philippines

In April 1946 I went again to Washington as a member of the Status Commission which was created by the Legislature of Puerto Rico and on which all the political parties with members in the Legislature were represented. Once more we tried to find a solution to the problem of status as we saw it. During that time hearings were being held before congressional committees on a bill to establish the economic relations which would exist between the United States and the Philippines when the latter became a republic. I read carefully the record of those hearings because of their obvious bearing on the question we were raising. It convinced me that Puerto Rico would never obtain the right to choose separate independence in a plebiscite except under economic conditions which would destroy any hope of continuing to improve their standard of living. The most important factor which led me to this conviction was the most-favored-nation clause found in trade treaties between the United States and many other countries.

The plan at the time was to give the Philippines economic treatment which would preserve for them the advantages of union with the United States for only eight years; this preference would be gradually reduced until the Philippines had no preference whatsoever in their economic relations with the United States. The principal reason for this treatment of the Philippines was the most-favored-nation clause in trade treaties to which the United States is a party. Under this clause the United States is required to give each nation with which it has a trade treaty containing the clause the most favorable economic treatment provided in a treaty with any other nation.

Obviously, the United States could not maintain its present good economic treatment of Puerto Rico, which is vital to our continued development, if we acquired a status which had all the legal paraphernalia of separate independence. It became clear that only under some form of status in association with the United States in which we retained our American citizenship could we preserve the good economic conditions which are necessary for our survival as a people. It could not be gainsaid that any status for Puerto Rico which connoted loss of American citizenship and disassociation from the American Union meant the discontinuance of our present favorable economic conditions, except perhaps for a few years on a diminishing graduated scale. The hard fact was that the present free trade between Puerto Rico and the United States could not be continued if Puerto Rico were a separate, independent nation. To provide for such free trade would require the same treatment for all the most-favored-treaty nations. And this, of course, was out of the question. Moreover, added to our economic situation was the affection and mutual respect which had developed between the peoples of Puerto Rico and the United States within our common citizenship.

We concluded that we must stop wasting time groping for a solution to the problem of political status which we knew beforehand was impossible for Puerto Rico to attain—impossible not for the American Union but for us. The Philippines with their greater territory and natural resources in relation to population, could manage under such stringent economic conditions. Our destiny lay in a different direction. It was incumbent upon us to devise creatively a realistically free form of political status which would not be at war with the solution of the economic problems of Puerto Rico and yet would protect the dignity of our people within our association with the American Union.

The Path of Progress

Once we forthrightly faced this task in the middle of 1946, things began to happen. The political status lost its role of enemy of the solution of our economic problems; instead we considered it in the light of and in harmony with the effort to solve the great economic difficulties of our people. We moved at an unprecedentedly accelerated pace which proved beyond peradventure that the log jam on status had finally been broken.

There had been no progress in self-government for Puerto Rico since 1917. Less than two months after this new approach to the problem of status had been adopted, the President of the United States appointed Jesús Piñero, who had been elected by the people of Puerto Rico as their Resident Commissioner in Washington, to the post of Governor of Puerto Rico. And it took only four years for Congress by Public Law 600 to offer to create a relationship between Puerto Rico and the United States based on a compact approved by the people of Puerto Rico and on a constitution written by the people of Puerto Rico themselves.

The wisdom of halting the divisive and futile debate on status, which paralyzed our progress towards self-government from 1917 until 1946, has been dramatically demonstrated by the swiftness of the events which occurred between 1946 and 1952. With this hindrance removed, the long-repressed political energy of our people soon created a new form of status, a new form of political relationship in the American Union and in all America, a new form of political harmony with the economic freedom of our people, in place of the rigid and sterile formulas which threatened the full development of Puerto Rico, which had immobilized for generations the great creative political powers of its people.

It should be made clear that what we have done has been to initiate a process of political creation in Puerto Rico, and not merely to invent just another formula. Precisely because it needs to grow in so many phases in its life as a people, Puerto Rico cannot become engaged in formulas. It must use its energy in development and continuous growth. Nothing could enslave us more than handicapping our great drive towards a happy future with a rigid, obsolescent, unprogressive, or inapplicable formula.

Interpretation of the Constitution

Every constitution is subject to different interpretations which are made in good faith. But our thesis is that by their votes in the referenda in which Public Law 600 and the constitution were approved, the people adopted the interpretations of these documents advanced by those who campaigned for their approval. We submit then that when the time comes for judicial review of the compact and the constitution, they should be interpreted in accordance with the understanding of the people as to their meaning and scope when they approved them. We are confident that such interpretations will prevail, and that they will yield the results which will be most favorable and liberal to Puerto Rico and which will promote fraternal understanding between Puerto Rico and the American Union.

"I LOVE MY COUNTRY"

[Despite the fact that the island's economy was on the move, and living standards were rising, not all Puerto Ricans were willing to peacefully accept the Commonwealth status as a solution to colonialism.

On July 4, 1950, President Harry S. Truman signed Law 600, which allowed Puerto Ricans to draft their own constitution under a Commonwealth form of government. On October 30, that same year, five armed Nationalists attacked La Fortaleza, the Governor's mansion in San Juan; there were bloody uprisings in other island towns, causing twenty-seven deaths and ninety gunshot injuries. On November 1, two Puerto Ricans —Griselio Torresola and Oscar Collazo—made an amateurish, but head-line-catching, attempt to kill President Truman in Washington. Despite this unrest, and despite the fact that many voters abstained in protest, the Commonwealth constitution was approved by a vote of 374,000 to 82,000 on March 3, 1952. But the Nationalists did not give up. On March 2, 1954—exactly thirty-seven years after Woodrow Wilson signed a law that made all Puerto Ricans citizens of the United States—headlines on the front pages of newspapers throughout the world screamed out that a band of Nationalists had opened fire in the halls of Congress of the most powerful nation on earth.]

A squad of Puerto Rican terrorists, led by a woman, fired a wild fusillade of pistol shots from a visitors' gallery into the crowded United States House of Representatives yesterday, and wounded five Congressmen, one so severely he was given only a 50-50 chance to live.

Critically wounded was Rep. Alvin M. Bentley (R.-Mich.), a freshman member. A bullet plowed into his chest, down through his abdomen, and out his side. . . .

The four other Congressmen, one with a flesh wound in the back, three with wounds in the legs, were all reported in good condition last night. . . .

The "suicide squad," a woman and three men, were identified by police as belonging to the Puerto Rican Nationalist Party. Two other party members had tried to assassinate President Truman in November, 1950, at Blair House in Washington. Police said the four yesterday bought one-way tickets from New York, expecting never to return alive. . . .

From Edward F. Ryan, *The Washington Post*, March 2, 1954, pp. 1, 12–13. © The Washington Post. Reprinted by permission.

All residents of New York, the four terrorists are: Mrs. Lolita Lebrón, 34, divorcee, of 315 W. 94th St., New York City; Rafael Cancel Miranda, 25, 120 S. First St., Brooklyn; Andrés Figueroa Cordero, 29, and Irving Flores Rodríguez, both of 108 E. 103rd St., New York City.

The woman boasted the shooting was planned on George Washington's birthday, was staged for Puerto Rican independence, and was timed to coincide with the opening of the Tenth Inter-American Conference in Caracas, Venezuela. . . .

In the wake of the attack, both Houses speedily adjourned while police threw heavy guards around the Capitol, and leaders ordered immediate extra security measures for future sessions.

In addition, extra guards were assigned to protect Vice President Richard M. Nixon and his family, as well as Interior Secretary Douglas McKay and Agriculture Secretary Ezra Taft Benson, both of whom canceled a scheduled joint visit to Puerto Rico.

The attack was without precedent in American history. One veteran legislator called it "an attack on representative Government."

The woman stood up without warning, waved a flag, and fired the first shot, according to her story to police. Her shot was the signal for the others to fire. There were a score or more of shots, fired staccato within a few seconds. The woman screamed, witnesses said, in Spanish. It sounded like "Vive La Mexico" to some and "Vive Puerto Rico" to others.

Their fantastic fusillade shattered the routine of the House of Representatives at 2:20 P.M.

The House was halfway through a vote on a resolution to permit debate on a bill that would authorize continuation of a program for admitting Mexican farm laborers for temporary employment in this country.

Speaker Joseph W. Martin, Jr. (R-Mass.) said "I had just finished counting the "ayes"—168—and was about to call the "noes" when I heard the first two or three cracks. I looked up to see what was going on and I moved back against the wall.

"The gunfire was coming from the back row of the gallery at the southwest corner. A women there was waving a flag and shouting. She was shooting too, and so were some men."

Members thought at first it was a demonstration with blanks. Then they started feeling bits of plaster hit them. . . . There was a sudden rush for the doors, while some members ducked behind chairs. Others hit the floor. . . .

Two bullets slapped into the majority leader's desk. . . . Other bullets hit the rear walls of the House, the ceiling, and punctured the chairs where members sit. . . .

A score or more of bullets had been fired in a few agonizing seconds. Then there was silence. A visitor in the gallery, Frank Wise, of Tacoma Park, Md., said he was five seats away from the

Puerto Ricans. When the shooting stopped, he jumped at one of the gunmen, and "pinioned his arms."

Wise said he rushed the man out of the Gallery and pushed him into the hands of people there. Then he turned just as a second man came through the door. "I grabbed him around the arms and said 'here, this man's got a gun, too.'"

Both men were disarmed in a wild melee.

Mrs. Lebrón and two men, Miranda and Cordero, were seized at the Capitol, while Rodríguez was picked up later at the Greyhound Bus Terminal, police said. Police also seized three other Puerto Ricans from Florida at the bus station, but concluded after questioning the Florida trio that they had nothing to do with the shooting.

According to Murray [Police Chief Robert V.—Ed.] Mrs. Lebrón said the quartet got together in New York on George Washington's Birthday and agreed to come to Washington to stage a demonstration for the freedom of Puerto Rico.

Murray said documents found in her pocket indicated she was a member of the Nationalist Party of Puerto Rico.

According to Tom Kennamar, House Doorkeeper, the woman's purse contained a note which said:

"Before God and the world, my blood claims for the independence of Puerto Rico. My life I give for the freedom of my country. This is a cry for victory in our struggle for independence which for more than half a century has tried to conquer the land that belongs to Puerto Rico.

"I state forever that the United States of America are betraying the sacred principles of mankind in their continuous subjugation of my country, violating their rights to be a free nation and a free people, in their barbarous torture of our apostle of independence, Don Pedro Albizu Campos."

On the back of the paper . . . was written:

"I take responsible for all."

. . . . Secret Service and FBI agents also questioned the four. Police had some trouble at the outset because all the group spoke broken English. Interpreters were called in to help question them in Spanish. . . .

Mrs. Lebrón and Miranda told newsmen in an interview last night that they shot the Congressmen to bring to the attention of the American people and the world that Puerto Rico is not free.

Mrs. Lebrón said as long as Puerto Rico is not free such a shooting "may happen again."

. . . . She said she was treated well by police. "Somebody has to be punished and I want the law to punish me," she continued. . . .

She said she came to the United States six years ago and was employed in a sewing machine factory in New York. She said she had an eighth grade education and was a Catholic.

Miranda, who said he was not sorry they shot the Congressmen, told newsmen he was jailed for two years in Puerto Rico as a draft dodger.

He said he left Puerto Rico about a year ago and now operates a punch press in a shoe factory in New York. . . .

Boyd Crawford . . . staff administrator of the House Foreign Relations Committee, was in the committee room when he heard the shooting. . . .

"I recognized it as gunfire and I tore out of the committee room to see what it was all about. I saw a small slender woman there and heard her scream something in Spanish and heard her say in English 'I love freedom, I love my country.' "

WORKER IN THE CANE

[While the industrialization program pushed ahead in the 1950's, Puerto Rico remained largely rural, and most of the country's working men still earned their "rice and beans" by toiling in the sugar cane fields. Anthropologist Sidney Mintz, who spent several years observing the lives of Puerto Rico's plantation workers, here provides a close-up view.*]

From the air the narrow coastal plain of southern Puerto Rico looks like an irregular green ribbon. It contrasts sharply with the blues and azures of the sea to the south, and with the sere vegetation of the uplands to the north. The plain itself is covered with sugar cane. A road cuts through the cane, paralleling the sea, and linking towns along the coast. Most of the people live in rural areas rather than in the towns: in shacks that hug the shoulders of the road or stretch around the bays and inlets; in barracks and houses around the plazas of the old-time sugar haciendas; or in company towns built up near the monster cane-grinding mills. The mills are the most conspicuous landmarks from the air: their chimneys cast long shadows over the shacks and across the cane. From the air, the workers' shacks look regular and neat. There is a picturesqueness about the thatched roofs, the waving palms, and the nearness of the sea.

But walking through a village destroys such impressions. The ground is pounded hard and dusty, littered with tin cans, paper,

From Sidney M. Mintz, *Worker in the Cane* (New Haven: Yale University Press, 1960), pp. 12–22. Copyright © 1960 by Yale University Press. Reprinted by permission.

coconut husks, and cane trash. The houses are patched with old Coca Cola signs, boards torn from packing cases, and cardboard. Only a few are painted. The seeming order dissolves into disorder and crowding. Large families are packed into tight living places. The houses are variously divided into two, three, or more sections by partitions which never reach the ceiling. The cooking is done in ramshackle lean-tos behind the living quarters. And all around the houses grows the cane.

Such a village is Jauca. The barrio called Jauca contains clusters of houses, some on the edge of the sea, some along the east-west highway, and others bunched around the centers of the *colonias* —the great farms of the corporations which control over 95 per cent of all the cultivated land in the municipality. In Barrio Jauca the largest aggregation of houses is along the highway; this village is called Poblado Jauca. The nearest large groupings are at the beach to the south and to the northwest near the plaza of the largest colonia in the barrio, Colonia Destino. There is a company store at Colonia Destino; 36 little two-room shacks provided rent free by the corporation to resident workers; a two-story house for the *mayordomo*, or overseer; two barracks left from slavery times and still occupied; and the ruined shell of the hacienda warehouse, now used to store machinery and fertilizer. The only trees in view are some palms growing near a point on the beach, the twin rows of tamarinds which line the approach to Colonia Destino, and a few scattered fruit trees among the houses of Poblado Jauca.

Poblado Jauca consists of a string of shacks lining the highway, and a substantial cluster of additional houses—on an acre plot of land called Palmas Orillanas—which extend from the road southward toward the sea. There are fewer than a dozen small stores and bars, two school buildings, and, at one end of the village, the crumbling mill and chimney of an old sugar hacienda. The village has standpipes along the road to supply its water, many of the houses are electrified, and the road which connects the village to the towns of Santa Isabel to the west and Salinas to the east is well surfaced. In its outward appearance, Poblado Jauca does not differ significantly from hundreds of other such "line" villages in the sugar areas of Puerto Rico.

At five o'clock in the morning Poblado Jauca is still and deserted-looking. An occasional touring car goes by on the coast road carrying passengers from Ponce to San Juan. The roosters crow and the dogs bark and the surf sounds softly. Every shack is shut tightly—the wooden shutters of the windows closed against the "night air," the doors barred. The cookhouses behind the shacks are cold; the sun is still low. An easterly breeze stirs the cane, rattles the Coca Cola signs, shakes loose a ripe nut in the palm grove near the water.

But by six o'clock the village comes to life. The first signs are the swinging back of the shutters that give on the back yard and the tendrils of smoke curling out of the stoves. The first need of the morning is food: the food, coffee. In the early morning the air has a deceptive chilly freshness. Everything is coolly damp and stimulating. In less than an hour the entire quality of the morning is transformed. By the time the men have drunk their coffee, tied their cuffs to their ankles with cords, and picked up machetes or hoes and the food for the midmorning breakfast, the sun is high and glittering; it weighs on the skin like something tangible, burns away the dampness from every surface, almost crackles as it grows hotter. The men leave the houses, carrying their breakfast and tools and dressed in rough work clothes, wide-brimmed straw hats, and old shoes. They go to "defend themselves" (se defienden) in the cane, which is their phrase for the struggle of making a living. These men have lived with the cane, most of them, from the time they were born. It grows up to the edges of the house plots. When it is in full glory it stands fifteen feet high, and the villages are choked in it. It litters the roads; during harvest the smell of it fills the air, the "hair" of its surface works into the skin like peach fuzz. Men who work in the cane speak of "doing battle" (bregando) with it.

From the thatch shacks along the beach, from the wooden ones along the highway, the men move toward the plazas of the old haciendas to get their work orders for the day. Some will form the cutting lines; others will lay rails for the wagons that are loaded in the fields or will do the loading. There are cultivators and seeders, seed cutters and winch operators, ditchers and gang bosses. Most of the jobs can be done by nearly everyone, but individual workers have preferences and some have special skills. Old Don Tomás, like many of the oldest Negro people in the barrio, is a palero—a ditcher—the most skilled, the highest-paid, and the most prestigeful "dirt" job in the fields. The cutters come mainly from the shacks at the beach; they are white men, most of them named De Jesús, whose families migrated to the coast from nearby highlands. The De Jesús are set somewhat apart by other Jauqueños. Some of them take their Catholicism seriously and go to church; they try to grow little vegetable gardens at the beach, and they fence their houses; they "marry cousin with cousin"; and unlike the old coastal working families, they prefer cane cutting on a piecework basis to most other jobs. Aníbal and Fredo are truck drivers; they were in the Army, and learned some skills there most Jauqueños, and especially the older ones, could never acquire. Truck driving pays relatively well and it is easy work compared to cutting or loading. Don Daniel likes to plant seed. It is a curious choice, for Don Daniel is very tall and seeding requires that one bend over continuously, setting and tapping the seed—which is not seed at all, but cuttings of cane stalk—into place.

By seven o'clock those who have work are out of the village. The children eat and start for school, or begin their jobs at home —toting pails of water, mopping the floors, tending the baby, ironing—or play in the yards with toys made of old tin cans and bits of wood. As the sun climbs, each woman begins to prepare the hot lunch which must be carried out to her man in the fields, no matter how far away he may be working. No Puerto Rican cane worker will settle for a cold midday meal. At nine o'clock he has his thermos of black coffee and a piece of bread smeared with margarine or topped with a slice of cheese or sausage —he feels it gives him the strength he needs to work till noon— but at noon someone must bring him a hot luncheon. Nests of pots hung on wire frames are the lunchboxes of the Puerto Rican countryside. Sometimes the pots hold noodle soup, or a quantity of starches such as boiled green bananas, taro, yams, and Irish potatoes; fish broths, cornmeal cakes, and salads mixed with bits of boiled salt cod are common. But no matter what else, one tin container is always full of rice, another of red or white beans in a mild sauce. Rice and beans are the staple of the lower-class Puerto Rican.

After lunch the cane workers pick up their machetes once more. Back home the wives are busy with the laundry. They scrub the clothes on washboards, remove stubborn dirt with scrapers fashioned from coconut shell, and hang the clean clothes on fences or stretch them over pieces of corrugated iron to dry. Then water is boiled for the afternoon coffee, and the youngest children must be bathed and dressed to await their fathers' return. By three or four o'clock the men have all returned, and the heat of the day has begun to abate slightly. The men bathe, crouching over the washtubs in the cookhouses or in showers fed from hand-filled tanks if they have them. It is in the late afternoon that the social life of the day begins. Men shave after their afternoon baths; young girls and boys put on their good clothes; the radios loudly announce the baseball scores, carry political discussions or Puerto Rican and other Latin American music.

Dinner is not eaten by the whole family seated at a table, but by each family member independently, down to the littlest, during a two-hour period. The father sits at the table and is served by his wife, who hovers about him, often with her youngest child in her arms. Again rice and beans and black coffee are the core of the meal but there may also be cornmeal slabs in fish broth; or stewed goat or beef; or boiled salt cod. Children eat standing in the kitchen, or sitting in the yard and feeding the chickens from their spoons. The dog and the chickens scour the floors and yards and follow the housewife about with friendly but cautious importunacy.

After dinner the street becomes the setting for conversation and flirting. Loafing groups gather in front of the small stores or in the yards of older men, where they squat and gossip; marriageable boys and girls promenade along the highway. Small groups form and dissolve in the bars. The women remain home; married couples rarely walk together, usually only on their way to revivalist prayer meetings. The more worldly young men—who have probably served in the Army and have a little money—may hail passing public cars and go to the movies in the nearby towns, or to see girls in neighboring villages. If it is a Tuesday or a Saturday night, illegal numbers-games sellers will be making their rounds, collecting bets placed on credit at an earlier time. The winning numbers (which are based on the winning numbers in the national *legal* lottery) will be announced the next morning over the radio, and nearly everyone in the village, knowing the favorite numbers of their fellows, will know who has won.

By nine o'clock—unless it is a Saturday—Jauca has grown quiet. Activity continues within the houses, the stores, and the Pentecostal chapel. Youths may prepare to hunt octopus and lobster on the cays, while their younger brothers are catching crabs in the cane fields, along the irrigation ditches. Couples in love say their good nights in the shadows. By ten even the stores are closed; one bar or two may still be open. The Pentecostals come home from their services. Only if there is a wake, a local political meeting, or a fight will activity continue outside the houses. The surf, scarcely noticeable during the noise of the day, can be heard again after ten o'clock, and the dogs and roosters vie with the gentle little croaking frogs—the *coquí*—in breaking the night's stillness.

During the course of the week the character of a day's activity varies. Saturdays are paydays, and Saturday nights are special. The nickelodeons play late into the night, and many people of all ages dance. Old Tomás Famanía, who has all his teeth and walks straight, though he carries a cane of *frescura* with a brass tip, and glories in his more than sixty years, comes up from his thatched shack at the beach to dance. He usually picks rumbas, and his partners will be Ceferino Hernández' daughters and granddaughters, none of them more than eight years old. The bachelors stand at the bar drinking their rum neat—each drink downed in a swallow from a tiny paper cup. The more affluent buy half pints of rum (called "Shirleys" after Shirley Temple) and finish them sitting at the tables. The teen-age males play pool on the much-ripped table in Cheo's bar and watch the girls walk by. Sometimes the barbecue pit at Cheo's will be going. A youth will crouch by the bed of hot charcoal, casually turning the long pole on which a whole pig is impaled.

On Saturday evenings during harvest the front doors of the houses are open. One can peer in to see the dimly lighted "parlor," which is separated from the "dining room" by a low wooden partition. There is the mother with one child nursing, another sleeping in her lap, a third perhaps drowsing at her feet or pulling at her skirt. The grandmother may be visiting, rocking in a chair, sometimes smoking a cigar. Conversation is animated and humorous: Don Fonso had to chase his mare two miles tonight down the main road; Barbino has nearly worn out the record called *Vuelve* (Return) at the bar, because his girl friend Wilma is leaving for "El Norte"; Don Fico hit on the *bolita* (numbers game) for $2,300 last Sunday; there is an elopement expected, or a revival meeting; how long will the *zafra* (harvest) last? The father returns from his visit to a *compadre* (godparent of one of his children) and greets his mother-in-law with respect and care. A man must maintain very good (but circumspect) relations with his mother-in-law. The children, those still awake, cling to him. He may put them to sleep by rocking and fondling them as the hours pass. When the front door is closed and the shutters are swung to, it is time for the parents to go to bed. One teen-age son may still be abroad; he will creep in after the house is dark, feast on the cold rice-and-bean leftovers from dinner, and crawl into bed, often alongside two or three brothers. And the bed may be a folding cot.

Sundays are quieter than weekdays, as Saturdays are noisier. The Pentecostal church has its day and its night services. Older people dress up on Sunday, though very few ever go to church. In the summer townspeople come to swim at the Jauca beach, to sit under the palms and drink soda or coconut water. Passing cars may stop in Jauca—a merchant or salesman seeks to purchase a dozen succulent land crabs to take home to San Juan. Jauqueños wander down to the beach to watch the townsmen swim. These are a different sort of people. They are not explicit about how they regard each other, but town and country are not quite the same, and the townsmen who come to swim or to buy crabs are not merely cane cutters who may live in town but storekeepers, civil servants, and teachers. And, parenthetically, it is not their color that sets them apart but their class.

Just as Saturday and Sunday differ from weekdays, so the harvest time differs from *el tiempo muerto*—dead time. From Christmas until early summer the cane is cut, and much cane is planted. The fields are alive with activity. Long lines of men stand before the cane like soldiers before an enemy. The machetes sweep down and across the stalks, cutting them close to the ground. The leaves are lopped off, the stalk cut in halves or thirds and dropped behind. It is a beautiful thing to watch from a hundred yards' distance. The men seem tiny but implacable, moving steadily against a green forest which recedes before them. When the cane has been piled and then scooped up, either by men who load it on carts brought into the fields on movable tracks, or by the new *arañas* (spiders), machines that load it on rubber-wheeled carts, the oxen may graze among the trash. And soon the field may be cleared for planting a new crop, which will be sprouting within weeks of the harvest.

From a distance, the scene is toylike and wholesome. Up close it is neither. The men sweat freely; the cane chokes off the breeze, and the pace of cutting is awesome. The men's shirts hang loose and drip sweat continuously. The hair of the cane pierces the skin and works its way down the neck. The ground is furrowed and makes footing difficult, and the soil gives off heat like an oven. The mayordomo sits astride a roan mare and supervises the field operations. He wears khakis and cordovan riding accessories. To see him ride past a line of men bent over and dripping sweat, to hear the sounds of the oxen in the fields behind, the human and animal grunting, and to feel the waves of heat billowing out of the ground and cane evoke images of other times. The men of Jauca grow drawn in the first two weeks of the harvest. This is the time to make the money to pay debts from the past dead time and to prepare for the next. It is a way of life that can make menial jobs in the continental United States seem like sinecures.

When the cane is entirely cut the intense activity ceases. The last trainload of cane, from the westernmost plantations serviced by the Machete and Aguirre mills, is pulled through Jauca by the little engine to the accompaniment of an unceasing whistling. The train is crying; the next day the whistles of Machete and Aguirre will cry. And then, people joke sourly, the people will cry. The nickelodeons play less. The drinkers of bottled rum turn back to *cañita*—"the little cane," the illegal white rum. Don Tomás has no more dancing partners, because there are fewer nickels. The little account books each Puerto Rican family has for its food purchases begin to carry more unpaid entries. *Fia'o*—credit—gets extended two weeks instead of one, or four instead of two. Back before World War II, when Puerto Rico was much poorer, dead time was marked by a sharp increase in infant mortality, supposedly from a disease diagnosed as gastroenteritis; the correlation with the cessation of income does not seem to have been a coincidence.

In dead time one hears more reminiscence, there is more fishing, the ways to turn an extra penny are given more thought. Around the houses one notices little treasures that were overlooked before because they mean much less during the harvest: the bedraggled chickens, a melancholy goat, perhaps even a duck. There is a lime tree behind Don Cosme's house, and it will yield large quantities of lime drink. And if coffee is really short, one can brew *hedionda*, which grows all over. Headache powders may be better, but some headaches do pass if you crush a leaf of *naranja,* dip it in oil, and press it to the brow. Cheo has a hive of bees; and if one has a compadre who is a fisherman, he may make a present of the *carey* (turtle meat) that he could not sell or use this morning. A little cornmeal will make the land crabs fatter, and one's sons keep the crab traps going throughout the rainy season. The land is crowded with the growing cane and the yards are dry and sterile, but there is a tree here and a bush there, one hen still is laying, and octopuses live in the rocks of the cay. Everything belongs to Corporation Aguirre, it seems; but there is a little left that belongs to the people.

The feast day of the patron saint of Santa Isabel—who is not Saint Elizabeth, despite the town's name, but Santiago Apóstol— comes in the summer, at a time when money is scarce. (Some wags have suggested that the town fathers should pick a new saint, preferably one whose birth may be commemorated during the harvest.) In October and November there is some work in the fields, for this is the planting period for the *gran cultura* (big growth) cane, which is allowed to stand fifteen or even eighteen months before it is cut. Some Novembers there are elections. The baseball season gets into swing. And when Christmas comes, the harvest is near once more. The year begins and ends with the swish of the machetes.

DON ABELARDO

[Not all Puerto Ricans worked on large sugar cane plantations, which are mainly located along the flat coastal plains of the island. Many others lived in the mountainous interior, where tobacco, coffee, fruits, vegetables, and livestock were important. Grinding poverty persisted in much of the countryside, and unsung heroes struggled to survive. Here, John Hawes—a long-time resident of the island—recounts an incident about a remarkable *barrio* leader, and the plight of strong men, with families, and without work.]

Don Abelardo Reyes Rivera is a fiery little fighting cock of a man. In his middle sixties, with a shock of white hair that stands straight up on his head, large observant black eyes, three remaining front teeth which have turned yellow with age, like old ivory, he has been President

John Hawes, *The Island Times,* San Juan, Puerto Rico, March 25, 1960, p. 24.

of the Barrio for twenty years. For twenty years he has acted as the intermediary between his neighbors, in the valley that makes up Barrio Flores, and the municipal authorities. He has judged minor offenses that never reached the police; found work, whenever possible, for those who needed it, and settled disputes. His only authority derives from the neighbors who chose him, and like the judges of medieval Castille, he judges by no set code of laws, but *por los sus sesos* (by his own wits and experience). His wits are sharp, and his experience encompasses most of life in Barrio Flores.

Abelardo was born in the Barrio, and he has spent all of his sixty odd years there. He has seen the days of the tobacco boom, when everyone had money in their pockets, and life was good and the times, after a hurricane passed, when people collected palm nuts and wild beans from the scattered weeds, roasted them, and made a substitute for coffee. He survived the terrible time when the great Northern Tobacco Companies went into bankruptcy, and men went about the hills at night, burning the barns that had tobacco in them, to maintain their strike for a chance to live.

As long as he may live, he will never forget the night when he heard muffled voices outside his house at midnight and roused himself to see who the intruders were. At the first flicker of the match that he started to light the lamp with, a familiar voice called to him:

"Don't light the lamp Abelardo, and don't open the door. We will kill the cow, because people are hungry, and we will leave a share for you, but we don't want to be forced to hurt anyone."

He would never forget it, just as he would never forget that they left the head and a filete for him, propped up on sticks, where the dogs couldn't reach them.

"Fair enough," he said. Needless to say, he never said anything about recognizing the voice of his midnight visitor. In times of really desperate need, anyone might do such a thing. When his midnight visitor died, 15 years later, Abelardo was President of the Barrio. He went to the wake early in the evening. At three o'clock in the morning, when a group of people were about to leave, they offered to accompany him to his house.

"No," he said, "we have something in common, the dead man and I. I'll see him through." He stayed through the night, and in the first clear light of dawn, he helped to carry the coffin over the tortuous mountain trails, up and down, but mostly down, leading to the town, and he was present when the grave was filled in.

These are things that people remember, and they are still mentioned in the neighborhood. Apart from these inevitable disorders, provoked by crises, in the world in which he lives, don Abelardo is familiar with ordinary weakness. He knows why the men who work all day, five or six days a week, on the steep slopes of the tobacco talas, or weeding and cutting the hill cane, get drunk at the end of the week. He knows why they fight with their wives, and quarrel with their children and neighbors. He knows how people get killed on such occasions, how sudden anger leads to death. He understands and sympathizes with the remorse of the murderer, at the same time that he sympathizes with the bereaved, but he is ,sentimental about neither. Violence is a mistake, but once started, it has to run its course like a canefire or a sickness. A man is killed—the killer must be punished. And the whole Barrio suffers in both instances. This might not be just, but it is the law. Abelardo shrugs and repeats the bitter proverb:

"For the poor, there is no justice."

Abelardo's moral judgment is firmly based on the teachings of the church, but with certain individual amendments, founded on his own experience and knowledge of his neighbors, that would shock a parish priest.

Underneath all of his patience and understanding, even his seeming resignation in adversity, Abelardo is a fighter. He has fought hard and well for the people of his Barrio. Flores is one of the poorest barrios in the municipality, and one of the most thinly populated. Lacking any rich and important residents who might raise their voices in the municipal councils, or a large number of votes that would compel the attention of politicians, the barrio might well be almost forgotten, were it not for Abelardo. Armed with nothing but his boundless energy, ready wit and love of reasoning, Abelardo sees to it that nobody forgets Flores.

People say that the Mayor winces whenever he sees Abelardo coming, but Abelardo's demands are never unreasonable, and he takes most of the unpopular decisions upon himself. In times of drought and hardship there is a fierce competition for the jobs that the municipality offers, repairing the roads, trimming the undergrowth and clearing the drains. It was Abelardo who established the principle that the roads in Barrio Flores should be tended by residents of the Barrio. This was clearly a popular decision among his neighbors, but he went further. No man who is not the father of a family, he decreed, may work on the roads. And more, in hard times, no man may work more than one day a week on the roads.

Not unnaturally, this decision was resented by some, but its essential justice made it acceptable to the Barrio. It was questioned, one night, in don Abelardo's little store. Feeling ran high,—and several of the participants were a little tight. Don Abelardo came out from behind the counter. He liked to fight in the open.

"Miren señores," he said, "is there anyone here who wants to go to New York?" He waited for a minute and a half. Someone in the back started to answer, was kicked by his neighbor, and kept quiet.

"We all want to stay here with our families, and there's only one way to do it." The little white-haired man stood in the glaring light of the electric bulb over the doorway. His big gnarled hands made an encircling movement. "We all want to live here. So we all have to sacrifice. I could pick you, and you, and you," his root-like finger indicated three men in the semi-circle that faced him, "and say that you are the best workers, and so," he shrugged, "you should have the jobs." He paused, and then his spatulate index finger pointed to the first man that he had picked out, "would you, *could* you, provide for your sister and all her children? No sir. You couldn't. It is better to have one day's work for the head of every family, so that everyone has something, even if it's only a little, than to have seven or eight prosperous families in this hunger-bitten barrio, and the rest starving to death. Am I right, gentlemen or am I wrong?"

For a long moment, the old man stood in the harsh light of the bare bulb, facing the half circle of neighbors, gathered around the counter. Then someone said:

"Don Abel, we're dry. Isn't there any beer here?"

Slowly, muscle by muscle, don Abelardo relaxed. "*Joven,* I have more than you could drink in a year." Two minutes later, Abelardo was behind the counter, providing drinks for the men and doling out eight cents worth of dried codfish to a small boy who had been sent on an errand by his overworked mother.

Many times Abelardo has threatened to resign as president of the Barrio. But Flores without Abelardo would be like rice without beans—like an asopao without olives, like bread without salt,—unthinkable.

THE STATUS DILEMMA

[The dilemma of Puerto Rico's political status, which has plagued the island since it was a colony under Spain, was not resolved by the granting of citizenship in 1917, nor

---

Selections in this chapter:

1. From Juan M. García Passalacqua, *San Juan Star*, February 3, 1970. Reprinted with permission.

2. From U.S. House of Representatives, Subcommittee on Territorial and Insular Affairs, Committee on Interior and Insular Affairs, Hearing on H.R. 5945 and other bills to establish a procedure for the prompt settlement in a democratic manner of the political status of Puerto Rico, May 17, 1963, p. 50.

3. *Ibid.,* pp. 128–30.

by the founding of the Commonwealth government in 1952. There still remained a growing minority that urged statehood, and an equally determined movement that condemned colonialism, and demanded independence.

In 1959, Muñoz Marín tried to rewrite the Commonwealth, adding greater powers of home rule, but he was ignored by Congress. In 1963, when John F. Kennedy occupied the White House, he tried again. Here, a former aide of Governor Muñoz tells what happened when the groundwork was being laid for a plebiscite.]

We have to go back once more to 1963. . . . Efforts were directed towards Congress to try and get a commitment that commonwealth could be permanent, to enable it to confront in a plebiscite the traditionally "permanent" solutions of statehood and independence. Promises of help were extracted from then-President John F. Kennedy. A bill was introduced in Congress that would have made commonwealth "permanent and irrevocable." Hearings were held in the House of Representatives on May 16–17, 1963. In the early afternoon of May 16, Governor Muñoz visited President Kennedy at the White House. The word spread among the faithful that the agreement to make commonwealth permanent if the people voted for it had been sealed. It was a very, very happy occasion.

On the afternoon of May 17 came a betrayal. Harold Seidman, acting assistant director for the Bureau of the Budget—the "acting" and "assistant" reinforce the importance that the administration gave to our issue—came before the committee. He was categorically clear: "We strongly favor the perfection of existing arrangements with the understanding, however, that actions taken now cannot and should *not* be considered to be binding for all time in the future. . . . We believe the words 'permanent union' as used in section 2 of the bill, may give rise to misunderstandings."

People who knew of the Kennedy commitment couldn't believe their ears. Even some members of the congressional committee thought for a moment that this could be a fourth-echelon bureaucrat let loose, and felt compelled to ask: "Do you know if there is a position from the Administration that you would like to state?" Without blinking an eye, and for posterity, the man answered: "I am here, I should make clear, representing the views of the Administration." That is historical fact. This writer was there. That was then, and (for all we know) is now, the *official* position of the United States of America. . . .

[During the 1963 hearings on political status, the Commonwealth status came under attack from various circles, including members of the U.S. Congress. This sharp exchange between Governor Muñoz and Representative John Saylor of Pennsylvania was one of the most dramatic.]

Governor Muñoz. I would say that the basic thing is to clarify the noncolonial nature of a commonwealth status. . . . The basic importance is to clarify a feeling, a relationship of dignity, of political dignity between Puerto Rico and the United States beyond any shadow of a doubt. . . .

Mr. Saylor. Governor, I was looking this morning at the statement of Mr. Crawford who, you will recall, was the eminent chairman of this committee when the basic legislation was passed. I have found it. What he said on the floor of the House on June 30, 1950, and what you are saying are as opposite as it is humanly possible to get. On page 9592 of the Congressional Record, Mr. Crawford, in addressing the House, said:

We are not offering the people of Puerto Rico anything except the right to vote on a constitution to be submitted to the President of the United States who in turn is to submit it to the Congress of the United States for approval—

and all of this commonwealth that you keep talking about, and the clarification, I am satisfied are things which have been built up under your administration in Puerto Rico and have not been the intention of Congress then, and I hope not now.

Governor Muñoz. Congressman, I have had a great friendship for Mr. Crawford, and I have a great respect for his memory, but I would not agree with him on that. If he was right, then Puerto Rico is still a colony of the United States. If it is still a colony of the United States it should stop being a colony as soon as possible, for the honor of the United States and for the sense of self-respect of the people of Puerto Rico. (*Applause and jeers.*)

[At the same hearings, congressmen heard the testimony of Juan Mari Bras, leader of the Pro-Independence Movement. The text incorrectly uses his second surname, calling him "Mr. Bras."]

Mr. Bras. . . . the forces of independence will not accept anything short of a full, unconditional transfer of all sovereign powers to the people of Puerto Rico. We do not deny the right of both Puerto Rico and the United States to enter into some type of association in the future. But, such association will not be valid if it springs from our present colonial status. Only free and independent nations can validly associate themselves.

And regarding the pretension of this bill to establish the permanency and irrevocability of the present colonial setup of the Puerto Rico–United States relationship; I warn you, in the name of thousands of patriots struggling for independence in my country, that the attempt to secure, on a permanent basis, the chains of our colonial subjugation, will only produce such friction and

struggle that the situation in Puerto Rico could very well degen-
erate into an American Algeria. . . .

. . . . We have never exercised sovereignty in the past. The
constitutional convention that we held in 1952 was not in the
exercise of sovereignty but in the exercise of the delegate powers
of Congress that asked the people of Puerto Rico to elect a convention and to submit through that convention a proposal for
a constitution that would again be approved by Congress.

Mr. O'BRIEN. Then your first step would be independence. If
Puerto Rico as an independent nation decided to water down or
even turn its back on complete independence, then you would feel
that would be the decision of a sovereign independent people,
and you feel that the steps that have been taken so far . . . have not
been taken by a sovereign independent people.

Mr. BRAS. That is right. . . . You cannot consent to a contract
if you don't have the freedom to do that. . . .

The same happened in the international law on politics. A colonial
people is like a minor. He is incapable of consenting to anything.
You should have to emancipate it in order to have some sort of
compact or treaty or agreement with that people. That is what
the United Nations have asked. It is very simple. Just relinquish
sovereignty, put it in the hands of the people . . . of Puerto Rico. . . .

Mr. GILL. I understand your position, However . . . you are pre-
determining the result. In other words, you would already be out
of the United States and then we will talk about your future
status. Did you not mention the unemancipated child who needs
to be set free? Take it another way. This unemancipated child is
now in our house. I don't feel free to kick him out in the cold
weather and say "Get out" if he doesn't want to go.

Mr. BRAS. The thing is, we are not in your house. You are in
ours. . . .

A YANKEE FROM MASSACHUSETTS

[Before a plebiscite
was held in 1967 to allow voters to choose between Commonwealth,
statehood, and independence, a detailed study was made of all aspects
of Puerto Rico. Public hearings were conducted. On July 28, 1965, the

From U.S. Senate, 89th Congress, 2d Session, Document No. 108, Vol. II,
"Status of Puerto Rico, Hearings Before the United States–Puerto Rico Commission on the Status of Puerto Rico, Social-Cultural Facts in Relation to the
Status of Puerto Rico," Washington: U.S. Government Printing Office, 1966,
pp. 109–11.

U.S.-Puerto Rico Commission on the Status of Puerto Rico heard Elmer Ellsworth, who had spent most of his life as a local farmer. In the 1940's, as a founding member of the Popular Democratic Party, Mr. Ellsworth also served in the insular House of Representatives. Here, he describes how times have changed in Puerto Rico—not always for the better—and he protests against the drafting of Puerto Ricans into the U.S. Armed Forces. "How many boys from this peace-loving island," he asks, "must now die in Vietnam?"]

Mr. ELLSWORTH. Honorable members of the committee, to introduce myself I must say that I am a Yankee from Massachusetts who has made my home in Puerto Rico for some 46 years. So I have come to put in my two cents' worth before this committee.

As many here know, I was associated with my old friend Luis Muñoz Marín in "la lucha" to set up the Popular Democratic Party and to win the elections in 1940, under the theme "Pan, Tierra y Libertad." Years later in the mind of Don Luis there emerged a brilliant solution to the status of Puerto Rico, the associated free state or Estado Libre Asociado. I never was sold; I couldn't buy it because basically it had an obvious fault which I never could stomach. Under this status Puerto Ricans will continue to be drafted into the Armed Forces of the United States. Coming from an old State that has a fame for its democratic tradition, it never appeared right to me that a people with second-class political rights should be forced to serve the mother country.

Don Luis is an intelligent man. I waited through the years to see him give some sign of appreciating that obvious defect in the status; but there was no word, there was not even a whisper. Not even when the awful tragedy of Korea in which Puerto Ricans, not rugged people, not rugged marines, but people generally of small physical stature from a tropical colonial country, were sent into the subarctic region of North Korea and were thrown into some of the most bloody sections of that terrible war. I don't know if any of you have ever had a chance to visit the Juliá Clinic: I have. And there I found scores of Puerto Ricans whose lives have been ruined by their battle experience in Korea. Scores of them, today, and how many years has it been since Korea? How many?

Now, that does not seem to be enough. Now, there is a new field for Puerto Ricans to be thrown into a slaughter—Vietnam. How many boys from this peace-loving island must now die in Vietnam? . . .

I am a farmer and have stayed close to the "jíbaro" of the mountain interior. . . . I know that they are not happy over this prospect of having their sons drafted and sent to Vietnam. But can they protest? What would happen? As everyone knows they would immediately be accused of being Communist. . . . Anyone with a deep feeling and understanding of democracy has to be outraged by this drafting of Puerto Ricans, without a voice, nor a chance to vote in approval or disapproval of the President of the United States who is making these dreadful decisions. Is this true democracy or simply an ugly hangover of the worst of colonialism?

Now I must tell you frankly, gentlemen, that I don't believe much in committees. I have seen a lot of them in my 46 years. How many committees have come to Puerto Rico about the status? And still no solutions. Don Luis himself tried to sell the people that this Estado Libre Asociado was at last the final permanent status of Puerto Rico. That illusion lasted him for a few years and then even he had to realize its temporary nature and how it had to evolve further.

Now, if anything is to come out of the committee, gentlemen, for God's sake, try to get an amendment through Congress to eliminate the drafting of Puerto Ricans until the final status of this island is decided or they have true representation in Washington. That's all.

The CHAIRMAN. Perhaps some of the members of the Commission would like to ask you questions, sir. . . .

By MR. FERRÉ:

Q. Just one question. Excuse me. Mr. Ellsworth, you have been in touch with the people of Puerto Rico at the grassroots for a long while. Do you feel that they are eager and anxious for Puerto Rico to become a State of the Union?

A. No. The people of Puerto Rico have been told for a number of years: "It is not status, status is not the problem; it is social justice." They have been sold on that for a long time and the Popular Party keeps saying the same thing. The people of Puerto Rico aren't very happy with anything going on in Puerto Rico today. I don't know how some of you leaders get around to talk to the people. But Puerto Rico today is not the Puerto Rico of 10, 15, or 20 years ago. I lived in a house in Manatí when I first came to Puerto Rico. I was a pineapple grower, I was the manager of a pineapple plantation. We lived in one old two-story big house under the mango trees, and we never shut the doors of that house in the 8 years I lived in it. In fact, when a new manager came and I went to live in Cidra—into the wilderness of Cidra—his wife was a little scared. She was afraid of the peons with their "machetes" in their hands; so she tried to shut the door at night but the doors were so warped out of shape they wouldn't shut.

Now, this status thing has been kicked around so long that there are other problems that are more pressing. Agriculture is dying in Puerto Rico, and a country without any basic agriculture isn't a happy one. The other day I went up by my old farm, which I had to sell because the town grew and crept up close to me. . . .

I ran into a man, a "trabajador" who had worked for me for many,

many years. He stopped me. He said: "Mister, las cosas están malas. Estamos ganando más chavos, pero ayer yo tuve que pagar más de un peso por un racimo de guineos verdes." *

Nothing has grown. The new laws which protect the "agregado" were passed with good intentions, but they were not practical. As a "patrón," which I was once, I insisted and urged my men to keep planting their crops. But now the "patróns" are fearful that there would be a problem when they wanted one of their agregados to leave. So now in general there are no more agregados and nobody plants food crops. So, today, two things mainly are being planted in Puerto Rico—cement houses and pangola. † True, human beings can eat the steers that the pangola produces and it produces good steers; but the only two phases of agriculture that are up in Puerto Rico are dairy and cattle raising. All the other phases of farming are down. This year we had a bad drought and "plátanos" were sold in Caguas for 12 cents a "plátano," and a miserable little fruit at that.

So, we are getting houses, automobiles, and all the gadgets of the great United States of America, but we are not growing much of any of our food. Yes, there are more and more automobiles, television sets, and every kind of gadget. There are also other things but there is not much food produced and there are not very many books.

So I say that this is not a happy country, because the happy man was the worker who had his wage and also had his bananas and "plátanos" and "yautía" and "malanga" and chickens and a pig or two. He never starved. There are urbanizations in Puerto Rico, as you may know, that they call Campbell, Urbanización Campbell, because the people live mostly on Campbell's soup.

"THE CONSCIENCE OF HIS PEOPLE"

[The decade of the 1960's was a turning point in Puerto Rico's history. In 1964, Governor Muñoz stepped down and nominated a younger man—his long-time aide, Roberto Sánchez Vilella—to run for the post. In the 1967 plebiscite, the Commonwealth status was favored by 60 per cent of the voters, while 39 per cent chose statehood, and a fraction voted for independence. In 1968, a pro-statehood candidate, Luis A. Ferré, won an upset victory for the governorship, and Muñoz Marín went into virtual retirement.

* "Mister, things are bad. We're earning more money, but yesterday I had to pay more than one dollar for a bunch of green bananas."

† Pangola grass is planted, with government cash incentives, for cattle grazing.

Translated from César Andreu Iglesias, *El Imparcial*, San Juan, April 24, 1965, p. 30. Reprinted by permission of the author.

It was also a time when the foremost modern figure in Puerto Rico's independence movement passed into legend. Pedro Albizu Campos, the militant Nationalist, died in San Juan on April 21, 1965. He had spent eighteen of his seventy-three years in prison. In April, 1936, Albizu was sentenced to ten years in Atlanta Federal Penitentiary after Nationalists killed insular police chief Francis Riggs. When he was pardoned, six years later, thousands of persons met his ship as it docked in San Juan. In 1951, Albizu was jailed after a Nationalist uprising broke out in several island towns, and an attempt was made on the life of President Truman in Washington. He was pardoned in 1953, but this was revoked the next year, after Nationalists wounded five Congressmen. Albizu suffered a stroke in 1956, which left him partially paralyzed. He was sent to Presbyterian Hospital in San Juan, where he remained until he was pardoned by Governor Muñoz in November, 1964. Journalist César Andreu Iglesias wrote this stirring epitaph shortly after Albizu's death.]

Don Pedro Albizu Campos entered into history before he died. Now the legend begins. . . .

It would be illusion to believe that Albizu's life has ended. It is just now beginning. His death marks the end of an epoch. He was, without doubt, the last vestige of our patriots of the previous century. Without that link, who knows if we might have lost our roots!

To define Albizu, a single word suffices. Albizu was the conscience of Puerto Rico. He was for those who followed him, and even more so for those who rejected him.

In deep crises, a single conscience can save a people. Puerto Ricans were lucky to have Albizu. What would have become of us without him?

Albizu accepted his role as his inexorable destiny. Nothing is more terrible than to be the conscience of a people. He spoke when it was necessary to speak. He denounced when denunciations were needed. He accused when it was necessary to accuse. And he was always ready to accept the consequences.

He knew no compromise or surrender. He acted as he was: an unyielding, absolute conscience. That is where the incomprehension began.

If Albizu had only spoken with less anger. If Albizu had only denounced with less fire. If Albizu had only accused with less passion. Ah! Then he would not have been our conscience.

Some have tried to minimize Albizu, saying that his people rejected his words, and repudiated his acts. But that is juvenile logic. It is quite unimportant whether he was repudiated or rejected at one time or another. What gives the measure of Albizu is the impact of his words and of his acts upon the conscience of all Puerto Ricans, to some degree. . . . That will last!

And that, precisely, is the difference between an apostle and a politician.

The politician is with everyone, or pretends to be. The apostle is alone, with his conscience. He is not with others; they are with him . . . to whatever extent and number that may be! . . .

The most important decision is that which each individual makes when he is alone with his conscience. Above the formal vote is the silent vote of the people. And as every critical moment has shown, at the eleventh hour, people and conscience reach an understanding.

Even the hardest-skinned Puerto Rican feels this, although he may not understand it. It is felt by those who adapt to circumstances, for their own good. It is felt by the politician who has not lost all his dignity. It is felt by the teacher, the lawyer, the laborer, the government clerk. . . . They feel it and know it—by intuition if not by conviction—rich and poor, men and women, young and old. And the proof is that no man inspired greater admiration from his people than Albizu.

It had to be thus, because Albizu is the conscience of all Puerto Ricans. And a conscience is seen and heard, even when we look the other way, and pretend to be deaf.

The person who represents the conscience of a people can hardly hope to triumph. His mission is not to save himself, but to save us. In that self-sacrifice is his victory: the final triumph of the cause to which Albizu devoted his entire life.

Part IX

EXODUS

> We have to share everything. We share
> poverty with the Negroes, religion with
> the Irish and Italians. We don't even have
> our slums for us alone.
>
> —JACK AGÜEROS, a Puerto Rican in
> New York City government,
> *New York Times*, April 23, 1968.
>
> I have great hope for their education and
> great fear of the streets.
>
> —ENRIQUE PAOLI, father of ten
> children, *Cleveland Plain-Dealer*,
> April 26, 1971.

Like the waves of
immigrants before them, Puerto Ricans came to the United States in
search of work. This is borne out by hard statistics over the years: each
time there is a recession or a slowdown in the U.S. economy, the number of migrants from Puerto Rico decreases; when the mainland economy "heats up," and jobs are plentiful, the northward flow of manpower
resumes.

Since the end of World War II, economic conditions in Puerto Rico
have improved immensely, but not nearly enough to employ all who
needed work to support their families. What was once a trickle of migration turned into a torrent when inexpensive air travel became available
between San Juan and America's industrial centers on the East Coast.

By the late 1950's, several American cities had large Spanish-speaking
barrios. Most of the newcomers were ill-prepared for their new way of
life, but they tenaciously held on to the hardest, poorest-paying jobs,
lived in overpriced substandard housing, and struggled to establish
themselves. Some fell by the wayside, into public welfare dependence,
or—far worse—into drugs and crime. Soon, U.S. newspapers began referring to "our Puerto Rican problem," in much the same way that
newspapers at the turn of the century complained of the "filthy He-
brews," or "the dangerous Italians."

Inch by inch, the Puerto Ricans have gained a toehold in America, but many of them have paid a terrible price. The following selections describe the exodus from Puerto Rico, and some facets of those first hard years.

THE EARLY DAYS

[Back in 1910,
there were a mere 1,513 Puerto Ricans scattered through 39 states of the
Union, according to the national census. A decade later, compared with
the mass of newcomers from Europe, the Puerto Rican community on
the mainland was still small: 11,811 islanders were reported to be living
in 45 states. Among these pioneers was Jesús Colón, born in the tobacco
region of Cayey. He worked his way north during World War I as a bus-
boy aboard a freighter—that soon afterwards was torpedoed to the bottom of the Atlantic by a German submarine. These excerpts are from his
book, which—in his words—offers "a modest attempt . . . through the
medium of personal experience to throw a little light on how Puerto
Ricans in this city *really* feel, think, work and live."]

It must have been around 1918. . . .

My brother's job was to keep the long, cold desolate platforms of
a subway station nicely clean, to wash the toilets and see that the
drunks didn't spoil his artistic brooming. Among his other multiple
little tasks he had to collect all the newspapers and press them
into bales that were stacked at the end of the station. For this he
got about sixteen dollars a week for working from seven to four
in the morning.

While he worked nights I worked days. So we hardly talked to
each other during the week.

But one thing we did every evening as I came in was for me to
hand him my working pants. He put them on, the pants still warm
with the heat of my body. Then he said "Hasta mañana" and left.
When he came at 4:30 or 5 in the morning I was fast asleep. At
seven in the morning I took back my working pants, put them on,
without disturbing his sleep and off to work I went until the
evening. When I came in at about six he took my—our—pants back.

The question might be asked: "And what did you do when both
of you would go out say—on Sunday?" To that I would answer that
we had our Sunday suits. I could not call them Sunday best, because
"best" implies that there were other suits in our wardrobe . . . we
had no other suits. Just two. His and mine. And a pair of working
pants for the both of us. Then again we could not call our suits
"Sunday best," because our two Sunday suits had seen their best

From Jesús Colón, *A Puerto Rican in New York & Other Sketches* (New
York: Mainstream Publishers, 1961), pp. 25–28, 115–17. Reprinted by permission.

days already many, many, years ago. They were two blue serge suits whose seat-shine seemed to have permanently permeated the other parts of the cloth. . . .

But the fact remained that we only had one pair of working pants between the two of us. And that was a fact for months, until the day when we were not too tired after one of us came from work, to go out and buy one pair of pants. By that I really mean, until we could spare the few dollars—the cost of a pair of good working pants—without disturbing the very delicate balance between what we earned and what we had to spend on room, food, and other incidentals. . . .

Early in 1919, we were both out of work, my brother and I. He got up earlier to look for a job. When I woke up, he was already gone. So I dressed, went out and bought a copy of the *New York World* and turned its pages until I got to the "Help Wanted Unskilled" section of the paper. After much reading and re-reading the same columns, my attention was held by a small advertisement. It read: "Easy job. Good wages. No experience necessary." This was followed by a number and street on the west side of lower Manhattan. It sounded like the job I was looking for. Easy job. Good wages. . . .

The place consisted of a small front office and a large loft on the floor of which I noticed a series of large galvanized tubs half filled with water out of which I noticed protruding the necks of many bottles of various sizes and shapes. Around these tubs there were a number of workers, male and female, sitting on small wooden benches. All had their hands in the water of the tub, the left hand holding a bottle and with the thumb nail of the right hand scratching the labels.

The foreman found a vacant stool for me around one of the tubs of water. I asked why a penknife or a small safety razor could not be used instead of the thumb nail to take off the old labels from the bottles. I was expertly informed that knives or razors would scratch the glass thus depreciating the value of the bottles when they were to be sold.

I sat down and started to use my thumb nail on one bottle. The water had somewhat softened the transparent mucilage used to attach the label to the bottle. But the softening did not work out uniformly somehow. There were always pieces of label that for some obscure reason remained affixed to the bottles. It was on those pieces of labels tenaciously fastened to the bottles that my right hand thumb nail had to work overtime. As the minutes passed I noticed that the coldness of the water started to pass from my hand to my body giving me intermittent body shivers that I tried to conceal with the greatest of effort from those sitting beside me. My hands became deadly clean and tiny little wrinkles started to show especially at the tip of my fingers. Sometimes I stopped a

few seconds from scratching the bottles, to open and close my fists
in rapid movements in order to bring blood to my hands. But almost
as soon as I placed them in the water they became deathly pale
again.

But these were minor details compared with what was happening
to the thumb of my right hand. From a delicate, boyish thumb, it
was growing by the minute into a full blown tomato colored finger.
It was the only part of my right hand remaining blood red. I started
to look at the workers' thumbs. I noticed that these particular
fingers on their right hands were unusually developed with a thick
layer of corn-like surface at the top of their right thumb. The nails
on their thumbs looked coarser and smaller than on the other
fingers—thumb and nail having become one and the same thing—a
primitive unnatural human instrument especially developed to
detach hard pieces of labels from wet bottles immersed in galvanized
tubs.

After a couple of hours I had a feeling that my thumb nail was
going to leave my finger and jump into the cold water in the tub.
A numb pain imperceptibly began to be felt coming from my right
thumb. Then I began to feel such pain as if coming from a finger
bigger than all of my body.

After three hours of this I decided to quit fast. I told the foreman
so, showing him my swollen finger. He figured I had earned 69
cents at 23 cents an hour.

Early in the evening I met my brother in our furnished room.
We started to exchange experiences of our job hunting for the
day. "You know what?" my brother started, "early in the morning
I went to work where they take labels off old bottles—with your
right hand thumb nail . . . Somewhere on the West Side of Lower
Manhattan. I only stayed a couple of hours. 'Easy job . . . Good
wages' . . . they said. The person who wrote that ad must have had
a great sense of humor." And we both had a hearty laugh that
evening when I told my brother that I also went to work at that
same place later in the day. . . .

It was very late at night on the eve of Memorial Day. She came
into the subway at the 34th Street Pennsylvania Station. I am still
trying to remember how she managed to push herself in with a
baby on her right arm, a valise in her left hand and two children, a
boy and girl about three and five years old, trailing after her. She
was a nice looking white lady in her early twenties.

At Nevins Street, Brooklyn, we saw her preparing to get off at
the next station—Atlantic Avenue—which happened to be the place
where I too had to get off. Just as it was a problem for her to get
on, it was going to be a problem for her to get off the subway. . . .

And there I was, also preparing to get off at Atlantic Avenue, with
no bundles to take care of—not even the customary book under my
arm without which I feel that I am not completely dressed.

As the train was entering the Atlantic Avenue station, some white man stood up from his seat and helped her out, placing the children on the long, deserted platform. There were only two adult persons on the long platform some time after midnight on the eve of last Memorial Day.

I could perceive the steep, long concrete stairs going down to the Long Island Railroad or into the street. Should I offer my help as the American white man did at the subway door placing the two children outside the subway car? Should I take care of the girl and the boy, take them by their hands until they reached the end of the steep long concrete stairs of the Atlantic Avenue station.

Courtesy is a characteristic of the Puerto Rican. And here I was— a Puerto Rican—hours past midnight, a valise, two white children and a white lady with a baby on her arm palpably needing somebody to help her at least until she descended the long concrete stairs.

But how could I, a Negro and a Puerto Rican, approach this white lady who very likely might have preconceived prejudices against Negroes and everybody with foreign accents, in a deserted subway station very late at night?

What would she say? What would be the first reaction of this white American woman, perhaps coming from a small town. . . . Would she say: Yes, of course, you may help me. Or would she think that I was just trying to get too familiar? Or would she think worse than that perhaps? What would I do if she let out a scream as I went toward her to offer my help?

Was I misjudging her? So many slanders are written every day in the daily press against the Negroes and Puerto Ricans. I hesitated for a long, long minute. The ancestral manners that the most illiterate Puerto Rican passes on from father to son were struggling inside me. Here was I, way past midnight, face to face with a situation that could very well explode into an outburst of prejudices and chauvinistic conditioning of the "divide and rule" policy of present day society.

It was a long minute. I passed on by her as if I saw nothing. As if I was insensitive to her need. Like a rude animal walking on two legs, I just moved on half running by the long subway platform leaving the children and the valise and her with the baby on her arm. I took the steps of the long concrete stairs in twos until I reached the street above and the cold air slapped my warm face. . . .

"WHAT IS PREJUDICE?"

[Bitter experience taught
the early migrants that in the United States there was racial prejudice
of an intensity unknown in Puerto Rico. In the 1950's, as thousands of
migrants flew north to seek jobs, the island government made sincere,
but feeble, attempts to prepare them for the "culture shock" that
awaited them. Part of this effort was a series of pamphlets that was distributed in rural areas of the island. Excerpts from one of these pam-.
phlets deal with the question of racial prejudice. The message is written
in simple terms, for people with little formal education.]

What is prejudice?
Prejudice is the judgment or opinion that one forms without having
enough information about something . . . without taking the truth
into account. Let us take an example:

If we don't know the Jews, but we insist that all Jews are
traitors, we are judging something without knowing it. We are
committing an injustice. We are being prejudiced. Why are we
prejudiced?

Well, perhaps we recall the Bible, where we read that Judas
betrayed Jesus. And Judas was a Jew. Then, without thinking or
reasoning, we say that Jews are traitors. Should all the Jews pay
for what Judas did? That wouldn't be just. Jesus himself was a
Jew. Would anyone dare to say that Jesus, being Jewish, was a
traitor? . . .

Let's suppose that in the United States a black American commits
a crime. There are many white Americans who are prejudiced
against the blacks. What happens? The act of a single black is paid
for by the others. Because people with prejudice say: "Look, that's
what the blacks do." And it isn't true. Because when a white
American kills someone, it doesn't occur to anyone to say that all
white Americans are killers. In the same way, the other blacks are
not guilty of what a single black did. . . .

The same thing can happen to the Puerto Ricans in the United
States, as it does with the blacks or the Jews. . . .

If one Puerto Rican steals, Americans who are prejudiced say that
all Puerto Ricans are thieves. If one Puerto Rican doesn't work,
prejudiced Americans say all of us are lazy. If one Puerto Rican

Translated from *Emigración*, Libros Para El Pueblo-Número Ocho (San
Juan: Department of Education, 1966), 2nd Edition, pp. 49–51.

throws his garbage into the street instead of into the trash can, prejudiced Americans say that all Puerto Ricans have filthy habits. So, each mistake by a Puerto Rican in the United States is paid for by all. How?

We pay, because a bad opinion of us is formed. And the result may be that they discredit us, they won't give us work, or they deny us our rights.

Of course, not all Americans are prejudiced. There, as in Puerto Rico, there are all kinds; good people and bad people, stupid people and intelligent people, honorable people and thieves. . . .

How can we defend ourselves against prejudice? Not with violence or insults. We cannot attack the prejudice of others with our own. One means of defense and attack against prejudice is to set a good example. Another is to have the knowledge of all our rights and duties as citizens.

But we must keep something else in mind. We must be alert, so as not to contaminate ourselves with the prejudices of some Americans.

Some Puerto Ricans have grown cowardly, in the face of prejudice in the United States. Their solution to the problem has been to believe in the prejudice of some Americans. There is nothing more terrible to see than a Puerto Rican in the United States who is contaminated by the prejudice there. He begins by attacking the American blacks, and winds up attacking his own Puerto Rican brothers. He betrays his own, and even winds up denying that he is Puerto Rican. That type of wrongly "Americanized" Puerto Rican is one of our worst enemies. . . .

LONG NIGHT'S JOURNEY

[The exodus of Puerto Ricans that began in the 1950's was so massive that the route between San Juan and New York soon came to be known as an "air bridge." Day after day, planeloads of migrants were lofted from their *patria*, and a few hours later descended the stairway to a new world, 1,600 miles to the north. During the flight, they were crammed together in planes that jounced about in the air like ships in a storm-tossed sea. It was a frightening, often nauseating, baptism. Dan Wakefield, the well known American journalist and novelist, who lived for more than a year in New York's Spanish Harlem, also made the trip.]

From Dan Wakefield, *Island in the City: The World of Spanish Harlem* (Boston: Houghton Mifflin, 1959), pp. 23–43. Reprinted with permission.

Ricardo Sánchez came from where the sugar cane is higher than a man to the plaza in old San Juan where the buses marked *Aeropuerto* stop. He came with his wife and two daughters and three suitcases and a paper bag and the promise from a brother in Harlem, New York, that there was work to be found in *fábrica*. The work in the sugar cane was over for the season and Ricardo had found nothing else. The government would pay him $7 every two weeks for thirteen weeks before the season began again, and then with the season he would get $3.60 a day for eight hours in the sun. He had done it before, as his fathers had done it, but this time he told himself he wanted something more. "It is," he said, "no good to be poor." His lean brown face was twisted in a grimace of disgust as he said the words, and remained that way, in the memory of poverty. slowly relaxing as he fingered the three fountain pens neatly clipped to the pocket of his new brown suit, and turned to face the dark from where the buses come.

Christopher Columbus, migrant by trade, stood by frozen in the stone of a statue, the accidental patron saint of the plaza that serves as a boarding place for those who go away. Even more practically, Columbus' weathered figure serves those who stay, for around it sit the old men who sit around the statues of the plazas of the world; these by the chance of Columbus' mistaken discoveries (and Ponce de León's mistaken hopes) speaking the language of his creditor the Queen. But the Queen is four centuries dead, and the island's highest ruler is a president from Kansas—a place whose name and language are totally foreign to the old men who sit by the statue.

Their fathers before them were Indians here, called Borinqueños, and Spanish followers of Ponce de León, seeker after gold and youth and captor of neither. His body is buried up the street. Their fathers were Negro slaves from Africa, brought here to fill the vacuum left when the Indians painfully vanished, by death and escape, from the Spaniards' rule. . . .

The city is quiet, and the old men who sit in the plaza seem unconcerned. Their fathers are gone and their sons are free to go.

For more than a century the sons have left the plazas and the dust-and-green towns of the interior to come to New York. Ricardo Sánchez is young, but his journey is old. The first Puerto Ricans came to New York in the early 1800's, along with other men of good hope from the underfed islands of the Caribbean who decided that "it is no good to be poor." From Cuba and Santo Domingo they came, from San Juan and Haiti and Jamaica. Some survived and others were lost, and in 1838 the men from Puerto Rico who had managed to make themselves merchants of New York City formed a Spanish Benevolent Society for those of their brothers who had failed and were hungry.

Others went west, and by 1910 there were Puerto Ricans living in thirty-nine states of the Union. Twenty years later the people of the island were in every state, though the great majority were still in New York City. The journey north from the Caribbean became a regular route for those seeking something better (and having the money to make the search), and for most of the first half of the twentieth century an average of 4000 came from Puerto Rico to the mainland every year.

No one seemed to notice. It was not until near the end of the Second World War that the quiet, steady migration became the great migration—the promise of the mainland suddenly expanding with more new jobs than ever before and the word passing on from relative to relative, friend to friend, employment recruiter to unemployed. During the war there was little transportation available for Puerto Ricans who wanted to leave the island, but toward the end of it the U.S. War Manpower Commission brought workers up in army transports to help fill the booming job market. In the first year after the war 39,900 Puerto Ricans came to the mainland, and the annual stream reached an average of roughly 50,000 in the postwar decade. As it has throughout its history, the Puerto Rican migration curve followed the business curve on the mainland, and the start of the greatest postwar recession in 1957 was reflected by a 28 per cent decrease in migration from the year before. Downturns in the volume of business on the continent have always meant downturns in migration from the island, and during the worst depression years of the thirties the flow of migrants actually reversed itself, with more returning annually to the island than came from it. But barring an extreme and prolonged depression, the total of 600,000 first- or second-generation Puerto Ricans in New York City in 1958 was expected to rise to a million by the early 1970's. And, for the first time, the great migration had begun to spread more heavily in cities and towns throughout the country. In 1950, 85 per cent of the entering migrants settled in New York City, but by 1956 and 1957 the average was down to 65 per cent, with others going to expanding Puerto Rican settlements in cities such as Philadelphia (New York's largest Spanish-language newspaper now carries a special column of Puerto Rican news from Philadelphia), Chicago, Cleveland, Ashtabula, Bridgeport, Milwaukee, and others farther west.

The journey from the island had become not only more promising because of the market for jobs after World War II but also much easier to make because of the airplanes that rose from San Juan and landed at Idlewild, New York City, 1600 miles up the ocean, in only eight hours and for only $75 on regular airlines instead of the former price of $180. Besides the approved commercial lines that opened up regular service after the war there were secondhand planes mak-

ing unscheduled flights for $35—they could charge that price be-
cause they were paid off later by men from the states who came to
Puerto Rico and charged "employment agent" fees that often consumed life savings sweated from sugar cane as payment for non-
existent jobs in New York City. Some of the victims never found
out because they first became the victims of ill-equipped planes that
crashed in the ocean. After several such tragedies the government
outlawed the small, unscheduled airlines from making the San
Juan–New York run.

But the regular, legal air travel flourished—not only giving a boost
to the old migration to the mainland cities but also opening up a
new migration. Cheap and fast plane travel made it possible to transport idle agricultural workers from Puerto Rico during the heavy
harvesting season on the mainland in the spring, and back again to
the island when the sugar-cane season began in the fall. A new
seasonal migration began on that basis after the war and has grown
to an annual flow of about 30,000 workers (not counted in the
regular migration figures of those who come and plan to stay).
Contrary to popular belief, the great majority of Puerto Ricans
who come to New York, and other U.S. cities, are not laborers but
city people who have held city jobs on the island.

Ricardo Sánchez, who waited in the dark for the bus marked
Aereopuerto, was one of the small but slowly growing number of
Puerto Ricans who have left the sugar-cane fields for the city. The
desire to escape from the backbreaking work of the cane cutting is
still not easily fulfilled, but the dream has become much more
widespread since many young men saw the world in service with
the U.S. Army in Korea, and returned home with higher aspirations.
Frank Ruiz, the secretary-treasurer of the *Sindicato Azucarero*
(Sugar Workers Union) in Puerto Rico says that it is harder now to
get the young men to work in the cane fields because "the army has
refined them."

Ricardo Sánchez was able to make at least a partial transition in
his work before the drastic change from the island fields to the New
York fabric shops. During the idle season a year before, he had
found a job doing piecework in a garment shop in the small town
of Vega Baja. But the work didn't last, and after another season in
the fields he decided to try his luck—and his brother's help—in the
fábrica shops of New York City.

Ricardo held for himself and his family tickets on the $52.50
night coach Thrift Flight to Idlewild airport. It leaves six nights a
week from San Juan at eleven o'clock and arrives the next morning
at Idlewild at seven. The adjective "thrift" is the only term of
distinction between this flight and the other night coach flight, which
costs $64, leaves a half hour later, and arrives in New York City two
hours earlier. The Thrift Flight is not recommended—or even sug-

gested at the ticket counters—to non-Puerto Rican travelers. English-speaking people who ask about it are told that it is better to spend the extra money and go on the eleven-thirty flight.

There were only Puerto Ricans on the *Aereopuerto* bus that Ricardo Sánchez boarded in the plaza of Christopher Columbus. They stayed together when they reached the San Juan airport, checking in baggage and then joining friends and relatives and watchers in the crowd on the observation deck. When the flight was called, it was as if a troop plane were leaving for a war, or a group of refugees being shipped of necessity out of their native country. It is that way every night around eleven o'clock at the San Juan airport—the women crying and the men embracing them; the old people staring out of wrinkled, unperceiving faces and the young engrossed with the wonder, rather than the pain of it, pressing up against the iron rail of the observation deck and squinting through the dark to watch the line of human travelers move as if drawn by a spell through the gate below and into the still, silver plane that swallows them, closing silver on silver to complete itself, and then slowly moves toward the dark and disappears.

Inside the airplane Ricardo Sánchez had seated his wife and one of his daughters on the left-hand, two-seat aisle, and taken his other daughter and himself across to the right in the three-seat row with a stranger. The flight was full, as these flights are nearly always full. . . .

The plane was hot—hotter than the 75° weather outside—and many of the men, already sweating, had taken off their coats. A young, dark-skinned woman in an aqua silk dress was crying softly and fanning herself with the plastic *Ocupado* sign from the pocket of the seat in front of her. The stewardess appeared at the head of the aisle when the door was closed and gave a demonstration while the steward explained on the loudspeaker, first in Spanish and then in English, the instructions for putting on life jackets in case of an emergency.

The engines began, swelled, and the plane crept forward. The woman in the aqua dress pressed her face against the porthole-style window, crying much louder now. The balcony of watchers grew smaller and darker; became a few white handkerchiefs waved in the night, and then was gone. Babies began to cry as the plane rose, moving above the red, white, and green pinpoints strung geometrically and sparkling in the pattern of the city and suburbs of San Juan. In several minutes the dark had covered it. The no-smoking and safety-belt signs in the plane blinked off, the overhead lights went out, and only the small, individual reading lights above the seats were on. The babies stopped crying, and the temperature of the plane began to cool. Seats were pushed back, and soon the thin beams of light from the few remaining reading lights were thickened with cigarette smoke. The stewardess came by and asked

Ricardo Sánchez if he wanted her to hang up his suit coat. The stewardess did not speak Spanish and Ricardo, looking at her quizzically and smiling politely, clutched his coat when she reached for it and held it folded on his lap. He leaned his head back against the seat, folding his hands on his lap, and stared straight ahead, the view slightly tilted with the angle of the seat; his mouth in a tight, tentative smile. After a while he closed his eyes.

The dull, steady roar of the engine was the single sound, growing louder and fuller as other sounds stopped, until, in its constant drone and throb, the sound of the engine became no sound at all, but a part of the plane's suspended life. It became a sound again several hours later when the screams woke Ricardo Sánchez from his tilted sleep:

"Ay, ay, *ayyyy!*"

The women screamed as the plane fell forward through the dark. The sound of the two engines heightened and throbbed. The plane leveled off from the drop, leaving the stomachs of the passengers with the sickening, overturned sensation that comes on a roller coaster during the sudden, steep descent. The steward hurried down the aisle with smelling salts.

Ricardo Sánchez leaned forward to look across the aisle at his wife. Her head was leaning across on her daughter, who sat in silence, her eyes widening to watch the steward stop by the seat and wave the smelling salts. Ricardo's mouth opened and his white teeth were clenched together as if he were being struck. He started up, but the safety belt was fastened on his waist. He looked at it a moment, then leaned back into his seat. The plane dipped again.

The steward stopped and explained to the only non-Puerto Rican passenger that the plane had hit a storm.

"We felt it quite a bit," he said. "The planes for this flight aren't pressurized. If you take the eleven-thirty flight—the $64 one—you fly above all this."

There was no announcement in Spanish about the storm. Ricardo Sánchez's wife, revived, pulled the white bag for vomiting out of the pocket of the seat and leaned into it. Lightning flashed as the plane pitched again in the dark—the tiny green light on the end of the wing was the only thing visible. Ricardo Sánchez tightened the safety belt of his daughter who sat next to him. She clutched at the arm of the seat, in silence, and pressed against the back of it, her thin legs sticking out with the shiny black patent leather shoes not touching the floor. Her father stroked her hair, then leaned back himself and touched the palms of his hands together, pointing upward, in his lap. Through the crack of the seat in front, the brown, large-veined hands of a woman twisted and knotted and pulled on a rainbow-colored silk handkerchief.

The dips became slighter and the screams lower, several becoming soft, continual moans that rose with the fall of the plane. A man walked back to the stewardess who sat reading a copy of the *Saturday Evening Post* and asked her in English if the worst of the storm was over. She looked up annoyed and said, "*I'm* not the pilot," touched her forefinger to her tongue, and flipped the page of the magazine.

A little after five o'clock in the morning the silver wings of the plane became visible, and then a layer of clouds below the plane. A pink strip grew at the end of the layer of clouds in the east, and an orange streak grew from the pink. The billowed layers of clouds below became blue-gray, then lighter blue. Ricardo Sánchez tapped his daughter's shoulder and told her to look. She leaned across on his lap and he explained, "It is dawn. Look—it is beautiful."

About six o'clock the stewardess came by with a tray of steaming paper cups and asked each passenger, in English, "Would you like some coffee?" Some didn't seem to understand so the stewardess repeated the question in more distinct tones, "Would you like some coffee?" There were those who still did not understand and the stewardess, seemingly annoyed, passed on. Some people nodded, or held out their hands, and were given coffee.

The woman in the aqua silk dress stood up in the aisle and pulled up her stockings. She sat back down, pulled a small bottle from her purse, turned it on her finger, and dabbed at her neck. The strong, sweet smell of perfume spread across the aisle. The plane had broken through the clouds and there was water below. Soon there was land—another island; this one, too, striped and set with rows of white lights and green lights, fewer lights in the growing gray dawn than were seen in the night above San Juan. The island that the plane approached seemed not so much larger than the island it had left. Lower, the land turned brown and barren, with a swamplike series of protrusions in the water, and the plane moved closer till the brown high grass on the land and the wind-ruffled waves of the water were clearly visible. The plane seemed about to touch the water and suddenly touched on land—the end of the Idlewild airstrip. The babies again were crying.

The plane stopped, and the passengers looked out the window at the quiet runways, the long, low buildings, and the high, silver lampposts that arched in a long and graceful curve like the neck of some thin and watchful animal, repeated row on row. The women stepped out of the silver door, clutching at their flimsy, bright-colored dresses, into the morning chill of New York and the gray, surrealistic landscape of Idlewild.

Friends and relatives waited at the gate with scarves and coats and kisses and handclasps and took the passengers out of the airport and into cars and buses to the Bronx and the lower East

Luis Muñoz Rivera (with straw hat, cigar, and cane) visiting a farm in the northwestern mountain country near Utuado in 1913.

Country women making hats from fiber at the turn of the century.

Pedro Albizu Campos, who was elected President of the Nationalist Party in 1931 and is now considered a martyr by pro-independence Puerto Ricans.

The Ponce Massacre on Palm Sunday, 1937, when police opened fire during a Nationalist parade.

Puerto Ricans from the island arriving at Philadelphia airport to harvest a tomato crop shortly after World War II.

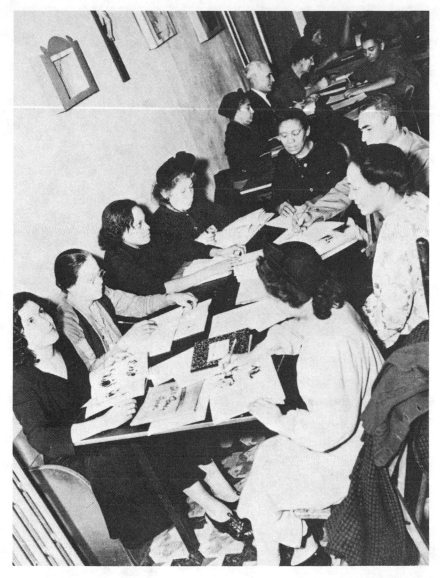

Puerto Ricans studying English at an East Harlem settlement in New York City in the 1940's.

Puerto Rico Information Service

Aerial view of modern San Juan.

Puerto Rico Information Service

Modern petrochemical complex on Puerto Rico's southern coast.

Spokesmen for the Young Lords, a group of young activists formed in New York City in the late 1960's.

Rafael Hernández Colón, who became governor of Puerto Rico in January, 1973.

Side and the upper West Side of Manhattan and also to New York's first large Puerto Rican neighborhood, known as Spanish Harlem.

"I'M FREEZING TO DEATH"

[The migrant soon learns that getting used to cold weather is just the first of several harsh adjustments. Next come finding a place to live, a job, a means to communicate, and a way to make your children respect you in a city where you yourself are insecure. Via the tape recorder, and exhaustive research, the late anthropologist Oscar Lewis spent a lifetime trying to "give a voice to the people who are rarely heard." Here, he listens to Puerto Ricans in New York City as they describe the dreams, and nightmares, of migration.]

Upon arriving, many informants experienced an initial feeling of dejection and a strong desire to return to Puerto Rico. They expressed disappointment and even disgust at the ugliness and dirtiness of the city. . . .

"The truth is that I was disillusioned when I saw New York because I thought that it would be a cleaner and prettier place and that the houses would be newer. I was disappointed to see so many slums. I thought, 'Puerto Rico is much prettier than this!' "

The cold weather bothered most people and they disliked the fact that New Yorkers lived "all shut in" even in the summer, in contrast to the open porches, doors and windows of the houses in Puerto Rico. . . .

"When I arrived I wanted to turn around and go right back to Puerto Rico because it was so cold. I came in January of 1961 and there had been a tremendous snowstorm. There were about seven inches of snow on the ground and it was below zero. I said to myself, 'Mmmm, I'm not liking this country very much.' But then I told myself, 'Go on, get off the plane. Let's see what it's like.'

From Oscar Lewis, A Study of Slum Culture: Backgrounds for "La Vida" (New York: Random House, 1966), pp. 126–28, 144–45, 160–61, 182–84, 201. Reprinted with permission.

"I came with nothing but a sweater and a suit, one of those wash and wear suits. I had written to my brother asking him to bring a coat to the airport because I didn't have one.

"As I was getting off the plane a girl said to me, 'Excuse me, can you help me carry this baby? I have two of them.' But I said to her, 'I'm very sorry, *señora*, but I'm freezing to death and I don't have a coat.'

"I got off the plane and ran to the terminal. My brother was waiting with a coat so I put on the coat over my sweater. I put on gloves, I put on everything!

"It was three o'clock in the morning and I kept looking and looking to see what kind of a country this was. Somehow we got to a subway, and that was a crazy thing. I thought they were the same as the buses in Puerto Rico and that when you wanted to get off you stood up and pulled the cord. But my brother told me, 'No, it's not like that here. This isn't a bus, it's a train, and it stops where it likes.'

"There were a lot of people on the subway, but I wasn't paying any attention to them. I kept looking out the window to see what the country was like. But what could I see? Nothing. The train was going underground! All I could see was the wall. I'll never forget that in all my life."

Complaints about the impersonality and anonymity of living in New York and its effects upon morality and behavior patterns are well illustrated by the following excerpt: . . .

"Here you may move into the apartment next to mine and it will be ten years before I find out you are there. When I go out to work in the morning I don't see my neighbors who live in the same building. I once saw an American girl in the building where I lived and I asked someone if he knew her. 'Why that girl lives right here,' I was told. Yet, as long as I had lived in that building, I had never seen her before.

"In Puerto Rico, it's different. Suppose you live somewhere in Río Piedras—everybody in the whole barrio knows you. If you move, there isn't one neighbor who can't tell me, 'She moved to Cantera, in Santurce.' . . . Even if someone wants to cheat you by moving away they can't, no matter how far they move. But here one can move two blocks away and even his nearest relatives can't find him. . . ."

There was a general feeling among our informants of being exploited and discriminated against—mainly, they believed, because of their language handicap.

"Hispanos are the only ones in New York who have to work

for practically nothing. The colored people are a bit better off than the Hispanos because at least they know English. Negroes are the laziest people you'll find here. They're born lazy. A colored man gets a job in a factory and the boss explains clearly to him what he is supposed to do. But suppose he's working at something and the boss says, 'Look, hand me that piece of paper.' He'll tell the boss, 'Pick it up yourself,' and go on with what he is doing. With an Hispano it's different. Like if the boss says, 'The only thing you have to do here is to dust that little chair,' you can be sure that before he's through they've made him scrub the floor, clean the toilet, wash down the walls. And if there's a heavy package to be carried, it's the Hispano who has to carry it. . . .

"What else can he do? He doesn't know the language and if he quits the job he will have a hard time finding another one. All because he doesn't know English. That's what keeps us down. In a factory we have to do all the odd jobs because we don't have the advantage of speaking English, and the Hispanos who do know English get the best of the others and hold them back instead of helping them out. When a boss tells an Hispano who knows English to order another man to do something and the other says, 'Tell the boss that if I am to do that he should pay me more,' the first will come back at him, 'If you don't like the pay, you can quit.' A man of one's own race!"

. . . many parents questioned the right of law enforcement officials to prevent them from beating their children. They believed that beatings were a necessary part of child discipline and they attributed much of the delinquency to overprotection of the young. . . .

"Here the children become very independent at an early age. If you give a kid a good wallop and his bruises show, the police can get after you. It's not like that in Puerto Rico. Here in New York one day I was giving my little boy a good strapping and a policeman came and warned me to stop beating him. . . . That happened because my boy took $20 from my purse and went to the dime store in the neighborhood and bought everything he could lay his hands on. When I found out about it, I took him back to the store and had him return the things and get the money back. And for each thing I gave him a good spanking. That's when the cops stopped me. But if I had let my son get away with that, God only knows what he would be like today.

"So anyway, when the policeman butted in, I said, 'You can warn me about hitting my child now, but when he's eighteen and you see him on the rooftops robbing apartments and acting shamelessly, don't say anything to me. Bring him down with a bullet and leave me in peace.' The cop never said another thing to me about spanking my child." . . .

Our informants were very critical of the manner in which Puerto Ricans behave toward each other. Although some insisted that there is no friction among Puerto Rican migrants, many others lamented their lack of unity and the presence of discrimination and exploitation within the group.

"The Hispanos also have a little—let's say a little—discrimination among themselves. Not actually because of color, you understand, but because some Hispanos are in better positions, they live in better sections of the city and earn more money than the rest of us. This class may own a business and wants to segregate itself from the other Hispanos. Sometimes they even disown us. They say that they're not Hispanos but South Americans or something like that. . . .

"If we had any kind of unity, all those things that happen to us here wouldn't occur. Instead of offering a hand, the ones that come first try to keep the others down. If a veteran Hispano is working as a salesman, he goes from door to door to exploit his compatriots rather than going to the houses of Americans who have money. . . .

"The trouble with the Puerto Ricans in New York is that each lives for himself and they're all scared to death. They don't dare to protest against anything. They won't picket a police station for fear of getting shot. Most Puerto Ricans here don't even dare speak up when the factory bosses make them work overtime and then don't pay for it. They belong to unions but the unions don't do a thing for them. They are afraid to complain to the Department of Labor for fear the boss will find out and fire them. They think they would starve if they did. They hold back and won't talk.

"I don't know what's the matter with our leaders! The leaders were all born and bred in the States. They have no feeling for Puerto Rico, nor for us Puerto Ricans who come here. They have gone to school here from the first, they live well, so what do they care about the rest of us? They think, 'Let the rest of them sink or swim. Why should I bother as long as I have what I want, earn a good salary, and live well? If the rest don't know how to get as far as I have, let them stay where they are.'

"If you go to them with your complaints, they are the first to rob you. You go to one of those lawyers because he speaks Spanish the same as you do, and the first thing he'll tell you is, 'Bring $50 or $60 and I'll see what can be done about your case.'

Suppose you want to bring suit against the company where you work. As soon as your back is turned, your man will seek out the company lawyer and you are out on the street, fired from your job. . . ."

So many of the families harbored hopes of returning to Puerto Rico that it suggests that Puerto Ricans were, psychologically speaking, not really immigrants at all, but migrant workers. . . .

"As soon as I can, I want to leave New York with all its 'modernization.' This 'modernization' doesn't go back with me. It's for those who have ability, money, education, and who are on their way up. Perhaps it's for my children in the future, but not for me. . . .

"When I leave here I'm going to take $800 or $1,000 with me to Puerto Rico. But I'm not going to live like a rich man in the center of San Juan. I'll work in San Juan but I'm going to take my family to live in the countryside, where I can have a little house of my own, even if it's made of planks and has a tin roof. At least I won't have to pay rent. I'll buy a few acres of land and I'll come home and raise my animals and cultivate something. I'll educate my children and perhaps the whole family can live peacefully. Of course it's always possible that it won't work out. And what I think now is that if luck is not with me, and I fail, I'll throw myself under a car."

AMERICAN-BORN "FOREIGNERS"

[The Puerto Rican migrant has much in common with the people of other ethnic groups who poured into America's "melting pot" during the past century: He is new, he must cope with a strange culture, and he is poor. Yet, in certain very important respects, he is unique: He is born an American citizen, he is often wrongly lumped together with the American blacks (with no consideration or understanding of his own heritage), and he rarely intends to settle permanently on the mainland. These important differences are explored by a former priest, who for many years was involved with Puerto Rican communities in New York and on the island. Since 1968, the author has directed the Center for Intercultural Documentation, CIDOC, in Cuernavaca, Mexico.]

From Ivan Illich, "Puerto Ricans in New York," *The Commonweal*, June 22, 1956, pp. 294–96. Reprinted with permission.

After the introduction
of the quota system in 1924, it seemed as if the melting process in
New York City were finally about to catch up with the number
of people tossed into the pot. Then, in the late forties, the city was
presented with a novel challenge, an invasion of American-born
"foreigners," the Puerto Ricans. . . .

These Puerto Ricans are not foreigners, and yet they are more
foreign than most of the immigrants who preceded them. About
this seeming paradox the well-meaning should be well-informed,
since to be received kindly because you are a foreigner is not
much different from being received kindly because, "after all,
all men are alike." In both cases, chances are that the man who
receives you is determined never to come to know you. . . .

This fallacy is at the bottom of the attitude of many well-
meaning people toward the Puerto Rican immigrants: Let them
do what the Irish or Italians did, or let them attempt what the
Jews attempted; let them grow gradually through their own national parishes, territorial ghettoes and political machines to full
"Americanization"; let them vociferously assert that they are as
good Americans as the man next door. These attitudes are very
common in New York, where the arrival of successive migratory
waves is taken for granted. It is too often gratuitously assumed that
the future novel about the Puerto Rican journey will be fashioned
after either *The Last Hurrah* or *Marjorie Morningstar*, or will be
a combination of both.

The welfare investigator who says to José Rivera, "My parents
went through the same experience," neither lies nor expresses
xenophobia—he just oversimplifies, like the politician who tries
again to use methods which worked when Italian was spoken
in Harlem.

When the Irish and the Germans came here a century ago, New
York City was faced with a challenge of a kind never experienced
before and of a size never to be duplicated. In 1855, one-third
of the city's population (500,000) consisted of immigrants who
had arrived in the previous decade; against this proportion the
one-fifteenth of the city's population which in 1955 consisted of
recently arrived Puerto Ricans (again 500,000) seems insignificant.

In the days of the heavy influx to America, wave after wave of
immigrants arrived, settled down and became accustomed to new
patterns. The newcomers spoke different languages, worshipped in
different churches, came from different climates, wooed in different fashions, ate different dishes and sang different songs. But
under these apparent differences they had much in common. They
came from the Old Continent and arrived as refugees or settlers
to become Americans and to stay for good. They brought their
own clergy, rabbi, priest or minister, and the symbols of past
millenia which were their own, St. Patrick, the Maffia or Loretto,

no less than the Turnverein. They settled in special sections of the city and kept to themselves for years before they ventured to take part in that experience new to all of them, life in a pluralistic society. They fell into a common pattern, and it is no wonder that those who had been here long enough to consider themselves part of a settled stratum fell into the habit of assuming *a priori* that each new incoming group would be analogous to theirs. This assumption, in fact, proved to be true until after the second world war, with the exception of two groups, the Orientals and the Southern Negroes.

Then, suddenly, the Puerto Ricans arrived en masse. New York had never before known such an invasion, an invasion of Americans who came from an older part of the New World into New York, which had been part of the diocese of San Juan long before Henry Hudson had discovered Manhattan. And New York had never had to deal with born American citizens who in their schools had learned English as a foreign language, yet who went to the polls to vote.

These strange Americans were sons of a Catholic country where for centuries slaves had found refuge, where the population of a little over two million is overwhelmingly white but where a difference in the shade of the skin is no impediment, either to success or to marriage. Yet theirs was the first sizable group coming from overseas into New York to be tagged by many as "colored," much less because of the racial heredity of some than for the vaguely sensed great difference between them and former new arrivals.

This was a new type of immigrant: not a European who had left home for good and strove to become an American, but an American citizen, who could come here for one harvest and return home for vacation with a week's salary spent on a coach ticket. This was not the fugitive from racial or religious persecution in his own country, but the child of "natives" in a Spanish colony or perhaps the descendant of a Spanish official in the colonial service; not a man accustomed to be led by men of his own stock—priest, politician, rebel or professor—but for four hundred years a subject in a territory administered by foreigners, first Spanish, then American, only recently come into its own.

The new arrival from Puerto Rico was not the Christian in his own right who received the Faith from the sons of his own neighbors, but the fruit of missionary labor typical of the Spanish empire. He was a Catholic, born of parents who were also Catholics, yet he received the Sacraments from a foreigner because the Government was afraid that to train native priests might be to train political rebels.

Even the physical configuration of the world from which he came was different. He was a man from an island where nature is provident and a friend, where field labor means much more harvesting than planting. When nature rebels every few decades, he is powerless; in the hurricanes he cannot but see the finger of God.

Until recently, nobody in Puerto Rico built a house with the idea that it should survive the elements with its strength or withstand the climate with its air-conditioning. What a difference from the Pole and the Sicilian, both of whom built to withstand nature, climate and time, both of whom built to separate their lives from that of nature. One might have come from the Russian steppe or the ghetto and the other from an olive-grove on the coast, but both knew what winter meant; they knew that a house was there to protect them from the cold, a place within which to make a home. It was easy for the Pole and the Sicilian to settle in tenements and to live confined there. But the new immigrant from the tropics knew no winter, and the home he left was a hut in which you slept, but *around* which you lived with your family. The hut was the center of his day's activities, not their limit. To come to a tenement, to need heat, to need glass in your windows, to be frowned on for tending to live beyond your doors—this was all contrary to the Puerto Rican's traditional habits, and as surprising to him as it is for the New Yorker to realize that for any immigrants these basic assumptions of his life should be surprising. . . .

Many a Puerto Rican does not leave the Island with a clear plan of settling on the mainland. How can a man who leaves on the spur of the moment, planning to make a fast dollar in New York and be back as soon as he has enough to buy a store, take roots in New York? I remember one woman who was in despair because her husband had disappeared on his way to the cane-fields, carrying his machete. She thought, of course, that a rival had grabbed him from her. And then, after a week, she got a money-order from Chicago. On the way to the cane-field he had run into a hiring gang and decided to try his luck—and that was the reason he neglected to come home for dinner. In a case like this, in which a man "drops in" on New York, with no intentions of staying but of eventually commuting "home," how can the transient have the same effect on his neighborhood in New York as the old immigrant who came to stay? Yet the statistical curve of emigration from the Island is in exact correlation with the curve of employment on the mainland. If employment is scarce, the reflux increases correspondingly. Many, even after years in New York, feel they got stuck there because of money.

With the arrival of hundreds of thousands from Puerto Rico and the other Central American States (it is estimated that more than one-fourth of N. Y.'s Spanish-American population is not

Puerto Rican), not only a new language but a new pattern of
living has been added to the city. Instead of the strangers speaking
only a foreign tongue who formerly arrived exhausted from the
long journey, American citizens, all of whom know some basic
English, arrive in airplanes within six hours * of leaving their
tropical island.

The old immigrants settled in national neighborhoods; the new
commuter spreads out all over the city; ten years after the beginning of the mass influx, Spanish has already become ubiquitous
in New York. Unlike European immigrants, all Puerto Ricans
know some English, and this helped, but there is another factor
that has contributed to this spreading to all quarters by South
Americans. In former times when a neighborhood became a center
for the newest immigrant, it was either a slum or tended to
become one. And once a neighborhood had deteriorated it hardly
ever was redeemed. The great immigration from Puerto Rico
started after World War II, due to such factors as cheap air
transportation, acquaintance with the mainland acquired by many
during service in the army, rising education under the new political
order on the island, and, last but not least, the growing pressure
of population which has more than doubled since the beginning
of the century. At that same time, the city was embarking on
its great slum-clearance program, and the first blocks to be torn
down were almost invariably those where the newest immigrant
had just settled. As a result, the Puerto Ricans began to be resettled
all around town in new projects, and on a non-discriminatory
basis.

Considering this dispersal and the tendency to commute to the
Island, it is no wonder that there are hardly any Puerto Rican
national neighborhoods in the traditional sense. One result is that
it is difficult for Puerto Ricans to develop local grass-roots leadership within their own group; either their concentration per city
block is too thin, or the intention to stick to the neighborhood
is absent, or the necessity to organize with their own is weak
because all are citizens who at least understand some English
and have official "protection" from the government labor office—the
first instance of something like a "Consulate for American Na-
tionals." And there is no doubt that another factor contributing
to the relative lack of neighborhood leadership is the lack of a
tradition in leadership, caused by hundreds of years of colonial
administration.

Thus Puerto Ricans in New York find it more difficult than
groups which came before them to form their own in-group leadership, if they do not find it completely impossible. This fact gives
them a very real advantage over former migrations in one way,

* By 1971, air time between San Juan and New York was three and one-half
hours.

because it almost forces them into an active participation in the established community. On the other hand, the sudden challenge of having to participate in a settled New York community proves too arduous for many who might have been able to become leaders in their own cliques. . . .

"HISPANOS" AND "MARINE TIGERS"

[Throughout the history of U.S. immigration, new groups—Italians, Russians, Greeks, Germans, Poles—have shed their old culture and mannerisms, as one would a ragged suit of clothes, as they eagerly tried to fall in step with "The American Way of Life." The children of Jewish immigrants from Europe, for example, sometimes denied their religion, or changed their surnames; a few even resorted to plastic surgery to straighten their "un-American" noses.

Puerto Ricans have also taken part in this sometimes pathetic process. Many, unable to "pass" as 100 percent Americans, created their own pecking order. They called themselves "Hispanos" or "Latinos." In this way, they tried to associate themselves with Spain or the Latin American republics, and to disassociate themselves from what some U.S. newspapers called "the Puerto Rican problem." The following book excerpt describes the situation in the 1950's, which is far different from today, now that a new concept of ethnic pride has emerged among different racial and national groups.]

Among Puerto Ricans . . . the terms "Hispano" and "Latino" are used and preferred to "Puerto Rican" for self-identification. . . .

In the past, Hispanos or Latinos were a small minority of intellectuals and middle-class professionals from Puerto Rico, Spain, and Latin America who lived in New York. By 1950, the Spanish-speaking socially mobile persons of lower-class origins, who now considered themselves in a higher social position than the recent lower-class migrants from Puerto Rico, were calling themselves Hispanos. More recently, the term has been extended to include all Spanish-speaking persons who reside in New York, regardless of their social and economic class.

In Puerto Rico, a Puerto Rican is someone born on the island, which is his country. He may be a member of the upper, the

From Elena Padilla, *Up from Puerto Rico* (New York: Columbia University Press, 1958), pp. 32–35. Reprinted by permission.

middle, or the lower class; he may come from either country or city; he may be a farmhand, a farmer, or a banker; he may be a millionaire, a salaried employee, or a wage earner. But whatever else he is, he is Puerto Rican and is not regarded as a member of an ethnic or minority group.

In New York, the terms "Hispano" and "Latino" have been substituted for that of "Puerto Rican," because the latter, in more ways than one, has become a "bad public relations" identification for New York Puerto Ricans. It is associated with unfavorable pictures of the behavior and respectability of Puerto Ricans, which are not necessarily true or real. Even when used in Spanish and by Puerto Ricans themselves, it may convey an assumption of undesirable characteristics of the persons referred to. . . .

When referring to friends, or to persons considered "decent and respectable," the term "Hispano" is preferred by Eastville * Puerto Ricans. Recently arrived migrants soon learn that they are to call themselves Hispanos and drop their identification as Puerto Rican. They will probably not deny their country, but will resort to the linguistic subterfuge of Hispano to protect themselves from being characterized in a derogatory manner. They will tend to emphasize their particular home towns and municipalities in Puerto Rico, for to be accepted among Hispanos, it is important to know something specific about one's past and where one came from. . . .

One of the common forms of relating personally . . . is by initiating a conversation in which one identifies oneself as Hispano, in the sense of Puerto Rican, and by establishing this clearly. This particular approach to personal relations suggests three major social features of the Puerto Rican group. First, that being Puerto Rican and referring to oneself as Hispano is an entree for social relationships, and second, that the participants in the relationship have to establish the authenticity of their being Puerto Rican by showing some particular knowledge of the island, such as being conversant with a specific *municipio*, town, or city, and then a particular street there. Thus the identification is narrowed down to a level that no foreigner can reach. . . . Third, the identification also calls for establishing that one belongs to a particular family. One's status must be defined and acceptable if a personal relationship of any continuity is to be formed.

Hispanos classify themselves into three major groups with reference to life-experience and time spent in New York City. Those who have lived here for many years (*los que llevan muchos años aquí*) are the first. Those who grew up in this country, including the second generation, *nacidos y criados* (born and brought up), and those born in Puerto Rico who come to New York in early

* Fictitious name used by author to denote a Puerto Rican community in New York City.

childhood comprise the second. Recent migrants, those who have come in the last several years from Puerto Rico, and who are referred to in derogatory terms . . . as "Marine Tigers" are the third. (*Marine Tiger* was the name of one of the Liberty ships which made a number of trips between San Juan and New York after the war, bringing many thousands of Puerto Ricans to the States. It lent its name to the new "greenhorns," and the name has continued to stick.)

DOWN THESE MEAN STREETS

[There are countless tales of horror about Puerto Rican migrant workers who have been misled, cheated, and abused. Some of the worst episodes occurred in the years immediately following World War II, when migrants knew little about the pitfalls of trusting smooth-talking employment agents.

In Chicago, in 1946, the Castle Barton and Associates employment agency imported 362 young Puerto Rican girls to work as housemaids, at about $60 a month. From this low salary, the agency deducted $125 as its fee, at the rate of $10 per month, and held an additional sum in escrow for each girl's air fare home. The girls were little better off than indentured servants. Lonely, underpaid, unable to speak English, a number of the girls were lured into prostitution; others took factory jobs, and others returned home disillusioned.*

In another notorious case,† sixty Puerto Rican men were promised jobs in the North Chicago Hardware Foundry. After deductions for room and board, employment agency fees, and compulsory allotments for their dependents back home, the already meager $34.50 weekly paycheck shrank to virtually nothing. The employer was housing the men, during the winter, in unheated railway cars.

Once Puerto Ricans settled permanently on the mainland with their families, some of the obvious abuses ceased. But there were other problems. The Puerto Rican was "the last to be hired, and the first to be fired." A lack of skills made it hard to secure good-paying work. And the color of a man's skin often proved more important than what he could do.

Piri Thomas grew up in Harlem, and, despite extreme poverty, and bouts with narcotics and prison, has become a successful writer. Being a dark-skinned Puerto Rican, while some of his friends and relatives were "white," taught him some hard lessons. He learned quickly that

* *The New Republic*, April 28, 1947, p. 7.
† *Ibid.*

From Piri Thomas, *Down These Mean Streets* (New York: Alfred A. Knopf), pp. 98–104. Reprinted by permission.

America is a black-white world; there is little tolerance for the poly-chromatic reality of Puerto Rican culture. This selection, from his first book, describes a job interview in 1945.]

YOUNG MEN, 17–30
GREAT OPPORTUNITY
LEARN WHILE WORKING
EARN WHILE TRAINING
Door-to-door salesmen in house-hold wares. Guaranteed by Good Housekeeping. Salary and com-mission.
603 E. 73 St.   2nd fl.—9 a.m.

"Dig, Louie, this sounds good," I said to my boy. "Let's go over in the morning. Hell, with our gift of *labia* we're a mother-hopping cinch to cop a slave."

"*Chévere,* Piri, man, we got all Harlem and we know plenty people. Bet we can earn a hundred bucks or more on commissions alone."

We went down the next day and walked into the office and a girl handed me and Louie each a paper with a number on it and told us to please have a seat. My number was 16 and Louie's was 17. Man, me and Louie were sparklin'. We had our best togs on; they were pressed like a razor and our shoes shone like a bald head with a pound of grease on it.

"Number 16, please?" the girl called out.

I winked at Louie and he gave me the V-for-victory sign.

"Right this way, sir, through the door on your left," the girl said.

I walked into the office and there was this paddy sitting there. He looked up at me and broke out into the friendliest smile I ever saw, like I was a long-lost relative. "Come in, come right in," he said. "Have a chair—that's right, sit right there. Well, sir, you're here bright and early. That's what our organization likes to see. Yes sir, punctuality is the first commandment in a salesman's bible. So you're interested in selling our household wares—guaranteed, of course, by *Good Housekeeping.* Had any experience selling?"

"Well, not exactly, sir, but—er—when I was a kid—I mean, younger, I used to sell shopping bags in the *Marketa.*"

"The what?"

"The *Marketa* on 110th Street and Park Avenue. It, er, runs all the way up to 116th Street."

"Ummm, I see."

"And my mom—er, mother, used to knit fancy things called *tapetes.* I think they're called doilies, and I used to sell them door to door, and I made out pretty good. I know how to talk to people, Mr.—er—"

"Mr. Christian, Mr. Harold Christian. See?" and he pointed a skinny finger at a piece of wood with his name carved on it. "Ha, ha, ha," he added, "just like us followers of our Lord Jesus Christ are called. Are you Christian?"

"Yes, sir."

"A good Catholic, I bet. I never miss a Sunday mass; how about you?"

"No, sir, I try not to." *Whee-eoo!* I thought. *Almost said I was Protestant.*

"Fine, fine, now let's see . . ." Good Catholic Mr. Christian took out some forms. "What's your name?"

"Piri Thomas—P-i-r-i."

"Age?"

"Er, seventeen—born September 30, 1928."

Mr. Christian counted off on the fingers of one hand . . . "twenty-eight, er, thirty-eight, forty-five—ahum, you were just seventeen this September."

"That's right. Paper said from seventeen to thirty."

"Oh, yes—yes, yes, that's correct. Where do you live?"

I couldn't give him the Long Island address; it was too far away. So I said, "109 East 104th Street."

"That's way uptown, isn't it?"

"Yes, sir."

"Isn't that, um, Harlem?"

"Yes, sir, it's split up in different sections, like the Italian section and Irish and Negro and the Puerto Rican section. I live in the Puerto Rican section. It's called the *Barrio.*"

"The *Bar-ree-o?*"

I smiled. "Yes, sir, it's Spanish for 'the place'—er—like a community."

"Oh, I see. But you're not Puerto Rican, are you? You speak fairly good English even though once in a while you use some slang—of course, it's sort of picturesque."

"My parents are Puerto Ricans."

"Is Thomas a Puerto Rican name?"

"Er—well, my mother's family name is Montañez," I said, wondering if that would help prove I was a Puerto Rican. "There are a lot of Puerto Ricans with American names. My father told me that after Spain turned Puerto Rico over to the United States at the end of the Spanish-American War, a lot of Americans were stationed there and got married to Puerto Rican girls." *Probably fucked 'em and forgot 'em,* I thought.

"Oh, I—er, see. How about your education? High school diploma?"

"No, sir, I quit in my second year . . ."

"Tsh, tsh, that was very foolish of you. Education is a wonderful thing, Mr. Thomas. It's really the only way for one to get ahead, especially when—er, uh—why did you leave school?"

My mind shouted out, *On account of you funny paddies and your funny ideas in this funny world*, but I said, very *cara-palo*, "Well, sir, we got a big family and—well, I'm the oldest and I had to help out and—well, I quit." Then, in a sincere fast breath, I added, "But I'm going to study nights. I agree with you that education is the only way to get ahead, especially when—"

"Fine, fine. What's your Social Security number?"

I said quickly: "072–20–2800."

"By memory, eh? Good! A good salesman's second commandment should be a good memory. Got a phone?"

"Yes, sir. Lehigh 3–6050, and ask for Mr. Dandy. He's my uncle. He doesn't speak English very well, but you can leave any message for me with him."

"Very, very good, Mr. Thomas. Well, this will be all for now. We will get in touch with you."

"Uh, how soon, about, Mr. Christian? 'Cause I'd like to start work, or rather, training, as soon as possible."

"I can't definitely say, Mr. Thomas, but it will be in the near future. Right now our designated territory is fully capacitated. But we're opening another soon and we'll need good men to work it."

"You can't work the territory you want?" I asked.

"Oh no! This is scientifically planned," he said.

"I'd like to work in Harlem," I said, "but, uh—I can make it wherever you put me to sell."

"That's the spirit!" Mr. Christian bubbled. "The third commandment of a good salesman is he faces any challenge, wherever it may be."

I took Mr. Christian's friendly outstretched hand and felt the warm, firm grip and thought, *This paddy is gonna be all right to work for*. As I walked out, I turned my head and said, "Thank you very much, sir, for the opportunity."

"Not at all, not at all. We need bright young blood for this growing organization, and those that grow with us will be headed for great things."

"Thank you. So long."

"So long, and don't forget to go to mass."

"No, sir, I sure won't!"

"What church you go to?" he asked suddenly.

"Uh"—I tried to remember the name of the Catholic Church on 106th Street—"Saint Cecilia's!" I finally burst out.

"Oh yes, that's on, er, 106th Street between Park and Lexington. Do you know Father Kresser?"

"Gee, the name sounds sort of familiar," I cooled it. "I can almost place him, but I can't say for sure."

"Well, that's all right. He probably wouldn't remember me, but I was a youngster when he had a parish farther downtown. I used to go there. Well, if you run into him, give him my regards."

"I sure will. So long, and thanks again." I closed the door carefully and walked out to where Louie was still sitting.

"Man, Piri," he said, "you was in there a beau-coup long-ass time."

"Shh, Louie, cool your language."

"Got the job? You were in there long enough for two jobs."

I smiled and made an okay face.

Louie cupped his hand to his mouth and put his head next to mine. "That cat ain't a faggot, is he?" he whispered.

I whispered back with exaggerated disgust, "Man! What a fuckin' dirty mind you got."

"Just asking, man," he said. "Sometimes these guys are *patos* and if you handle them right, you get the best breaks. Well, how'd you make out?"

"In like Flynn, Louie."

"Cool, man, hope I get the same break."

"Number 17," the girl called.

"Here I go," Louie said to me.

"*Suerte*, Louie," I said. I gave him the V-for-victory sign and watched his back disappear and dimly heard Mr. Christian's friendly "Come right in. Have a—" before the door closed behind Louie.

Jesus, I thought. *I hope Louie gets through okay. It'll be great to work in the same job. Maybe we can even work together. He'll cover one side of the street and I'll cover the other. As tight as me and Louie are, we'll pool what we make on commissions and split halfies.*

"Hey Piri," Louie said, "let's go."

"Damn, Louie, you just went in," I said. "You only been in there about five minutes or so. How'd Mr. Christian sound?"

We walked down the stairs.

"Okay, I guess. Real friendly, and he asked me questions, one-two-three."

"And?"

"And I'm in!"

"Cool breeze. What phone did you give?" I asked.

"I ain't got no phone. Hey, there's the bus!"

We started to run. "Fuck running," I said, "let's walk a while and celebrate. Man, you could've gave him Dandy's number like I did. Aw, well, they'll probably send you a telegram or special delivery letter telling you when to start work."

"What for?" Louie asked.

"So's they can tell you when the new territory is opened up and when to come in," I said. " 'Cause the other territory—"

"What new territory?"

I opened my mouth to answer and Louie and I knew what was shakin' at the same fuckin' time. The difference between me and Louie was he was white. "That cat Mr. Christian tell you about calling you when some new territory opens up?" Louie said in a low voice.

I nodded, "Yeah."

"Damn! That motherfucker asked me to come and start that training jazz on Monday. Gave me a whole lotta shit about working in a virgin territory that's so big us future salesmen wouldn't give each other competition or something like that." Louie dug that hate feeling in me. He tried to make me feel good by telling me that maybe they got a different program and Mr. Christian was considering me for a special kinda job.

"Le's go back," I said coldly.

"What for, Piri?"

"You see any colored cats up there?"

"Yeah, *panín*, there's a few. Why?"

"Le's wait here in front of the place."

"*Por qué?*" asked Louie.

I didn't answer. I just watched paddies come down out of that office and make it. "Louie," I said, "ask the next *blanco* that comes down how the job hiring is. There's one now."

Louie walked over to him. "Say, excuse me, Mac," he said. "Are they hiring up there—you know, salesmen?"

"Yes, they are," the guy answered. "I start Monday. Why don't you apply if you're looking for work? It's—"

"Thanks a lot, Mac," Louie said. "I might do that." He came back and started to open his mouth.

"Forget it, *amigo*," I said. "I heard the chump."

We waited some more and a colored cat came down. "Hey, bruh," I called.

"You callin' me?"

"Yeah. I dug the ad in the paper. How's the hiring? Putting guys on?"

"I don't know, man. I mean I got some highly devoted crap about getting in touch with me when a new turf opens up."

"Thanks, man," I said.

"You're welcome. Going up?"

"Naw, I changed my mind." I nodded to Louie, and he came up to me like he was down for whatever I was down for.

"Let's walk," I said. I didn't feel so much angry as I did sick, like throwing-up sick. Later, when I told this story to my buddy,

a colored cat, he said, "Hell, Piri, Ah know stuff like that can sure burn a cat up, but a Negro faces that all the time."
"I know that," I said, "but I wasn't a Negro then. I was still only a Puerto Rican."

HARLEM SI, TAMMANY NO

[This article describes the victory of the first Puerto Rican district leader in New York City, in 1961. Since then, other Puerto Ricans have been elected to posts at the city or state level, and one man—Herman Badillo—has reached the U.S. Congress. But Puerto Ricans still remain a very feeble political force in America.]

I want there to be a sign on Tammany Hall that says Aquí se habla español.   —CARLOS RIOS

Fifteen years after the death of Fiorello La Guardia, and a decade after Vito Marcantonio's enigmatic empire crumbled into disillusionment, a new phenomenon has begun to stir the impoverished multitudes of East Harlem. It is a phenomenon that preaches tenants' councils, literacy tests in Spanish and a $1.50 city minimum wage. The cradle of this phenomenon is the East Harlem Reform Democratic Club, an anomaly among the city's reform clubs, since it is neither white nor middle class, and its only contact with eggheads is a charcoal drawing of Pablo Casals that hangs on the wall.

On September 7, the club's volunteer brigade of teen-age enthusiasts, student socialists and working-class Puerto Ricans rose up to smite the once invincible Tammany machine, and elected Carlos Ríos the first Puerto Rican district leader in the city's history. The victim of this patchwork crusade was John Merli, the incumbent of fourteen years. The social forces that achieved the victory were those of Puerto Rican representation and a decade's accumulated hatred of slum landlords. The regular Democratic organization in East Harlem, either through venality or stupidity, counterposed itself to these forces.

Heart, brains and founder of the East Harlem reform club is thirty-three-year-old State Assemblyman Mark Lane, who launched

From Jack Newfield, "Harlem Sí, Tammany No, " *Commonweal*, Sept. 29, 1961, pp. 10–12. Reprinted by permission.

the club in the winter of 1960, after spending five years in Spanish Harlem, where he waged war on landlords and police brutality, and took up the cause of minorities and civil liberties, generally in the same case. . . .

In March of 1960 Lane won the reform nomination from Manhattan's Tenth Assembly District, which extends from 74th Street to 106th Street, and from the East River to either Third, Park or Lexington Avenues depending on how badly a specific block has been gerrymandered. All three reform clubs in the 10th A.D. voted Lane their endorsement, but only after he was subjected to grueling attacks on his past left-wing and Marcantonio associations by the membership of the club in the 10th A.D. Middle, and after the female co-leader of the club in the 10th A.D. South had resigned when Lane received an 82-3 vote of confidence.

Lane won the June 7 primary by 900 votes, and in November Kennedy's coattails helped elect him much less than the 3,100 Puerto Ricans the East Harlem club registered for the first time during one week in October.

Prior attempts to bring the thousands of unregistered Puerto Ricans of the community into politics had all ended in failure. In 1957 the Council of Spanish Organizations estimated that only 85,000 of the potential 266,000 eligible Puerto Rican voters in New York City were registered. Any attempt to pin this apathy to the Puerto Rican culture, however, was shattered by the eighty-three per cent turn-out in the island's 1960 gubernatorial elections.

The causes of the small registration in East Harlem were numerous. Many Puerto Ricans sensed the insincerity of every candidate who tramped across the East Harlem landscape between Vito Marcantonio's death in August of 1954, and Lane's campaign of 1960. Then, too, the dominant Merli organization understandably made no effort to bring them into politics. But the major roadblock was the requirement that registrants pass the literacy test in English. Many Puerto Ricans were embarrassed to try; others were warned not to try.

The three major groups of unregistered voters consisted of elderly people who had lived their entire lives not voting; those who withdrew from politics in disgust after the three major parties formed an alliance to purge Marcantonio from Congress in 1950; and those who had moved into the neighborhood since 1955.

The number who withdrew after Marcantonio's defeat has never been calculated, but is probably a considerable figure. Running on the American Labor Party ticket in 1951, Manuel Medina, Marcantonio's protégé, polled 28,000 votes to Merli's 35,000 in a race for the City Council. When this is compared to the 5,500 votes polled by José Loman on the Liberal ticket in 1957, in a race against Merli, the depth of Marcantonio feeling in the Puerto Rican community becomes apparent.

But there are reasons why the registration drive of 1960 succeeded in East Harlem where others had failed. One was the youthful zeal of the campaign workers, who provided baby sitters, transportation and moral support in order to prod, convince and cajole more than 3,000 Puerto Ricans into registering for the first time. The same drive also enrolled 1,100 new voters who were not Puerto Rican.

The principal reason, though, was that Lane turned the registration drive into a frontal assault on the literacy test requirement, as he argued from every street corner in East Harlem: "The Spanish-speaking people who read *El Diario* or *La Prensa* are infinitely more informed on the issues than anyone who reads the *Daily Mirror.* . . . This test is blatantly discriminatory." And he cited a federal survey which charged New York State (along with Georgia and Mississippi) with discrimination in voting rights.

Lane was so anxious to test the legality of the literacy test that he broadcast the answers to it from a sound truck, daring arrest, and he maintains now that even more new voters would have been enrolled if it weren't for harassment by desperate Merli poll watchers on the last day of registration. . . .

That registration drive, coupled with Lane's victory, set the stage for Carlos Ríos to challenge Merli's district leadership for the first time in a primary struggle. Ríos came to East Harlem from Puerto Rico in 1949, and for twelve years his mournful eyes gazed upon the daily, unremembered tragedies that are the history of every slum. He saw rat-infested schools that made no provision for the hundreds of children who spoke only Spanish. And he became the secretary of a P.T.A. He saw sweatshops that flourished in the community. And he became an organizer for the Cap Makers Union. He saw the youth of the community clubbed by police and seduced by narcotics pushers. And he became a lay preacher with the East Harlem Protestant Parish. He saw Puerto Ricans cheated out of political representation. And he became a candidate for district leader.

The tempo of the campaign modulated slowly, like a bolero, through the scorching summer. When the petitioning period began on June 21, more than half of the 10th A.D. North's sixteen election districts were bereft of captains. Ríos, who was recovering from a mild heart attack, suffered while helping move the furniture of an evicted friend, was unable to campaign. Funds were low and campaign workers scarce.

But in early July the New York chapter of the Young People's Socialist League committed a dozen of its less sectarian members to work in the campaign. Several days later, the F.D.R.-Four Freedoms Club, a band of twenty-eight idealistic high school students, entered the campaign, and quickly became the backbone of the club, their members often staying to four and five in the morning to get out a mailing. And then individuals began walking into the club.

The intense magnetism the club holds for the youth of the city is the wellspring of the phenomenon of East Harlem. One of the reasons for the attraction is that the club offers a unique opportunity for day-to-day contact with men and women who carry the scars of exploitation and bigotry. To read in a textbook that East Harlem has twenty per cent chronic unemployment or the highest rate of narcotics addiction in the country is one thing. To walk through the hot, ugly streets and see these statistics etched in the faces that stare out from every open window is something else. . . .

On July 28th the campaign reached its first crest, when Mayor Wagner, wed to the reform movement three days before at a shotgun ceremony, reluctantly accepted Lane's plea that he tour the block of East 100th Street, between First and Second Avenues, a block of 4,200 people crammed into twenty-seven rotting tenements.

The Mayor of New York came to the city's cruellest slum in the middle of a hot afternoon. He saw rats, roaches and vermin. He saw junkies lounging in hallways. He saw mounds of decaying garbage in backyards. Lane took Wagner into an apartment at 311 East 100th Street where rats had eaten the stuffings out of the sofa. He took him into another apartment where the toilet bowl overflowed a foul smelling river each time it was flushed. He took him into a backyard where the stench from rotting garbage was intolerable and a swarm of mosquitoes buzzed around the mayor's head.

As Wagner walked back towards his shiny limousine, he was approached by a craggy-faced man carrying a cigar box. He told the mayor he was trying to collect enough money to pay for the funeral expenses of his eighteen-month-old son, who had toppled from a fifth floor window the day before. On July 30th the block was declared a Play Street, and a volleyball net was set up in the middle of the street, presumably to exterminate the rats and cure the junkies.

By the first week of August the club had borrowed sound truck equipment from the A.D.A., and whenever they could borrow a car (mostly Lane's) the mobbed streets of East Harlem echoed the sound of Ríos' speeches, delivered in hoarse, passionate Spanish, and the pungent lyrics of Gil Turner's folksongs. The repetitive themes of the street corner oratory were discrimination, housing conditions and Puerto Rican representation. "Ninety-sixth Street," Lane would shout a dozen times a night, "is the Mason-Dixon line of New York City. . . . Housing is more segregated here than it is in Jackson, Mississippi."

One night a policeman ordered the truck off the streets because it was 10:30. "Leave it alone," a ten-year-old told the cop on the beat, "they're for the tenants. Go chase Merli's truck, he's for the landlords."

The campaign moved into its last weeks, building relentlessly towards the crescendo of primary day. More tenants' councils were organized. More petitions for reductions in rent were filed. Money began to trickle in from the wealthier reform clubs as the scent of possible victory floated downtown. More mailings went out.

And so too did the tempo of the Merli campaign increase. His sound trucks nightly roared "The truth about slimy Mark Lane, that racist who went on a Freedom Ride only to spread more hate and bias . . . that pro-Communist who wants to destroy The House Un-American Activities Committee . . . that Jew whose real name is Levine." The references to Ríos were less frequent. They said he was "only for the rich Puerto Ricans," and that he preached his sermons "dressed in a tuxedo." They put up posters depicting him as Lane's puppet.

On August 21, while Lane was attending a special session of the Legislature in Albany, four men charged into the Ríos headquarters and threatened several campaign workers with a lead pipe. On August 29, while riding to a rally with Eleanor Roosevelt in an open car, Lane was struck with a beer can hurled from a rooftop. Four stitches were required to close the wound in his scalp. The incident, which received considerable coverage in the daily press, proved to be a potent weapon during the last days of the campaign.

The outpouring of voters on primary day dwarfed everything in the turbulent history of East Harlem politics. In some election districts the vote was as high as eighty per cent. The Ríos poll watchers, not one of whom was over thirty years of age, successfully challenged hundreds of non-residents who tried to vote, while squads of "pullers" worked frantically to get out the favorable voters.

By 10 p.m. when the polls closed, a noisy clot of five hundred people was crammed into the tiny reform clubhouse. By 10:15 the first three election districts, with large Italian and Irish populations, had reported. They showed Ríos and Merli running neck and neck. Next came the returns from two heavily Puerto Rican districts. Ríos carried them handily. Then Roberto Verdejo, captain of the populous 50th election district, raced into the clubhouse waving his tally sheets. Ríos had carried his district by a margin of 5 to 1.

At 10:28 Lane stood on a chair and shouted "We've won." The final results showed Ríos carried twelve of sixteen election districts, winning 2,839 to 2,038.

Then followed a jubilant parade through the streets of East Harlem. Gil Turner, riding on a sound truck, led the marchers, and hundreds of others standing on fire escapes and street corners, in tuneless but wildly enthusiastic renditions of "East Harlem's My Home," and "Que Bonita Bandera." By the time the parade reached a delirious midnight climax, the ranks of marchers had swelled to almost 1,000.

On 100th Street a woman raced out of a tenement hallway and

grabbed Lane in a violent embrace. "Today is our Independence Day," she screamed in Spanish.

But September 7th was really only the beginning. One district leader and one Assemblyman do not make a social revolution. . . .

"MY PARENTS, THEY CRY WITH JOY"

[Like a huge magnet, New York City attracted the vast majority of Puerto Rican migrants until the late 1950's. Today, about 40 per cent of migrants from the island settle outside New York. Most Puerto Rican communities are clustered on the eastern seaboard, in New York, New Jersey, and the New England states. But a substantial number of Puerto Ricans—perhaps 130,000—have settled in the Chicago area. As a Chicago journalist reports, "many have made it here," but "there are serious problems of poverty and alienation." Significantly, Chicago was the spawning ground for the Young Lords, a Puerto Rican street gang that evolved into a militant social activist movement.]

Many have made it here in Chicago. Many find disappointment and become caught in circles of despondency. How severe their problems are is virtually impossible to express in numbers. The welfare roles and unemployment statistics don't have entries under "Puerto Ricans." No one really knows the extent of Puerto Rican misery in Chicago.

"There aren't any figures," says one Puerto Rican, Mrs. Isabel Collazo, veteran case worker in the Wicker Park office of the Cook County Department of Public Aid. "But naturally since there are more Puerto Ricans than ever, the caseload is up, way up. The problems certainly are bigger. Credit buying is quite a temptation to people who've had little; all those pretty things. Then there's garnisheeing of wages. . . . When you dig into why someone is applying for help it so often turns out that the newcomer got in over his head and leaving his family was all he could think to do." . . .

There are serious problems of poverty and alienation here. The Latin American Defense Organization, a largely Puerto Rican group, stormed the Wicker Park headquarters of the Cook County Department of Public Aid in disgust and frustration with the welfare system. . . .

From John Adam Moreau, "The Puerto Ricans: Who Are They?", *Midwest Magazine, Chicago Sun-Times*, September 21, 1969. Reprinted by permission.

Something is clearly the matter in the Puerto Rican community if a former street gang, the Young Lords Organization, declares its contempt for its elders and capitalism and says that it patterns itself after the radical Black Panthers. . . .

It is the Lords who participated in May in the occupation of the administration building of McCormick Theological Seminary to publicize demands that McCormick and the city do more for the poor on the Near North Side where the Young Lords live.

It was the Lords who in June took over the Armitage Ave. United Methodist Church at No. 834 on that street, managed not to be thrown out, and who in August opened a day-care center in the church basement.

And it was the Lords who took over urban renewal land at Armitage and Halsted to make a People's Park, and who used physical force to break up a meeting of the Lincoln Park Community Conservation Council to protest possible use of urban renewal land for a tennis club.

In every instance the Lords argued they acted on behalf of the poor and because the city is not "responsive" to the needs of the poor in its area.

Underlying their fervor and aggressiveness . . . is a conviction that some kind of socialism is the answer to the nation's woes, and that class, not race, is what divides the nation.

The Lords are relatively impotent and have no strength resembling that of some of the black youth gangs. . . . For months there have been abortive talks among the Lords and other gangs about some kind of coalition but there has been little progress. There are, by police count, 13 predominantly Puerto Rican street gangs, a potential but as yet little exploited source of power. . . .

One of the greatest weaknesses of the Puerto Rican community is that it is not organized politically, partly because there are so few professional men—probably no more than 50 in the entire Chicago area.

No Puerto Rican has ever held a major office in Chicago. . . . In short, the Puerto Ricans are the only major ethnic group in this country which has not become a pressure group.

"Whenever you see some Puerto Ricans getting power," says Mike Barreto, a Puerto Rican who is executive director of the Spanish Action Committee, "you see them begin to sell out." . . .

Barreto mentions names like Manuel Toledo, director of the Division St. Urban Progress Center, and Carlos Caribe Ruiz.

"I admit I'm a patronage worker," Toledo replies, "but when we talk the city listens. I push when it is needed. The Puerto Ricans who have gotten some influence with the city got it because they are strong leaders."

Says Caribe Ruiz, executive director of the Puerto Rican Congress: "Believe me, I understand what groups like these Young Lords feel. I believe they mean well. They want a slice of the pie just like I did when I came here. But you never get anything by marching, like Barreto and his people. . . . These people couldn't have broken the communications barrier with the city, the police, the schools, but we have."

There are few Puerto Rican precinct captains in Chicago and except for a pitifully incompetent and ill-timed effort last March during the special aldermanic race, no Puerto Rican has run for political office. . . .

Says Marcelino Díaz, a prominent real estate man: "You Anglos tried to put Puerto Ricans on a reservation, but they're beginning to get out. . . . We're here only 18 years and the machine overcomes us because of our disunity. . . . We're going to have to fight for a long time."

Shortly after the Division St. riot of 1966, the city fathers planted saplings on that street near Damen, where the trouble broke out. A few of the trees have died, and the rest have grown irregularly. A tiny minority of the Puerto Ricans (and there were non-Puerto Ricans involved, too) took part in the riots. . . .

One wonders . . . whether Puerto Ricans in Chicago are better off in 1969 than they were in 1966. The statistics are not there and the answer depends on to whom you talk. . . .

Marcelino Díaz says:

"I know I'm selling more real estate to Puerto Ricans." . . .

Claudio Flores, successful publisher of the newspaper *El Puerto-rriqueño*, co-owner of a restaurant in Niles, and owner of travel agencies, sees betterment everywhere.

"I ought to know," he remarked, "because I file a lot of income tax returns for Puerto Ricans." . . .

From the standpoint of Jorge Prieto, a Mexican-American physician who works in Spanish-speaking areas, "things have gotten much worse since '66."

"Malnutrition among the Puerto Ricans is practically universal," he contends. "As a result, the rule—not the exception, but *the rule* —in almost every pregnancy is some kind of abnormality in the prenatal period, during delivery or during the first year. . . . This is because they're too poor to take care of themselves. City health facilities are adequate but under-used because of the language problem. No Puerto Ricans have any influence with the Board of Health, of course."

And James Fernández, of the Chicago office of the Commonwealth of Puerto Rico's Economic Development Administration, says, "You'd have to prove it to me that things are better. A little here, a little there, but it's still mostly a life of factory work and dishwashing. The Puerto Rican still does a lot of your dirty work." . . .

The 1960 census said there were 35,000 Puerto Ricans in Chicago, 25,000 of them born on the island. There are many more today. Luis

Machado, of the Chicago office of the commonwealth's Department
of Labor, estimates 70,000. Other sources say 80,000 to 100,000. . . .

"In the strong trade unions like plumbing, electrical work, car-
pentry and bricklaying," says Thomas Pietrantonio, a Puerto Rican
born on the mainland who is editor of the National Labor Journal,
"The Puerto Rican doesn't stand a chance. They won't let him in.
But he's welcome in the machine shops where there's a lot of risk.
Take a look sometime when you're down on Division St., and if you
don't see a couple of guys within an hour's time with a finger or
two missing, I'd be surprised."

"Puerto Ricans don't like to go to classes and union meetings and,
of course, they tend to fear recriminations from employers," says
Alicea Martínez, a staff representative for the United Steel Workers
of America, who came in 1954 intending to make money and go
home, but who got a good job as a welder and . . .

And made it.

Like Carlos Caribe Ruiz, 41, executive director of the Congreso
Puertorriqueño, an umbrella organization of social and civic groups.
In 1947 Caribe Ruiz left his parents and 16 brothers and sisters in
Cabo Rojo.

"I sold my bicycle and chickens and took off," Caribe Ruiz recalls,
"and I studied for a while at the Juilliard School of Music in New
York."

Now Ruiz is a real estate agent.

"In those days," he went on, "it wasn't like now. We were discriminated against everywhere we went. You'd buddy up with a guy
for protection. I lived in an 8-by-10 room. It cost me $22 a week."

Things got better for Caribe Ruiz. For $12,000 he bought on con-
tract a house worth $3,000—that's the method whereby you can lose
everything if you miss a payment. He is enormously proud of the
home at 1901 W. Erie. There he has raised or is raising five children,
three already in college.

"I don't think I'm particularly bitter against Anglo society," he
says today. "It's been hard but better than I expected. But I remember things, a beating I got once—and the way the Italians
treated us when we moved in over on Erie, for example."

And Manuel Toledo, 37.

He is president of the Board of Coordinators of Puerto Rican
Affairs, and he holds a patronage job from the Regular Democratic
organization: director of the Division St. Urban Progress Center.

Toledo came here from his native Lares in 1951, became a factory
worker, eventually rose to foreman, and now owns a house. "If I
had stayed in Puerto Rico," he says, "I probably would be ignorant
and poor . . . Today I feel like a king."

And Marcelino Díaz, 45.

Díaz had some formal education before he left Cidra and came to

Chicago in 1949. He finished his schooling at Valparaiso University. Like his father, he is a real estate man.

And Cayetano Vallejo, 28.

Vallejo couldn't better fit the model for the role of office manager at American Dream Corp. He arrives here in 1959 from San Lorenzo, is befriended by a Polish-American man, works for him, learns cabinetmaking—"I didn't know anything about wood; I had worked in a beauty parlor"—saves $7,000, buys machinery, borrows more money from the Small Business Administration, and opens a factory for making display equipment on S. Wabash.

Many have known first-hand themselves what Vallejo has gone through: 10 to 12 hours of work a day, seven days a week, your heart in your mouth, your future uncertain.

"I was cheated once along the way," Vallejo said one day, "but I got smart after that. Everything legal, in black and white. I have never been more happy."

Vallejo owns a home in Bellwood, where his parents, who were farm people, live. There are five sisters and four brothers, ages 21 to 37. True to the contemporary Puerto Rican pattern, two sisters married Puerto Ricans from here and returned to the island with them to help set up a grocery store and a television repair shop.

These are, of course, the people who have succeeded to the extent of having enough money to live in dignity, the people who can afford to have ever bigger aspirations.

They and Puerto Ricans like them are the newest link in the ethnic chain. They have sat down to the great American banquet. They are the newest newcomers, hankering to become something and somebody, to have cause for a joy like that of Vallejo who, when he recalls setting up in business, says:

"My parents," Vallejo says, "they cry with joy when they hear I open my own place."

"EL BARRIO'S WORST BLOCK"

[As the years pass, old and new generations of Puerto Ricans fan out into other cities of the United States; a growing number, particularly in the New York metropolitan area, have moved to middle-class suburbs. But El Barrio in Spanish Harlem is still a point of reference for Puerto Ricans, just as New York's Lower East Side was for the thousands of Jews who

From David and Sophy Burnham, "El Barrio's Worst Block is Not All Bad," *New York Times Magazine*, January 5, 1969, pp. 24–25. Reprinted by permission.

came to America from Eastern Europe. El Barrio is still an impoverished ghetto that holds one of the largest single concentrations of Puerto Ricans; it is a point of entry for many of the poorest newcomers, a trap for those unable to escape, and a home for those who know no other home. This article shows how, in the midst of the most hostile conditions, people struggle to survive—and how some do.]

A block in El Barrio—Spanish Harlem—despite all the speeches and studies and community-action programs of the last years, remains remarkably foreign to most Americans, who have never lived in the crowded, dirty world of aging, six-story tenements, or talked to the people who live there—the parents, the children, the wage-earners, the welfare-takers, the healthy and the sick. Another reason why the area is hard to understand is that most studies of this world have focused on only one of the dark aspects of its life—the lack of family stability, or the drug addicts, or unemployment, or the obviously unsuccessful schools—and failed to portray the stable families, the industrious working fathers, and the teen-agers who have rejected drugs, the large numbers who grow strong and survive. . . .

[One block in El Barrio] has been more completely portrayed. The work was begun four years ago by Dr. Bernard Lander, a New York sociologist, his brother Nathan and Dr. H. P. O'Brien of Notre Dame, and was supported by a series of grants. . . . A rare picture has emerged by now of one period in the life of the block and some changes in the life-styles of its residents.

The 25 tenements facing the 630-foot street are red brick, most of them blackened with grime. They seem to press in on the street. Two buildings have been abandoned, their windows broken, their insides gutted by fire and emptied by thieves. Between some of them are sudden open spaces where a building has been torn down and the empty lot has become filled with rubble and beer cans. In contrast are five freshly painted tenements on one side of the street which are being renovated by a local housing organization, Metro-North.

When the study began, 2,500 people in 640 families lived on the block. Today, after the removal of a few tenements, there are 400 families of 1,750 individuals. Three out of every five residents are Puerto Rican, almost all the rest Negro. The population is far younger than that of the city as a whole; every other person is under 21. . . .

Two of every three families are headed by men; the rest by women. Of these family heads, more than half had not finished school, more than half were unemployed, a quarter were on welfare, a third made less than $60 a week. Rent, compared with the rest of Manhattan, seems low; two-thirds of the families pay between $25 and $45 a month for a three- or four-room apartment.

The block was built in 1906 to accommodate a wave of Jewish immigrants from the lower East Side (upper Manhattan was opened to construction two years earlier with the completion of the first subway). The houses were "new-law" tenements. Among other reforms, every room had to have at least 70 square feet of space. Every room had to have a window.

The Jews were supplanted by the Italians and the Italians by the Puerto Ricans and Negroes, but the housing did not begin to get really bad until 1953, when the city designated the block for public housing, and then did nothing. The landlords, awaiting renewal, stopped making repairs; and during the next 15 years the block gained its reputation as a "bad" block.

Sixty per cent of the people on the block have lived there for 10 years or more, despite the fact they say they want to move, and most look back to a golden past: "It's not the street. It's the people who moved into the street. See, 'cause . . . it was a very good neighborhood. I mean it was quiet. It was, I couldn't say it was clean, but it was quiet, and they didn't have a lot of burglars and murders that they have now. It's just the dope and the marijuana that's being brought into the street that's messing up the street. . . ."

The poorest people tend to remain on the block; and the poorest are also those with the least education, the least resistance to and the fewest outlets for frustration, the highest incidence of ill health, mental disturbance and unemployment. The interior of the housing on the block has often been described: brown hallways with their rotten stairs and the acrid smell of garbage; cold apartments with overflowing toilets and moist, peeling paint. Housing probably is the worst problem because it is always with you. . . .

None know this better than the people who live there. About eight years ago the neighborhood formed Metro-North to do something about housing in a seven-block area. This organization is completely self-supporting, financing its two offices, supplies and phone bills with bus outings, dances and private donations. In the last three years it has fought the city bureaucracies, organized the tenants in rundown buildings, obtained vacate orders from the buildings department, relocated numerous families from dangerous buildings, and finally acquired about $12 million in private grants to buy and renovate 17 tenements—an example of concerned citizens' action that would make any middle-class family proud.

Though most of the work of Metro-North is in housing, in 1965 it persuaded the city to build a vest-pocket park on the block. It is a bare asphalt slab, more like a parking lot than the usual leafy image of a park, but to the residents of the block it is an achievement. . . .

But this, of course, is only a beginning; the block's major problems remain. The fighting gangs are gone now, and apparently there are fewer crimes of violence, but the street—almost without shops, seemingly deserted on a cold winter day—is a marketplace for drugs. A bookie hangs out here. A numbers racketeer. Two pushers. Youths watch for fags to service for $5, money that immediately will be converted into a bag of heroin. Girls walk the streets. You can find almost anything here, and the activities permeate the lives of everyone, whether they participate and approve or not.

The fact is that the majority of the people on the block do not participate even peripherally in the life of crime, beyond a regular bet on the numbers. . . . On this block, if there is considerable crime . . . there is also a surprisingly conservative, even middle-class, morality.

Of the 50 teen-age members of the old fighting gang that was centered on the block . . . three are now in rackets, eight or ten are addicts; but three are members of the police force, one is a lieutenant in the Marines and the remaining 30 or 35 have also "gone straight." It seems to be a matter of growing up.

Look at Angelina, the 19-year-old mother of an illegitimate child, who admitted she smoked pot when she was 14, shoplifted, roamed the streets. She doesn't do that anymore.

"It's not lady—it's not for a woman. That's men's stuff. Boys' stuff."

The block is composed of 1,750 individuals as different as characters in a good novel. There is the short, heavy woman, a social worker, with direct brown eyes and a finely arched nose, strong, proud, self-sufficient. She has lived on the block with her husband and four children for 40 years. She sent one son through college. And there is the woman whose two daughters are lesbian—and it is a sad commentary on the neighborhood that the third will probably be one. (There seems to be a lot of lesbianism on the block. Many girls are drawn to it, either from fear of the hit-and-run tactics of the boys, or else because they grew up in state institutions where homosexuality is common. . . .)

A large number of people on the block believe that ability is more important than pull or "who you know." Many of the 25 per cent on welfare are ashamed of receiving it, though others accommodate themselves to it quite cynically. . . .

If some people abuse the welfare agency, the agency sometimes returns the favor. One caseworker, for example, tried to dissuade an ambitious youngster from learning a trade. "He say to me, 'Why don't you just go to work and forget the problem of going to school?' I told him if I go to work . . . I'm going to get a job washing dishes, somewhere, going for 15 dollar. That's what he requested I do." This youth is now working on a B.A. degree at City College.

Perhaps drugs have the most to do with the evil reputation of the block. One-twentieth of all the deaths from overdoses in Manhattan in 1967 (20 out of 400) occurred on this block, and despite continued and frequent arrests, the block has maintained its reputation as a place to get heroin. Cars with Jersey plates cruise down the street, looking for a connection. Yet only a small proportion of the block's population, less than 2 per cent, uses heroin. . . .

While Lander found that during the four-year period of his study one-third of the kids began taking heroin, he also discovered that about one-third of those with a drug history—22 out of 60 addicts and former addicts—had quit. It seems they reached their late 20's and early 30's and simply stopped. On the average they had been off drugs for three years or more. All but three stopped without the assistance of the various government programs. . . .

Many on the block, especially the young people, admit that they commit illegal acts on a fairly regular basis. For the teen-agers, for example, the weekly shoplifting trip down to Macy's or up to Incredible Alexander's in the Bronx is a regular Saturday entertainment, like going to a movie.

"Why do you steal?"

"To get what we wanted. Pocketbooks and clothes." . . .

They rarely are caught, partly because they are very adept, partly because the stores find it cheaper to accept a certain amount of shoplifting than to hire enough clerks to wait on each customer. One store detective estimates that his staff catches one of five of the shoplifters, about half of whom are middle-class. When the slum kids are caught, he said, "the Puerto Ricans break down and cry; the Negroes are cool and tough." . . .

If surprisingly small numbers are arrested on the block, an even smaller proportion ever get to court or prison. According to police records, only 11 percent of the boys between 11 and 20, and only 30 per cent of the adults who were arrested ever went on to court. . . . There is an almost unanimous lack of respect for the police there, a widespread belief that they are corrupt and brutal.

"One of my friends got killed by a cop," a pretty young Puerto Rican girl remembered. "The cop was drinking and they say he came out of a bar on 103d Street, and the kid was running and some lady was yelling, and he got shook up and he shot him in the back and got him killed, and he died."

"Had your friend done anything?"

"I don't know. You really don't know what happened 'cause the cop told his story and that's all the story. It was still wrong 'cause he coulda shot him in the leg or something, but he shot to kill."

She added: "Cause you're a Puerto Rican or Negro, they just take you in the car and beat you up and then take you to the precinct and everything." . . .

A young man was asked whether the police accept bribes.

"Oh sure, they do that all the time."

"Have you ever seen it yourself?"

"Giving them money? Oh sure."

Who would it be?"

"Bookies. All over. Everything."

A runner for the numbers racket was even more definite. "They, you know, they come around the first of every month. There is the cop which you call the captain's man and he comes around and he picks up for the captain and then the cop on duty he gets paid, too."

"Aren't there any honest cops?"

"Yeah. You get an honest cop on Fifth Avenue someplace. You can't have honest guys around a block like this."

BILINGUALISM IN EL BARRIO

[How well a mainland Puerto Rican speaks English or Spanish depends largely upon education, and length of time in the United States. Today, the mainland community is greatly divided in terms of language ability. Those who are truly bilingual—mastering both Spanish and English—are in the minority. As a rule, Puerto Ricans who migrated to the mainland as teenagers or adults speak far better Spanish than English, which may be an obstacle to them in economic terms. Those who arrived as infants, or were born on the mainland, possess a better command of English than Spanish, and sometimes speak no Spanish. This can result in serious communications gaps, not only with parents and grandparents, but with the whole ethos of their ancestral homeland. Quite frequently, mainland Puerto Ricans are linguistically ambivalent: They speak poor English and Spanish, and blend both languages in the same sentence. This problem is explored in the following excerpt from a taped interview with Puerto Rican high school students in New York City.]

Fishman. How come your father knows English better than your mother?

Ramón. Well, because he's always been working, so once you have to learn English there's no doubt about it. Then he attended school for some time and he learned English there and I would speak English to him all I want and he'll understand me.

From Joshua A. Fishman, Robert L. Cooper, Roxana Ma, *et al.*, *Bilingualism in the Barrio*, U.S. Department of Health, Education and Welfare, Office of Education, Bureau of Records, Contract No. OEC-1-7-062817-0297, August, 1968, I, pp. 228–57.

F. Why do you speak Spanish to him sometimes?
R. He wants me to. He wants me to. I tell him something in English and he says to tell it to him in Spanish. . . . Que me hable en español. You know he wants to hear me speak Spanish. . . .
Mike. My mother and my father they speak perfect English and my father knows about twenty words in Spanish and my mother knows Spanish quite well. But in the house I hardly ever speak Spanish unless it's to my grandfather and he's a Spaniard. He's always correcting me. I hate that. . . . Like I might say I'm going to "trabajar," I'm going to work . . . Tu va a trabajar. In Spanish he'll translate for me. He'll repeat what I said, not in the present or past. And like if I go to my grandmother's, she's another Spaniard, and she would want me to speak to her in Spanish but she speaks English also. But my grandfather, like for instance, everytime I come from school I stop off where my grandfather works and like I'll have 10 to 15 minutes of speaking to him in Spanish, but other than that I hardly ever speak in Spanish. . . . Up until I was 10 years old my grandmother used to take care of me a lot. My mother used to work so she would take care of me; that's where I learned most of my Spanish. Then after I got into my mother's hands she destroyed it. I don't know as much Spanish as I did before. . . . And you just forget Spanish if you don't practice it and also like Tommy I get an urge to speak Spanish once in a while.
F. What's this urge like? I don't understand the urge.
Tom. We just naturally come out speaking Spanish. Your mother might be home cooking something and you'll just go and if you have something to tell her or ask something you'll just naturally talk in Spanish. I guess that would be the urge. But let me clear just one thing up. My parents do speak Spanish at home all the time. . . . When I speak to them in English, if they don't reply in English they'll always reply in Spanish so that they are always speaking Spanish to each other. . . .
M. There was an instance yesterday where my Spanish saved me from a fate worse than death. . . . I work in Alexander's and I'm a shoe salesman and yesterday was my first day selling shoes so I wasn't that fast in getting the shoes. So this Spanish couple about 19, 18, 20, they asked me to get these 4 pairs of shoes and since I don't know myself that well around there it took me a little while. When I got back they started talking in Spanish, you know, about me. This dirt is no good, taking his time about it, making me wait so much time. . . . Before they actually said anything real bad I came out. I said something in Spanish. I said, "pues aquí están los zapatos." They said, "Oh, no." Their attitude changed because they knew that I knew what they were saying. They said, "Oh another one that knows how to speak Spanish." And when I put on a suit and tie I don't look Spanish at all; in fact most of the time

I don't look Spanish and most of the people in Alexander's in the shoe selling business are Spanish. And I think one or two more. One looks Spanish and the other one doesn't and me I don't look it at all. So they don't expect you to be Spanish and if you are Spanish they expect you to speak Spanish. So like they'll tell you off in Spanish without you knowing about it. They'll smile, you dirty no good; and stuff like that, you know. . . .

Liz. In my house my mother and father speak to each other in Spanish all the time. I speak to my father in Spanish all the time 'cause his English is atrocious, and he is lost speaking it and understanding it. My mother, she can speak English a little bit better 'cause she works and in order to communicate with her fellow workers she has to use it. But I usually speak to her in English or I talk to her in Spanish. My problem is that sometimes I start in Spanish and I'll end in English or vice versa. . . . by the time I finish what I have to say the whole meaning of it is lost somewhere in the air. And that's one reason why there's a great lack of communication. . . .

M. Did you ever think of a problem such as mine? I don't know very much Spanish and I have to go to her [Liz] house every once in a while and I'm there trying to translate my English into Spanish when I don't know my Spanish that well. . . . Like I'm very talkative and when I go to her house I only say about ten words and that's that.

L. My mother thinks he's a very shy boy and I laugh because he's not that way at all and my father comes from Colombia so he speaks very good Spanish and he always corrects me but he doesn't do it to him as often when he [Mike] comes over because he's afraid that if he does correct him he'll [Mike] keep quiet altogether. And, but he's very quiet when he comes to my house, and we always have arguments over that because I want him to talk and my parents think that, oh my goodness, he's so shy and everything and he's not shy at all. . . .

Gil. I speak it [Spanish] all the time at home. I hardly ever speak it except to my brothers really—with my family it's hard to get across a point without speaking Spanish in my house. Even if they, you know, part of the family knows English, but they just can't take to it very well. . . .

F. Your father knows English but you speak Spanish to him. . . .

Gil. Yes. Maybe once in a while I might let loose some. . . . I guess it's because I was always adapted to it since I was small, to talking Spanish to him since I, you know, whatever I learned in school, I used to talk English in school, not at home. . . .

R. . . . my uncle . . . knows English like my father would know it. He could speak to anyone and hold a conversation, but when he comes over to my house, I'd prefer to speak to him in Spanish, because I know he prefers me to speak in Spanish. . . . I think he'd feel better, you know—he'll say, "Ah, he's speaking to me in Spanish." Although he knows English and he knows that I know English, but, you know, it's like cursing almost, because I know although he knows English he knows Spanish much better, and well, let's say, well, he went to high school in New York so he knows English pretty well, although he comes from Puerto Rico, but he feels a lot better when I speak to him in Spanish. He feels that I'm being more courteous, let's say. . . .

George. Yes, I know a lot of people in my building—a lot of relatives. Like my uncle for instance. He's 56 and he came when he was 15 from Puerto Rico. . . . So he went to elementary school, he went to Junior High School, he was in the army until 1945. He speaks perfect English but I only speak Spanish to him. . . .

M. . . . my mother likes . . . me to speak Spanish to her, but I never, unless I get the urge, I won't speak Spanish. . . . Like she owns a beauty parlor and once in while this urge hits me and I'll enter the beauty parlor. She'll be working on a customer and I'll start speaking in Spanish to my mother. My mother would tell me don't speak Spanish because the lady might think you're saying something bad about her, so I have to stop right there and I have to start with the English and I have to translate what I said. It's just, just the urge, that's about it. I don't think I can explain myself. And I'll speak it the whole day. . . .

R. Well, I work in a drug store and when people come in if they are elderly I speak Spanish to them, not very well, but I try, and when you want to talk to somebody and you don't want the boss to listen in, you speak Spanish and when you want to fool around, or with customers, which you can't do in front of the boss in English, I do it in Spanish and I only speak Spanish most of the time only in the store and it's to my older relative I speak Spanish. Up until then I use English all the time. . . . My father speaks in Spanish. When I want a favor, I'll speak to him in . . . I'll speak to him in Spanish. . . . When I want money or something . . . I'll speak to him in Spanish, you know, first. I'll have a little conversation with him in Spanish. I'll put him in a good mood and then I'll strike him for the money, you know. . . .

M. I do [the same] with my grandfather mostly. You know he has an old saying, "the best friend is a dollar in the pocket." In Spanish it is, "el más buen amigo es un peso en el bolsillo," so every time that I'm going to ask him for money I say I need a friend. . . . Eh, "necesito un amigo o necesito cinco amigos." Five friends, ten friends, as many friends as I need, I would say that. Well, he says, well I can't. How about two? When I say five he says two. I'll say three and he'll two-fifty. We'll cut it down and make it about half.

I. Well, there are things that you just naturally, you know, feel like asking in Spanish. My father, when I need money from him,

well I'll just say, Pop, can I have two dollars? something like.
I'll say it in English, but for instance when I'm playing with my
father, like if I want to borrow the car, I'll tell him I want to
borrow your car. I don't have my license yet, but I'll say, "préstame
el carro." You know that's just playing with him and he'll react. . . .
Gil. They feel nice. It's just the way you say it sometime. You say
it with a certain little ting to it that they like.
F. Like, like what, what do you mean like a ting?
Gil. I don't know. You know, you talk to, let's say, grandmother,
right?—you tell her, "Mira mija ven acá," you know, "y plánchame
esto aquí te doy una pecita ahí," you know, things like that, you
know, little jokes, you know, and they just do it for you because
they just know your jokes, they make them laugh, and right away
you get it. You gotta do it a certain way though. If you said it
in English, if they don't understand it very well, you know, even
if they know both languages, but it wouldn't have that little
feeling to it.

NEO-RICAN JETLINER

[Jaime Carrero's bilingual
"*Jet Neorriqueño*/Neo-Rican Jetliner," was probably the first literary
mention of the concept of Neo-Ricanism. "Neo-Rican" is now a term
commonly used to describe the "in-between" product of Puerto Rican
and North American culture, a hybrid person who speaks and thinks in
both languages, sometimes simultaneously, but is a stranger in both
lands. There are, today, probably a few hundred thousand Neo-Ricans
in America; still others have returned to the island of their birth, or
their parents' birth, where their children are being taught Spanish for
the first time. Neo-Ricanism involves more than language; it encompasses a complex set of attitudes, set forth in the following poem.]

> Ticket please
> *Me recuerda ese señor*
> *a* Dick Tracy
> *a Trucutú*
> (Alleyoop *en inglés*)
> *Ahí viene otra vez*
> *con el 'no se ponga de pié*
> *por favor'*

From *San Juan Review*, April, 1965. Also appeared in a private edition,
printed in San Germán, Puerto Rico in 1964 at Inter-American University.
Reprinted by permission.

Fasten your seat belt
Ahí viene esa señorita
con el 'abróchese el cinturón
en seguidita please'
please' por favor
plis
plis
No smoking *señor*
Is this seat taken?
No. Please.
Thank you.
Are you from over here?
No Sir from New York
But you look Puerto Rican.
I'm not I'm not born in New York
born in New York
No smoking please
My name is Raúl.
From Puerto Rico?
Jes an'now from Noo Jork.
Muee bieeen senhor
Raúl is may name *señor*.
American— you look American
blond
you don't look Puerto Rican:
Raúl *señor* my name is Raúl.
R-A-U-L u.u.u.
Like the U you find in fool?
Jes. U.U.U. fool.
Fasten your seat belt fasten your seat
Fasten your fasten fast fast fast
F-f-f-f-s-s-s–t-t. . . . .

Vuelo A

New York the center of the world is big the dream my father
had when the sugar cane died of drought Sir and bad fertilizing
Sir did its job to force his wings open to search for the greatest
money on earth the dream my father had.

Conversación I

Hey boy
Le tengo miedo a esa voz.
'We the people of the United States
in order to form
Hey boy

I am scared of that voice with the
Hey boy
'a more perfect union,
Hey boy
'establish justice,
Me duele esa voz con el
Hey boy
Me duele esa voz como un SUR
Hey boy
'insure domestic tranquility
Me duele el color de esa voz
                    con
                    el
Hey boy
and so on
and so on
promote the general welfare,
Hey boy it is it
and so on
and so on
'over the land of the free
Me duele, me duele esa voz. . .
. . . .
Hey boy did you see
                    did you see   ?

Vuelo B

New York Sir the center of the world gave birth to my little
kid sister yeah and you know the doctor said and the nurse said
when the other doctor and the other nurse showed up with my
kid sister Sir that no other baby was as big Sir as my kid
sister Sir was.

Conversación II

My friend is big man
a new man man Neo-Rican
a big man man
Big man, my friend is big
Neo-Rican
A Jetliner man
Big man, my friend is big
big as fire man
As big as I can say mountain
  as I can say sky
  my friend is big
  big man big

                    as the dry season
                    as the rain
                    big I say
                    my friend is big
                    big man big
            As big as I can say Manhattan
                    my friend is bigger
                    the size of God
                    The Jetliner
                    Neo-Rican
                    MAN . . .

Vuelo C

New York the center of the world taught me law-stick ball pool
the street money man—the wings my father saw but forgot to
take when he saw them there man everywhere anyway in the law
in the street in the money.

                    Conversación III

            La primera vez que la escuché
                    en mi primer viaje
                    me sonó poética
                            esa frase
                            o gráfica
                    algo así
                    S.O.B.
            Yes Raol like *CERVEZA*
                    the word to me
                    is a girl
            Oh Raol you're nuts
            . . . .
            Man you spelled his name bad
            . . . .
            How?
                    R-A-U-L like fool
            Jes like foool
            Ah Raool sounds like fool
            a U like fool
            Jes fool U like foool
            U U U   fool

Vuelo D

New York the center of the world taught me law yes Sir the
color of the wings my father found when he came to forget his
land yes Sir and decided the wings money can buy were better than
the land.

Conversación IV

A ver mi hermana he venido
Hace tiempo no la veo
Slow please did you say NANA
    No señora hermana dije hermana
                 Sister *dije* sister
That I come to see her
                         you see?
    La pobre no se levanta
Is she sick?
    Sí señora.
Is she old?
    yes yes *no se puede mover*
I am sorry to hear that.
    podía caminar
    la última vez que la vi
Is she sick?
    yes yes
Is she old?
    yes yes
I'm sorry to hear that

Lamento 3

This Puerto Rican is silent
This Puerto Rican is sad
        to be silent and sad
        I feel something big
            or low
            or dark
            is going on
            in the back
            of the mind man.
This Puerto Rican is silent and sad.
The color no white man dares to ask.

Lamento 2

I was born in New York new blood.
I was born in New York
I'm not a Jones Act Puerto Rican.
yeah?
I'm a Neo-Rican man   new flash.
yeah?
I known what I know no Jones Act man
yeah?
. . . .
what was that   ?

Lamento 1

Hay horas de espalda: sin terminar
Jetliner warned—you're high
Hay horas de frente: ahí puestas, tranquilas
Jetliner cracks
Hay horas de día: que hay que caminar
Overshoot — too high
Hay horas de hombre: volar
cracks open
Hay horas . . .
CRASH   in the dark

Lamento 0

On the fringe of trouble if you ask
          ¿por qué señor
          por qué?
On the fringe of trouble I say
          ¿olvida el Jones Act?
On the fringe of trouble I say.
          a chance sir do we have
          a chance sir a chance?
We cannot solve your problems I say
On the fringe of trouble again
On the fringe   . . .

Part X

THE DIVIDED NATION

> What appears to be taking place . . . is a
> growing movement of young Puerto Ricans
> back and forth between the island and the
> United States. They come back looking for
> a job, but rarely find one. They had been
> reminded in the United States that they
> were Puerto Rican, but here they are told
> that they speak Spanish with an "English
> accent," that "you are not really one of
> us." The young Puerto Rican may well ask
> himself, not only "Where am I going–"
> but "Who am I?"
>
> —A. W. MALDONADO, *The Nation*,
> March 16, 1964.

> I am proud of my accent, I don't want to
> drop it.
>
> —CARMEN OLIVERI, a New York-born
> Puerto Rican student, *New York
> Times*, April 23, 1968

After seventy years
of United States rule, Puerto Rico is still the poorest community under
the American flag, and its sons and daughters who have migrated to
the mainland still comprise the lowest paid, poorest housed and least
educated minority group in the nation.

About twenty-five years ago, former island governor Rexford Guy
Tugwell wrote, of Puerto Ricans:

I am ashamed of my country, sometimes, for not having cared enough
to do something for them besides hand out relief and use them for
political advantage. I am humiliated that, having been Governor for
almost five years, I have not been able to make some considerable
change in this. . . . Puerto Rico comprises one of those small groups
of people, of whom there are many in the world, who are tied by
destiny to a larger entity. The process of working out a satisfactory
organization of the relationship is a matter in which only a few of us

happen to be interested. . . . Something will happen in the case of Puerto Rico, but it seems awfully slow in coming.*

Since those words were written, more economic and social change has occurred in Puerto Rico than in the previous four centuries. Some of this change was generated by Mr. Tugwell, the last—and by far the best—American to govern the island. But most of it took place when the federal government relaxed its colonial leash a few notches, and allowed Puerto Ricans to play a more active role in running their own affairs.

The same phenomenon is slowly, agonizingly, developing in the *barrios* of America's cities, where second and third-generation Puerto Ricans are educating and organizing themselves, and starting to demand their fair share of power.

A large question that remains, however, is not how quickly—but *where*—Puerto Ricans are heading.

A final decision on the island's political status will have far-reaching consequences. Puerto Ricans disagree strongly about the political future of their island. Even if they eventually reach a consensus, they will not be the only ones to drive the final bargain. U.S. businesses have a $3 billion stake in the island. The U.S. Army, Navy, and Air Force maintain bases there, and, although modern technology makes these bases less crucial than they were during World War II, Puerto Rico still occupies a strategic location.

As if matters were not complicated enough, about one of every three Puerto Ricans now lives on the U.S. mainland; there is constant back-and-forth migration, and cross-pollination of customs and attitudes.

The mainland community was once dispersed and silent, but it is now coming into its own. Until recently, for example, the most important Puerto Rican on the mainland was the island's Resident Commissioner in Washington. Today, he is overshadowed by Congressman Herman Badillo, whose constituency is in New York, where he was raised. Thus, *Palante*, the New York-based paper of the Young Lords, is not incorrect when it calls Puerto Rico today a "divided nation."

As time goes by, the island will become more urban-industrial, and the cultural gap with the United States will narrow. Over a long period, it may narrow to such a fine divide that political assimilation will not imply any drastic surrender of cultural values.

On the other hand, as Puerto Rico slowly gains more home rule, the island's leaders may balk at relinquishing their hard-earned control to a centralized government in Washington. Today, at a time when America's minority groups are putting unprecedented emphasis upon ethnic pride, mainland Puerto Ricans may be the first to protest against full assimilation. They may, instead, relish the fact that there is still a *patria* to which one can return, or at least dream of.

* Rexford Guy Tugwell, "In Defense of Puerto Rico," *The New Republic*, April 15, 1946, p. 512.

"NATION AND HOMELAND"

[In November, 1968, wealthy industrialist Luis A. Ferré surprised many experts—and himself as well, he admitted—when he won the governorship of Puerto Rico. For 28 years, island politics had been dominated by the Popular Democratic Party, led by Luis Muñoz Marín. But many voters, particularly those in the middle-class suburbs that ring San Juan, were clamoring for change; also, the Popular Democrats were weakened by bitter internal struggles. Ferré took advantage of this, and mounted a vigorous, well-planned campaign. For the first time in Puerto Rican politics, television was employed to market a candidate as one would a household product. The air waves were saturated by spot commercials showing a firm, paternalistic Ferré, promising *La Nueva Vida*, The New Life, to the island's citizens. He barely won, with 44 per cent of the votes, compared with 42 per cent for the Popular Democrats.

Because Ferré had long been identified with the pro-statehood cause, Puerto Rico was polarized into two hostile political camps. Many advocates of the middle-of-the-road Commonwealth status began to sound like *independentistas*, as they warned of the dangers of statehood. Ferré did little to allay the fears of his opponents; in a speech seven months after his election, he supported the presidential vote for Puerto Ricans, a step that would immerse the island in the U.S. political system.

As the rhetoric grew more heated, and violence shook the University of Puerto Rico campus, Ferré adopted a more conciliatory tone. His New Progressive Party proposed the concept of *jíbaro* statehood; meaning political, but not cultural, assimilation with the United States.

Ferré's views on how Puerto Rico could join the Union, without surrendering its unique personality, are outlined in a speech given in San Juan on October 12, 1969, to mark Columbus Day. In Puerto Rico, it is known as *Día de la Raza*, Heritage Day; the island also celebrates its discovery by Columbus on November 19, 1493. (Note: In November 1972, Ferré lost in his bid for re-election as governor; the winner was Rafael Hernandez Colón of the Popular Democratic Party, which espouses Commonwealth status and increased autonomy.)]

Puerto Rico has warmly hailed our New Life, but there are noisy voices hawking that it will result in the cultural disappearance of Puerto Ricans.

From *Speech Delivered by the Governor of Puerto Rico, Hon. Luis A. Ferré on Heritage Day (Día de la Raza), October 12, 1969.* Commonwealth Department of Education, Santurce, Puerto Rico, 1969. The text is in both Spanish and English.

Those who say so are basing their position on hackneyed arguments. . . .

We are Puerto Ricans. At a glorious moment in the first decade of the 19th Century, the patriot Ramón Power and Bishop Arizmendi managed to congeal the awakening of our conscience as a people. From that moment we move . . . to the Lares Revolt [1868] and to the achievement of the Autonomic Charter [1897]. The people of Puerto Rico slowly achieve a greater conscience of themselves and greater powers of self-government. Then there comes the change in dominion. Puerto Rico is shaken by the impact of the American presence.

In this century, after having overcome a naive and mistaken colonialist policy, our people take up a new struggle to obtain more powers of self-government, a struggle which peaks a half century later with the election of the Governor and with the drafting, by ourselves, of our own Constitution. I feel honored to have been able to make at that Constitution . . . my modest contribution to this process of the definitive quest for our own values and our own governmental powers. But I am further honored to have been able to contribute to this stream of development of our values which set us apart from the other peoples of the world.

There is a simple definition of what it means to be a Puerto Rican. Hostos gave it in his diary and I want to share it with you. The great Teacher told us: "Whence does that come and why is it so? Why do we cling so tenaciously to the native land? I think I have found the answer. I set it down here in order to come back to it and think about it some more. We love our land because it is for us a reference point. Life is a journey; reason would not know how to find the starting point were it not for the piece of earth whose image is before our eyes everywhere."

I tell you that, as it is for Hostos, Puerto Rico is my starting and reference point. It is also yours.

Once the journey of life has begun, we may ask ourselves where we are going. It is also Hostos who can best answer that question. Writing in Paris on the fifth of August in 1868 he speaks of heading immediately for Europe to—and I quote: "free myself from the struggle with shameful hunger and thence take me on to Puerto Rico and grant myself a month of oblivion and hope and place myself in my theatre of operations, in that America to whose future I have pledged my own."

I have come before you, my fellow citizens, young people of Puerto Rico, to extend to you the invitation for us as people and as men, collectively and individually, to follow the example of Hostos and consecrate our future to the future of America.

The American world, the entire hemisphere from Alaska to Tierra del Fuego, must make a superhuman effort so that men in it may unchain themselves from poverty, oppression and hunger so that the children of today's poverty shall not become the parents of tomorrow's poverty. Puerto Rico may very well become the leader in this humanitarian effort. We have established an ever closer union with the United States of America. We want to be a part of the United States forever. But we want to be so not with the attitude of one who seeks admission into another's house, but with the attitude of one who comes home and has something of himself to offer also.

I conceive of our participation in the great task of hemispheric integration as the best contribution which we Puerto Ricans may make to our fellow citizens of the North. A fulcrum of two cultures, a center for change and adaptation of what is best in both, Puerto Rico has in this Hemisphere the paramount task of contributing to the understanding between the United States and Latin America. We have such an ability and we should exercise it. We should offer Puerto Rico as a center of work where the United States of America and our neighbors on the rest of the Continent may learn together how to live in harmony and how to solve without violence their problems and how to work out for themselves a better and more just future.

To bring about this ideal of Latin and North American harmony, Puerto Rico has to make a special effort to understand its own nature and to show, by its everyday life how a people of a great cultural richness can also make use of the most modern concepts of technology. We can show how an essentially Latin people can, at the same time, be perfectly American. We must feel as Puerto Ricans, operate like Americans and dream of a united America where we will have been the home and seat of both cultures.

I now want to address myself most specially to our youth. . . . To be Puerto Rican is the most significant achievement before us as a people. It is precisely that quality of being a culturally united people which gives us the credentials to improve understanding between Latin American culture and North American culture.

But Puerto Rico has also achieved the technical proficiency of the American people and you, the young, are experiencing that. That ability is of great value in this task. Both abilities, the ability to feel as creatures of Hispanic culture and the ability to perform as beings of Anglo-Saxon culture, are the two which permit us to make our mark in the Hemisphere. To do so we must develop ourselves as a people in both directions at once.

We must understand, my dear young fellow citizens, that in order to better serve this purpose of understanding of which Hostos spoke, that we must give a new dimension to progress. During the last 20 years there has been a revolution in the communications media, radar, television, satellites. The world has grown smaller and we men can communicate with each other faster and easier than we ever dreamed. But, in spite of this easier com-

munication, we have made precious little progress in comprehension
and understanding. That is the new dimension which we must add
to progress. Man must learn to understand himself better and to
understand his fellow man better. We need a revolution for understanding. Here, the Puerto Rican, because of his understanding
of the two cultures of America, has the ability and also the obligation to serve in achieving the Hostosian dream of a united America,
through a greater understanding.

And that is why I conceive as one of the principal duties of the
New Life that of preserving, promoting and perpetuating the
Puerto Rican being. This is not a new posture in my life. I have
always held up and have always defended the values of our land.
On July 27, 1963 I pointed out: "To be an American does not mean
to speak English or to be the son of a Yankee. The United States,
today with a population of 180 million, has received throughout
its history more than 40 million immigrants of all races—English,
German, Italian, Polish and Jewish. For Puerto Ricans to be
Americans, as for millions of the children of other races which
today make up the American nation, is to be true to the principles
of democracy which are set forth in the Constitution, and to feel
one with other American citizens in the protection of our freedoms
and our national life."

It is moved by this knowledge and, even more, by that feeling in
my soul that I now add: "Nation" is a concept of political, social
and human identification. "Homeland" (*patria*) is the heart's affection for the place of birth. Our Nation, the United States. Our
homeland, Puerto Rico.

I have had occasion during my life to propitiate and defend the
values which make me feel proud to be a Puerto Rican. You will
remember that during the deliberations of the Status Commission
a prominent U.S. senator took the following position—and I quote:
"The people of Puerto Rico represent a rich and old culture. We
gladly welcome diversity; therefore, the characteristic culture of
Puerto Rico, as such, is no barrier to statehood. However, the unity
of our structure of federal states requires a common language. . . .
The recognition and acceptance of English as the official language
must be a previous condition for statehood." Faced with this
absurd position, born of a poor understanding of what the American
nation is, I made it clear then that if assimilation was to be made
a condition *sine qua non* for statehood, then it would be impossible
to accept. . . .

History has proved me right. Sociologists, psychologists, and
even the large communication media in the United States recognize
that diversity, not *assimilation,* is the nerve and essence of the new
American culture. This very week a well-known national magazine
says:

The hard truth is that the celebrated American melting pot has never worked quite so well in life as in nostalgic myth. As Nathan Glazer and Daniel P. Moynihan pointed out six years ago in "Beyond the Melting Pot," Americans tend to maintain their sense of ethnic identity far more tenaciously than was once supposed.

But over and above that, the nation's Supreme Court said:

Congress could very well have concluded that as a means of promoting the intelligent use of the vote, the ability to read or understand Spanish is as effective as reading English for those who have access to newspapers and programs in Spanish.

The opposite, the demand for assimilation, in the words of the judges of the nation's highest court, would be "an abominable crime."

Fellow citizens . . . this is the moment for diversity within the unity of the great American nation. Let us make our contribution to this precious moment in her history! . . .

I . . . invite you to serve in this noble endeavor: that we come before history to promote two fertilizing and enriching streams of our past and our future which have been the source of our achievements as people. Let us follow the road of Puerto Ricanism. Let us follow the road of unity with the United States. Following these two paths of noble and generous projections which transcend our naturally limiting boundaries as an island and enable us to contribute to the achievement of hemispheric peace, solidarity and progress, we will arrive at our rendezvous with history.

"FROM A JAIL IN PUERTO RICO"

[In the preceding article, Governor Luis A. Ferré appeals to Puerto Rico's youth "to feel as creatures of Hispanic culture" and "to perform as beings of Anglo-Saxon culture," which is the essence of his concept of *jíbaro* statehood.

But many of Puerto Rico's young people, particularly those on the college campuses, are attracted to the views of men such as Rubén Berríos Martínez, the youthful president of the Puerto Rican Independence Party.

From *New York Times*, April 28, 1971, p. 43. Reprinted by permission.

Berríos was imprisoned for three months during the spring of 1971, for violating a federal injunction that ordered him to leave the U.S. Navy's firing range in Culebra, an offshore municipality of Puerto Rico. Since World War II, the Navy has used Culebra, and some of its surrounding islets, for naval and aerial target practice. In 1971, naval plans to secure more land on Culebra collided with resistance from the island's 600 residents, who claimed that they were being forced to abandon their birthplace.

The issue became an international controversy. Culebrans received support from virtually every political group in Puerto Rico, as well as from sympathetic congressmen, lawyers, and activists in the United States. The Navy has since announced plans to reduce its Culebra operations, and to gradually phase them out. Berríos and his followers, who adopted a tactic of "militant nonviolence," were among the leaders of the "Save Culebra" movement. Unarmed, they "invaded" the island in a small boat, and erected a Christian chapel right on the very beach that was used as a target for naval cannon. Berríos wrote the following letter while serving his prison sentence; when he emerged from jail, he was greeted by a large crowd, and it was generally conceded that he had gained the sympathy of many persons not formerly identified with the independence cause.]

SAN JUAN—I am writing from a jail in Puerto Rico, the last classical colony in Latin America. The slave-master relation, in whatever form, negates that which separates human beings from animals: freedom.

I am writing in an American newspaper because the American people are our potential allies. To become independent, Puerto Ricans must make it more convenient for the United States Government to leave than to stay in our land, and in that endeavor, free Americans can be of great help.

In a country where 13 per cent of its scarce arable land is occupied by foreign armed forces which also make an atomic arsenal of its territory; where its youth is ordered to fight in the wars of a foreign nation, thus making the cry of "taxation without representation is tyranny" a sigh compared to this blood tribute; where the laws of a foreign parliament apply without the consent of the governed, thus making a mockery of the most elementary rules of representative democracy, the fight for national liberation has become the duty of every self-respecting man and woman.

If to these abusive political conditions one adds a 28 per cent unemployment rate, vast squalid slums populated by 25 per cent of our families, prices higher than those in New York with incomes of less than $300 per capita for one-third of our population, an abysmal maldistribution of income whereby 9 per cent of the families receive 40 per cent of the net income and 40 per cent receive 9 per cent of the net income, yearly returns of $450 million for American investors and a $1-billion deficit in the balance of payments in favor of the United States, then the fight for social revolution becomes part of the obligation of every Puerto Rican.

It is not surprising that the Americans are starting to hear about a different Puerto Rico. The widely publicized occurrences, such as the Navy's abusive bombardment of Culebra Island, the university riots, the more than 150 acts of sabotage that have plagued American enterprises in Puerto Rico during the last two years, are the symptoms of a deeper problem. To the institutionalized violence of the colonial system some respond with nonviolence, others with violence, and, sad to say, some still respond with collaboration.

Genuflecting, the collaborators will apologize and reassure Americans that "independentistas" constitute a minority in a community of loyal American citizens. As proof they will submit the thesis of colonialism by consent.

And in a sense, they might have been right. Classical manipulations of colonial masters, division of spoils with local tories, propaganda bombardment through American-controlled television and newspapers, an educational system destined to instill Puerto Ricans with a feeling of inferiority, impotence and dependence, and direct persecution of independence forces have occurred. The United States Government managed in the past to divide Puerto Ricans and confuse and suppress their urge for liberation.

But now the colonizer-colonized contradictions, particularly the incompatibility between social justice and colonial status, have become evident. And the independence forces have directed their energies toward erasing the traditional psychological misconception whereby the mass of the Puerto Rican people, through constant indoctrination, believed the republic to be equivalent to hunger. By uniting the fight for national liberation with the fight for radical social change, by answering the question—why independence?—our fight for freedom has ceased to be an élite movement and is being transformed into a mass movement.

Besides realizing the need for a radical change, Puerto Ricans see the possibility of such a change. This is due, in large part, to the declining prestige of the United States, and to the effective addition to our methodology of nonviolent tactics. These are particularly suited to situations like ours where the balance of physical power is disproportionate and the colonized nation is forced, by internal and international policy considerations, to wear a mask of democratic respectability.

Colonized, exploited, ideologically prepared, and full of hope, our people are on the road to freedom.

"CANCIO AND COMPASSION"

[Should a Puerto Rican
who believes in independence be required to serve in the U.S. military,
which he considers to be a "foreign" army? For that matter, should a
resident of Puerto Rico, who considers himself loyal to the United
States, be required to serve, if he cannot vote, either for the President,
who is Commander-in-Chief of the Armed Forces, or for members of
Congress, which has the power to declare war? The issue of the military
draft is one of several which remains unsolved, because of Puerto Rico's
anomalous Commonwealth relationship with the United States. Here, a
Puerto Rican journalist describes how one U.S. federal judge on the
island wrestled with his own conscience in deciding the case of a conscientious objector to the draft.]

Almost inevitably,
a judge leaves his imprint on the court over which he presides.
Some judges are lenient in their interpretation of the law, others
are strict. Some judges go about their job in a matter-of-fact way,
others like to add a touch of drama. Through their interpretation
of the law, either liberally or conservatively, judges sometimes
make decisions that change the course of a nation's history. Witness,
for example, the 1954 decision of the U.S. Supreme Court, under
Chief Justice Earl Warren, outlawing segregation in the public
schools.

Federal Judge Hirám Cancio has definitely left his mark on the
U.S. District Court over which he presides. Cancio's emphasis on
Puerto Rican values, his sometimes unorthodox approach to his
job and his flair for the dramatic has distinguished his four years
as a federal judge. Now, Cancio's dramatic announcement that he
was reducing the sentence of convicted draft evader Edwin Feliciano
Grafals from one year to one hour has brought him once again into
the public spotlight.

Cancio has his admirers but he also has his critics. His out-
spokenness has sometimes brought charges that he has exceeded
the authority vested in him as a judge. For example, in March 1968,
Cancio delivered an impassioned plea against the death penalty to
a jury which could have ordered Mrs. Carolyn O. Wilkins sentenced
to death on a first degree murder charge. Cancio told the jury:

Frank Ramos, *San Juan Star*, January 30, 1970, p. 33. Reprinted with permission.

"The vast majority of the people of Puerto Rico do not believe in the death penalty. That is the reason why the Constitution of Puerto Rico clearly prohibits the death penalty. Unfortunately, the Constitution of Puerto Rico does not apply in this jurisdiction. Therefore, you have a great responsibility in your hands. You are to decide whether this lady is going to live or whether this lady is going to die. . . ."

Cancio's plea brought charges that he was interfering with the right of the jury to reach its own conclusions. But it also reflected Cancio's compassion for those persons who are brought before him on trial. People at federal court tell the story of the old man who was brought before Cancio on a charge of capturing and selling canaries and nightingales.

It seemed the old man had violated a long-standing statute that prohibited the capture of migratory birds. When Cancio learned that the old man lived on the verge of poverty and that he depended on the sale of these birds for his livelihood, Cancio persuaded the U.S. attorney to drop the case.

Moreover, when he learned the man had spent his last cent in coming to San Juan for the hearing, Cancio gave him several dollars of his own funds so he could take a público home.

Cancio's compassion was undoubtedly a factor in his decision to reduce the sentence he himself had originally imposed against Feliciano Grafals. He felt that Feliciano Grafals was technically guilty of violating the law but morally innocent. Had he written the law, Cancio said, he would have declared persons like Feliciano Grafas to be true conscientious objectors. Cancio's concern was best expressed by the judge himself in a statement he made to the accused shortly before imposing the original one year sentence. He said:

"Judges often suffer when sentencing human beings, even though those human beings happen to be hardened criminals. In your case, my suffering has been the greatest of all the cases before me. It has been the greatest because I do not believe you are a criminal but a person who for ideas and ideals in which he firmly believes, has chosen to violate a law which he believes unjust, invalid and unconstitutional.

"I know that you love Puerto Rico. I love Puerto Rico as much as you do. The only difference is that we disagree as to what is best for our country. I wish you would have given me the opportunity to avoid this sentence by having accepted probation. I think I know why you would not voluntarily accept any conditions, but I am very sorry not to have been able to avoid sentencing you as I did. Good luck."

Cancio's statement not only reflected his compassion but also his concern for Puerto Rico and its future. The idea that Puerto Rico is a distinct entity, with its own culture and value, is a theme that has emerged time and time again during Cancio's tenure as judge. It was this feeling that led Cancio to deliver a eulogy from the bench praising Puerto Rican composer Rafael Hernández the day after his death. More recently, Cancio's concept of the island's distinct character led him to deliver a speech urging that Spanish should be the preferred language used in the U.S. District Court in San Juan.

In the Feliciano Grafals case, Cancio's concern for the island caused him to dwell at length on Puerto Rico's status dilemma. Although he expressed his belief in the validity of the island's present status, he acknowledged in his ruling that some people might have good reason for thinking otherwise. He said:

"There is today a respectable number of respectable people, some of them to be found even among the defenders of commonwealth status, who honestly believe that the United States governs in Puerto Rico in the limited form allowed it by the Puerto Rico Federal Relations Act without there having really been consent of the people of Puerto Rico."

Cancio's statement on status was intended as a warning light to Congress and the island government to resolve, once and for all, the perennial problem of status. Cancio suggested that the problem could be resolved in three ways: statehood, independence or a clarification of commonwealth status, in which the powers of the U.S. and Puerto Rican government would be clearly defined. In the absence of a new pact clarifying commonwealth status, Cancio said, Congress could approve a law granting that the penal provisions of the Selective Service Act and other federal laws would not apply to the island without the expressed consent of the island's Legislature and Governor. Until the status question is resolved, the judge concluded, there will be persons like Feliciano Grafals who will question the applicability of compulsory military service and other federal laws to the island.

Cancio's plea may or may not stir Congress and the Puerto Rican government to action. In the long run, its possible impact on the U.S. Supreme Court may be even more significant. Should the high court decide to hear an appeal of the Feliciano Grafals case, and most informed people feel there's a strong possibility that it might, then it could provide the high court with its first real opportunity to consider some of the questions concerning the island's political status that are raised by Cancio.

THE CUBAN INVASION OF PUERTO RICO

[The Cuban Revolution has had a stunning impact on Puerto Rico—most of it negative. Puerto Rican tourism prospered when Havana ceased being the Caribbean's most popular resort town. But Cuba's shift to Marxism has been used time and again as a "warning" that Puerto Rican independence could lead to a "Castro-Communist style dictatorship." Also, a large colony of Cuban refugees has settled in Puerto Rico since 1959; Cubans now hold key positions in the island's business world, and in its communications media. This competition has created resentment against Cubans by many Puerto Ricans. Also, Puerto Rico's press—never a bulwark of liberalism—has turned decidedly conservative, and its anti-Castro propaganda ranks among the most strident in the world. Culturally, Puerto Rico and Cuba were very close throughout centuries of Spanish colonial rule, and until the late 1950's. But once the United States severed relations with the Castro regime, Puerto Rico was totally sealed off from its Caribbean neighbor. One must understand all of these factors in order to appreciate the bizarre incident in June, 1966, when Castro's Cuban athletes "invaded" Puerto Rico.]

In June over 300 Cuban athletes "invaded" San Juan for the Tenth Central American and Caribbean Games and, according to one old-timer, "there hasn't been so much *exitación* around here since Carlos Lindbergh landed!"

If the Cubans won no other medals, they were guaranteed from the start with a prize for the most flamboyant mode of arrival.

Months ago, it was doubtful whether the U.S. Government would grant entry visas to the Cuban athletes. But Gen. José Clark Torres of Mexico, the representative of the International Olympic Committee for the Games, warned that there would *be* no games unless Cuba were allowed to participate. Finally, the U.S. granted entry visas, to the relief of Puerto Rican government officials, who had stood by like spectators in the political ping-pong game.

Just prior to the opening of the Games, the Cubans had still not announced how they'd travel to Puerto Rico. Cuba suggested flying in directly via Cubana Airlines. The U.S. said that it would not permit direct travel from Cuba to Puerto Rico because Castro's

Kal Wagenheim, "The Cuban Invasion of Puerto Rico," *The Independent*, New York, September, 1966, pp. 1, 4.

government would not allow several hundred American citizens living in Cuba to go to the U.S. on refugee flights operating into Florida. The U.S. then said that Cuba was free to reach Puerto Rico by flying to Mexico or Madrid, and entering via commercial airliners.

This sounded fairly sensible, but in the game of political ping-pong being engaged in, the Cubans felt that they would lose points by following the *"yanqui"* suggestion. The situation remained tense. How—everyone in Puerto Rico wondered—would the Cubans arrive?

Suddenly, on the morning of Thursday, June 9, members of Puerto Rico's *Movimiento Pro-Independencia* reported that the Cubans were coming via ship. U.S. Coast Guard and Navy authorities denied any knowledge of this. Undaunted, an MPI delegation set forth in a hired motor launch to welcome the Cuban ship. Four hours later, the MPI launch chugged back to San Juan Harbor. The result: one MPI member had become terribly seasick, and MPI leader Juan Mari Bras, taking advantage of the pleasant hours at sea, had pulled in a impressive haul of fish. But no Cubans.

On Friday morning, the day before the opening of the Games, near-chaos broke loose in San Juan. Autos jammed the ocean drive along Muñoz Rivera Avenue near the entrance to Old San Juan. There, out in the mist, just before the horizon, was a ship! A Cuban *Communist* ship! Within sight of Puerto Rico! The Showcase of Democracy in the Caribbean! And the Cubans on board were looking right at the Showcase!

The traffic jams were tremendous as onlookers gaped right back at the mysterious vessel, which stood offshore, its motors idling ominously on Russian petroleum. U.S. helicopters and reconnaisance planes flitted busily about in the air. U.S. Navy ships made wide circles around the Cuban vessel. San Juan radio and TV stations crackled with the news. The Cubans were "invading."

Puerto Ricans and Cubans of every imaginable political shade began to make plans. Later in the afternoon, at the baroque pink-and-mustard U.S. Customs Building in Old San Juan, the battle lines were ready. A contingent of MPI members stood by, holding aloft placards welcoming the Cubans. Not far away, pro-Statehood students from the University of Puerto Rico bore placards denouncing the Communists. Lurking on the perimeter were Cuban exiles. Each group was armed with transistor radios, blaring out the latest news on the Cubans.

Meanwhile, the Cuban ship, the *Cerro Pelado*, remained offshore, safely beyond the international limit. The U.S. Coast Guard had warned the Cubans that they could not enter the harbor. Not to be outdone by the Cubans' flair for drama, the Coast Guard had resorted to a novel—if not downright swashbuckling—means of communication. The message was delivered by a Coast Guard plane which swooped low across the deck of the *Cerro Pelado* and dropped it, in a wooden bottle. . . . "We thought it was a new game and we wondered how to play it," a Cuban athlete later told an Associated Press reporter.

Next crisis: how would the Cubans get ashore? The Coast Guard offered three of its vessels. Come ashore in ships flying the "yanqui" flag? Never, said the obstinate Cubans. One wag suggested that they swim. Finally, it was agreed that a private tugboat, The Peacock, would deliver the 357-man Cuban delegation in two trips. But it began to rain ("The Cubans brought Hurricane Alma with them," said one spectator. "No!" said another. Presidente Johnson is making it rain!"), the sun disappeared and the landing was postponed until the next day.

So time-consuming was the red tape involved in the checking of the visas that only part of the Cuban group (about 100) arrived at Hiram Bithorn Stadium in time for the official inauguration, where 22,000 spectators greeted them with mixed applause and boos. There were some touching scenes when exiled Cuban newspapermen met face-to-face with their Communist Cuba colleagues. After a few awkward moments, it looked like a family reunion.

In the following days, one could not turn on the radio without hearing something about the Olympic Games, and especially about the Cuban athletes. Exiled Cuban families flooded the airwaves with offers of food and lodging to any athlete who wished to remain in Puerto Rico. (At this writing, three Cubans—all athletes—have sought political asylum and plan to live in the U.S.A. A star Cuban baseball pitcher, however, when offered a considerable sum to sign a U.S. baseball contract, refused and commented that he planned to stay in Cuba, "where I aspire to be a Communist, which is very difficult."

A few Cuban exiles made daring efforts to recruit the athletes. One tried to accost a young cubana as she was leaving a tennis court. Another drew a gun and threatened an athlete with "Exílate!" (Go into exile!). At some of the sporting events, the Cuban athletes were subjected to strong verbal abuse, causing the Games officials to render an apology to the Cuban delegation and prompting newspaper editorials pleading publicly with the exiles not to "discredit the traditional Puerto Rican reputation for hospitality to its visitors."

One radio show, El Pueblo Opina (The Public Gives its Opinion), became a hotbed of controversy as Puerto Ricans called to criticize "the Cuban exiles who abuse the hospitality of their hosts by mixing politics with sports." One Puerto Rican woman said: "If we want these young people to exile themselves and stay in Puerto Rico, we ought to show them what democracy is really like; we shouldn't abuse them." A Cuban woman called and said that the entire Cuban exile colony shouldn't be judged by the action of a few hotheaded individuals. Then a Cuban man called and angrily denounced all the other callers, as well as announcer Teófilo Maldonado, as "pinkos, if not Reds."

Another radio station, which claimed to have a secret "commando" inside the Olympic villa, announced that "the player with Number 27 on the Cuban baseball team is a *spy*, not a player. All he does is *spy, spy, spy*. Watch out for Number 27!"

Meanwhile, a San Juan newspaper columnist gravely pronounced that Fidel Castro is "not really a Communist, but a nationalist," that "nationalism is the blood brother of dictatorship, and that Cuba had reduced its athletes to "pawns of political propaganda" by forcing them to travel by sea and "create a scandal."

And a scandal it was. On the day the Cuban athletes were supposed to arrive, newspapermen from all over the world, stationed in Santo Domingo to observe the crisis there, had been flown here to cover the Cuban's arrival.

One of them, a sunburned reporter from London, smiled and kidded me: "I say, you Americans are supposed to have invented advertising, but it looks as though Fidel has really pulled a fast one. By the way, exactly what kind of relationship is Puerto Rico's with the United States? I've heard that it's autonomous, somewhat like Australia or Canada are from England. Yet I've been trying to get a peep out of the Puerto Rican government officials about the arrival of the Cubans, and they keep telling me to ring up the bloody U.S. Navy. Who the devil calls the signals around here anyway?"

"That's a long, long story," I said, as we headed towards the little bar near the Cataño ferry.

A DAY AT THE BODEGA

[The dream of many a hardworking immigrant is to save a little money and open a store. The Spanish-speaking *barrios* of the United States are dotted with *bodegas*, or *colmados*, as they are known in Puerto Rico. The owners of these small grocery stores, caught in the vicious circle of poverty, are often as much victims as their clients. In his exhaustive study of the impact of America's inadequate welfare policies upon the poor, Brooklyn-born writer Richard M. Elman spent a day in one *bodega*. As he observes, many of these small entrepreneurs "are abused and hated by the very people they serve, and in the course of the day's business they

From Richard M. Elman, *The Poorhouse State: the American Way of Life on Public Assistance* (New York: Pantheon Books, Random House, 1966), pp. 217–30. Reprinted by permission.

will hate and abuse their customers in turn." The *bodega* owners in the slum may perform a "vital function . . . but at what expense to themselves and their lives!"]

Antonio Ubas has been the owner of a . . . *bodega* on Clinton Street for the past six years. In all that time he has still not managed to sell off any of the huge pyramid of canisters of kosher salt that were in his store windows the day he gave $150.00 key money to its former occupant, Mr. Alex Colmar. Antonio has a wife and two children. He lives in a project, considers himself a good manager, and is generally well liked in the neighborhood. To his kosher salt display he quickly added the standard array of Puerto Rican delicacies—chick peas, guava shells, nonalcoholic malt beers, and tamarind juice—and then he ran leaders on such items as rat poison and cockroach powders, which are also staples among the urban poor; but he has never yet been able to do as much business on the register as he can usually show in his little black book. Antonio's is that kind of tiny, close establishment, a storefront deep, with shelves going up to the ceiling. The place gives off a deep, rich smell, and you feel you could reach up with his wooden pole hook and pull down exquisite delicacies. Not so! Paying $80.00 a month rent and $20.00 more for his telephone and utilities, Antonio has been in such a tight squeeze over the past six years that most of his top shelves are still crowded with old Mr. Colmar's dusty boxes of Quaker Oats and Oxydol.

As he puts it, "You build up a lot of credit and you hope that people will start repaying you so you can buy more goods and sell more. Sometimes they just don't. It's hard. I'm not complaining. Some of these people have it worse than me, but it's hard . . .

"When a person comes in and it's not the first time, he don't ask permission," Antonio continued, explaining the rules by which he must do business. "He will take this. He will say he wants something like that. Then he will say, 'Write it down!' Well, Macy's can write it down and the Welfare will say okay, because they have people who make up the bills and it looks good, but all I have is this little book. How do they know whether I am telling the truth? If I say it's not all right to such a person, she will only go to the place down the street, and then maybe when she has a little money she won't come back here. I give people what they want . . . and all month long they give me back a little at a time. It's not so nice because sometimes I can't do that with my jobbers. It just seems like I have to be here for these people, and they are sometimes very inconsiderate. They run up a big bill . . . maybe $25.00 . . . and then they disappear.

"Well, if you go to Welfare about such a person they will say, 'It is your own fault, for being so greedy. We give such people

cash so they should buy with cash. If you want to take risks with
people like that it is your own fault.' "

It hardly seems fair to call Antonio Ubas a greedy person. Once,
a few days before Thanksgiving, I was talking to him when Brownleaf came into the store. Brownleaf nodded to me with the blind
side of his face and then went over to browse among the shelves,
as if in some lending library.

"Watch this," Antonio winked at me.

When Brownleaf showed up at the counter, he unburdened himself of a large can of turkey, two small cans of cranberries, a
frozen turkey TV dinner, a loaf of bread, a bottle of hard cider, and
four bananas. Antonio wrote up each item on his pad and added up
the total, which came to $2.59, but he wouldn't put anything into the
bag.

"And two packs of Salems," Brownleaf added then.

Antonio stared down at his fists which were digging into the sticky
counter.

"I'd like those cigarettes," Brownleaf said.

Antonio smiled. "I don't even know your name . . ."

"You know me," Brownleaf said. "My wife is here all the time . . ."

"I don't know you," Antonio insisted. "Tell me your name."

"Come on," Brownleaf said. "You know me."

"What's your name, Mister?"

Brownleaf said, "Are you being funny?"

Antonio did not act as if he were being funny. He was putting
all the groceries away under his counter.

"Holy shit," Brownleaf said. "You want me to spell it out? It's
Brownleaf—B . . r . . o . . w . . n . . l . . e . . a . . f . ."

"I still don't know that name," Antonio said "Are you sure I
know your lady?"

"You know her. She comes in all the time with the kids."

"You got to do better than that. A lot of people do that." Antonio
was smirking as he put the purchases into a bag and handed them
across the counter to Brownleaf.

"What about my Salems?"

"I don't like people to go hungry," Antonio smiled. "But I don't
see why they got to smoke . . . I don't smoke . . ."

Brownleaf said, "Cocksucker," and he went out the door with
the package in his hands.

"So that's what I am," Antonio said. He found a page marked
Brownleaf in his little book and wrote down $3.00 next to the date.

I asked, "What was all that about?"

"What do you want me to do?" Antonio exclaimed. "Call the
police?

"I know that guy. Sure," he added, "he and his wife . . . they're
coming in here all the time just like he says. Look at this!" He

showed me the page in his ledger with a long column of scribbles on it. Brownleaf seemed to owe at least $20.00. "He knows I know him. Sure," Antonio said then, slamming his book shut. "We just play this little game sometimes. It's just a little thing he's got with me . . ."

"An expensive thing," I said.

"*That?*" Antonio was blushing. "He doesn't mind that. He's a pretty good guy most of the time and he pays his bills. It's just that I've got to take care of my customers and so they've got to pay a little extra for the service."

"So you two knew each other all the time?"

"You don't understand anything," Antonio said, turning back to his book.

Antonio Ubas is a small, plump, fair-skinned little man with shiny black curly hair and soft brown eyes. He always wears a clean white shirt with sleeves rolled up to the elbows, and his arms are firm and thick but hairless. If Antonio were not so plump, he would be handsome, like his fifteen-year-old son Dickie, who is sometimes pressed into helping out in the store. One Jewish holiday, when school was out, I stayed with them from 8:00 A.M. until closing time to keep a log of the day's business. Here are my notes.

7:51 A.M.: I arrive. Store open. Dickie loading milk in fridge. Antonio sweeping.

8:35 A.M.: Antonio sends Dickie for three containers sweet coffee. First customer arrives. Young bohemian girl in slacks. Buys milk, a box of chocolate doughnuts, Kents. Pays cash.

8:40 A.M.: Man buys Luckies, cash.

8:42 A.M.: Woman buys three oranges, a pound of margarine, a pack of frankfurters, and cigarettes. Asks for credit. Dickie comes back with coffee as Antonio is writing down purchases. Woman is reminded that she needs coffee. Antonio grinds a pound of beans. Woman says, "That's a nice smell."

8:51 A.M.: Boy buys toothbrush, chocolate milk. Pays cash.

9:03 A.M.: Bill collector buys cigarettes. Woman with three children gives Antonio a slip of paper with a big order. They seem to know each other well. She asks if he will send Dickie with the packages. Dickie, who is playing with her kids, looks up frowning but agrees to go. Antonio puts slip with order next to register, asks if she will pay. She hands him $5.00, which he pockets. "I owed you this. Now I'll have to owe you some more."

9:35 A.M.: Antonio completes order, sends Dickie with delivery. Total sale: $6.75. He writes it in the book and then subtracts $4.75. "I want to be able to give Dickie something for his trouble," he explains. Woman comes in, buys sugar. Pays cash.

10:03 A.M.: Antonio is putting away the rest of the milk when Dickie returns. He asks, "Was she all right?"

"I got a dime," Dickie says.

Antonio throws him a quarter. "For school!" He smiles at his son warmly.

Dickie says, "I think that man is back with her—"

"She better watch out," Antonio says. "I can't carry her like that last time."

10:37 A.M.: Antonio has been telling me about his army service in Korea, which he enjoyed, he claimed, because it gave him a chance to see a lot of things.

Dickie is reading *El Diario*, looks up, says, "Tell him about Japan."

Then a customer walks in, Spanish-speaking, asks for Drano. Antonio hasn't got it. Offers to send Dickie down the block. Woman shrugs, walks out. Antonio writes down Drano on a pad next to register and then starts adding up due bills. Man in work clothes comes in, obviously a friend. He and Antonio chatter together in Spanish. Dickie asks if he can take a break. Man goes to counter. Orders a half-pound of bacon, bread, eggs, a chocolate bar, and a large bottle of orange soda. Pays cash—$2.15.

"She got her check today. She'll pay what she owes," the man says in English as he leaves.

11:07 A.M.: No business at all. Antonio working on due bills. Beer truck arrives. Dickie goes to unload cases. Delivery man buys a pack of Camels and some gum, hands Antonio an invoice, which he signs.

"Tomorrow I will have it," he tells the man, who says, "I won't be back until next Monday."

11:23 A.M.: Dickie putting away beer. Goes to lunch. No business for half an hour. Then a sudden flurry: Spanish-speaking woman buys can of beef stew (charges); boy buys rice, can of spaghetti, bread, and a jar of peanut butter (charges $1.39). Boy also wants cigarettes. Antonio says no because he is under age. Negro man buys a large bottle of beer. Pays cash. Fast-speaking woman gives large order in Spanish for bread, milk, rice, beans, fishsticks, condensed milk, teabags, sugar, half pound of butter, hot chocolate, three tomato soups, a pound of hamburger, box of Tide; she says she wants to charge everything, and she adds bananas, Brillo pads, and another container of milk; but when Antonio says no, she finds $3.00, which he pockets, and then he lets her charge the rest. Other women waiting. One wants soap. One wants chocolate doughnuts. Both cash. Delivery man arrives with soda. Antonio asks, "Where the hell is Dickie?"

1:00 P.M.: Dickie has returned. Still busy. Mostly school children. They each buy a different can for lunch . . . corned beef hash, spaghetti, beef stew, baked beans. One kid insists on Franco-American. Antonio doesn't think he has any. Too busy to make sure in the back room. Six children, six different credit sales . . . total

$1.46. Antonio sends Dickie out for more coffee, eats a banana and a Drake's cake. Offers me some.

2:15 P.M.: Very, very slow. Antonio turns on radio. We listen to news in Spanish, then he switches and we listen to English-language news. Bohemian girl wants Gauloises. Antonio hasn't got any. Woman buys Tampax and toothpaste. Friend of Dickie's drops by. They go for a walk. Creamery truck arrives. Antonio waiting on customer with thick Jewish accent, wants *Yartzeit* candle. Antonio hasn't got. Creamery man presents bill for $25.00. Antonio looks in the register, gives $15.00 on account. Policeman comes by. They chat about a certain Mr. Box, whom I don't know. Maybe Antonio's landlord? Woman buys Ivory soap, a can of chick peas, a roll of toilet paper. Pays cash. Man buys Mars bar, flips dime against counter. Antonio all out of pennies. I volunteer to go next door . . .

2:50 P.M.: I have come back to busy store. Children buying ice cream; women buying potatoes and chopped meat, onions, fish-sticks, detergents. Children pay cash—$.60. Women pay cash—$3.05 and $2.55, but one woman realizes she must charge—$4.50. Afterwards Antonio looks in book. He is very angry! Woman now owes $32.00. Dickie comes back.

"Where the hell you been?"

Dickie shows father that he has bought *El Diario*. Antonio smiles, sends Dickie with order to Mrs. Cabeza.

"Be sure you collect!"

He takes a bag of potato chips and offers me some. I buy a bottle of coke for each of us—$.20 cash sale. Antonio waits on Negro man who wants link sausages and half a dozen eggs. Pays cash—$1.02. Dickie comes back with $9.00. Antonio gives him another quarter. Pleased, Dickie starts to sweep up. Antonio yawns. Man buys Winstons. Woman buys English muffins. Antonio grinds coffee and tells Dickie to take it home to wife.

He says, "You got the rest of the day off. Take your sister to a show."

Dickie runs away. Antonio yawns again. Goes to back of store. Calls a number. His wife. They are talking in Spanish.

Antonio comes back. "You think this is interesting?"

I try to duck his question. Customer walks in wearing big heavy coat. Asks for Carbona. Antonio hasn't got. I look at watch. 4:15 . . .

6:03 P.M.: Very slow. One woman wanting fish balls for cash. A man to whom Antonio won't sell. Mrs. Ubas comes with stew for Antonio's dinner in double boiler. She says children all went to movies. She is going to see her sister. Will Antonio stay open late? He shrugs, starts to eat dinner. Wife wishes me good night. Dark outside now. Man comes in to buy milk. Pays cash. Woman wants a lemon and a bottle of Clorox. Antonio won't charge. Woman puts back Clorox but buys lemon with cash.

Antonio says, "She is a terrible woman."
Won't tell me why. Antonio's sister-in-law calls. Could he lend her
a few dollars tomorrow? He says he will give it to his wife in the
morning, but she mustn't come to the store. Man wants to know if
Antonio can cash Welfare check for $39.00. Antonio hasn't got
enough in register. Offers to hold the check and lend him $15.00 on
account until tomorrow, when he will give him the rest.

Man says, "You give me $20.00 and the rest is for my wife's bill."
Antonio smiles and looks into register. It's a deal. He hands man
$20.00 in singles from register and sticks check in pocket. Only two
or three bills now in register. Antonio marks off $19.00 from man's
account. Still plenty more on the bill. Man breaks bill to buy
Luckies . . .

7:19 P.M.: Very, very slow. Kid wanting correct time. Woman
pays for phone call. Buys milk and a square of cream cheese. Antonio's supper cold. Empties out double boiler. Says he has heart-
burn. Asks if I would go next door for tea. As I leave, he turns on
radio again . . .

7:30 P.M.: Antonio too busy to say thank you when I return with
tea. Radio blaring. Spanish-speaking man with big order: rice, beans,
sardines, anchovies, eggs, bread, canned tomatoes, olive oil, Malamar
cookies, Ajax, canned peaches, pineapple cubes, milk, and frankfurters. Also thinks of buying guava shells but decides no when
Antonio gives him price. Pays cash—$9.15.

8:05 P.M.: Antonio and I have been talking about all the airplane
crashes lately when Drano woman comes back. She has Welfare
check for $55.00. Can Antonio cash? He tells her he hasn't got. She
becomes angry. Curses. Leaves store. Antonio picks up *El Diario*.
His eyes are a little bloodshot, and it looks as if somebody has just
dabbed shoe polish underneath the lower lids. I go to get a sand-
wich . . .

9:12 P.M.: Come back to Antonio's store. Door open. Lights on.
No Antonio. Finally he appears from back carrying heavy case
marked "Franco-American."

"I just knew I had some . . ."

Sweating and panting, he tears open the case, puts all the cans
on the shelf, and asks me to throw the cardboard box in the can
outside.

"Any more business?"

"A woman with a nosebleed," Antonio smiles. "I sold her Kleenex."

9:36 P.M.: I feel as if I have been here forever. Antonio is very
silent. I don't think he has much patience with my hanging around,
although he seemed pleased at first. He asks me when I intend to
leave, and I say whenever he closes down.

Antonio says, "Won't be long now."

He opens up the register and starts to count his money. There is
not too much to count, but he knows he has a few dollars in his

pocket. Three teenagers come in. Antonio slams register. Boys want cigarettes. Antonio sells a pack of Camels and a pack of Kools for cash. Third boys buys cupcakes. Cash.

Antonio sings *"En mi corazón . . ."* as he goes back to register.

Spanish-speaking man comes in. Very timid. Looks over at me once as he talks, and Antonio finally sells him large box Kotex—man pays cash.

"No me burlas," Antonio starts singing again.

Woman enters store. Buys milk and Easy-Off. Pays cash.

Antonio asks, "You new around here?"

"I just moved in."

She buys cockroach powder and a stick of gum. Goes out and then comes back in. She lives across the street. Her name is Helen Dugan. She needs a bed.

"Where is a good place to buy a bed?"

Welfare gave her the money, but they didn't tell her where to go. Antonio says he doesn't know but he will ask his wife if she will come back tomorrow.

She says, "Why not? I live right across the street."

10:45 P.M.: I am getting very groggy. Antonio also seems to be feeling the strain. Once I catch him dozing against the counter. At 10:15, a phone call. A woman wants him to deliver. Antonio says he can't. At 10:25 teenagers. Cigarettes again. A man buys a pound of coffee. A man in work clothes buys cigarettes and a Mounds bar. Another man comes into store.

Antonio says, "I've been waiting for you."

Man hands him check. Antonio takes out book, crosses out column of figures. Writes down balance: $14.00. Goes to register and gives man five singles.

Man says, "My wife will be in tomorrow for a big order."

Antonio nods sleepily. Man breaks single to buy Kents. Antonio goes to center of store and pulls switch on light. Starts sweeping up, but won't lock door. Man drops by. Shows Antonio paper.

"No," he adds, "I don't know of such a family."

Man buys cigarettes and leaves.

Antonio says, "I bet he's from the Welfare . . ."

Negro woman comes in. Buys a can of tuna, a jar of mayonnaise, some onions, and a bar of chocolate Halvah. Pays cash—$1.25.

Antonio says, "Don't you want bread?"

When she doesn't answer, he goes to empty out register. Man comes in. Doesn't seem to know what he wants. Walks from shelf to shelf.

"I'm closing," Antonio says.

Man has hands in pockets. Antonio repeats that he is closing, in Spanish. Man comes over to counter. Buys a loaf of bread. Pays cash. Fat man comes in. Has Antonio got fresh ham?

"I'm closing," he says.

Man buys a pound of frankfurters. Wants to charge. Antonio asks for name and address. Man lives right above store. Produces Welfare card. Antonio okays sale but copies down serial number in book. Man then buys cigarettes and orange soda.

When he leaves Antonio says, "Now I'm really closing." Bolts front door.

"I hope you know why you stayed here," he says, "because I don't."

I offer to buy him a beer but he says that he is just too tired. I buy a pack of cigarettes. Antonio wants me to pay wholesale. We argue. I look at my watch. It's 11:27 . . .

By working nearly a hundred hours a week Antonio Ubas is likely to gross in the neighborhood of $1,400 a month, from which he will net about $350 to $400. About one in ten dollars will go directly to his pocket so he won't have to report them to the government. As much as 20 percent more of his business will consist of credit, on which he will charge a small premium, probably no greater than the inflationary trend. Antonio will carry his people just so long as they continue to pay him back every couple of weeks, and his jobbers will endeavor to carry him in the same way. Twice monthly he will need large sums of cash on hand to redeem Welfare checks that will be proffered as partial repayment on bills. In 1964 he filed a federal income tax return showing $4,160 gross income on which he paid $450 in taxes. There were also state taxes and licensing fees amounting to perhaps $100. He sent $10 a month to his mother in Puerto Rico and supported his family on a budget of approximately $55 weekly, which he earned at a rate of less than $1.00 per hour. Antonio has GI life insurance worth $10,000 and a small savings account, which is used to pay taxes and licensing fees, to forestall creditors in a pinch, or to cash Welfare checks. In any week his margin of profit is usually the few extra pennies he can wring out of his clients through credit. This tends to make his attitude toward people on Welfare somewhat ambivalent. On the one hand, he recognizes with a certain bitterness that some people are not working yet are doing nearly as well as he. On the other hand, he sees that his chief *raison d'être* at present is to provide a service that the larger stores refuse to provide. The following morning, after my visit, Antonio was at work by 8:00 A.M. I didn't arrive until 11:00. He looked a little tired but was in good spirits. His sister-in-law's husband had just found work through the State Employment.

"That's a load off my back," he smiled, and began to thumb his way through the pages of his ledger.

It was a school day. Dickie would not be coming to help out. He was going to close early because he wanted to take his wife shopping. How early was early? Antonio scratched his head. He explained that he wasn't quite sure when he would actually be able to close down. This guy owed him a lot of money and he had just gotten his check, but he was in the Bronx and would be there all day. Antonio would would just have to wait until the man got downtown after suppertime.

"THEY LOSE HEART"

["I want my kids to go to school, so they don't have to sweat for a living like me." Poor, hardworking parents from every migrant group to America have made similar statements, and Puerto Ricans are no exception. Puerto Ricans display a great faith in education, and this faith is beginning to bear fruit. More and more young Puerto Ricans are graduating from America's high schools, and many go on to college. At several universities, bilingual and remedial training programs and courses in Puerto Rican studies have begun to take hold. Despite notable progress in the past decade, a shockingly high percentage of Puerto Rican children drop out of school. As this study indicates, Puerto Rican children in U.S. public schools "tend to learn less, lose heart more, and drop out sooner than their classmates." Some of the reasons why are explored in the following article, which is part of a study commissioned by a Puerto Rican agency that assists students in furthering their education.]

No one can say precisely how many Puerto Rican children are enrolled in public schools in the United States, but anyone who has examined their predicament knows they tend to learn less, lose heart and drop out sooner than their classmates. It is true that their classmates, mostly poor and often black, fare none too well either. The Puerto Rican child and the Negro child share many humiliations, not the least of which is a system of even-handed injustice dispensed by big-city school administrations throughout the North. But the Puerto Rican child carries additional burdens all his own, his status as a stranger in our midst being perhaps the heaviest, and these have been sufficient to keep him at the very bottom of the educational pyramid.

The observer can but dimly discern the everyday frustrations which many Puerto Rican schoolchildren have come to take for granted: their imperfect grasp of English, which often seals both their lips and their minds; their confusion about who they are (what

From Richard J. Margolis, *The Losers: A Report on Puerto Ricans and the Public Schools*. Commissioned by Aspira, Inc., New York, May, 1968, pp. 1–5. Reprinted with permission.

race? what culture?), a confusion compounded by the common ravages of white prejudice; * their sense of being lost, of traveling through a foreign country with a heedless guide and an undecipherable map. The list of frustrations is long. They may not reveal the whole truth, but they do illuminate many of the consequences.

The many Puerto Rican parents who complain that their children "are not being taught to read or do their arithmetic" are usually right. No new study is required to confirm their anxieties; findings in the Coleman Report on *Equality of Educational Opportunity* are sufficiently eloquent. They indicate that Puerto Rican children in the United States lag behind both urban whites and urban Negroes in verbal ability, reading comprehension and mathematics.

Test scores of sixth grade students, for example, place the average Puerto Rican child about three years behind the average white child in all three categories of achievement, and about one year behind the average Negro child. In the later grades, the gap between Negroes and Puerto Ricans narrows, but the gap between whites and the two minority groups becomes wider. Relatively speaking, the longer a Puerto Rican child attends public school, the less he learns.†

The less he learns, the more he despairs. One of Coleman's tests, designed to assess the student's sense of control over his life, contained this statement: "Every time I try to get ahead, something stops me." Almost a third of the Puerto Rican children agreed with the statement, compared to about a fifth of the Negroes and only one-eighth of the whites.

* An exchange, during a routine shakedown on the streets of Philadelphia, between a white policeman and a Puerto Rican teenager may shed light on this subject. "Are you a spic or a nigger?" the policeman asked.
"I'm a Puerto Rican, cop."
The policeman hit him. "Don't you know you're not supposed to call me a cop?"
"Excuse me, officer, don't you know you're not supposed to call me a spic?"
The teenager told this story, on tape, to a white interviewer. It may or may not be accurate in every detail, but the message is clear.
† Dentler summarizes the overall results of the three tests as follows:

Test	Group	6th grade	9th grade	12th grade
Verbal Ability	White	6	9	12
	Puerto Rican	3.3	6.1	8.4
	Negro	4.4	6.6	8.7
Reading Comprehension	White	6	9	12
	Puerto Rican	2.9	5.7	8.3
	Negro	4.2	6.4	9.1
Mathematics	White	6	9	12
	Puerto Rican	3.2	5.6	7.2
	Negro	4	6.2	6.8

Answers to another test statement—"Good luck is more important than hard work for success"—were just as revealing. Nineteen per cent of the Puerto Rican children agreed; nine per cent of the Negroes; four per cent of the whites.

"Shallow men believe in luck," wrote Emerson. So do deeply hurt children. If many Puerto Rican children feel they lack control over their environment—and therefore over their own destinies— the reasons are not hard to find. Here are some very routine examples of helplessness, chosen from many I came across while visiting schools and families:

• A six-year-old was roundly scolded by his teacher for wetting his pants. All morning he had been trying to tell her—in Spanish!— that he had to go to the bathroom.

• José González, a kindergartener, has given up trying to tell his teacher his name is not Joe. It makes her angry.

• An honor student asked her counsellor for a chance to look at college catalogues. "Is that Italian or Spanish?" asked the counsellor, looking at the name on the girl's card. "Spanish? Now this is just my opinion, but I think you'd be happier as a secretary." *

• A vocational student hoping to become an electrician did the same wiring job for four consecutive years, over and over and over again.

• A "phys ed" instructor noticed that one of the girls was wearing a new gym suit. "Oh," he said loudly, "did the welfare check come?"

• A junior high school student was accused by his teacher of lying because he averted his eyes when speaking to her, a sign of respect on the island.

• A little girl couldn't wait to get her first report card. But when she got it there was nothing written on it except two big letters: "LD". Language Difficulty.

• A teenager told his principal he would have to drop out if he wasn't given protection from assaulting gangs whose turf lay between home and school. The principal referred him to a psychiatrist. †

But I am running ahead of my story.

Things being what they are, it is not surprising to hear from some teachers and administrators that Puerto Rican schoolchildren have nowhere to go but up. Yet there is little support even for that faintly comforting notion. It would be more accurate to say that Puerto Rican children have nowhere to go but *out*—out of the schools and into a world for which they are unprepared. This they

* In yet another of Coleman's tests, high school seniors were asked: "Have you ever read a college catalog?" A "Yes" response was given by 45 per cent of the Puerto Ricans, 59 per cent of the Negroes and 73 per cent of the whites.
† After enduring more beatings, he did drop out—a healthy response to a most unhealthy situation.

are doing in large numbers. The public schools are like a giant sieve, sifting out all but the strongest, the smartest or the luckiest.

Many school administrators insist they have no serious dropout problem among Puerto Rican students. Some attribute the low high school enrollment totals to the newness of the Puerto Rican community. "Their kids haven't reached high school age yet." High school principals also like to say that Puerto Rican students who leave school are not really dropouts—they are simply "transfer" to another school. "We have a mobility problem, not a dropout problem."

There is probably something to be said for both these explanations, but not much. Experience in cities where the Puerto Rican community has had time to produce its share of teenagers makes it clear that the dropout syndrome cannot be explained away. For example, in 1966 in New York City public schools, Puerto Ricans comprised more than one-fifth of the total enrollment but less than one-eighth of the academic high school enrollment. On the other hand, non-Puerto Rican whites accounted for about half the total enrollment and about two-thirds of the academic high school enrollment.

Plainly, a lot of Puerto Rican elementary students are disappearing before they reach high school. The picture is similar in Newark, where there are more than five-thousand Puerto Ricans in public schools. They account for eight per cent of all elementary students but only four per cent of all high school students. The comparable figures for non-Puerto Rican whites is 19 per cent for elementary school and 36 per cent for high school.

As for the claim that dropouts are really transfers to other schools, one must ask: What schools? Surely none of those I visited. Somewhere in America there may be a Shangri-la high school into which Puerto Rican teenagers drop. If so, it is overcrowded.

The widespread policy of putting back teenage Puerto Ricans to lower grades (because of their language difficulties) is one reason they drop out. The teenager is likely to feel both foolish and bored among children three and four years his junior. Rather than be left back he may prefer to be left out altogether.

We get an inkling of these difficulties by looking at Hoboken's dropout figures for 1967. Of the 149 students who dropped out, 131 "left to seek employment." *Almost half the dropouts left before the tenth grade.* We have no way of knowing how many of these were Puerto Rican—they comprise more than a third of the overall school population—but it seems likely that only a Puerto Rican would be old enough to drop out of the eighth grade in order to look for a job.

Not all school systems deny that dropouts exist—New York and Hoboken, if not exactly outspoken on the subject, at least don't look the other way—but many prefer obfuscation to clarity, apparently on the theory that what they don't know can't hurt them.*

The picture becomes still murkier when we try to discover how many Puerto Rican high school students go on to college. No school system I visited has bothered to count, but in some high schools they answer not by the numbers but by the names. So few Puerto Ricans are going to college that a principal can usually count them on one hand. †

All of which suggests that today's ghetto school, in its commerce with Puerto Rican children, is failing to do the job which the nation has traditionally assigned to it, that of assimilating newcomers into the American mainstream. The long-range implications of this failure are depressing in the extreme.

THE YOUNG LORDS

[The Young Lords, an organization of street-wise young activists formed in the late 1960's, reflects the growing maturity of the Puerto Rican migrant community on the U.S. mainland—which was once a voiceless appendage of the island, and is now developing its own institutions. Until recently, militant political leaders in the Puerto Rican *barrios* of America belonged to either pro-independence groups in Puerto Rico, or to left-wing U.S. groups. But the Lords emerged from the *barrios* where they were raised; they borrowed some of their original impetus from the Black Panthers, but have since evolved their own style. They have avoided violent conflict, and have focused instead on dramatic, issue-oriented ploys: the sudden takeover of a *barrio* church for a free children's breakfast program, or the "hijacking" of a New York City mobile clinic to examine slum children for tuberculosis. The Lords are a new ingredient in the history of the Puerto Rican protest movement. On the island, leaders of far left and/or pro-independence groups have usually come from middle- or upper-class backgrounds, and their styles of action and oratory have

* "The most vicious attribute of urban school systems, until recently," observes Peter Schrag, "has not been their consistent failure with the disadvantaged, but their refusal to produce honest data on that failure. In case after case, they pretended . . . despite statistical evidence to the contrary, that it was individual children, not schools, that failed."

† Those holding high school degrees are often ill-prepared to compete in the job market. In Newark a group of volunteer lady tutors found that many Puerto Rican girl graduates who had majored in secretarial studies were incapable of filling out a job application form.

From Michael Abramson, *Palante: Young Lords Party* (New York: McGraw-Hill, 1971), pp. 34–36. Copyright © 1971 by Michael Abramson and the Young Lords Party. Reprinted with permission of McGraw-Hill Book Company.

been in the traditional Hispanic mold. By contrast, the Lords are mainly the children of poor migrants; they have been raised in urban ghettos, and English is their first language. The "official 13-point program and platform," published frequently in *Palante*, the newspaper of the Young Lords, outlines their basic goals. They want "a socialist society" and "oppose capitalists and alliances with traitors." They want "liberation and power in the hands of the people, not Puerto Rican exploiters." They want self-determination and liberation, not only for Puerto Ricans, but also for "all Latinos" and "all third world people." Thus, the Lords are not strictly a Puerto Rican party, but a socialist movement that has sprung up from within the poor Puerto Rican working class on the mainland, where blacks, Chicanos, Dominicans, Haitians, and poor whites all suffer together. The thrust of most protest groups in Puerto Rico is nationalistic, and strongly defends traditional Puerto Rican culture; the Young Lords—while demanding "a true education of our creole culture and Spanish language"—are more ideological than nationalistic.

The following excerpt—the story of a Young Lord named Georgie—tells of his upbringing in New York's junglelike *barrio*, and of his growing political awareness.]

I think if I would have been raised up upstate, man, in a good community, I would've never become a gangbuster, I would've never shot nobody, I would never have stabbed nobody—but since I was raised up in this community, this is what it, oppression, teaches you—kill, stab, steal, and shoot dope—like, now the thing is dope, mainly. I got a lot of brothers out there, man, that are shooting dope—they used to jitterbug with me. They used to call me Little Man, 'cause I always was really small for my age. But smallness to me didn't mean nothin', because wherever there was a bat, it used to make me always the same size as the other person.

When I was a little kid, around seven years old, they used to have what they called the Lightnings. Later on, they became the Lightning Dragons. You know, little kids see those big guys and say, "Wow! Man, when I grow up I wanna be like them." Because that's all there is to do in your neighborhood—like if you don't learn how to be a pimp, you learn how to be a jitterbug. Those were the two big things then, because at that time there wasn't that much drugs around the neighborhood. I always wanted to be a pimp, because the pimps they were always clean, they had shoes, a lot of wing-tips, a lot of sharkskin, mohair suits, and they always had money in their pockets. I always used to say to myself, "Oh, man, when I grow up I want to be a pimp."

I started all my fighting when I was really young. My father used to have a very nasty attitude—anybody that looked at him, he would go up to them and say, "Have I got a monkey in my face or somethin'?" If it was a little kid, he would put me to fight against him. And I got into the habit of always fighting in the block—as a matter of fact, when the older guys wanted to play stickball in the block I used to tell 'em. "No, man, you people ain't gonna play in the block—me and my fellows are playing." And, my fellows were all guys six years old, seven years old, you know, against guys eighteen. And, since we wanted to be like them we used to, like, put on a show, and we thought we were *bad* 'cause we had stickball bats and shit.

My father and my mother used to give me everything I wanted. Except my father—he always told me, like, the only two things that he wouldn't give me in life was roller skates and bikes, because I might get killed by a car. And, that's where my trouble really started, because when I was around nine years old, like, I wanted a pair of roller skates *so bad*, and my father would never buy them for me. I remember, five of us went to Central Park and we dug these guys rollerskating. I was nine years old and I wanted some skates—and there was five of us, and we seen these guys skating down the thing, and like, we beat 'em up and we took off their skates. Anyway, the pigs came, and me and my brother got busted for the skates and shit, and I went to the Youth House for a few months.

The next year I got busted again—this time for robbing *La Marqueta* and I did five years in Children's Village.

When I came out I was tired. On 111th Street they had the Viceroys and the Dragons then. At first I really didn't want to join them. I said, "Oh man, if I join one of them, I'm just gonna go back upstate again."

But I used to live in Viceroy turf, right across from where their center was. I was raised up with a lot of those guys and I always wanted to hang out with them. A lot of the debs, the sisters, used to go for me, too. What happened was that the Dragons saw me hangin' out with the Viceroys, and thought I was in the Viceroys—you couldn't blame them, you know.

In P.S. 83, where I was going, they had around two Viceroys, and maybe fifty Dragons—so you know where that was at. One day I was playing dice and all these Dragons surrounded me and asked me, "Hey, man, are you a Viceroy?" I told 'em, "Look, man, I'm not no Viceroy," and I tried to explain to them that I had just come out of jail, but they thought I was bullshitting them.

I remember they hit me all the way from the schoolyard—for a whole block they were hitting me. And then they got me in this telephone booth and broke a telephone right over my hand. So now I was mad, but I still didn't want to join the Viceroys. Another time I was with this guy named Bimbo—he used to be an old Viceroy, he was from my neighborhood. Anyway, they caught me and Bimbo in the train station and they came over to us, and they told me, "Look, man, this is the second time we catch you—the

last time we bust your ass, man, and you tell us you wasn't a Viceroy. And every time we see you, we see you with Viceroys."

What they did was, they waited around a minute before the train
came and threw me on the train tracks. And I got up and I ran, you
know. I said, "Damn, man, these guys are fuckin' me up every time
they see me—so I'm gonna join the Viceroys, man. I might as well
join them."

We used to jitterbug, right. Some times we used to go down to
103rd Street and, like, go up to the block and shoot up the candy
store or shoot up the guys that were around. Sometimes we used
to stab guys, sometimes we used to get stabbed. We wasn't thinkin'
about the other guys being Puerto Ricans. Like, now we're political,
but at that time Puerto Ricans were Puerto Ricans—if he was your
enemy, you kill him.

When you used to go to school, like, the teacher used to tell you,
"Oh, man, you dumb—like, you nothing but a little boy," and
shit like that. So all the young brothers used to have that complex
of the teacher calling them a boy, and they wanted to prove it to
themselves they were a man. And they would go to any means to
prove it.

When I first started jitterbugging, a brother named King Kong
got shot at 117th Street. When he got killed I was hurt—that was
my main man, you see, one of my brothers. A week after that, the
Dragons came down to 112th Street in a car and they started shooting at us. We had a gun on us, so when they started shooting, one
of the brothers was gonna run over to the car to, like, to shoot the
Dragons. But the Dragons they shot him in the arm with a .38 and
he fell. So this guy named Chico grabbed the gun. This other guy,
Nate, opened up the door from the car and Chico shot the Dragon
in the head, you know, shot him in the head. He fell against the
horn dead, and the car went out of control and went into that store
on the corner of 112th Street and Madison. Even though I knew
Chico had killed this dude, I felt bad about it. You know, you say,
"Ah, fuck it, yeah we killed a motherfucker, man." But inside, you
really say, "Man, one of these days they probably come up to me
and shoot me. . . ."

Some of us been lucky, that we stabbed a lot of guys, right, but
never killed nobody, and we not doin' time. But some of the
brothers, like, they're unfortunate—they're doin' life in jail. And
right now I feel sorry for a lot of these brothers, even the Dragons,
man. I know if they had another chance to live, they would never
jitterbug no more or kill another brother. You know, they might
turn political like I did and Bobby did, right—because, like, I
cooled down.

I stopped jitterbugging because my enemy became my best
friend. Like, they got this guy named Feather, from the Young
Dragons—right now, man, he's like my brother—I love that cat,

I love him. If anybody would try to hurt me, I know he'll kill for me—if anybody try to hurt him, I know I'd kill for him, man. Me and him were real together in jail. A lot of Dragons that I met there, some of them are more friends of mine than my old, old friends the Viceroys, you know. And you go ask the Dragons, man—Dragons will tell you the same thing.

I guess it's because we got to know each other and that's what the Young Lords is really about, man—to show you you don't fight against brothers, because you might be angry against your brother today, and tomorrow he might be your best friend. Tomorrow, he might be the guy that saved your own life.

THE YEAR 2000

[Will Puerto Rico, by the year 2000, be the fifty-first state of the Union? Will it become an independent republic? Or, will it continue under the present Commonwealth status? What about the Puerto Rican community on the U.S. mainland, which will number more than 2 million persons by that time?

Peering into the next century is difficult, because a host of variables can nudge the course of history into surprising directions.

A few things appear certain. The Puerto Rican community in the U.S. is changing, as new layers of first, "bridge," second, and third generations are added to the mixture. The experience of Puerto Ricans on the mainland will also "naturally color" the views of their Caribbean brethren concerning political status, according to the author of the following article.

Joseph Montserrat has been involved in Puerto Rican community affairs for many years. He directed the Migration Division of the Commonwealth Department of Labor in New York City, and later was President of the New York City Board of Education. He calls for an "alliance" of Puerto Ricans everywhere, of all generations, "to help solve each other's problems." Montserrat echoes the feelings of many other community spokesmen, who call for unity, for a collective vision.]

The Puerto Rican experience in the United States will play an important role in shaping the future of the Island. In turn, what happens on the Island will influence the Puerto Rican experience here. There is

From Joseph Montserrat, "Symposium on Puerto Rico in the Year 2000," *Howard Law Journal*, Washington, D.C., Fall, 1968, XV, No. 1, pp. 12–27. Reprinted with permission.

a dynamic relationship, although it may not be overly apparent, between the two Puerto Rican populations. . . .

First, it must be remembered that the great majority of Puerto Ricans residing in the United States have lived here for less than 15 years.

Second, almost 50% of the United States Puerto Rican population is under 21 years of age.

Third, among those Puerto Ricans born in the United States of Puerto Rican parents, about 84% are under 14 years of age.

There are presently approximately one million Puerto Ricans residing in the United States. The present estimated population of Puerto Rico is 2,700,000. In other words, of a total 3,700,000 Puerto Ricans, some 27 per cent of them live in the States.

By 2000, the population of Puerto Rico, given the present rate of natural increase, will have reached at least 5,000,000 persons. During the same period of time, the Puerto Rican population in the continental United States, based on natural increase alone, will have doubled. It is also reasonable to estimate that the United States Puerto Rican population will have grown at an even faster rate than Puerto Rico's because migration during that period will have continued at a rate no less than its present rate—about 30,000 persons per year. This is provided, of course, that during the next 30 years we will not experience any major recession or depression. Thus, we can estimate that by the year 2000 there may be 2,000,000 Puerto Ricans residing in the United States. . . .

Although we speak of Puerto Ricans as a single group, the reality is that Puerto Ricans in the States constitute at least three different groups. These can be roughly defined as the *first* generation, the *bridge* generation, and the *second* generation.

The *first* generation is composed of Puerto Ricans born, raised and educated in Puerto Rico. Although they have made adjustments to their new environment, their value system, thought patterns and emotional reactions are still primarily rooted in Puerto Rico. . . .

The *bridge* generation are those Puerto Ricans who were born in Puerto Rico, spent part of their lives and received some of their education in the Commonwealth, but migrated at an early enough age to complete their education in the States. They also have lived in cities for a significant part of their lives, and have acquired and assimilated more of the values, life patterns and emotional reactions of the United States than have members of the *first* generation.

Because of age and the other demographic factors of which I have spoken, the *second* generation Puerto Rican is not yet as important a segment of the Puerto Rican community in the States as he will be by 2000. It is he that will have an important hand in determining the future relations of Puerto Rico and the United States as well as the nature of Puerto Rican society here and on the Island. To understand how he will grow and develop in the United States we must look to his roots in the United States to isolate the factors that will bear most heavily on his growth. One of the most important of these is his forebear's experience in the United States. This will be his legacy. And the story of Puerto Ricans here is really the story of their migration and experience here. . . .

In New York City today Puerto Ricans are a symbol. They symbolize—indeed personify—the basic problems of the city. Today, even as one hundred years ago, New Yorkers facing the problems of rapid community changes rarely reason abstractly about the cause of these changes.

Puerto Ricans come to New York because New York has jobs that need to be filled; because New York needs Puerto Ricans. However, because of one of its basic problems—lack of planning— New York is no more ready to receive Puerto Ricans now than it was to receive the immigrants it needed a century ago. New York is not unique. Neither Chicago, Cincinnati, Milwaukee nor any other city is ready to receive the new blood needed to keep it economically healthy and culturally alive.

Therefore, rather than viewing the problems of its Puerto Rican population as reflecting the problems of this country's urban centers, Puerto Ricans are themselves viewed as presenting a problem to the cities. Thus, we have, "The Puerto Rican Problem." This is nothing more than seeing an effect as a cause. It is also a means of developing a scapegoat for the conscience of established groups and interests in the cities. . . .

There is another important element in this picture.

Racism is inherent in American society. It is an American cultural trait. It is not an aberration, but rather the norm.

But we look to the wrong source for the origin of racism. We seek to explain what is regarded as this unusual phenomenon in the character of minority groups. We believe that the disease originates in a specific organ rather than realizing that the entire body is shot-through with virulence. When blacks are excluded from the opportunity to advance, we look at the blacks and ask what is wrong with them that they cannot attain the fundamental blessings of American life—a good job, a good education and a good home. We should ask what is wrong with American life that the blacks cannot attain what others have.

As the recent report of the President's Commission on Riots and Civil Disorders eloquently point out, the riots in the City did not begin in the ghetto tenements, plotted in cellars by several desperate men. They began in the comforts of suburban and urban homes, unconsciously formulated by well-meaning men who see nothing in the adverse conditions they promote, and from which they benefit, that can lead to rioting. . . .

It is within this spectre of racism in the United States that Puerto Ricans find themselves. No issue will have a greater effect upon the Puerto Rican communities of the States than the present struggle for equality that is so frequently referred to as the Black Revolution.

The reality, however, is that this profound social revolution is more than just Black. It involves many groups—one of these is Puerto Ricans. The Puerto Rican involved in the struggle has two special problems:

First, although many of his fellow Americans know intellectually that he is a citizen, emotionally he is regarded as a foreigner, with all this term implies for Americans.

Second, and perhaps most important, Puerto Ricans are not a race—they are an ethnic group in which some members are "white" some "black" and some so-called "mixed."

In other words, in a sense, Puerto Ricans are the only racially integrated group in the United States, as we have come to know the meaning of the word integrated. As such, they suffer the peculiar problem of not being understood either by their black brothers or by their so-called white neighbors.

To black men, Puerto Ricans are trying to "pass." They do not understand why Puerto Ricans have not joined them in a more militant manner in the Civil Rights struggle.

For too many of his white neighbors the Puerto Rican is seen as a non-white person with all that this implies within the American reality. What neither black nor white Americans understand is that Puerto Rico has never had what we in the United States call a minority group. In Puerto Rico the only people who are called a "minority" are those members of political parties that fail to win an election.

Puerto Ricans, therefore, whether black, white or mulatto have not received the same conditioning in this regard as have both the American black and whites.

This is not to imply that there is no prejudice among us Puerto Ricans. However, in our history as a people prejudice has been limited primarily to relations between individuals, and has never been socially instituted. In our history of more than 450 years, we have never had a broad scale system of *institutionalized* discrimination.

Puerto Ricans, whether black or white, have never had to bear the horrendous burden of fighting those who would make them feel or believe that they were lesser human beings because of skin pigmentation, or for that matter, for any other reason.

There has never been a race riot in Puerto Rico.

This, then, is one of the major differences between the blacks and the Puerto Ricans in the United States: that all Puerto Ricans are not "colored," and that even among those who are, color is not a major issue in Puerto Rican life.

Another significant difference is that Puerto Ricans represent a whole, unlike the blacks, who represent a part or minority of a whole. For this reason, Puerto Ricans are accustomed to seeing other Puerto Ricans at work at all levels, from low-income farm workers to the rich landowner who hires them; from the teacher who teaches them to the head of the University; from the district political leader to the Governor, the members of the Cabinet, and the members of the House and Senate. . . .

The Black Revolution today is first of all a struggle to secure the self respect and dignity due blacks because they are human beings. This self respect and this dignity Puerto Ricans have had for centuries. They have it in Puerto Rico (part of the American Union) and they insist on keeping it wherever they go.

For the Puerto Rican, therefore, particularly for those of the *first* and *bridge* generations, his struggle today, and increasingly so in the next thirty years, is and will be to *retain* the rights he has always had, rather than to *attain* rights he has never had.

For Puerto Ricans anywhere to accept the values, or more correctly the state of mind that color represents in the United States, would be to introduce into their way of life a racism that has never existed in the form in which it exists in the United States. To accept this racism would mean—figuratively and literally in some cases—to split the Puerto Rican family down the middle. This is true today, particularly among the *first* and *bridge* generations.

At this point I would like to speak briefly about the second generation Puerto Rican—the Puerto Rican born in the States of Puerto Rican parents. I will hereafter call him the New Puerto Rican.

The New Puerto Rican is a phenomenon who might add a new dimension to the concept of pluralistic democracy. Second genera-tions of the past, at great psychic costs, resolved their problems by giving up, in order to become "Americans," the values, culture, religion and sometimes even the name of their parents. It is interesting to note that the United States is one of the few coun-tries of the world where a man can consider himself educated and speak but one language. This, despite the fact, that the United States, perhaps more than any other country in the world, has received thousands of people who have spoken all of world's languages. It may well come to pass that the New Puerto Rican may break this traditional, historical reality, both for the better-ment of American life and its world image as well as for his own psychic salvation.

To understand the New Puerto Rican we must appreciate the fact that to be Puerto Rican in the United States is very different from being Puerto Rican in Puerto Rico. This is particularly true for the New Puerto Rican. He is Puerto Rican because he cannot be anything else. He does not have, as does his father of the *first* generation and his older brothers of the *bridge* generation, the knowledge, experience or security of knowing what it is to be a Puerto Rican in Puerto Rico. He has been raised in a setting where he is a minority, where he is different, which in the reality of the United States has always meant to be "less than," i.e., inferior to others.

Unlike his brothers in Puerto Rico, he is not just a child in school; he is a Puerto Rican. He is also something else. When I was being raised in East Harlem, I was frequently called a "spik." I am no longer called a "spik." I am now referred to as being culturally deprived, socially disadvantaged and a product of the culture of poverty. This too is the reality of the New Puerto Rican.

Furthermore, he is an unknown quantity, and an unknown reality to his cousins in Puerto Rico, who because of their conditioning cannot fully understand the peculiar and particular reality of their stateside equivalent.

Although there is much discussion regarding the problem of identity in Puerto Rico, it becomes academic when compared to the identity problem of the New Puerto Rican. No Puerto Rican in Puerto Rico need constantly remind himself that he is Puerto Rican. The New Puerto Rican, on the other hand, must almost literally remind himself every minute of every day that he is Puerto Rican. If he does not constantly remind himself of this fact, there are many others who will not let him forget it. His dilemma is that he is most certainly not Puerto Rican in the sense that he would be if he resided in Puerto Rico. He cannot be. The stimuli and values around him as well as the ever-present reality of his minority group position, among other reasons, make this impossible.

Frequently, the New Puerto Rican has never even seen Puerto Rico and quite frequently does not even speak Spanish. But, to all those around him, he is Puerto Rican. And indeed he is—he is the New Puerto Rican! There are those who, at this time, might point out that second generation groups of the past have also found themselves in a similar position. . . .

There are however, a series of variables that separate the situation of the New Puerto Rican from that of other Puerto Ricans in the United States, and that also hinders understanding among the various groups. One of these is citizenship. The same citizenship status among Puerto Ricans here and on the Island causes a unique dilemma.

As a citizen of the United States, the Puerto Rican born in the Commonwealth of Puerto Rico, a part of the American Union, need never learn English nor lose his cultural identity. He need never become a carbon copy of something he is not. If, however, he were to migrate from one part of the Union—Puerto Rico—to another part of the Union, New York City, this is exactly what he is expected to do.

That he should learn English, both as a tool for realizing the aspirations that motivated him to leave home, and as a means of expanding his knowledge and to further fulfill himself as a person, needs no discussion. But, at the same time that he is asked to learn English, he is asked to depersonalize himself by giving up the values and culture that give meaning and reality to his life. This is tantamount to a tacit judgement that his culture and values are inferior. He is told by words at times and by inference at other times that the values he holds dear are not worthy of his children. This represents the essence of denigration.

The New Puerto Rican does not fully understand the dilemma of his *first* generation father and *bridge* generation older brother. He sees in that which his father represents the cause for his not being accepted as part of the whole and as the reason why he must constantly be reminding himself that he is Puerto Rican although he is not sure what that means.

As I have demonstrated, much of Puerto Rico's future will turn on the relationship that is yet to be established with the United States. A key role in determining this relationship will fall to Puerto Ricans in the United States, especially the New Puerto Rican who by 2000 will compose a major portion of the Puerto Rican population here. His growth will take place within the context of American society. The primary elements that will influence his growth are the migration experience of his father and the legacy of problems stemming from migration that become incorporated into his heritage.

In addition, the American culture, and the racism that runs through it, will also be key factors in determining the New Puerto Rican's world view. These factors will naturally color the manner in which he views what is best for Puerto Rico, and therefore, the manner in which he exerts his influence on Congress toward an ultimate solution of Puerto Rico's political status.

Many possibilities exist for how his view of Puerto Rico's situation will be colored. The New Puerto Rican may feel that his suffering is due to being an outsider in America. This may cause him to project a statehood solution onto Puerto Rico, thinking that through statehood his problem of being considered an outsider will disappear. He may project an Independence solution, hoping thereby to erase the position of limbo in which he finds

himself. Thus through Independence he may attempt to demonstrate to the society that stigmatizes him that he has made his
choice.

Finally, he may take the path leading toward a more dynamic
Commonwealth status, one that fully realized the hopes of Puerto
Ricans on the Island and those here who see in maintaining the
link with their birthland a means of gaining strength from their
culture to combat the problems they face here.

All of these paths are fraught with danger because the ultimate
status of Puerto Rico should be wrought in the hands of the
Puerto Ricans on the Island—the Puerto Ricans who will be most
affected by the status and the ones who are closest to the dynamics
of their own society. Only Puerto Rico can judge what solution it
wants for itself.

If the bitter experience through which the *first* generation, *bridge*
generation and the New Puerto Ricans pass causes them to project
a solution for their situation onto the ultimate solution of Puerto
Rico's political status, they will do great harm both to themselves
and to their brothers on the Island. They cannot use their political
strength in favor of a status solution different from that which
their compatriots on the Island wish.

All generations must, therefore, maintain the bonds that the
first and *bridge* generations have with their Puerto Rican brothers
on the Island. Only by so doing can they keep each other informed
of the realities of the two countries and the differing needs of
the Puerto Rican populations. The Puerto Ricans of both countries
will gain the necessary resolve through their alliance to help solve
each other's problems.

TRADE OR TREASON

[In the two decades
since this book was first published (1973), much has changed in Puerto Rico.
The island's population is up to 3.5 million. Income is up, and signs of material
progress (new homes, highways, new cars) are abundant. But at least half of
Puerto Rico's people remain below the U.S. poverty line, and receive federal
food stamps. Unemployment hovers in the 15-20% range. Increases in drug
usage, violent crime, and the scourge of AIDS have contributed to a marked
deterioration in the quality of life. The debate over political status continues to

---

From Kal Wagenheim, *San Juan Star*, May 31, 1986, p. 18. Reprinted with permission.

obsess the leadership in Puerto Rico, as it has since the 19th century under Spain (the average voter, however, is more concerned about crime, jobs, and housing). With pro-independence sentiment estimated at about 5% of the electorate, the remaining 95% is split about evenly between supporters of Commonwealth and those who seek U.S. statehood (support for statehood has grown steadily since the 1950s, but may still fall short of a solid majority). In the six gubernatorial races held every four years since 1972, the pro-Commonwealth party has won three times, and the party which supports U.S. statehood has also won thrice. The following article discusses a problem which limits Puerto Rico's political and commercial relations with its Caribbean neighbors.]

At times, when I receive my copy of The San Juan Star up here in *el norte*, and I read certain statements made by some of the island's public figures, I think we are living on separate planets. The planet where I—and most others—reside is shrinking. It is becoming, in the words of Marshall Mcluhan, "a global village."

People in all nations are traveling across borders, either for pleasure, or business.

The State of Florida, for example, has become a major player in Caribbean-Latin American trade.

Its governor, a U.S. citizen, travels widely in the region, and frequently welcomes business and government leaders from all nations of the hemisphere, to Florida.

The Florida Commerce Department, in fact, has a special Caribbean Basin Division, which sponsors "business opportunities missions" for its citizens, who travel throughout the region, and help feed Florida's already booming economy with increasing doses of foreign trade.

The government of the city of New Orleans also is active in organizing links between its port facilities and the business communities of Central America and the Caribbean.

The Port Authority of New York and New Jersey organizes investment and trade missions to all parts of the world, including the Caribbean. These activities also help keep the New York-New Jersey metro area alive with commerce.

All of these international activities—by states, cities and port authorities—are carried out with the approval, support and enthusiastic blessing of the United States government.

Why? Because international trade helps generate jobs.

And why am I writing about this obvious fact?

Because some poor misguided souls in San Juan, Puerto Rico have, in recent months, been trying to make it sound as though efforts to promote international trade are somehow disloyal to the concept of being an American.

These poor narrow-minded souls happen, also, to be advocates of U.S. statehood for Puerto Rico.

Statehood is not the issue here.

At issue is the following point: is growing international trade good for Puerto Rico, whether it remains a Commonwealth, becomes the 51st state of the Union, or becomes an independent republic?

Ask any economist. He'll tell you that it is.

Ask the White House. Ask the Office of the U.S. Trade Representative. Ask the U.S. Department of Commerce.

They will affirm the fact that if Puerto Rico can strengthen its economy by building up commerce with its Caribbean neighbors, it will be good not only for the island, but also for the region and the hemisphere.

But these poor misguided souls are alarmed when government or private sector leaders from Puerto Rico travel to Costa Rica, or the Dominican Republic, or Japan, or Argentina, to generate economic activity that will help to put bread on the table of families in all of these countries.

They call such globe-hopping *"jugando a la república"* ("making believe we're a republic").

These poor misguided statehooders claim that Commonwealth is a colonial condition.

Yet, by regarding all forms of international commerce as being somehow akin to betrayal of U.S. citizenship, they reveal a colonial mentality that is quite sad to behold.

By their misguided condemnation of Puerto Rico's legitimate role on the international scene, they are saying, by implication, that it is only "patriotic" to do business with New York, Miami, New Orleans, and other parts of the United States.

In the meantime, government and business leaders from New York, Miami, New Orleans and elsewhere in the U.S. blithely hop around the Caribbean and Central America, engaged in the apparently "treasonous" activity of international trade.

These poor misguided statehooders apparently believe (or say they believe) that it is disloyal to do business with foreigners, unless one receives explicit permission from some bureaucrat in Washington.

That's not what being American is all about. They've got the wrong idea. Ronald Reagan won an overwhelming mandate from the American people when he told them that Washington was intervening too much in their lives. The American spirit is one of individual initiative, self-reliance, not of dependence on or approval from Washington.

The political status debate—between Commonwealth, U.S. statehood and independence—is certainly legitimate.

But please, *señores estadistas,* let's leave international trade out of the debate. Let's declare it irrelevant.

Please, come join the rest of us on this planet and recognize the obvious: Puerto Rico, no matter its eventual political status, will *always* be a small island smack in the middle of the Caribbean. It has linguistic, cultural and geographic links with the rest of the region. It is only natural for any reasonably alert Puerto Rican to be aware of the fact that, while airplanes fly from San Juan to New York and Washington, they can also fly to Kingston, Santo Domingo, Caracas, San José, and even Tokyo. Ships reach most of those places, too. One can buy bread and wine, and cars, and pay for mortgages, not only with dollars, but also with pesos, colones, bolívares, and yen.

Don't take my word for it. Ask David Rockefeller if it's OK to trade in the Caribbean and Latin America. He'll tell you.

A COMPLEX REALITY

[Perhaps the most dramatic change in Puerto Rican life during the past few decades has been the explosive growth of the Puerto Rico population in the continental United States, particularly in comparison to the population on the island. Between 1960 and 1990, the number of persons of Puerto Rican birth or origin residing in the U.S. has soared from 887,000 to more than 2 million. The island's population has grown at a much slower rate during the same period, from 2.3 million to 3.5 million, largely because of continuous out-migration. If current trends continue, Puerto Ricans in the U.S. will outnumber their compatriots on the island by early in the 21st century. Today, roughly half of all Puerto Ricans in the U.S. reside in New York City, but the rest of the migrants and their children have spread out throughout the U.S. Social scientists and the press often describe Puerto Ricans as the poorest ethnic group in the U.S., but as the following article explains, the reality is far more complex, and approximately 70% of Puerto Ricans in the U.S. are above the poverty line.]

For years, we have been hearing from social scientists, who cite official data from the U.S. Census Bureau, that Puerto Ricans in the United States are the poorest, most down-trodden minority group in the nation.

The same data, however, if more carefully analyzed, reveal a far more complex reality, including hidden strengths and positive signs.

Let me refer to a recent Census Bureau report, based on March 1989 surveys, which has been summarized and disseminated by the Institute for Puerto Rican Policy Inc., a New York-based research, advocacy and networking group.

Item: Puerto Rican males in the United States in 1988 had median

From Kal Wagenheim, *San Juan Star*, August 4, 1990, p. 19. Reprinted with permission.

annual earnings of $16,122. This was *higher* than earnings for Mexican males in the United States ($12,107), for Central and South American males ($14,930), and all other Latinos ($16,030), except for Cubans ($17,572). In other words, the typical Puerto Rican male worker (a member of the so-called poorest minority group in the United States) earned only $28 a week less than the typical Cuban male worker (who is part of the group considered to be among the most successful immigrants to the United States).

Item: Puerto Rican women in the United States in 1988 had median annual earnings of $11,241. This, too, was *higher* than the earnings of Mexican female workers ($8,110), Central and South American women ($9,936), and, in fact, about the same as the earnings for all non-Latino women in the United States ($11,245).

If we look at educational attainment, which often correlates closely with income, these data are not totally surprising, since 54 percent of all Puerto Ricans in the United States, age 25 or above, have high school degrees (compared with 49.8 percent of Mexicans and 50.9 percent of all Latinos), and 9.8 percent have four years or more of college (compared with 6.1 percent of Mexicans and 9.9 percent of all Latinos).

Why, then—if Puerto Ricans are at least as well educated as other Latinos in the United States, and if Puerto Rican workers earn more than other Latinos—is the Puerto Rican community considered the poorest?

Because, depending upon how you interpret the data, that is also true.

Item: Median family income for Puerto Ricans in the United States in 1988 was $18,932, *lower* than that of all other Latino groups: Mexicans ($21,325), Cubans ($26,858), Central and South Americans ($24,322), and other Latinos ($23,666).

Item:30.8 percent of all Puerto Rican families in the United States lived in poverty in 1988, more than all other Latin groups: Mexicans (24.9 percent); Cubans (16.9 percent); Central & South Americans (16.6 percent); and other Latinos (20.6 percent).

How can Puerto Rican workers earn more, yet be poorer than other Latino groups?

Because we have overlooked one important piece of data: the question of single-parent families, most of which are headed by a female. Such families of all ethnic and racial groups are often among the poorest in the nation, because mothers are frequently required to care for young children, meaning they must rely on public assistance, or are less likely to qualify for high-paying jobs.

In this category, regrettably, the Puerto Rican community in the United States is a leader. 39.6 percent of all Puerto Rican families in the United States are headed by a single parent/female, and 58.3 percent of these families are mired in poverty. By contrast, this is the case for only 19 percent of Mexican families, 17.7 percent of Cuban families, 25.0 percent of Central and South American families, 23.1 percent of other Latino families (And 16.1 percent of non-Latino families).

With this data, we can see why there is no contradiction between higher-paid individual workers and worse degrees of family poverty.

It appears, then, that one can identify two major economic categories in the Puerto Rican community: the clear majority, who are working and competing quite well with other Latinos (and presumably with immigrants of other ethnic groups), and a troubling large minority of female-headed families that are trapped at the bottom of the socio-economic ladder.

Why are there more female-headed single-parent families in the Puerto Rican community than among other Latinos and non-Latinos? Is there something unique about the dynamics of family relationships in this group? If many are migrants from Puerto Rico (as I suspect is the case), is there a selective process at work which provides incentives for women in this situation to come to the United States?

We simply don't know. Some social scientists have begun to look at this question, but I am not aware of any comprehensive study that would provide us with meaningful data.

Without such data, how can policy makers and advocates hope to adequately address the problem?

BIBLIOGRAPHY

This list is designed to be of maximum assistance to both the student and the general reader. Many fine materials on Puerto Rican history are available only on the island, and it would be an exercise in futility to cite them here. Therefore, emphasis is given to English-language materials that are widely available.

The reader is urged to explore the *New York Times Index* and the *Reader's Guide to Periodical Literature*—both commonly found in libraries—which contain many hundreds of listings about Puerto Rico.

Entries in this list are divided according to the ten part divisions of the book, and arranged in approximate chronological order.

In addition, the interested reader should examine back issues of the following publications: in Puerto Rico, *El Mundo, San Juan Star,* and *Claridad;* in New York, *El Diario-La Prensa, Unidad Latina, Palante,* the *New York Daily News,* and the *New York Post.* In Puerto Rico, the most extensive collection of pertinent material—including newspapers no longer published today—is found in the *Colección Puertorriqueña,* University of Puerto Rico Library, Río Piedras campus. An essential source book found there is Antonio Pedreira's *Bibliografía Puertorriqueña (1493-1930),* (Río Piedras: Universary of Puerto Rico Press, 1934).

GENERAL REFERENCE WORKS

BRAMELD, THEODORE B. *The Remaking of a Culture: Life and Education in Puerto Rico.* New York: Harper, 1959.

BRAU, SALVADOR. *Historia de Puerto Rico.* San Juan: Editorial Coquí, 1966 (1st ed., 1904).

FERNANDEZ MENDEZ, EUGENIO. *Historia Cultural de Puerto Rico, 1493-1968.* San Juan: Ediciones El Cemí, 1970.

FIGUEROA, LOIDA. *Breve historia de Puerto Rico.* Vol. 1, "From the Beginnings Until 1800"; Vol. 2, "1801-1898." Río Piedras, Puerto Rico: Editorial Edil, 1969.

FREIDRICH, CARL J. *Puerto Rico: Middle Road to Freedom.* New York: Rinehart, 1959.

HANSEN, MILLARD, and WELLS, HENRY, eds. *Puerto Rico: A Study in Democratic Development.* Philadelphia: American Academy of Political and Social Science, 1953.

HUNTER, ROBERT J. *The Historical Evolution of the Relationship Between the United States and Puerto Rico: 1898-1963.* Pittsburgh: University of Pittsburgh, 1963 (thesis reprinted by Xerox in 1970).

LEWIS, GORDON K. *Puerto Rico: Freedom and Power in the Caribbean.* New York: Monthly Review Press, 1963.

MALDONADO DENIS, MANUEL. *Puerto Rico: una interpretación histórico-social.* Mexico City: Sigo 21, 1969.

MUNDEN, KENNETH, and GREENBAUM, MILTON, eds. *Records of the Bureau of Insular Affairs Relating to Puerto Rico, 1898-1934; a list of selected files.* Washington, D.C.: U.S. National Archives, 1943.

SEDA BENILLA, EDUARDO. *Requiem para una cultura: ensayes sobre la socialización del puertorriqueño en su cultura y ámbito del poder neocolonial.* Río Piedras, Puerto Rico: Editorial Edil, 1970.

STEWARD, JULIAN H., ed. *The People of Puerto Rico.* Urbana: University of Illinois Press, 1956, 1966.
U.S.–*Puerto Rico Commission on the Status of Puerto Rico.* Washington, D.C.: U.S. Government Printing Office, 1966. Five volumes.
WAGENHEIM, KAL. *Puerto Rico: A Profile.* New York: Praeger, 1970.

PART I: DISCOVERY AND CONQUEST

ALEGRIA, RICARDO. *Discovery, Conquest and Colonization of Puerto Rico: 1493–1599.* Translated by Kal Wagenheim and Luis Muñoz Lee. San Juan: Colección de Estudios Puertorriqueños, 1971.
COLL Y TOSTE, CAYETANO. *Prehistoria de Puerto Rico.* Bilbao, Spain: Editorial Vasco Americana, 1967.
FEWKES, J. WALTER. *The Aborigines of Porto Rico and Neighboring Islands.* 25th annual report of the Bureau of American Ethnology, 1903–4. Washington, D.C.: Government Printing Office, 1970.
MASON, OTIS T. *The Lotimer Collection of Antiquities from Porto Rico in the National Museum.* Washington, D.C.: Smithsonian Institution, 1899.

PART II: THE COLONIZATION

COLL Y TOSTE, CAYETANO. *Leyendas y tradiciones Puertorriqueñas.* Bilbao, Spain: Editorial Vasco Americana, 1969.
CRUZ MONCLOVA, LIDIO. *Historia de Puerto Rico.* Vol. 1, 1808–68. Río Piedras: University of Puerto Rico Press, 1952.
HAKLUYT, RICHARD. *Hakluyt's Voyages: The Principal Navigations, Voyages, Traffiques and Discoveries of the English Nation.* Edited by Irwin W. Blacker. New York: Viking, 1965 (1st ed., 1600).
MAYNARDE, THOMAS. *Sir Francis Drake, His Voyage in 1595, Together with the Spanish Account of Drake's Attack on Puerto Rico.* Vol. 7. London: Hakluyt Society, 1849.
MORALES CARRION, ARTURO. *Puerto Rico and the Non-Hispanic Caribbean.* Río Piedras: University of Puerto Rico Press, 1952.
SIGUENZA Y GONGORA, DON CARLOS DE. *Infortunios de Alonso Ramírez.* San Juan: Libros del Pueblo, Instituto de Cultura Puertorriqueña, 1967 (1st ed., 1690).

PART III: THE SPIRIT OF NATIONHOOD

ALONSO, MANUEL A. *El gíbaro: cuadro de costumbres de la isla de Puerto Rico.* San Juan: Instituto de Cultura Puertorriqueña, 1967 (facsimile of 1849 edition).
CRUZ MONCLOVA, LIDIO. *Historia del año 1887.* Río Piedras: University of Puerto Rico Press, 1958.
———. *Historia de Puerto Rico.* Vol. 2, 1868–85; Vol. 3, 1885–98. Río Piedras: University of Puerto Rico Press, 1962.
PEDREIRA, ANTONIO S. *Hostos: ciudadano de America.* San Juan: Instituto de Cultura Puertorriqueña, 1964.
TURNBULL, DAVID. *Travels in the West. Cuba; with Notices of Porto Rico and the Slave Trade.* New York: Negro University Press, 1969 (1st ed., 1840).

Newspapers & Periodicals

QUASIMODO. "The Earthquake at Puerto Rico." *New York Times,* December 28, 1867, p. 8.
"The Man from Bayamón." *San Juan Review,* April, 1964, p. 36.

PART IV: MANIFEST DESTINY

BERBUSSE, EDWARD J. *The United States in Puerto Rico: 1898–1900.* Chapel Hill: University of North Carolina Press, 1966.

BRYAN, WILLIAM S. *Our Islands and Their People.* New York: N. D. Thompson, 1899.
DALLEK, ROBERT. *1898: McKinley's Decision: The United States Declares War on Spain.* New York: Chelsea House, 1969.
GREENE, THEODORE P., ed. *American Imperialism in 1898.* Boston: D. C. Heath, 1955.
HERRMAN, KARL S. *A Recent Campaign in Puerto Rico by the Independent Regular Brigade, under the Command of Brig. Gen. Schwan.* Boston: E. H. Bacon, 1907.
KELLER, ALLAN. *The Spanish-American War; A Compact History.* New York: Hawthorn, 1969.
KIDDER, FREDERICK E. *The Political Concepts of Luis Muñoz Rivera of Puerto Rico.* Gainesville: University of Florida Press, 1965 (thesis reprinted by Xerox in 1970).
REID, WHITELAW. *Making Peace with Spain.* Edited by H. Wayne Morgan. Austin: University of Texas Press, 1965.
U.S. War Department, Division of Insular Affairs. *Immigration Regulations for the Island of Porto Rico, June 7, 1899.* Washington, D.C.: U.S. Government Printing Office, 1899.
WHITE, TRUMBULL. *A Graphic Account, Descriptive and Historical, of the Tropic Islands of the Sea Which Have Fallen Under Our Sway.* Vol. 1. Chicago: J. S. Ziegler, 1898.

Newspapers & Periodicals

CARROLL, HENRY K. "Porto Rico: How Shall it be Governed?" *Forum,* XXVIII (November, 1899), p. 257.
CHAPMAN, CARLTON T. "How the Stars and Stripes Came to Arroyo." *Harper's Weekly,* XLII (September 3, 1898), p. 874 (*see also* p. 863).
DAVIS, RICHARD HARDING. "The Porto Rico Campaign." *Scribner's Magazine,* XXIV (November, 1898), p. 514.
EMERSON, J. E. "Alone in Puerto Rico; a War Correspondent's Adventure." *Scribner's Monthly,* LVI (September, 1898), p. 666.
HENRY, MRS. GUY V. "Porto Rico From a Woman's Point of View." *American Monthly Review of Reviews,* XX (July–December, 1899), p. 177.
New York Times, July 5, 1898, p. 6. "Invasion of Puerto Rico: Thirty Thousand Men, with Cavalry and Artillery, to be Sent under Gen. Brooke."
———, July 18, 1898, p. 2. "Trade of Puerto Rico."
———, July 22, 1898, p. 1. "Miles Off for Puerto Rico."
———, July 23, 1898, p. 2. "Puerto Rican Junta's Views."
———, July 28, 1898, p. 1. "Miles is Pushing Onward to Ponce."
———, July 29, 1898, p. 6. "The Puerto Rican Campaign."
———, July 30, 1898, pp. 1, 6. "Ponce Yields Without a Shot."
WEINER, C. "Financial Wrong in Porto Rico." *North American Review,* CLXVII (December, 1898), p. 754.
WILCOX, MARRION. "From Guayama to St. John." *Harper's Weekly,* XLII (October 15, 1898), p. 1010.

PART V: "CITIZENS OF PORTO RICO"

First annual report of Charles H. Allen, governor of Porto Rico, covering the period from May 1, 1900 to May 1, 1901. Respectfully submitted to the Hon. William McKinley. Washington, D.C.: U.S. Government Printing Office, 1901.

Newspapers & Periodicals

ADAMS, T. S. "Independence Day in Porto Rico." *Nation,* LXXIII (July 18, 1901), p. 46.
BURCH, H. R. "Suffrage in Porto Rico." *Annals,* XIX, No. 3 (1902), p. 425.
DEAN, F. "Going to the Opera in Porto Rico." *Bookman,* XXXV (March, 1912), p. 31.

FALKNER, R. P. "The English Language in Porto Rico." *Forum*, XLI (March, 1909), p. 206.
GLASSFORD, W. A. "Porto Rico and a Necessary Military Position in the West Indies." *Journal of the Military Services Institution*, XXXVII (1905), p. 43.
HILL, ROBERT T. "Porto Rico or Puerto Rico?" *National Geographic*, X (1899), p. 516.
Independent, LXXI (October 26, 1911), p. 932. "Denationalized, Unpatriated."
ROWE, LEE S. "Political Parties in Porto Rico." *Annals of the American Academy of Political and Social Science*, XIX, No. 3 (1902), p. 351.

PART VI: AMERICAN CITIZENSHIP

VELEZ AQUINO, LUIS A. *Puerto Rican Press Reaction to the Shift from Spanish to U.S. Sovereignty: 1898–1917*. New York: Columbia University Press, 1968 (thesis reprinted by Xerox in 1970).

Newspapers & Periodicals

GATELL, FRANK. "The Art of the Possible: Luis Muñoz Rivera and the Puerto Rican Jones Bill." *The Americas*, XVII, No. 1 (July, 1960), p. 1.
MORALES CARRION, ARTURO. "The Loneliness of Luis Muñoz Rivera." *San Juan Review*, July, 1966, p. 17.
New York Times, March 3, 1917, p. 8. "Wilson Signs Citizenship Bill."
———, March 9, 1917, p. 6. "V. Balbas, Editor, Says No to U.S. Citizenship."
Outlook, CXV (March 14, 1917), p. 447. "Porto Ricans Are Made Americans."
SHAW, ALBERT. "Porto Ricans as Citizens: Some Observations Regarding Their Political Future." *Review of Reviews*, LXIII (1926), p. 483.

PART VII: THE GRIM YEARS

BENNER, THOMAS E. *Five Years of Foundation Building: The University of Puerto Rico, 1924–1929*. Preface by Jaime Benítez. Río Piedras: University of Puerto Rico Press, 1965.
CLARK, VICTOR S., ed. *Porto Rico and its Problems*. Washington, D.C.: Brookings Institution, 1930.
CORDOVA DAVILA, FELIX. *Maladministration of Governor E. Mont Reily in Porto Rico*. Speech in the U.S. House of Representatives, April 4, 1922. Washington, D.C.: U.S. Government Printing Office, 1922.
———. *Conditions in Porto Rico*. Speech in the U.S. House of Representatives, March 4, 1925. Washington, D.C.: U.S. Government Printing Office, 1925.
———. *Home Rule for Puerto Rico*. Speech given in the U.S. House of Representatives, March 24, 1926. Washington, D.C.: U.S. Government Printing Office, 1926.
CORRETJER, JUAN ANTONIO. *Albizu Campos*. Montevideo: El Siglo Ilustrado, 1969.
GAYER, ARTHUR D., et al. *The Sugar Economy of Puerto Rico*. New York: Columbia University Press, 1938.
MEDINA RAMIREZ, RAMON. *El movimiento libertador en la historia de Puerto Rico*. San Juan: Imprenta Nacional, 1950, 1954, 1958. 3 volumes.
OSUNA, JUAN JOSE. *Education in Puerto Rico*. New York: Columbia University Press, 1923.
PEDREIRA, ANTONIO S. *Insularismo*. Madrid: Tipografia Artistica, 1934.
RIBES TOVAR, FEDERICO. *Albizu Campos: Revolucionario*. New York: Plus Ultra, 1971.
U.S. Congress. House. Committee on Insular Affairs. *Hearings to Amend the Organic Act of Porto Rico*. 68th Congress, 1st session, January, 1924.
VILLARINI, ANGEL R., and HERNANDEZ CRUZ, JUAN E., eds. *Pedro Albizu Campos: vida y pensamientos. Escritos y reseñas políticas, 1930*. Vol. 1. San Juan: Editorial de Educación Política, Puerto Rico Independence Party, 1970.

Newspapers & Periodicals

APPLETON, CAROLINE DAWES. "Porto Rico: A Study in Colonial Courtesies." *Review of Reviews*, LXXII (September, 1925), p. 301.
BARCELO, ANTONIO. "American Rule in Puerto Rico: 1899-1924." *Current History*, XXI (January 17, 1925), p. 511.
BERLE, A. A. JR. "Puerto Rican Independence." *Survey*, XLVI (September 24, 1921), p. 704.
CUESTA, J. ENAMORADO. "Porto Rico's Devastation by the Recent Hurricane." *Current History*, XXIX (November, 1928), p. 319.
IGLESIAS, SANTIAGO. "Porto Rico's Onward March." *American Federationist*, November 24, 1924 , p. 894.
——. "Why Puerto Rico Does Not Want Independence." *American Federationist*, October, 1937 .
LASTRA CHARRIEZ, ALFONSO. "I Accuse." *Nation*, CXV (September 6, 1922), p. 236.
MELENDEZ MUNOZ, M. "The Significance of Tobacco in the Economic Life of Porto Rico." *Tobacco*, LXXV (December 28, 1922), p. 5.
MUNOZ MARIN, LUIS. "A 98 Per Cent American in Porto Rico." *New Republic*, XXIX (January 4, 1922), p 151.
New York Times, April 10, 1931, p. 4. "Republic of Porto Rico Bonds Issued by Nationalist Party."
VILLARD, OSWALD G. "Liberty and Death in Puerto Rico." *Nation*, CXLIV (April 3, 1937), p. 371.
WARNER, A. "Porto Rico's Workers Awake." *Nation*, CXVI (April 11, 1923), p. 419.

PART VIII: "¡JALDA ARRIBA!"

AITKEN, THOMAS H. *Poet in the Fortress.* New York: New American Library, 1964.
ANDERSON, ROBERT W. *Party Politics in Puerto Rico.* Stanford: Stanford University Press, 1965.
ANDREU IGLESIAS, CESAR. *Muñoz Marín: un hombre acorralado por la historia.* San Juan: Editorial Claridad, 1964.
APONTE-HERNANDEZ, RAFAEL. *The University of Puerto Rico: Foundations of the 1942 Reform.* Austin: University of Texas, 1966 (thesis reprinted by Xerox).
BARTON, HUBERT C. *Puerto Rico's Industrial Development Program: 1942-1960.* Cambridge: Center for International Affairs, Harvard University, 1959.
BROWN, WENZELL. *Dynamite on Our Doorstep: Puerto Rican Paradox.* New York: Greenberg Press, 1945.
BROWNBACK, ANNADRUE HARRIS. *Congressional and Insular Opposition to Puerto Rican Autonomy.* University of Alabama, 1966 (thesis reprinted by Xerox in 1970).
FERNOS-ISERN, ANTONIO. *Addresses of Antonio Fernós-Isern, Resident Commissioner of Puerto Rico to the United States.* Washington, D.C.: Office of Puerto Rico, 1947.
GALBRAITH, JOHN K. *Marketing Efficiency in Puerto Rico.* Cambridge: Harvard University Press, 1955.
GONZALEZ, LUIS MANUEL. *The Economic Development of Puerto Rico from 1898-1940.* Gainesville: University of Florida Press, 1964 (thesis reprinted by Xerox in 1970).
GOODSELL, CHARLES T. *Administration of a Revolution: Executive Reform in Puerto Rico Under Governor Tugwell, 1944-1946.* Cambridge: Harvard University Press, 1965.
HACKETT, WILLIAM H. *The Nationalist Party.* U.S. House Committee on Interior and Insular Affairs. Washington, D.C.: U.S. Government Printing Office, 1951.
LANDY, DAVID. *Tropical Childhood; Cultural Transmission and Learning in a Rural Puerto Rican Village.* Chapel Hill: University of North Carolina Press, 1959.
LUGO-SILVA, ENRIQUE. *The Tugwell Administration in Puerto Rico, 1941-1946.* Río Piedras: University of Puerto Rico Press, 1955.
MARQUES, RENE. *Ensayos: 1953-66.* San Juan: Editorial Antillana, 1967.

MATHEWS, THOMAS G. *Puerto Rican Politics and the New Deal.* Gainesville: University of Florida Press, 1960.
PERLOFF, HARVEY S. *Puerto Rico's Economic Future; a Study in Planned Development.* Chicago: University of Chicago Press, 1950.
REIMER, EVERETT W. *Social Planning: Collected Papers, 1957–58.* Cuernavaca: Centro Intercultural de Documentación, 1968.
TUGWELL, REXFORD G. *The Art of Politics as Practiced by Three Great Americans: Franklin Delano Roosevelt, Luis Muñoz Marín and Fiorello H. LaGuardia.* New York: Doubleday, 1958.
——. *Puerto Rican Public Papers of R. G. Tugwell, Governor.* San Juan: Service Office, Government of Puerto Rico, Printing Division, 1945.
U.S. Congress. Senate. *Independence for Puerto Rico.* Hearings Before the Committee on Territories and Insular Affairs. 79th Congress, 1st session, on S. 227. Washington, D.C.: U.S. Government Printing Office, 1945. 2 vols.

Newspapers & Periodicals

BENITEZ, CELESTE, and REXACH, ROBERTO F. "The Problem of Puerto Rican Identity." *San Juan Review,* August, 1964, p. 21.
BOORSTIN, DANIEL J. "Self Discovery in Puerto Rico." *Yale Review,* XLV (1955–56), p. 229.
CARDENAS, FLORANGEL. "El Fanguito: A Hell on Earth." *San Juan Review,* April, 1964, p. 9.
Fortune, XLI (May, 1950), p. 86. "Profit Hunters in Puerto Rico."
KAZIN, ALFRED. "In Puerto Rico." *Commentary,* XXIX (February, 1960), p. 108.
LEWIS, GORDON K. "A Puritan in Babylon." *San Juan Review,* October, 1964, p. 46.
MUNOZ MARIN, LUIS. "Plight of Puerto Rico." *New Republic,* CVIII (January 11, 1943), p. 51.
New York Times, October 31, 1950, p. 1. "Revolt Flares in Puerto Rico; Soon Quelled With 23 Dead."
San Juan Review, October, 1964, p. 12. "A Talk With the Candidates."
——, November, 1964, p. 12. "The Addict: A Confession."
VIENTOS GASTON, NILITA. "The Problem of Puerto Rican Identity: Part II." *San Juan Review,* October, 1964, p. 37.
WAGENHEIM, KAL. "Vieques: Tragic Island." *San Juan Review,* June, 1964, p. 7.

PART IX: EXODUS

BERLE, BEATRICE. *80 Puerto Rican Families in New York City; Health and Disease Studied in Context.* New York: Columbia University Press, 1958.
CHENAULT, LAURENCE R. *The Puerto Rican in New York City.* New York: Columbia University Press, 1938.
CORDASCO, FRANCESCO, ed. *Puerto Rican Children in Mainland Schools.* Metuchen, N.J.: Scarecrow Press, 1968.
GALINDEZ, JESUS DE. *Puerto Rico en Nueva York: sociología de una inmigración.* Buenos Aires: Editorial Tiempo Contemporáneo, 1969.
GOLUB, FRED T. *The Puerto Rican Worker in Perth Amboy, N.J.* New Brunswick: Rutgers University, Institute of Management and Labor Relations, No. 2, 1956.
HANDLIN, OSCAR. *The Newcomers: Negroes and Puerto Ricans in a Changing Metropolis.* Cambridge: Harvard University Press, 1959.
KOSS, JOAN D. *Puerto Ricans in Philadelphia: Migration and Accommodation.* Philadelphia, 1965. (Thesis).
LEWIS, OSCAR. *La Vida: A Puerto Rican Family in the Culture of Poverty—San Juan and New York.* New York: Random House, 1966.
MASSIMINE, E. VIRGINIA. *Challenges of a Changing Population; a Study of the Integration of the Puerto Ricans in a West Side Community in Manhattan.* New York: Center for Human Relations, 1954.
MILLS, C. WRIGHT. *The Puerto Rican Journey.* New York: Columbia University Press, 1948.

SEXTON, PATRICIA CAYO. *Spanish Harlem: An Anatomy of Poverty.* New York: Harper & Row, 1965.
SPIAGGIA, MARTIN. *Self-Group Devaluation and Prejudice in Minority-Group Boys.* Ann Arbor: University of Michigan Press, 1959 (thesis reprinted by Xerox in 1959).
U.S. Congress. House. *Communist Activities Among Puerto Ricans in New York City and Puerto Rico.* Hearings before the Committee on Un-American Activities, 86th Congress, 1st session. Washington, D.C.: U.S. Government Printing Office, 1960.

Newspapers & Periodicals

BERGER, MEYER. "Assassins' Kin and Friends are Rounded Up in the Bronx." *New York Times,* November 2, 1950, p. 1.
BORDERS, WILLIAM. "Puerto Rican Population Swells in Connecticut." *New York Times,* August 26, 1967, p. 29.
GLAZER, NATHAN. "New York's Puerto Ricans." *Commentary,* XXVI (December, 1958), p. 469.
KOCH, JOSEPH E. "The Puerto Ricans Come to Youngstown." *Commonweal,* LIX (October 9, 1953), p. 9.
MALDONADO, A. W. "Migration Reverses." *Nation,* CXCVIII (March 16, 1964), p. 255.
MONSERRAT, JOSE. "Literacy Tests." *New York Herald Tribune Magazine,* October 13, 1963, p. 9.
New Republic, CLIV (June 25, 1966), p. 7. "No Hablo Inglés: Police Blamed for Puerto Rican Riots."
Newsweek, June 27, 1963, p. 23. "Chicago Riot: 'Venganza!'"
O'BRIEN, R. W. "Hawaii's Puerto Ricans: Stereotype and Reality." University of Hawaii, *Social Process in Hawaii,* XXIII (1959), p. 61.
ROBERTS, CHALMERS M., and LEWIS, ALFRED E. "Assassin Slain, Another Shot at Truman's Door." *Washington Post,* November 2, 1950, p. 1.
SOTO, PEDRO JUAN. "The Pentecostals." *San Juan Review,* March, 1964, p. 11.
WAGNER, GEOFFREY. "Puerto Rico in Harlem." *New Republic,* CXXXI (August 23, 1954), p. 16.

PART X: THE DIVIDED NATION

FERNANDEZ MARINA, R.; VON ECKARDT, U.; and MALDONADO SIERRA, E. *The Sober Generation: Children of Operation Bootstrap.* Río Piedras: University of Puerto Rico Press, 1969.
GARCIA PASSALACQUA, JUAN M. *La crisis política en Puerto Rico: 1962–66.* San Juan: Ediciones Edil, 1970.
——, ed. *Papers on Puerto Rican Studies.* San Juan: Puerto Rico Junior College, 1970.
GONZALEZ, ANTONIO J. *Economía política de Puerto Rico.* San Juan: Editorial Cordillera, 1967.
HAMILL, PETE. *Irrational Ravings.* New York: Putnam's, 1971.
HERNANDEZ, JOSEPH W. *The Sociological Implications of Return Migration in Puerto Rico.* Minneapolis: University of Minnesota, 1964 (thesis reprinted by Xerox in 1970).
JESUS, ALFREDO DE. *Problems Faced by the Spanish Community in the City of Boston and the State of Massachusetts.* Boston: Mayor's Office of Human Rights, May 13, 1971.
LIEBMAN, ARTHUR. *Children of Their Fathers: The Politics of Puerto Rican University Students.* Berkeley: University of California, 1967 (thesis reprinted by Xerox in 1970).
NIEVES FALCON, LUIS. *Diagnóstico de Puerto Rico.* Río Piedras: Editorial Edil, 1971.
PARRILLA BONILLA, ANTULIO. *Puerto Rico: iglesia y sociedad, 1967–69; conferencias, discursos, entrevistas.* Cuernavaca, Mexico: Centro Intercultural de Documentación, 1970.
ROGLER, LLOYD H. *Trapped: Families and Schizophrenia.* New York: Wiley, 1965.

SILEN, JUAN ANGEL. *We, the Puerto Rican People: A Story of Oppression and Resistance*. Translated by Cedric Belfrage. New York: Monthly Review Press, 1971.

U.S. Department of Labor. Bureau of Labor Statistics. *The New York Puerto Rican: Patterns of Work Experience*. New York: Regional Report No. 19, May, 1971.

U.S. Senate. *Equal Educational Opportunity for Puerto Rican Children*. Hearings before the Select Committee on Equal Educational Opportunity. 91st Congress, 2d session. Washington, D.C.: U.S. Government Printing Office, 1970. Part 8, pp. 3683–3973.

Young Lords Party, and ABRAMSON, MICHAEL. *Palante: Young Lords Party*. New York: McGraw-Hill, 1971.

Newspapers & Periodicals

BURKE, EDWARD C. "35 Puerto Ricans Freed, Ending Hoboken Strife." *New York Times*, September 7, 1971, p. 43.

ESZTERHAS, JOSEPH. "The City's Forgotten Minority." *Cleveland Plain Dealer*, series, April 25-30, 1971.

FESBURGH, LACEY. "Violence at the Parade." *New York Times*, June 14, 1971, p. 1.

GREEN, LARRY; CANFIELD, DAVE; et al. "Chicago's Latins: The Community Nobody Knows." *Chicago Daily News*, series, July 31, August 2-5, 1971.

LAGUERRE, ENRIQUE. "If I Had It All to Do Over." *San Juan Review*, June, 1965, p. 41.

New York Times, January 2, 1969, p. 23. "Ferré Becomes Governor of Puerto Rico Today, Ending an Era."

———, November 8, 1969, p. 67. "13 Puerto Ricans Injured in Clash."

———, March 12, 1971, p. 1. "Three Die in Riot at Puerto Rico U."

ROSARIO, RUBEN DEL. "Is Spanish in Danger?" *San Juan Review*, June, 1965, p. 59.

SUAREZ, MANUEL. "Puerto Rico Faces a Language Trial." *New York Times*, May 23, 1971, p. 19.

VAZQUEZ, JUAN M. "Many From Puerto Rico Flee City for Homeland." *New York Times*, February 28, 1972, p. 1.

WAGENHEIM, KAL. "Copper: The Billion-Dollar Secret." *San Juan Review*, January, 1965, p. 5.

INDEX

Abbad y Lasierra, Fray Iñigo, 33
Agriculture, 30–32, 38–44
Albizu Campos, Pedro, 167–73, 179–82, 223–25
Autonomy, 54, 73–76, 79–80, 126–27, 157

Badillo, Herman, 258, 284
Baldorioty de Castro, Román, 54, 73–76
Barbosa, Dr. José C., 75
Barceló, Antonio R., 136–37, 141, 152, 175–76
Berríos, Reuben, 289–91
Betances, Ramón Emeterio, 53, 59–62, 64–67, 75–76, 89
Bilingualism, 272–81
Black Americans, x, 243–45, 252–58, 271, 307, 317–22
Bonilla, Frank, xii
Bracetti, Mariana, 66

Cáncel Miranda, Rafael, 204–7
Cancio, Hiram, 292–94
Carrero, Jaime, 276
Castro, Fidel, 295, 298
Chicago, Puerto Ricans in, 252, 263–67
Citizenship, U.S., 110, 112–14, 123–39, 186, 318, 320–21
Coll y Cuchí, Cayetano, 143–46
Collazo, Oscar, 204–7
Colón, Jesus, 229–32
Columbus, Christopher, 1, 3–4, 13, 20, 235
Commonwealth status, 142, 152–53, 195–203, 204, 217–20, 221, 285, 292–94, 322
Coolidge, Calvin, 152–53, 171
Córdova Dávila, Félix, 139, 150–51, 153
Corretjer, Juan Antonio, 62
Cuba, 67–71, 72, 74–75, 77–79, 81–83, 87–88, 89, 295–98
Cubans in Puerto Rico, 295–98
Culebra Island, 289–90
Culture, 110–12, 121–22, 159–60, 161, 177–78, 276–81, 285–89, 315–22

De Diego, José, 99–100, 123–24, 126, 136–37
De Las Casas, Fray Bartolomé, 3
Discovery of Puerto Rico, 2–4

Drug addiction, 270–71, 312

Economy, 29–33, 38–44, 83–84, 107–8, 115, 147–49, 157–59, 162–67, 170, 183–84, 188, 195–96, 236, 298–307
Education, 31, 111, 129, 130, 144–45, 148, 161, 163, 302–11
Elections, 132–34, 175, 258–63
Ellsworth, Elmer, 220–23
English language, 101–2, 111, 122, 144–45, 163–64, 170, 259, 272–76, 288, 307–11, 319–22

Feliciano Grafals, Edwin, 292–94
Ferré, Luis A., 222–23, 285–89
Figueroa Cordero, Andrés, 204–7
Flores Rodríguez, Irving, 204–7
Foraker Act of 1900, 110, 116–17, 127, 130, 157
Fortas, Abe, 189

Geigel-Polanco, Vicente, 190
Gore, Robert, 174–78
Grito de Lares revolt, 61–67, 76

Harding, Warren G., 141
Hernández Colón, Rafael, 285
Hoboken, Puerto Ricans in, 310
Hoover, Herbert, 168

Immigration to Puerto Rico, 53
Income distribution, 290
Independence, 55, 59–61, 61–67, 69–73, 75–76, 82, 86–88, 90–91, 105, 124–26, 135, 136, 138–39, 141–43, 150, 160, 167–73, 179–82, 186, 190–94, 197–202, 219–20, 223–25, 289–94, 321–22
Indians of Puerto Rico, 1, 3, 15–26
Invasion of Puerto Rico by U.S., ix, 54, 80, 89–103, 169
Invasions by European powers, 28
Irving, Washington, 1, 19
Isabella, Queen of Spain, 1, 18, 19

Johnson, Lyndon B., 297
Jones Act of 1917, 125–26, 126–39, 280–81

Kennedy, John F., 218

Labor conditions, 147–49, 165–66, 229–32, 252–58
Larrinaga, Tulio, 114–19
Leahy, Admiral William D., 185
Lebrón, Lolita, 204–6
Lewis, Oscar, 241–45
Lindbergh, Charles, 151–52
Llorens Torres, Luis, 122
Lodge, Henry Cabot, 89

McKinley, William, 86, 89, 98, 166
Mari Bras, Juan, 219–20, 296
Miles, Maj. Gen. Nelson A., 92–96
Military service, 113, 145, 193, 221–22, 292–94
Montserrat, Joseph, 315–22
Muñoz Marín, Luis, 153–61, 176, 183, 186–87, 195–203, 218, 221, 223–24
Muñoz Rivera, Luis, 62, 74–75, 99–100, 106, 110, 124–36, 153, 196

Nationalism, 53–76, 167–73, 179–82, 204–7, 223–25
Neo–Ricans, 276–81, 319–22
New York City, Puerto Ricans in, 228–32, 236–50, 252–63, 267–76, 311–22
Newark, Puerto Ricans in, 310–11
Nixon, Richard M., 205

O'Reilly, Field Marshal Alejandro, 29–33

Padilla de Sanz, Doña Trina, 122
Pané, Fray Ramon, 4–5
Piñero, Jesús, 203
Plebiscite of 1967, 220–23
Political status under Spain, 53–54, 59–61, 71–73, 79–80, 115–16
Political status under the U.S., 86–88, 95–96, 110, 114–19, 150–53, 167, 190–203, 283–84, 315–22
Politics on U.S. mainland, 258–63, 315–22
Ponce de León, Juan, 1, 16–17, 25–26, 235
Ponce Massacre of 1937, 179–82
Population of Puerto Ricans on the island, ix, 30, 39, 53, 68, 83, 115, 315–22

Population of Puerto Ricans on the U.S. mainland, ix, 227–81, 265–66, 315–22
Power y Giralt, Ramón, 53

Race relations, 33–38, 44–51, 57, 67–73, 112, 137–38, 212, 231–34, 242–45, 247, 250–58, 271, 307–11, 315–22
Reilly, E. Montgomery, 141–42, 174
Religion, 37–38, 45, 247
Ríos, Carlos, 258–63
Rivero, Captain Angel, 99–103
Roosevelt, Franklin D., 174, 176, 185–89
Roosevelt, Theodore, 89, 98, 112–14
Roosevelt, Theodore, Jr., 168, 171–72, 174–75, 178

San Juan City, 55–58, 71–73
Sanchez Vilella, Roberto, 223
Sandburg, Carl, 77, 96–98
Saylor, John, 218–19
Slavery, 18–22, 27, 30, 34, 38–51, 57, 61, 63, 64, 67–71
Slums, 267–72
Spanish-American War, 77–103
Statehood, 124–25, 131, 138–39, 143, 150, 161, 166, 200, 285–89, 296, 321
Sugar cane industry, 162, 164–65, 207–14, 236–37

Taft, William Howard, 114, 119–20
Thomas, Piri, 252–58
Todd, Roberto, 75, 87
Torres, Jose, x
Torresola, Griselio, 204
Tous Soto, José, 152
Treaty of Paris, 132, 134
Truman, Harry S., x, 187–88, 204, 224
Tugwell, Rexford G., 184–88, 283–84

University of Puerto Rico, 177–78

Vizcarrondo, Julio, 74

Welfare, 270, 299–300, 306
Williams, Eric, 67
Wilson, Woodrow, 121, 136–38, 145
Winship, Blanton, 180–81

Young Lords, 263–65, 311–15